Authoritarian Power
and State Formation
in Ba'thist Syria

Authoritarian Power and State Formation in Ba'thist Syria

Army, Party, and Peasant

Raymond A. Hinnebusch

Westview Press
BOULDER, SAN FRANCISCO, & OXFORD

Westview Special Studies on the Middle East

Published in 1990 in the United States of America by Westview Press, Inc., 5500 Central Avenue, Boulder, Colorado 80301, and in the United Kingdom by Westview Press, Inc., 36 Lonsdale Road, Summertown, Oxford OX2 7EW

Library of Congress Cataloging-in-Publication Data
Hinnebusch, Raymond A.
  Authoritarian power and state formation in Ba'thist Syria : army,
party, and peasant / Raymond A. Hinnebusch.
    p. cm. — (Westview special studies on the Middle East)
  Includes bibliographical references.
  ISBN 0-8133-7590-8
  1. Hizb al-Ba'th al-'Arabī Al-Ishtirākī (Syria) 2. Syria—
Politics and government. 3. Political socialization—Syria.
4. Power. (Social sciences) I. Title. II. Series.
JQ1825.S873B31975 1990
320.95691—dc20   89-29074
                                                                      CIP

Printed and bound in the United States of America

The paper used in this publication meets the requirements
of the American National Standard for Permanence of Paper
for Printed Library Materials Z39.48-1984.

10   9   8   7   6   5   4   3   2   1

To Tsunaki and Yoshiko Ohyama
and my wife, Nancy,
for their invaluable support

Contents

Abbreviations

ABSP   Arab Ba'th Socialist Party
GFP   General Federation of Peasants
ha.   hectare (equivalent to 2.471 acres)
IBRD   International Bank for Reconstruction and Development
L.S.   Lira Suri, or Syrian Pound (worth about $0.11 in 1988)
SAR   Syrian Arab Republic

Preface

This book examines the rise of the Syrian Ba'th Party and the subsequent formation of the Ba'thist state. It interprets the Syrian Ba'th regime as a case of a particular kind of political formation quite prevalent in the Arab world, namely, the authoritarian-populist state. It seeks to understand the forces that produce the populist orientation of these regimes and the processes and structures through which their authoritarian power is consolidated. Although the vast majority of work on Syria focuses on elite politics or foreign policy, this study stresses the centrality of the linkages between elite and society in understanding authoritarian-populism and state formation there.

The book explains the rise of the Ba'th as the product of the vulnerabilities of a fragile traditional order split by great urban-rural gaps and of the crises unleashed by Syria's incorporation into the world capitalist economy and state system; these processes set off the de-legitimation of the old regime, a deep-rooted agrarian crisis, the rise of class conflict, and the mobilization of anti-system forces, particularly from the village. The analysis shows how the Ba'th's origins in a profound urban-rural conflict and its special road to power shaped its populist ideology and the authoritarian, but mass-incorporating, character of its rule.

The study also analyzes the struggles through which authoritarian power was concentrated and expanded. The formation of the Ba'th state is interpreted as the outcome of a dual strategy: (1) a revolution from above and the forging of Leninist political structures incorporating the rural population; and (2) the consolidation of a semi-patrimonial regime center through the emergence of a dominant leader who inserts kin and clientelist networks at the levers of coercive power. The outcome is a presidential monarchy presiding over three main institutions of rule—the Syrian army, the Ba'th Party, and the state bureaucracy—and resting on a village base.

The story is carried a step further in a companion volume to this study, *Peasant and Bureaucracy in Ba'thist Syria: The Political Economy of Rural Development* (Westview, 1989). That book examines agrarian policy under the Ba'th and the consequences of Ba'thist rule for socio-economic development in the villages from which the party came.

This study is based on a multitude of sources. Research in Syria, including elite interviews and village expeditions, was conducted in 1973–1974 and in the summers of 1977, 1979, 1982, 1985, and 1988. There is a small but important body of published primary sources, including Ba'th Party and government documents and personal accounts by "insiders" such as Razzaz, Safadi, Sayyid, and al-Jundi. A respectable corpus of scholarly literature has accumulated; some of it is by Syrian scholars, including economic analyses (Arudki), political and sociological studies (Hilan, Akhrass, Keilany, Jabbur, Allush, Hanna, Hamide), and village ethnographies (Ismail, Khalaf). I would like, in particular, to acknowledge the village study by Sulayman Najm Khalaf on which this book drew for its analysis of rural change in the Syrian East. The growing body of important works by Western scholars is indicated in the bibliography. I have tried to synthesize these disparate resources, organizing the data according to the concepts developed in the introductory chapter.

I thank the many Syrian officials, intellectuals, and friends who have helped make this book possible and the Fulbright Program and the Bush Foundation for financing the research.

Raymond A. Hinnebusch

1

Political Theory and the Syrian Ba'th Case

The Ba'th Party's 1963 seizure of power marked a major watershed in modern Syrian history: the collapse of the "old regime" which had inherited power in the first independent Syrian state and its replacement by a counter-elite which set out to forge an entirely new type of state and development strategy. Whether this amounted to a revolution as the Ba'thists insisted is a matter of controversy. The dominant views hold that it was a mere coup, although there is divergence on the nature of the post-1963 regime. Some hold that the Ba'th regime amounted to unstable praetorian military rule, others that it coalesced into neo-patrimonial rule by sectarian minorities. Some view the regime as a mere petit bourgeois nationalist reaction to imperialism which quickly evolved into a state bourgeoisie isolated from the masses. All these "schools" share the view that the regime, lacking political institutions capable of incorporating significant support, is narrow based and survives chiefly through repression; the mere creature of sectarian, military, or class elites, it is thought to have little advanced state formation in Syria.

Yet, this view seems strangely at odds with the record. The Ba'th Party, far from being rootless and ephemeral, has been entrenched as the dominant political force in Syria for decades and, indeed, became the vehicle of a major system transformation. Syria, historically plagued by a weak unstable state, has been ruled since the early sixties by the same party and since 1970 by the same leader, Hafiz al-Asad. Not only durable, this state also appears "stronger" than its predecessors if this is measured by the central-ization of power, the expansion of functions, the density of structures, the ability to contain a more mobilized opposition, and growing capabilities as an international actor. This is not readily explained by the dominant views. Each of them undoubtedly captures a different aspect of Ba'th rule—military, sectarian, class—but to the neglect of other equally crucial dimensions, namely the rural populist roots and the institution-building achievements of the regime.

Authoritarian-Populism

This study will argue that the key concept which gives the most adequate insight into the rise, durability, and nature of the Ba'th is *authoritarian-*

populism. Authoritarian-populism has been a characteristic feature of the post-colonial world, a particular kind of solution to the challenges facing new states being incorporated as subordinate players in the international state system and dependents of world capitalism. It seeks to establish the authority of a strong state autonomous of the dominant classes and external powers and to launch national economic development aimed at easing dependence and subordinating capitalist forces to populist goals.

Authoritarian-populism is a distinctive subset of authoritarianism. Authoritarian regimes typically start out by concentrating decision-making power in the hands of a small elite, often headed by a personalistic, frequently military leader, and rule with the support of the army, through the bureaucracy, and with little tolerance of political pluralism and few mechanisms of accountability; this is true of the populist variant, too. But the establishment of authoritarian power normally has a specific social rationale: such regimes arise out of social conflicts, and, initially at least, take sides in them, excluding and disadvantaging certain social forces to the benefit of others. Authoritarian regimes must thus be distinguished by the particular social interests which shape their ideological orientation. While conservative authoritarianism originates in a bid of the dominant class to block challenges to privilege from below, the populist variant originates in nationalist struggles against imperialism and revolts by middle class or plebeian elements, often from the periphery, against an upper class order. Populist authoritarianism seeks to exclude the old oligarchy from power and challenges dominant interests in the name of nationalism and equality (Huntington 1968:344–396; Almond and Powell 1978:376–381; Malloy 1977). While authoritarian-populist regimes often originate in military coups, to prevail over the powerful interests they challenge, they must mobilize their potential popular constituency. The personal charisma of a populist leader may temporarily bridge the state-society gap but unless routinized in political institutions, this support mobilization is unlikely to be durable. A regime pursuing a populist course against the dominant classes in the name of deprived groups requires a structure able to close the privileged political access of the former and organize the support of the latter: it is therefore likely to adopt some elements of the Leninist single party system, while stopping well short of forging a communist socio-political order. In the Arab world, this has widely resulted in a mixed military-party state which, though authoritarian, is shaped by its populist roots and develops the political organization to incorporate a certain mass base. But such populist regimes have also widely proven vulnerable to transformation in goals and alteration in structure. As they mature, they normally enter a more conservative *post-populist* phase in which they seek stabilization and accommodation with powerful interests and may abandon limited Leninization for limited liberalization which re-opens political access for the dominant classes.

In the following introduction, the argument of the study will be prefigured and located within the relevant traditions of political development theory. It will focus on two problems: (1) the origins and social base which shape the populist orientation of the regime; this will draw on the literature on political instability, popular and peasant movements, military intervention in politics and the formation of political identities in developing countries; and (2) the regime's power consolidation strategy and outcome; this will rely on Weber's concepts of authority, functionalist work on institution-building and a critique of conventional authoritarian theory. The discussion will also try to anticipate how the authoritarian-populist interpretation of the Syrian regime can be accommodated to the central but changing roles of sect, army, class, and national struggle in Syrian politics.

Populist Revolt: The Origins of the Authoritarian-Populist State

An authoritarian-populist regime typically originates in a revolt against established elites by relative "outsiders" in the name of subordinate social forces; going well beyond a mere coup from within the establishment, it makes a substantial break with the past, but it also stops far short of mass revolution from below. There are many studies of military intervention and of great revolutions, but little explicit treatment in the literature of this very important intermediate domain of anti-regime revolt.

The intermediate domain itself embraces movements which vary in the level of political mobilization and the extent of change they impose on society. One pole on this continuum could be marked by Huntington's (1962; 1968:198–208) *"reform" or "breakthrough" coup* and Trimberger's (1978) *"revolution from above"* in which a military coup against the old oligarchy opens the political arena to the middle class and to major social structural reform, but in the absence of major mass mobilization. At the other end is what Walton (1984) calls *national revolts,* mass uprisings which, being more uneven and less intense than full scale mass revolutions, do not take on the same anti-system dimensions or end in the same radical trans-formations, but nevertheless have important consequences. Reality can be yet more complex, mixing elements of these cases. Radical coup-makers could stimulate mass mobilization from above; mass forces could infiltrate and capture part of the state apparatus, and then launch a simultaneous coup and mass revolt; rebellion from below could radicalize the officer corps, precipitating a radical coup. Such cases, combining a radical coup and state-led "revolution from above" with aspects of popular revolt from below will be termed *"populist revolt"* and can be considered a typical road to power of an authoritarian-populist regime. While such a revolt can take place with far less than the massive mobilization of a great revolution, its success requires a wider coalition of forces than a mere faction of the officer corps, small group of urban intellectuals or single primordial group. Some form of anti-oligarchy alliance between a radicalized middle class, including strategic elements of the officer corps, and politicized segments of the peasantry must produce or develop around the populist leadership and this combination depends on a significant incidence of crisis and conflict in a society. This study will argue that the Ba'th's rise to power approximates this phenomenon.

But what are the conditions which make possible the combination of radical military coup, expressive of a middle class "breakthrough," and peasant revolt? Certain generalizations to be found in the literature on these questions have relevance to the Syrian case.

1. Third World revolt almost universally takes place within a context of imperialist domination, dependency, and nationalist reaction to it. National and social crises are interlinked: imperialism may buttress dominant classes but also undermine their traditional legitimacy; and imperialist penetration is a major source of social crisis, typically blocking autonomous national capitalism. National movements need not assume the radical social character of populist revolt; but where the imperialist impact is especially damaging or durable or the nationalist struggle prolonged they are more likely to do so. The intensity of struggle mobilizes ever more plebeian elements and calls forth ever more radical solutions, including the transformation of indigenous society. Leadership, thus, typically passes from the traditional or liberal upper and upper-middle classes into the hands of petit bourgeois radical intellectuals who, lacking a stake in the status quo, view national independence and social transformation as inseparable and the revolutionary mobilization of the masses as a condition of both; this situation may well lead to the radicalization of the officer corps and mobilization of the peasantry. While this reaches its extreme in modern mass revolutions, in the case of populist revolt it takes a lesser but significant form; Syria fits this category.

2. Social conditions for the rise of a radicalized middle class are typical of many Third World countries, but particularly so in the early stages of modernization when a state leadership rooted in the agrarian bourgeoisie still dominates. Modernization undermines traditional authority, creates a salaried new middle class with rising aspirations, and generates an intelligentsia from which counter-elites may be drawn (Halpern 1963:51–78). If, as is common in cases of delayed dependent development, economic expansion fails to keep pace with social mobilization, and especially if economic growth falters after a period of expansion and expectations are frustrated, a sense of relative deprivation feeds middle class political discontent. As, in these conditions, capitalist development enriches the agrarian-commercial bourgeoisie and exacerbates inequality, conflict over the proper course of development may divide the ruling class and the new middle class (Deutsch 1961; Gurr; Walton 204; Huntington 1968:39–59). Syria in the fifties was a classic case of middle class alienation, a condition which propelled the rise of the Ba'th.

3. The military is normally elitist and hostile to mass movements but under special conditions army officers may be radicalized. This is most likely: a) where the military establishment is autonomous of the dominant landed class and lacks a strong tradition of corporate elitism. b) where it is recruited from the new middle class or yet lower strata in a society dominated by a traditional elite; military radicalism is most associated with officers of lower middle class background, of a marginal ethnic group, from the hinterland, with personal experience of economic crisis or deprivation and interaction

with radical civilian associates, and of younger age. c) where the nation faces exceptional pressure from imperialism or a severe external threat and the military, naturally nationalist, embraces radical reform as the key to national power (Wolpin 9–26, 114–116; Berger 361–398; Halpern 1962; 1963: 251–280; Trimberger; Huntington 1962; 1968:192–237). All these conditions existed in Syria.

4. As Moore (1966) and Huntington (1968:292) argue, the peasantry, the decisive mass force in the outcome of political development in agrarian countries, plays a crucial "swing role:" if peasants are radicalized and mobilized, they provide the shock troops of revolution, but if they remain traditional, they are an anchor of conservative regimes. Between the extremes of peasant revolution and traditional passivity there are, however, many middle cases: peasant revolt or mobilization short of revolution can still affect outcomes and, in particular, may, as part of "populist revolt," facilitate the emergence of an authoritarian-populist regime. The study will argue that this is so of Syria.

Peasant revolt takes place in a total societal context, but a specifically *agrarian* crisis provides essential conditions and grievances. This crisis is a function of capitalist penetration of the countryside, making land a commodity, disrupting the village community and issuing in land concentration, tenancy, proletarianization and urban migration. The cash nexus replaces patriarchal or patronage relations. In these conditions, if the landed elite neglects agricultural modernization, while simply extracting a greater surplus from the peasantry, and the growth of population and landlessness generates an intense land hunger, violent landlord-peasant conflict is likely. Smallholders threatened by debt or landlord encroachment may take the lead in peasant mobilization because they possess the necessary independence of landlord control. Share-croppers are likely rebels since this tenure is a zero-sum relation and the landlord dispensable. Peasants threatened with proletarianization have little to lose by anti-system mobilization. A regime which fails to address the agrarian crisis faces, in its peasantry, a permanent reservoir of potential support for system-challenging movements (Russett; Shanin; Wolf; Zagoria; Walton; Paige).

5. Rapid social change and crisis provide conditions for the rise of an anti-system movement, but it takes leadership to translate them into political mobilization. In its early phase, "men of ideas" arise, intellectuals promoting a counter-ideology; critiquing and de-legitimizing the status quo and offering a vision of a better society, they raise the political consciousness of the public. At a later stage the thinkers give way to "men of action" and charismatic leadership may arise to turn ideas into a movement. Militant followers are recruited from the new groups created during, but unsatisfied by, modernization: students and intellectuals, products of the spread of education; the "marginal men" resulting from social atomization—newly- or half-educated persons of modest origins uprooted from traditional communities and insecure, ex-peasants who have recently migrated to the city, the "overeducated" "spiritually underemployed," white collar employees in

dead-end careers. Finally, it takes the party organizers, the technicians of a new political technology, to give broad scale and durability to the movement (Koury). Effective peasant mobilization, in particular, depends on such "outside" leadership which provides the ideology (nationalism, agrarian populism) and organization to break through the local encapsulation of the peasantry and generate broader peasant identifications. Radical intellectuals or "ex-peasant" urban migrants who become students or workers may provide this linkage (Hobsbawm; Walton).

6. The failure of the political system and its legitimacy are important ingredients in populist revolt. Ruling elites which fail to permit evolutionary change and refuse to open existing political institutions to middle class participatory demands are likely to face revolutionary ferment. In the face of radical challenges, they may lose their cohesion and ability to command, or military defeat and nationalist failure may shatter or render unreliable the repressive apparatus. Whether objective grievance-generating conditions actually translate into anti-system peasant mobilization depends on the strength of traditional socio-political structures. If the ruling landed elite enjoys class cohesion and retains strong links to the land and local political functions, it may contain the crisis, but if its local roots are fragile or undermined, the stability of the rural order depends on the coercive capacities of the state apparatus (Moore; Anderson 1974). Middle Eastern countries appear historically distinguished by sharp urban-rural gaps and the vulnerability of the ruling center to periodic revolt and renewal from the periphery; this heritage may make them especially fragile in the face of modern rural discontent (Ibn Khaldun). This study will argue that Syria's pre-Ba'th political order was exceptionally fragile and vulnerable.

7. Although all these ingredients are, more or less, part of "populist revolt," for it to happen they must come together in sufficient degree to overthrow the old regime and yet not lead into revolution. But why should they? First, full scale revolutions are rare, but, as Walton argues, many of the same factors which explain them also commonly give rise to lesser revolts. In the latter cases, the ingredients are less potent or combined in less explosive ways; in particular, peasant mobilization, compared to cases of revolution, is likely to be less intense and more uneven. This may be because of the heterogeneity of society, the unevenness of modernization, and the difficulty of putting together an anti-regime coalition which bridges the urban-rural gap. But if regimes are especially fragile it may not take mass revolution to sweep them away. If the old regime lacks nationalist legitimacy, a strong rural base, and effective political institutions, and if, in particular, its repressive apparatus is radicalized, it may be overthrown by a revolt stopping well short of full scale peasant revolution and, indeed, in the relatively earlier stages of modernization when the middle class has been radicalized but the mass periphery is only partially mobilized. The consolidation of the resulting populist regime, however, depends on subsequent mass mobilization and populist reforms which satisfy middle class and peasant grievances. Under these conditions, populist revolt may be a substitute for revolution. The study will argue that these conditions obtained in Syria.

8. Finally, the road to power taken by a populist regime, particularly the nature of the political mobilization out of which it arises, has important consequences for its capacity to consolidate power and sustain populist revolution from above. While the heights of state power are usually seized in a coup, the more the coup is preceded, accompanied by, or followed by mass mobilization and political conflict, the stronger the regime is likely to be. The greater the depth of social crisis and conflict out of which the regime arises, the higher the levels of mobilization likely to be achieved and the wider the regime's support base is likely to be. The more intense the mobilization and struggle for power, the more likely a strong shared ideological orientation will bind the populist movement's diverse elements, hence the greater the possibility of elite cohesion after the rise to power, and the more durable the regime's populist orientation is likely to be (Huntington 1974; Skocpol). In the Syrian case, the regime seized power in a coup, not mass revolt, but the coup was a delayed outcome of prior system crisis and mobilization which the regime was subsequently able to exploit to build a support base.

Populist Movements and Communalism

But how can the notion of populist revolt as an explanation of the origins of the Ba'thist regime be accommodated to the sectarian dimension of Syrian politics? Clearly populist revolt took place in a special setting, namely a mosaic society without a long-established indigenous national-state, a situation where communalism is likely to be an important factor. Yet, to the extent communal identities channel political mobilization, the grievances of modernization are likely to be diverted into particularistic conflict among a fragmented elite and its clientage networks or into separatism or civil war, precluding the cross-communal class-based coalitions and universalistic ideology necessary for successful populist revolt. Key to understanding populist revolt in a multi-communal setting is how class structure and communalism determine political mobilization.

The "nation-building" literature (Deutsch 1953; Lerner) argues that social mobilization, insofar as it erodes particularistic ties and generates the interaction needed for class and national consciousness, provides the conditions for modern nation-building and secular politics. Yet, it may also merely subsume the most parochial identities (kin, village) in larger but still subnational communal ones which, as self-sufficiency gives way to societal competition for scarce resources, become the vehicles of political conflict (Geertz; Harik 1972b). Whether political mobilization takes such a communal form depends on a variety of factors: it is most likely where communal differences (language, race, religion, etc.) are sharp and reinforcing, where there is no core culture attractive to minorities, where class differences are not developed enough to displace communal ones, where assimilation had not advanced prior to social mobilization, where no secular nationalism develops out of the independence struggle or through national institutions, and where political elites cultivate "natural" communal constituencies and seek ethnic hegemony instead of constructing cross-communal political bases and satisfying the equity demands of competing communal groups (Deutsch 1953; Anderson et. al. 1967:15–83; Weiner 1965; Coleman).

While analyses of these variables can help in identifying the broad tendencies in a society, actual cases of populist revolt in a mosaic society are likely to be complex *mixtures* of class and communal conflict. Where both class and communal identities are important, as in Syria, it is necessary to understand how they *interact* and three sorts of observations provide a starting point for understanding this case. First, communal consciousness does not exclude broader identities. Indeed social mobilization tends to engender the *simultaneous* development of several new identities—with communal group, occupation, class, and state; individuals are thus likely to have *multiple identities* and which takes precedence may depend on the issue or situation. Hence, in most countries, pure communal and class forms of conflict are less likely than mixtures: class and communal mobilization may take place side by side, may overlap, or may alternate in time. Second, while the *cross-cutting* of class by communal cleavages may often retard populist mobilization and make class coalitions fragile, where low class status is associated with certain minorities or deprived communal groups, that is, where cleavages *overlap*, not only will conflict be particularly intense, but communal mobilization may take a radical universalistic form. Deprived communal groups may identify with broader deprived classes and view class revolution as the solution to their particular deprivations. Third, the unevenness of mobilization is likely to result in unbalanced communal representation even in secular class or national movements. In Africa, for example, certain communal groups were disproportionately in the forefront of nationalist movements as a result of uneven change, that is, differences in the degree traditional communities were disrupted by modernization and exposed to education. This was due to accidents of geographical location or the pressure of overpopulation in certain areas or to greater receptivity to innovation in less stratified communities (Coleman 30–34). These three observations point to a certain possibility: that where minority status overlaps with class deprivation, minorities, particularly where uneven mobilization affects them earlier, may appear disproportionately in the vanguard of national or class based populist movements. In this case universalistic ideology may submerge communal identities while, nevertheless, never wholly effacing them. But if a particular minority group acquires, by virtue of its prior mobilization, a dominant political position and uses it to exclude other groups, communal identities are likely to revive and the populist class coalition erode or fragment. The mix of populist revolt and sectarian politics in the Syrian case suggests that it is such a complex case.

The Formation of the Authoritarian-Populist State

If populist revolt is to succeed it must be institutionalized in a state. Perhaps because they are typically products of divided societies lacking consensus where the perceived problem is to *concentrate* reformist power in the face of established interests and communal fragmentation, such states, particularly in the Middle East, usually take an authoritarian form. Power is forcibly seized and populist policy imposed. Durable power, however, must be legitimized. While legitimacy ultimately rests in consent, it has, as Weber shows, many sources besides procedural democracy—i.e. personal or primordial loyalties, charismatic leadership, ideological mission, or bureaucratic legality—and all of these are compatible with authoritarian rule. Moreover, as Blau (1964) shows, power can also be generated by some "exchange" of benefits between ruler and ruled. The use of coercion in the concentration of authoritarian power may, thus, be accompanied by a variety of legitimacy sources and "exchanges." The particular mix of these resources is a central key to the very nature of the regime. Nevertheless, to consolidate a new order, a populist regime must go beyond the *concentration* of power and *expand* it and this requires some institutionalization of participation (Huntington 1968:140–147).

The Concentration and Legitimation of Power

The concentration of power is the first test of regime formation. It begins with the seizure of the state center, often through a military coup; but there is initially little governing power in the system and it is usually fragmented by an intra-elite power struggle between cliques of officers and politicians, perhaps exacerbated by the communal differences typical of mosaic societies. The new regime's challenge to established interests may also unleash a struggle among wider—but normally urban upper and middle class—social forces. A zero-sum struggle is waged with Machiavellian methods—coercion, ruse, divide and rule, by which opponents are eliminated and coalitions of followers, allies, and coopted opponents built and established in command of inherited or newly created levers of bureaucratic command and coercion. This phase of "primitive power accumulation" corresponds to Huntington's "radical praetorian" regime.

To be durable, concentrated power has to be transformed into a system of legitimate leadership and intra-elite decision-making, without which the regime center is vulnerable to fragmentation and paralysis. The initial attempt at authority legitimation in authoritarian-populist regimes usually mixes charisma and ideology. As Weber (1964:358–363; Bendix 298–328) and Ibn Khaldun (1967) argued, a religious-ideological vision is often the force which unites fragmented primordial factions, typically from deprived or peripheral sectors of society, in a state-founding movement; an "ideological revolution" has been, in some sense, the crucible of populist regimes in the modern Middle East, too (Binder 1964). But to the degree ideology is merely "expressive," lacking a programmatic content, it may not provide sufficient consensus for unified decision-making or to cement intra-elite cleavages (Moore 1974). If it is intense, the elite may split between moderates and radicals over doctrinal interpretations or it may overreach itself in challenging the old order and bring on a damaging reaction. Charisma and ideology soon run up against an intransigent reality and must be moderated and routinized in institutions if the new state is to survive.

Charisma and ideology could, thus, lead into or be mixed with a legal-rational strategy in which the distribution of decision-making power is institutionalized in procedures, offices and assemblies at the center. This is the most stable approach to power concentration but is at odds with the logic of "primitive power accumulation," and presupposes an intra-elite consensus which must normally first be established by ideological or personal leadership: but such leadership militates against impersonal power sharing. Legal-rational rules in a culture without such a tradition may generate insufficient solidarity to bind a multi-communal elite, making the center vulnerable to fragmentation. As Weber (363–373; Bendix 308–328) suggests, however, if the routinization of charisma and ideology in legal-rational institutions fails, charismatic or personal leadership gives way to patrimonial rule.

Indeed, traditionally, as Bill (1984: 74–176) argues, ruling cores in the Middle East have been consolidated though patrimonial methods: the use of personal, kin, and ethnic loyalties—*asabiya,* as Ibn Khaldun puts it—combined with material payoffs for clients. In a mosaic kinship culture where tribal, communal, and sectarian rivalry was historically endemic and interpersonal trust limited to primordial groups, only persons "close" to a leader could be trusted in struggles for power. While loyalties to a universalistic ideology or impersonal institutions must be painstakingly forged, webs of primordial based personal links are "natural" ready-made sinews of association and hence power concentration; power probably cannot be built without some recourse to the basic associative tissue of the culture. In a mosaic society, resort to such a strategy is certain to translate into the use of communalism to cement an elite core. This strategy may create binding ties which muffle elite factionalism, but, as the Ottoman practice of eliminating the Sultan's brothers indicates, the closest primordial proximity is no guarantee of elite solidarity. Moreover, a personalistic elite core is wholly dependent on the personal vigor and competence of the leader. In a multi-communal society, elite core-formation must accommodate some kind of "ethnic arithmetic" or risk a very narrow base and communal counter-mobilization, but a "neo-patrimonial" strategy tends to exclude less trusted groups. It is useful to concentrate power but cannot mobilize enough actors to expand power much beyond the favored in-group. Though elites may initially use *asabiya* as a means rather than an end, followers recruited on this basis may turn the state into a "patrimony" used for the private ends of those with power, stimulating resentments and possibly rebellion by those excluded.

The liabilities inherent in each of the "pure" approaches to authority building typically results in combining universalistic with more exclusionist strategies. Weber himself argued that concrete cases were likely to be mixes, not pure forms, of his legitimacy types. In transitional societies where political association is a mix of particularistic and universalistic ties, state building strategies are likely to mix personal leadership, primordialism, ideology, and the creation of new formal structures. Indeed, the multiple sources of power developed by mixed strategies may lend greater versatility and adaptability to a regime. There may also be built-in contradictions: if for example, a patrimonial strategy is used to construct the elite core, can effective mass incorporating institutions be built or will they be enervated by clientelism? Between a closed exclusionist regime and wholly open universalistic institutions, there are many middle possibilities and mixed strategies are likely to give rise to such intermediate kinds of outcomes.

The outcome of a successful power concentration has typically been a powerful executive headed by a dominant leader relatively unconstrained by law or custom. The relations between the leader and the military, ruling party, and bureaucratic elites become the sinews of power in the regime. Elite recruitment typically turns on cooptation by incumbents from above. Policy-making is highly centralized, taking the form of personalistic, bureaucratic or ideological factionalism within the elite. But depending on the regime's mix of power building strategies, the leader may be accountable to and share power with the ruling party or parliament, the military may be more or less under legal authority, and the orientation of the regime may be more or less patrimonial, legal-bureaucratic, or ideological. A regime may, of course, fail to successfully concentrate power or get beyond the radical praetorian stage and, if so, it is unlikely to long endure.

In the Syrian case, the outcome is, in fact, typically ambiguous. Despite attaining a certain ideological legitimacy, the failure to establish a cohesive center led to resort to patrimonial techniques resulting in a Presidential monarchy which shares power with military and bureaucratic elites and party institutions. But patrimonialism continually threatens the legitimation of authority and the institutional dimension of rule.

Power, Institution-Building, and Participation

A stable regime depends on the creation of effective structures of power linking state and society. Authoritarian-populist regimes, often initially military, typically attempt some structural development through a strategy of limited Leninization. Power comes to rest on three central institutions, the army, the ruling single party (and its mass auxiliaries), and the bureaucracy. Creating a place for the military in the system capable of subordinating military violence to political procedures is essential to stability and a strong party system is crucial to incorporating a mass constituency.

The Military: The role of the military is typically central, given the importance of force and the absence of consensus in the imposition of authoritarian regimes. Historically, the military has been central to state formation, everywhere initially a function of security imperatives. In fragmented societies the army is often the most organized, national-oriented social force, with the largest stake in the state and best equipped to impose order. In societies lacking a dynamic bourgeoisie it may also be a modernizing force and sufficiently autonomous of the traditional ruling classes to take the lead in social change (Janowitz 1964:63; Halpern 1963:251–280; Halpern 1962; Horowitz 90–150; Trimberger 1975).

But whether the military has a positive impact on state formation depends on its incorporation into a system of established authority. In authoritarian regimes, its role varies widely. At one extreme is the "praetorian" case in which the military dominates, a politicized officer corps fragments among competing factions, subjecting the state to coups and countercoups or a general establishes a personal dictatorship (Be'eri 1970:463–481; Perlmutter 1981:18–19, 128–135, 147–159). At the other extreme is the Leninist model where the military is the creation and instrument of a strong ruling party; although one of the most powerful interest groups within the regime, it normally pursues its interests through legitimate institutions, excluding the gun from the political process (Wolpin 68–102). A whole range of intermediate cases are possible in which officers play a central political role but avoid the worst features of praetorianism. A dominant military leader may use his authority to create or stabilize political institutions. Or, the military may be a partner in a civil-military coalition, its role constrained by civilian political groups or institutions. While the officers may provide leadership in such regimes—becoming themselves politicians—the military institution, per se, not readily adaptable to political functions such as interest aggregation and mass mobilization, often shares power with a party through which civilian participation is incorporated (Huntington 1968:237–263). It will be argued that Syria falls in the intermediate category. Attempts to establish the Leninist model failed, but the military is partly incorporated into a system in which its role is constrained by a dominant leader and a Leninist-like party; praetorianism is contained but not eliminated.

The Party System: If the military is crucial to the concentration and defense of power, the single or dominant party is the key to its expansion. The party is a framework for the maintenance of elite cohesion and an instrument for mass mobilization and control. According to Perlmutter (1981:2–5), the creation of such a political infrastructure to channel mass participation is the chief feature distinguishing modern from traditional authoritarianism.

Ruling parties obviously vary widely, however, in their power to facilitate the concentration and expansion of power. The Leninist party with its core of ideological militants and mass auxiliaries penetrating society is the prototype of a "strong" party (Huntington 1968:334–343; 1974). To the extent a party approaches this model, it performs crucial functions: policy-making, elite recruitment, interest aggregation, mass mobilization. At the other end of the scale is the very fragile or subordinate party which is a mere facade for clientelism or a purely bureaucratic instrument of control (Harik 1973). Between the Leninist and the weak party are a whole variety of middle cases where parties are central to the political process but fail to attain the hegemony and capabilities of Leninist parties. Regimes seeking radical change require a strong party—an organizational weapon capable of penetrating and mobilizing mass support and smashing opposition—while regimes satisfied with the maintenance of order need much less. Authoritarian-populist regimes start out seeking radical change, but they vary in the extent to which they give priority to party-building; where they enjoy charismatic leadership, they may, in fact, neglect it. Moreover, to forge the strong ideological commitments of the Leninist-like party, it takes a sharp polarization between the party and its enemies and probably a long period of struggle for power from below and populist regimes vary considerably in this regard. It will be argued that Ba'thist Syria developed a fairly strong party.

In summary, authoritarian regimes vary widely in the extent of their institution-building capability. Observers often relegate such regimes to a praetorian or patrimonial category, sharply distinguished from institutionalized regimes, whether communist or democratic. But, in fact, many Third World states, including authoritarian ones which attempt some institution-building, probably fall somewhere in a middle category (Chalmers 23–43) in which *partial institutionalization* is characteristic. Rules, roles, offices, and structures do channel and constrain political action; but because they lack the fixity of constitutional regimes, they are vulnerable to manipulation and bureaucratization by the power elite and because they lack a transformative capacity comparable to totalitarian regimes, they are vulnerable to subversion by traditional culture. To the extent an authoritarian-populist regime subordinates the military and develops a strong party system it can be considered to achieve limited institutionalization.

Mass Incorporation and Power Expansion: The amount of power in a political system depends on the "number and intensity of influence relations" (Huntington 1968:143): the more participants and the more intensely mobilized they are, the more potential power. Expanding power means the mobilization of new actors into legitimate institutions. But can authoritarian regimes so mobilize support? In conventional theory, they are distinguished precisely by their inability to accommodate political participation. But while this is certainly true of their most primitive forms (purely personalistic or military no-party states), is it so of developed ones with reasonably strong parties?

Some argue that a single party, especially where it shares power with the military or is chiefly an elite-created instrument, cannot institutionalize authentic mass participation. Certainly it does not permit the choice needed to make participation fully meaningful for all; tolerance of opposition is so low and political rights so constrained that it can absorb only a limited spectrum of participatory demands. Even party activists usually have no strong mechanisms to punish elite abuse of power. Thus the regime is vulnerable to elite corruption and to participation crises and, to the extent institutional channels are clogged, demands will be expressed through clientelist connections or anti-regime protest (Almond 1966:311–313).

Yet between the democratic *ideal* and a participation *vacuum,* there is a wide middle ground. Huntington argues that an effective single party is uniquely capable of both concentrating power and expanding it through "mobilized" participation and Nelson questions the conventional dismissal of "mobilized" participation as inconsequential. Conflict between the single party and anti-regime opposition, may, Huntington argues, function as a kind of surrogate for party competition. Skocpol shows that authoritarian states originating in revolutions enjoy a much widened "mass-incorporating" capacity, that is, the ability to stimulate pro-regime activism and absorb wide parts of the previously passive population into their political structures (Huntington 1974; Huntington and Nelson 1976:7–10; Nelson 1987; Skocpol). It is, thus, reasonable to hypothesize that authoritarian regimes with roots in populist revolts which develop strong party structures may have a certain mass-incorporating potential. To survive in the face of the hostility of the previously dominant socio-economic classes they have a particularly strong incentive to mobilize a mass base. The conditions of populist revolt—agrarian crisis, mass alienation from the old order, the breakdown of traditional mass encapsulation, etc.—provide special opportunities to incorporate the peasantry, the majority social force in most Third World societies. Indeed, populist regimes typically attempt, through some combination of ideology, party organization, patronage, and land reform to mobilize the deprived non-participant masses, and thus widen and shift the balance of power in the political arena in their favor. They may thus achieve an institutionalization of *limited participation.*

Even a regime which starts out with populist ambitions may, of course, neglect institutional links to society, resorting instead to primordial loyalties and clientelism and if a party exists it may be nothing but a facade. But such patrimonialized regimes, unable to implement social reform or modernization, normally end up relying on alliances with local notables for mass linkage, leaving the villages and urban neighborhoods under their influence. Such a "Neo-patrimonial" regime, lacking an incorporated base to expand its power and sustain populism, is likely to end either in stagnation and the corrupt appropriation of the state for private elite ends or as, in time, political mobilization exceeds the modest absorptive capacity of its structures, in praetorian instability (Eisenstadt and Lemarchand 1981; Eisenstadt 1964). Yet, a mix of patrimonialism with institution-building strategies might produce a case where a viable party exists and, though infected by patrimonial traits, retains a certain mass incorporative capacity.

It must also be acknowledged that even a successful institutionalization of limited participation is no guarantee of stability for authoritarian-populist regimes. Given their relatively modest capacity, compared to totalitarian and democratic regimes, to either eradicate or accommodate opposition, it typically becomes a permanent challenge to their legitimacy; and in populist authoritarianism opposition is likely to include groups controlling a significant portion of societal resources. Moreover, modernization tends to create a more diverse and mobilized society harder to control and incorporate. In the face of precarious legitimacy and permanent opposition, the regime typically attempts to maximize its coalition through some combination of ideology, patronage, and populism and to control the opposition through a mix of concession and repression. If it stresses support maximization and inclusion, this tends to keep it responsive to the wider public, but may strain its resource base at the cost of economic growth. To sustain a strategy of repression, the regime must either have a strong constituency of its own, society be at a low level of mobilization, or the opposition fragmented. And the more a regime must depend on the apparatus of coercion, the more likely the ruler will become its prisoner (Migdal 1987). Thus, while an authoritarian regime may very effectively concentrate power, there may be built-in limits to its capacity to expand it; ultimately, wider power-sharing may be the only way to create a stronger regime.

Power, Public Policy, and Social Reform

The authoritarian-populist state is "modernizing" and reformist in orientation and this is crucial to its consolidation of power. In its early phases, class-shaped populist ideology animates plebeian elites and "revolution from above" is deployed to break the power of foreign interests and of the oligarchy. Attack on the oligarchy's control of the means of production through nationalizations and land reform curbs its social power and with it much mass dependency; power over the economy is also thereby concentrated in the hands of autonomous state elites. The regime may consciously seek an alternative to private capitalist development, either in the form of state capitalism in partnership with a subordinated private sector or through a socialist—public sector, cooperative—alternative. A fluidization of the formerly rigid class structure typically results as property (e.g. land) is more widely distributed and new opportunities (through education, state employment etc.) for upward mobility are opened up. Thus, regime policy spawns or broadens certain social forces—typically the salaried petite bourgeoisie, the small-holding peasantry, and a new "state bourgeoisie." Such re-stratification, the demolition of old distributions of wealth and status and the creation of new regime-sanctioned ones, is crucial to consolidating a new order (Apter 123–133). Thus, the regime uses reform and economic power to forge an alliance of the state-dependent middle class and peasantry which, if institutionalized, typically broadens the class composition of the state and may impart considerable durability to its populist policy thrust.

The ultimate fate of populist states is, however, intimately linked to their longer run ability to foster development and cope with the crises of modernization. But are they "weak" or "strong" states in their capacity to manage development? The concentration of power and exclusion of opposition may initially give authoritarian regimes a greater capacity to impose difficult decisions and major reforms against vested interests. Bureaucratic expansion advances the regulatory, extractive, and entrepreneurial functions of the regime. But the assumption of new functions may outrun the capacity of the bureaucracy. The dictates of power maximization may subvert economic rationality: the extension of state control over the economy, the use of patronage and tolerance of corruption to solidify the elite, and populist distributive policies all put economics in the service of power instead of the opposite; if carried too far, this is self-defeating, turning the "strong" state "soft" and depleting its resource base. Statism reduces the power of dominant classes but the regime must still tolerate autonomous societal centers—whether "traditional" or private capitalist—which, being naturally hostile, often obstruct its policies. Typically unable to establish full command of the economy through statist or "socialist" economic institutions capable of displacing an often alienated private sector, the regime will in time probably have to make concessions to foreign and private capital at the expense of populism. But the reforms it has carried out and the enhanced autonomy of the state may make the return to capitalism a less inequitable game than hitherto.

The Evolution of the Authoritarian-Populist State

Authoritarian-populist regimes undergo a fairly typical evolution in which four major variations (or mixes of them) may (but need not all) appear, distinguished by their level of institutional development and relative ideological orientation, as indicated in Table 1.1.

1. The *radical praetorian* regime denotes the early populist phase of power seizure and concentration when ideology, shaped by the elites' middle class or plebeian origins, drives the pursuit of radical reform. The regime, locked in conflict with the dominant classes, seeks the mobilization of mass support. There is also typically a certain intra-elite struggle for power out of which a dominant leader may emerge. Resting chiefly on charismatic leadership and/or army backing, the regime is unstable. The routinization of ideology and charisma needed for stabilization may proceed in either a legal-rational or patrimonial direction; but the expansion of power needed to consolidate a new order depends on the incorporation of a plebeian class coalition into political structures.

2. The regime may evolve through *limited Leninization* into a consolidated authoritarian-populist regime. Power remains concentrated in a mixed civil–military elite, but new participants, plebeian beneficiaries of radical reforms, are mobilized and organized through an ideological party, expanding power and consolidating the regime against the conservative opposition. A dominant

TABLE 1.1 The Forms of Authoritarian-Populist Development

Ideological Orientation	Level of Structural Development	
	Low	High
Radical	Radical Praetorian (Charismatic/ Ideological)	Authoritarian-Populist/ Limited Leninization
Conservative	Neo-Patrimonial	Authoritarian-Post-Populist/ Limited Liberalization

Source: Author

executive emerges, resting on the army and a one-party system incorporating some mass participation.

Once the revolution is so institutionalized, and once reforms have redressed the social crisis and achieved social restratification, the regime's orientation toward radical change is gradually displaced by a preoccupation with the management of the new order. The elite begins to identify its interests with the "state" and, seeking to maximize state autonomy, begins to balance rather than take sides between social forces. A "state interest" tends to supersede ideology as the determining factor shaping elite behavior. Just how this state interest is defined depends on what social forces are incorporated into it. It will certainly be expressed as an elite determination to defend the legitimacy, capabilities, resource base, etc. of the state. But in a statist/populist regime, the definition of state interests may also be shaped by a certain institutionalization of populist ideology in the ruling party, and will likely accommodate bureaucratic interests with a stake in the public sector and those of the corporatist syndicates through which the regime is linked to its populist constituency. In the mature stages of this form of authoritarian-populism, the earlier character of the political process as a class conflict over the direction of society is gradually superseded by a bureaucratic politics in which institutions and interest groups compete, inside the regime, over patronage, jurisdictions, and incremental policy change.

3. Alternatively, the regime may seek consolidation through patrimonial strategies. A *neo-patrimonial* regime concentrates power but cannot much expand it and lacks modernizing and reformist capability. Alternatively, a regime may begin with institution-building ambitions but regress into patrimonialism, ending in the loss of ideological energy, elite corruption, re-traditionalization of political structures, and mass de-mobilization.

Because pure patrimonial and institution-building strategies each have liabilities, regimes often mix them. The outcome is frequently a mixed Bonapartist/Leninist regime headed by a personalistic leader who presides over a collegial party and military leadership linked to him by clientelist ties. Once radical ideology ceases to play a leading role, the development of such mixed regimes is determined by the contrary pulls of patrimonial and rational-legal forces.

4. In a later *post-populist* evolution, the state tends to seek accommodation with the dominant classes at the expense of its populist constituency. The more the following conditions, which seem to drive this change, hold, the sooner and the more completely the regime will enter the mature post-populist phase.

a) *Elite transformation:* A radical elite in time exhausts its ideological energies: ideology and charisma must come to terms with everyday, especially economic, realities (Weber), radicals overreach themselves and are chastened by a conservative reaction (Brinton), and leadership vigor gives way to self-serving corruption (Ibn Khaldun), especially given the lack of accountability mechanisms in authoritarian regimes. The resulting *embourgeoisement* of the elite gives it a stake in new inequalities (Michels), inducing a conservative transformation of its ideology. This elite transformation is likely to advance most rapidly where there is no strong party to institutionalize ideology and replenish the elite with plebeian elements.

b) *Economic constraints:* Populist regimes, as they mobilize previously inactive mass sectors through an "inclusionary" and redistributive policy, foster consumption at the expense of accumulation and alienate the "haves" whose cooperation may be essential to growth (Malloy:3–17, 47–87). Efforts to create alternative socialist-like institutions typically fail: inefficiency, corruption, and politicization enervate use of the public sector as an engine of investment. The strain of populist policies on the resources of the state, economic stagnation, and vulnerability to external pressures, may force an opening to private and foreign investment and a good investment climate requires a certain rollback of populism and statism.

c) *Class formation:* In an statist regime, elite aggrandizement and the corrupt manipulation of state-market interactions tends to generate a new "state bourgeoisie" inside the regime. Under economic liberalization, it may strike alliances with and, in time, even amalgamate with the private bourgeoisie including the remnants of the old oligarchy. This may spell a bourgeois recapture of the state and the deployment of state power in the interest of capitalist development.

In the post-populist phase, authoritarian structures initially persist but are now used for conservative ends (Apter 357–390). This may mean increasing patrimonialization, the more so the stronger the patrimonial component of regime power consolidation, unless limited liberalization gives wider social forces scope to check this decay. Indeed, if a capitalist strategy is adopted in earnest, long run success probably requires accommodating bourgeois demands for access to policymaking through "limited liberalization:" typically, the single party system is dismantled, legal protections (especially of property rights) strengthened, and a revitalized parliament becomes the vehicle for power-sharing with the executive. A certain power diffusion takes place, mostly to the bourgeoisie; policy is thus bound to move in a conservative direction favoring the dominant economic forces in society. Because resistance to this course is likely, the core of authoritarian power is maintained, albeit now directed at radical counter-elites. If resistance is intense, such a regime could evolve into a full-blown authoritarian-conservative one (e.g. Pinochet's Chile) in which state power represses and demobilizes the masses in the service of capitalist interests. Egypt is a pioneer in post-populist evolution, but the seeds of it exist in the Syrian case.

There are also forces which work against post-populist transformation and which may delay this development indefinitely, e.g. leadership preferences, the easing of economic constraints by petro-rent, factors unfavorable to capitalist investment, such as war or instability, or barriers, such as communal cleavages, to the amalgamation of the old and new bourgeoisies, etc. Moreover, insofar as parts of the regime's initial populist ideology become customary legitimacy standards and insofar as incorporation of its populist base is institutionalized, post-populist development is likely to be gradual and the outcome possibly less inegalitarian than that found in pure conservative authoritarianism.

Plan of the Book

In the following pages, the preceding concepts will be brought to bear in an analysis of the rise and formation of the Baʿth state. Chapter 2 explains the crisis of the old regime as a product of Syria's historical development; it analyzes the traditional agrarian structures whose inequalities generated the grievances on which the Baʿth rose and the *ancien regime* whose fragility debilitated alternatives to Baʿthism. Chapter 3 looks at the forces of social change which undermined the old order and produced the middle class alienation, agrarian crisis, and peasant politicization from which the populist coalition arose. Chapter 4 examines the vehicles of populist revolt, looking at the radicalization of the army and the formation of the Baʿth Party; it then traces the political mobilization and conflict which brought the Baʿth to power. Chapter 5 examines the post-1963 formation of a new authoritarian-populist state. The initial struggle for power, its concentration and use by radicals to launch a revolution from above, and the consolidation of the new order through limited Leninization and the forging of a Presidential Monarchy, are analyzed. Chapter 6 looks at the structures of power on which this regime rests, army, party, and state bureaucracy, showing how each harnesses the village and contributes to regime power consolidation. Chapter 7 interprets the Baʿth-created peasant union as part of a populist variant of corporatism, linking the regime to its village base. Chapter 8 uses an array of village case studies to illustrate how the regime rooted itself in the countryside and how it affects village politics. Chapter 9 looks at the consequences of the regime's failure to incorporate the urban public: the rise of Islamic opposition. The final chapter relates the evidence in the bulk of the book to the concepts in this introductory chapter and draws some generalizations from the Syrian experience useful in understanding Middle Eastern politics.

2

Lord and Peasant in Traditional Syria: The Historical Roots of System Crisis

Although the Ba'th Party came to power by military coup d'état, it represented far more than a handful of rebellious officers. The rise of the Ba'th was rooted in a crisis of the agrarian structure and the failure of the traditional elite to consolidate its rule after independence. These developments, in turn, were a product of Syria's long history as a fragmented society split by a great urban-rural gap; Syria labored under a system of "oriental feudalism" established by generations of conquerors and transformed into a parasitic agrarian capitalism by its incorporation into the world capitalist system.

The Historical Shaping of Syrian Society

Syria's geography has shaped her historical fate. Syria's location at a strategic landbridge between three continents and amidst desert and steppe exposed her to continual movements of diverse peoples and invasions of nomadic tribesmen which left behind an extraordinary socio-cultural heterogeneity. The country's geographical complexity—a land of plain, desert, oasis, and mountain—provided the ecological bases for a socio-economic diversity which reinforced this cultural differentiation. This diversity, constant tribal penetration of society (with its endogamous marriage practices), localistic production on small holdings, and the primitiveness of transport and communication, produced and preserved a segmented, profoundly fragmented social structure and no unifying river system provided integrating counterforces. Nor, perhaps because of its exposed position, the prize of rival empires, did an durable indigenous historic state emerge capable of unifying this centrifugal society.

Syria's "mosaic" society was fragmented into a multitude of self-contained rival families, clans, tribes, villages, religious sects, and ethnic groups. The identifications and social existence of the individual were firmly rooted in these segments, most strongly in the patriarchal family, to an ever declining degree in each of the successively larger social segments in which the former was embedded. This segmentalism was associated with a culture of "ardent particularism," endemic conflict between the units of the "mosaic" and a feebleness of horizontal types of social association. Vertical ties of tribe and clientelism, although discontinuous and unstable, constituted the most effective social cement. A great center-periphery cleavage divided the dominant Sunni Muslim elite in the cities, controlling the state and much of societal wealth, from the mass of peasantry and tribesmen in their patriarchal communities, including a great variety of minority communities ranged along the periphery. In the Latakia Hills were Alawites, Christians and Isma'ilis; along the northern border, Kurds; on the desert fringe, Isma'ilis, Circassians, Turkomans and Bedouin; in the eastern Jazirah, Kurds and Bedouin; in the south, Druzes and in the southwest, Druze and Circassians. As the minorities were predominately peasant, the urban–rural cleavage reinforced communal divisions.

Geography also shaped the economic bases of Syrian society, making it a mixed world of precarious agriculture, trading cities, and nomadic pastoralism. Traditional Syria was predominately agrarian, but its ecology placed important limits on agricultural development and on the density and prosperity of peasant society. Agricultural development was limited by the scarcity and unreliability of the water supply and the mediocrity of much of the soil, eroded and exhausted by centuries of exploitation (Weulersse 1946:43–49, 52–53). Only about 1.8 million hectares of Syria's (post-independence) six million hectares of cultivable land is good soil suitable for intensive cultivation (IBRD 299). Only 10% of the total land surface receives a supply of rainfall adequate to support stable dry-farming and another thirty percent enough for extensive grain cultivation vulnerable to periodic drought; except with irrigation, there were major obstacles to crop intensification and diversification in most of Syria (Petran 21; IBRD 35, 41; Warriner 1948:81–82; 1962:57). It is true that, compared to neighboring countries like Egypt and Iraq, Syria has enjoyed a favorable man-land ratio, but this was in part a reflection of its highly extensive forms of cultivation as compared to their developed river-valley cultures. As Warriner (1962:57) put it, the "Fertile Crescent" is fertile only by comparison to the desert which surrounds it. Under these conditions, the land required great labor for a meager return and could only be made highly productive by a high level of technical and social organization, but this was largely lacking.

Irrigation, of course, held the potential to raise production by many times and relieve it of dependence on unstable rainfall, but, with some exceptions such as the Ghouta of Damascus, it was not practiced after ancient times on any significant scale. According to Thoumin (37–113), even where irrigation was undertaken it did not give rise to the large scale social organization of a "hydraulic society." Given the fragmentation of society and the lack of a strong state, it remained largely an individual or small group enterprise, a matter of a spring here, a waterwheel there, at most a village undertaking. Conflict over scarce water further fragmented society. Water rights, often poorly defined and subject to the balance of political power, were surrounded by an insecurity and arbitrariness which bred, according to Thoumin, a profound conservatism, defense of custom and unwillingness to innovate or agree to a more rational distribution: peasants feared any changes would be to the benefit of the larger landowning families. "A narrowness and force attaches to the spirit of private property [in water rights] despite the demands of a greater good." The scarcity of water created a zero-sum mentality which made social cooperation difficult; but it was, in part, the weakness of such cooperation which inhibited the hydraulic development for want of which much of Syria's limited water resources were wasted (Weulersse 1946:41–43, 162; Warriner 1948:92–95; Epstein 598).

The dominant mode of production in the absence of large-scale irrigation, extensive grain cultivation, was technologically primitive and of low productivity, yielding little surplus for accumulation and development. Extensive grain cultivation probably had, as well, long term cultural consequences, providing little impetus for development of a village work ethic, attachment to the land, or traditions of collective association which might have produced a more dynamic agriculture. Where man lacks the means to mold his environment, it molds him: in this environment of scarcity, the result was a deeply rooted culture of fatalism and a particularism that precluded the large scale social association needed to master a demanding ecology. Weulersse argued that the primitive level of technology was well adapted to Syria's unpromising ecological and social conditions, but it permitted only a primitive level of life which had crystallized for centuries (Weulersse 1946:26–27, 52–53; Warriner 1948:81–82).

At least until recent times, Syria's geography also put her astride major and lucrative international trade routes; the surplus derived from this middleman role gave rise to an urban civilization, only partially dependent on and to an extent isolated from its rural hinterland. The desert supported yet a third distinctive nomadic form of life. The existence of these alternative sources of wealth, together with the poverty of the agrarian base, produced a dominant culture hostile to work on the land. Rather, a strong merchant culture, with its stress on exchange instead of production, and a tribal culture more interested in honor and plunder than the creation of wealth, pre-dominated; thus, the cultural disposition to agricultural development was retarded (Hannoyer 1980:273; Weulersse 1946:121–122, 173; Warriner 1962:60–61; Bonne 150–151).

Syrian society was thus made up of three nearly separate and generally antagonistic "worlds," the city, the desert, and the sown (Holt 6). The city was historically dominant although occasionally the nomad contested its exploitation of the subordinate village. The city was the residence of ruling elites, in good part the residue of generations of outside conquerors; significantly, even landed elite families resided there, not in the countryside (Warriner 1962:67). The city had some political identity and form: the urban masses were linked to the elite through guilds and the ulama' and at times even armed and organized for self-defense. Hence, they could not easily be exploited and, indeed, because of their greater political power, the government tried to keep food prices low at the expense of the cultivator (Volney 215–216). But, being the residence of the landed military elite, the orthodox religious establishment, and traditional merchants and artisans, the Syrian city, unlike the free cities of the West, was a center of conservatism, not dynamism or radicalism.

A great gap divided the city and the village. The bulk of the urban population was, according to Weulersse, less a product of migration from the countryside than from other cities and, to an extent, from the desert. Syria was an "urban society with a tribal mentality" (Hreib 23); the dominant city values considered agriculture the proper work of subjects and peasants objects of scorn. Even Islam failed to bridge the urban-rural gap for the religion of the cities was high orthodoxy, an urban creed, which reinforced urban domination (Planhol 104). The religion of the countryside was a low folk Islam or some variety of heterodoxy; frequently the village lacked an imam and even when he existed there was little in the way of organized links between him and the Islamic establishment in the city (Sweet 48; Weulersse 1946:66–71, 85–87, 173–174, 227; Epstein 605). Indicative of the sharp gap between city and village was the absence of many smaller towns between them, a symptom, according to Planhol (105) of a semi-arid environment with an intrinsically vulnerable rural life. Few bonds of interdependence bridged the urban-rural gap. Urban life was less dependent than elsewhere on its rural hinterland, the irrigated gardens on its periphery supplying, except for grains, much of its food, the long-distance trade its wealth (Weulersse 1946:85). But this did not prevent the city from extracting a surplus from the village to satisfy the imperial treasury, pay its soldiery, and enrich the notable who held the tax-farm. The city took a great deal but rendered the countryside (*rief*) little in return. The city consumed and traded but produced little except for the artisanal production destined for urban markets; manufactured goods from the city were, thus, rare in the village. Nor did the city provide what is sometimes its justification, security and justice: the government apparatus was controlled by great urban families who used their "absolute political primacy" to encroach on and exploit the peasant. Much less did the city deliver social services, education, or health (Warriner 1957:56; Weulersse 1946:87–88).

If the supremacy of the city rested on wealth and government, in the tribal world of the desert nomad, where the sway of government hardly reached and where the nature of a pastoral economy put limits on the accumulation of wealth, physical force, mobility, and courage were the keys to supremacy. Here the camel-herding warrior aristocracy was master, living on plunder, tribute, and caravaning. To these lords of the desert the lesser non-noble sheep-herders paid tribute for protection. The mobility and violence of the nomad had long given him equality in his relation with the city and mutually beneficial relations existed; for example, urban merchants invested in herds entrusted to the nomads and divided when they reached maturity. In the relation of desert and sown, however, the dominant theme was the struggle between the two for living space, and in this contest the peasant was at a great disadvantage. Lacking the mobility and ferocity of the "man of the tent," the peasant was subjected to tribute or plunder or both.

Weulersse (1946:62), in a trenchant passage, describes the joy of the nomad in "returning to the liberty of the desert that which culture has enslaved" and the "terror of the peasant in the face of the man of the tent, master of everything he can take since he has nothing to lose." In the long periods when the state was weak, the nomad pushed back the boundaries of cultivation. But even when agriculture was on the advance this was accompanied by tribal settlement which infected peasant society with a nomadic spirit inhospitable to work on the land, a profound improvidence and an exaltation of lineage over the love of the land typical of the peasantry elsewhere (Weulersse 1946:60–66; Warriner 1962:60–61; Hourani 1946:66).

The village, the center of rural life, was, thus, caught between city and nomad. By comparison to them—except in mountainous areas where their sway could not reach or where the peasantry was tribally organized—the village was defenseless and "open to the strongest" (Weulersse 1946:80, 249–250, Ziadeh 247); the rural population was scattered and immobile, lacking any extra-village identity or leadership. The village, being the weakest of the three worlds, was forced to carry the burdens—taxation and plunder— imposed by the others. Yet, in this pre-capitalist society, land and man were nevertheless united: as long as the peasant paid his taxes and cultivated the land, there was no legal sanction for expelling him from it until the penetration of capitalism in the 19th century. Moreover, the villages, or alternatively their constituent clans, were vibrant units of social life and solidarity. In some villages, especially those of small proprietors in semi-arid areas, musha' tenure held, collective control of land in which individually worked parcels were periodically re-distributed to prevent outside intrusion, maintain equality, and minimize individual insecurity. In a few villages (e.g. in the Kalamoun Mountains between Damascus and Homs) strong community life was forged around the building and management of collective irrigation works. Where collectivist forces existed, the council of elders was a strong village-wide leadership and there were powerful pressures for the maintenance of equality and against individual initiative and aggrandizement.

Atop this divided society rested the ruling military-bureaucratic elites of the patrimonial conquest states of which Syria was for most of its history a province, including the last four hundred years under Ottoman Turkish rule. As Muslims, these elites enjoyed some legitimacy as long as they maintained order in a chronically insecure society. But because they were largely foreign in origin and constantly replenished from outside Syria, they never put down strong roots in the countryside or developed into a stable landed aristocracy able to integrate state and society.

Indeed, in the *rief* the patrimonial state was little more than an apparatus for the extraction of the already slim economic surplus. Under this system of "Oriental Feudalism," private property in land, reflective of nomadic tradition, was not recognized and the conquered land was in principle the sole property of the prince or state. The prince initially distributed the land among his retainers as fiefs or benefices in return for military or administrative service, though self-sufficient peasant villages remained in actual possession and use of the land. But typically this gave way to tax-farming by urban notables or functionaries: in practice theoretical state ownership and peasant usufruct obstructed the emergence of a hereditary landed class and encouraged instead "commercial rights of absentee exploitation" and the divorce of the ruling elite from the land. Under the Arab empires, the *iqta'* was a parasitic fiscal device quickly separated from military service; the Ottoman *timar* system was the most coherent effort to link land rights and military service, but it did not foster a true knightly class controlling hereditary estates with political-judicial functions over peasant society and, in any case, timars were established only briefly and in certain areas, almost none in Syria. Instead, the local pashas became chief tax-collectors, allowed to squeeze as much as they could from the peasantry while a class of urban notables (*ayan*) arose, thriving on tax-farms without performing any political or military service. The tax-farmer/notable held his benefice at the pleasure of the Sultan, unable to acquire legal right of private property over the land assigned to him and vulnerable to dismissal from his *iltizam* according to the vagaries of court politics. This instability of tenure made it in the interest of the notable to squeeze the peasant in order to amass a fortune as soon as possible or to placate the growing demands of the imperial treasury. Since the tax system took a proportion of the product rather than a fixed sum and increases in production would only increase taxes, the system discouraged work and land improvement on the part of the cultivator. The tax-farming system, combined with the nomadic origins (Arabia, later central Asia) and urban residence of the ruling elites, the lucrativeness of trade, and the inhospitableness of the area to agriculture militated against the development of an interest among the elites in the development and protection of rural life; plunder and taxation were simply too easy, agriculture too risky and alien to their traditions.

One result was that the conquering elites failed to become a political leadership in the villages capable of legitimizing the state and representing agrarian societal interests to it. Rather than being heads of manors on their ancestral soil, with personal links to the village communities, the elite lived in the city where the culture they valued and the power and office needed to get and protect their tax farming concessions were concentrated. On the other hand, a strong stable local gentry, performing political functions, did not arise from the land itself; this would have perhaps required a richer agrarian base and a greater willingness by the state to accept such a development, but these conditions only obtained in certain more fertile and inaccessible areas such as the Lebanese mountains. While the state did rule through local mediators and gatekeepers such as the tribal-like *zu'ama* or sectarian leaders and while in times of greatest state weakness they acquired real autonomy in the less accessible areas, these leaders, fragmented by segmental rivalries, never acquired any of the corporate cohesion of a true aristocracy and the state never legitimized a political/representative role for them independent of its sway. Instead, it embraced a theory of bureaucratic absolutism in the belief despotic rule was necessary to hold a fragmented society together. Hence an enduring elite-society gap translated into an inherently fragile state (Akhrass 45–46; Anderson 365–373, 508–513, 515; Baer; Hitti 215–217; Ma'oz 1968:152–154, 158–163; Hourani 1946:66–67; 1966:25; Issawi 71–72; Karpat 71–79; Bonne 30–35; Musallim 11–17).

The ruling elite also failed to lead and in some respects actually retarded economic development. The lack of an authentic landed class discouraged agricultural development. No gentry or estate managerial class responsible for development of production comparable to those in both the West and East Asia emerged. The absence of those who controlled the land from the countryside translated into little concern by state or lord to protect or develop the agrarian base of society, and only a strong state, interested in and capable of containing the nomad and maintaining irrigation networks, could sustain agrarian prosperity in Syria (Hamide 398). Significantly, only in the garden areas around the cities, which alone were held as private property (*mulk*), was there investment and development of production. Elsewhere, caught between the exactions of city and nomad, agriculture suffered a largely uninterrupted decline from the days when the area was the granary of the Mediterranean world: the anarchy and invasions of the 11th–14th centuries, followed by the decline of order in the 17th and 18th centuries led to the desertion of numerous villages, their numbers falling according to Bonne (377) from 3400 to 400 by the mid-nineteenth century. The pervasive insecurity from climate and nomad and the exploitation by city and state all discouraged the technical innovation and investment which in the West led to an agricultural revolution providing the base for capitalist development. Moreover, the dominance of the ruling elite, essentially oriented to war, over the cities, combined with the instability and, at a certain point, decline in the trade routes, blunted the emergence of a secure and independent commercial bourgeoisie as well.

Lacking a firm base in agriculture, vulnerable to instability from shifts in the international trade routes and to recurrent nomadic devastation, and deprived of an indigenous leadership committed to development, Syria's economy generated no sustained processes of accumulation and innovation. Thus, at a time when the requisites of capitalism were coming together in the West, this society was in a long decline rendering it incapable of autonomous development. Economic stagnation, the great state-society gap, and a divided and unmobilized society made the Ottoman domains, including Syria, especially vulnerable to the rising power of the West. Syria's lack of a dynamic indigenous leadership able to develop its slim resource base would leave it crippled, not only in facing the West, but in trying to build a new state in the years after independence. (Anderson 501–502; ad-Dahr 110–112; Volney 213; Ma'oz 1968:131–133, 163–165; Klat 47–50; Hourani 1946:25–26; 64–66; N. Lewis 1955).

Imperialism, Capitalist Penetration, and the Crystallization of Agrarian Structure

More than a century of imperialist threat, economic penetration, and political occupation reshaped traditional Syria. In the late Ottoman period, pressures from the West led to the *tanzimat* reform movement which forged a stronger more penetrative imperial state. But this state could not guard its economic frontiers and Syria was gradually incorporated as a dependency into the world capitalist market; while the potential for independent capitalist development was thereby retarded, "dependent capitalism" nevertheless began to reshape society. Integration into the global market undermined local artisanal industries, but it stimulated the beginnings of commercial agriculture for export, the growth of the grain trade, and a semi-legalization of private property in land by the Land Code of 1858.[1] This gradually resulted, albeit unintentionally, in the formation of large land-holdings in the hands of notables who extended their control into the rural hinterland, eroding the peasant's previous right of usufruct and laying the foundations for the great latifundia of the twentieth century. Combined with the gradual decline in the old long-distance trade routes and the growing monopolization of external commerce by foreign merchants and the Christian clients of the West, this development created a local elite far more dependent on agricultural revenue than hitherto. (Harik 1972a; Karpat 84–90; Warriner 1962:68–70; Hourani 1946:24–26; 1966:28–29; Issawi 206–207; Hannoyer 275; Petran 47).

The unfolding of these changes in the late Ottoman era had ambiguous consequences for Syria's development. The emergence of a class of urban notables with more secure control over landed property meant the rise of a potential indigenous ruling class, a nascent Syrian bourgeoisie, landed, commercial and official in character; its roots in local society, though still shallow, made it a potentially integrating force. Commercial agriculture also began to forge economic bridges among formerly autarkic cities and villages. But because private ownership and commercial agriculture were merely imposed on the pre-capitalist subsistence forms of production, they stimulated no agricultural revolution; as European manufactures destroyed local handicraft industries there were, moreover, few opportunities and little disposition until much later to invest the profits of commercial agriculture in local industry. As such, early capitalist penetration failed to stimulate much economic development. At the same time, as the class structure, formerly always very fluid, began to clearly crystallize, class conflict between the new landlords and the peasantry at whose expense they were established, began to develop. And, the growing need of the Ottoman government for revenue to cover the expenses of modernization and its mounting foreign debt, increased the tax burden on the common people; in places where the state was extending its penetration and exactions—e.g. the Hauran—repeated peasant revolts were touched off (Schatkowski-Schilcher 23–24). The local notables, enriching themselves on the remnants of the tax-farming system, were often perceived as accomplices in the central government's extraction from local society, made all the more onerous because little of the revenues sent to Istanbul ever found their way back in the form of expenditures for local services or development (Hourani 1968:63–64; Shamir 351–381; Ma'oz 1968:87–107; Schatkowski-Schilcher 13–14, 17).

The French occupation consolidated the formation of an indigenous ruling class and further crystallized the new class system developing in Syrian society. The French accelerated the development of the large private landed class. The final replacement of tax-farming by a regime of private property in land gave it secure tenure and allowed it to keep much more of the agrarian surplus (al-Dahr 95). While French policy made a few half-hearted efforts to protect small peasants, its general effect was accelerated encroachment of the landed notability on the peasantry and on the substantial state and *waqf* lands in the country. At the same time, the patina of legitimacy accorded to the "feudal" order under Muslim Ottoman rule was shattered and the association of land concentration with alien rule only reinforced its lack of legitimacy in mass eyes; indeed, it was widely believed that the French aimed to create a friendly landed elite which would support dependence on France. In addition, the reinforcement of security, which in good part amounted to a virtual disarming of the peasantry and tribesmen, increased the relative power of the notability (Akhrass 7; Warriner 1948:94; Hamide 197; Hanna 35–36, 41–43, 222–223, 243, 368; Petran 70; Lerner 271; Arudki 20–23).

The development of large landed property and a certain "modernization" of Syria's notability transformed it into a full-fledged agrarian bourgeoisie. It acquired Western education and its sons went into the modern professions or senior posts in the new bureaucracy established by the French. The French discouraged industrial development, retarding the emergence of a national bourgeoisie, but a Westernized professional and white collar middle class began to emerge out of the lesser commercial bourgeoisie. These developments introduced fundamental contradictions into Syrian society. The French fostered new Westernized classes but discouraged the industry needed to meet their needs, sowing the seeds of economic dependency and social instability; imperialism brought the village under increased urban control, but in Westernizing the new upper and middle urban strata, widened the cultural gap between them and the rural masses. The French also introduced the formal structures of a modern liberal state which provided the framework (parliament, parties) for a new class cohesion among the notability and became the focus for a growing nationalist movement, of which the most advanced wing of the agrarian bourgeoisie assumed leadership. But this alien-imposed regime would ultimately prove too fragile to contain the contradictions imperialism had generated in the heart of society.

What is most crucial is that when a true large land-owning elite finally developed in Syria, it came at the recent expense of the peasants, and, being historically late, was detached from traditions of political leadership in the local community as well as economic management on the estate. Although its leading wing developed into a semi-modernized agrarian bourgeoisie with a certain national character, it never achieved legitimacy in the countryside. Indeed, its formation sowed the seeds of landlord-peasant conflict on which the old regime would ultimately falter. In the remainder of this chapter, the social and political structures of the traditional regime, as they emerged in the late Ottoman and French periods and crystallized in the early post-independence years, are examined in greater detail.

Agrarian Structure Under the Old Regime

Landed Property: The Separation of
Ownership and Cultivation

If, by the twentieth century, agriculture provided the dominant economic base of Syrian society, the relations of agricultural production and exchange constituted the skeleton of the whole traditional social structure. The central pillar of this system was the control of landed property and its most salient characteristic was a great inequality in land distribution and a consequent separation between ownership of the means of production and the producer. Table 2.1 estimates the distribution of land among the agrarian population around 1950.

At the apex of the agrarian structure were the great estates of the landed notability, averaging 700 ha. in size (Mourad 26). Half the land was concentrated in large (100+ ha.) holdings owned by less than 1% of the agricultural population. These figures may actually understate the concentration of ownership since several holdings, while separately registered, may have been controlled by the same landed family; in the Ghouta, for example, 100 big landowners controlled 250 large holdings and the Quwatli family alone controlled 28 of them (Bianquis 1980:47–52). The lack of distinction between irrigated and unirrigated holdings (producing vastly different revenues) may also bias the figures; in many areas control of water, hence the ability to irrigate, was also concentrated in the hands of a few. Khader (1975:66) reports that 209 holders possessed 500–1000 ha. irrigated estates, and 95 owners ones of over 1000 irrigated ha., a formidable chunk of the nation's agricultural wealth.

About another third of the land surface was made up of medium sized holdings many of which were controlled by the urban and rural middle classes and not usually personally cultivated. Urban merchants and civil servants with extra income tended, in a society lacking an investment market, to buy land and much of the land around the cities was owned by them (Latron 218); each time a burst of commercial prosperity created a strata

TABLE 2.1 Pre-Reform Distribution of Land Ownership

Holdings (in hectares)	% of Agricultural Population	% of Land Surface
Large (100+)	<1%	50%
Medium (10 to 100)	9%	37%
Small (<10)	30%	13%
None (Landless)	60%	00%

Source: Hinnebusch 1989:88, 119-120.

of new rich in the cities, they sought to buy up nearby villages (Hamide 200). Other middle holdings were controlled by rich peasants and frequently not personally cultivated; if a peasant accumulated enough land and wealth, he would typically let the land to sharecroppers, move to the poor quarter of a nearby town, and take up commerce or money-lending (Latron 129–130). Even richer peasants who stayed in the village often hired a client-laborer to work their land (Weulersse 1946:114, 121; Hanna 69).

In all, more than two-thirds of the land was owned by persons who did not personally cultivate it. In contrast, owner-cultivators on small holdings, the vast majority of owners, controlled only around 13% of the surface. In consequence, almost two-thirds of the peasants owned no land. This was expressed in the traditional folk-saying: "He who owns does not work and he who works does not own" (Klat 52).

Several forces contributed to this separation between land and cultivator. The great proprietorships seldom originated in purchase. Some can be traced to grants made by the Ottoman Sultans to clients and great officers of state. But many were formed and most consolidated during the extended process under which land, previously public but held by peasants under rights of usufruct, was registered as private property in the name of tax-farmers or notables under late Ottoman rule. The Ottoman land registration project was beyond the understanding of the peasants who typically believed it was to facilitate tax collection or conscription and who were convinced to allow registration of their holdings in the name of a notable who promised to protect them against these exactions. Other land concentration had its beginning in the need of peasants, in times of insecurity, for a patron-protector against nomadic depredations, urban encroachment, or during intra-village conflicts; initially, a share of the product was paid in return for this protection, but in the process of land registration such patronage relations tended to be transformed into ownership by the patron. Land registration officials were easily swayed by bribery or the prestige and power of the notable to register land in his name. Moreover, the process of registration gave rise to endless litigation in which the peasant could not compete unless he had a patron to represent him in court, and even in this case he might end up losing his land to his "protector" anyway. Given the novelty of the notion of private property and the uncertainty of title in the long absence of a good cadastral survey, property rights became a matter of power and influence. The notable-tax-farmer who had previously taken 2/3 of the crop, passing on 1/3 to the government, had, with the consecration of private property only to pay a 10% land tax, but as landlord he still often took the customary two-thirds of the crop (ad-Dahr 95; Warriner 1948:86; Klat 50; Weulersse 1946:95–96, 116–117; Musallim 16–20; Naaman; Latron 213–214, 230).

After the fall of Ottoman rule, private appropriation of waqf and remaining state lands (including those of the Ottoman Sultan), continued to be a major source of land concentration. The French sought through cheap sale or grants of such land to consolidate and win over the landed class. Since this land was often cultivated by peasants who enjoyed virtual right of usufruct, this process was to their detriment and was feared and opposed by them (Naaman; Hanna 41–42, 47, 65; Keilany 1980:209); 20,000 families in 854 villages had their land bought up beneath them during French rule. Such private appropriation, combining nominal purchase and fraud, continued well after independence. In addition, where entrepreneurs brought supposedly uncultivated state land under the plow for five years, they could acquire title to it (Warriner 1962:101).

Debt was another mechanism of land concentration. All the factors which prevented the peasant from accumulating a surplus—extensive, low productivity cultivation, the exactions of nomad or notable, the peasant's own improvidence—made him very vulnerable in the inevitable lean years to dependence on urban merchants, money-lenders or notables for the wherewithal to tide him over; but these same factors normally made it impossible to repay such debts except by ceding his land to and becoming the tenant of his creditor (Warriner 1948:45; Weulersse 1946:114–515; Naaman). The process of land fragmentation encouraged by Islamic inheritance practices also began, as population growth resumed, to generate unviable microholdings whose owners were especially vulnerable to debt (Klat 53). The breakup of communal tenures tended not only to differentiate landholding among the peasants, but to give outsiders a foothold in small-holding villages which were typically enlarged through debt and power (Latron 220–239). Indicative of the extent to which the debt mechanism fueled land concentration was the outcome of one effort by the French to quell rural unrest in eastern Latakia by buying up several estates and distributing the land to the cultivators; within a few years the peasants had again lost their land through debt (Weulersse 1946:196–197; Latron 92–100).

The process of tribal settlement also gave rise to large landed property. The tribal chief was typically given—as the price of his political loyalty—personal title to tribal lands previously collectively owned; sometimes tribal members were thereby transformed into tenants on the chief's land, but in other cases the chieftain imported submissive peasants to work it or rented it to urban investors, while the tribesmen lost their grazing grounds and, little accustomed to settled agriculture, were left to fend for themselves (Shakra 47–48). Frequently, the chief moved to the city and assumed the life style of the great notability. Many of the tribesmen however, were reduced to abject poverty: merchants exploited them because they were too proud to haggle, rich peasants hired them at a pittance to watch their herds (Hanna 86–87; Weulersse 1946:117–118; Warriner 1948:49, 94).

Finally, in some areas of recent tribal settlement and among the mountainmen of the minority communities such as the Alawites, Druze, Isma'ilis and Kurds, a form of production relationship, which could be called "tributary," linking small-holders to patriarchal leadership, sometimes gave rise to differentiations in land-ownership. In these communities, the patriarchal community leader traditionally received a share of the product, either from common or individually held properties in recompense for religious, military and political leadership. Communal, kinship and political solidarities inter-locked with production relations making for relatively strong bonds between lord and peasant. Yet, the long-term tendency in some of these communities, especially after the crystallization of private property in land and in areas closer to the cities, was the differentiation of patriarchal leadership into a landlord stratum and the reduction of the free peasantry to sharecropping; then, even after the za'im ceased to perform political and judicial functions, his share of the crop continued as rent (Warriner 1962:60). Weulersse (1946:118) considered these formations midway between political sovereignty and property rights and observed that as the first relation was weakened the za'im would try to establish the second. As this happened, conflict between lord and peasant tended to erupt. These notables might, in turn, end up in the hands of urban usurers, thus becoming conduits for extraction of peasant wealth by the city; in this way the Kurdish mountains were drained of the benefits of their olive culture by Aleppine money-lenders who got the proud and idle aghas, used to spending everything they had on arms, vendettas, alcohol and gambling, in their grip (Hamide 524).

The process of land concentration went on pretty much unchecked from the mid-19th to the mid-twentieth century. According to Harik (1972a:356), small holdings represented 75% of land in the whole Ottoman domain in 1839 (but probably less in Syria); and they may still have controlled 25% in Syria in 1913 (Hannoyer 288; Musallim 17). By 1945, small peasant ownership amounted to little more than about 15% of the land while more than one-half of the peasantry worked on the big estates (Shakra 65). According to the IBRD (1955:355) study, 38% of the surface was in holdings over 100 hectares in 1946–1947 while at the end of 1952 this had risen to 49%.

Peasant proprietorship tended to survive under two conditions. In the mountainous regions, such as the Alawi, Kalamoun, and Druze mountains, where land was less desirable and less accessible or peasants more politically organized and less vulnerable to nomad or notable, small-holdings persisted. Secondly, peasant proprietorship survived in areas where the peasant could accumulate a surplus and achieve greater independence because rainfall or security was better or because irrigated garden or orchard culture, more prosperous and less suitable for large estates, existed. This was so in the Damascus Ghouta, in Idlib, the olive center, and in western Aleppo province where, relatively free of drought and the nomad, peasants were less fatalistic and more enterprising. But on the great central plains and on the desert fringes given over to extensive grain growing, vulnerable to drought and nomad, and open to the power and supervision of the notable, small ownership could not generally survive (Hamide 171, 345; Latron 114; Weulersse 1946:97, 120–121).

Landlord, Merchant, Peasant:
The Relations of Agricultural Production

The modest scope left to peasant proprietorship meant most peasants were either share-croppers or, to a lesser extent, agricultural laborers on the great estates. Typically, the estates were divided into small parcels worked by a sharecropper and his family using primitive technology and with little involvement by the owner-notable. The sharecropping tenure, in its modal forms, provided that the peasant receive 50% of the crop if he provided labor, water, seeds, implements and animals (*al-sharika al-hamwiya and al-halabiya*). In the common cases where he could provide only labor and the landlord provided draft animals, seed, and paid the taxes, the cultivator got 20–25% of the crop (e.g. *al-sharika al-muraba'*). Generally, if labor was scarce or the notable distant or checked by a rival, peasant bargaining power increased and his terms improved. Under the *sharika al-khamsa*, the landlord provided land, a house, and paid the taxes, while the peasant provided labor, draft animals and seed entitling him to 70–80% of the crop (Hamide 215–216; Hanna 51–54). In the case of garden culture (olives, vines, fruit-trees), long-term enterprises requiring peasant diligence and thus a bond of mutual interest between owner and cultivator, the peasant's status approached that of an actual "partner." When a proprietor furnished land, animals, and irrigation for established garden culture, he usually split the crop with the peasant, though in Ma'arrat an-Nu'man where landlord power was unrivaled, he took 2/3; where a proprietor enlisted a peasant partner to start a new garden under the terms of contracts called *mugharasa*, the cultivator received not only a share of the trees or vines he had raised at their maturity, but sometimes the land with them (Hamide 218–219). Moreover, in garden cultivation the owner was much more likely to invest in the land, thus contributing to the common prosperity of the partners and increasing the bond of mutual interest (Weulersse 1946:129–130). These favorable relationships were, however, a-typical, and, at the other extreme where the peasant's bargaining power was low (perhaps due to overpopulation), he might receive as little as 16% of the product (Latron 47–90).

Because it was common for the weighing of the harvest to be in the hands of the landlord and his men, the peasant frequently got less than he was entitled to. Moreover, he might be obliged to render various services to the lord such as working part of his estate without recompense, gathering firewood for the estate house, or sending his daughters for unremunerated domestic service there. In some areas the situation of the peasant was comparable to personal servitude; he might need the permission of the lord to marry and the latter enjoy the "jus primae noctis" (Hanna 61–62; Weulersse 1946:124; Fedden 207). On the larger estates it was common for the landlord to employ an overseer or *wakil* to supervise the sharecroppers; in this case, the measure of semi-independent self-management which made the sharecropping contract preferable to wage labor for peasants was negated. The interest of the wakil was to increase his own wealth at the expense of peasant and master: "for the peasant he is another parasite to feed and serve and one who needs to make his fortune" (Weulersse 1946:126–127). Some landlords policed their estates with armed retainers. Many believed they had the right to beat their peasants or kill their cattle and indeed, with the local gendarmerie in their pocket, in practice they often did: the peasant was expected to accept the landlord as "your ruler, your judge" (Seale 40).

The tenant had no security of tenure, protection against eviction, or right to compensation for improvements he made to the land when the tenancy was terminated (Klat 54; Warriner 1948:87). His house, even when he built it himself, did not belong to him. If labor was plentiful, landlords often made a practice of expelling sharecroppers to prevent development of peasant solidarity against them and keep them submissive; e.g. in Ma'arrat an-Nu'man and Salqine landlords expelled Mawali tribesmen and replaced them with more docile Alawis (Hamide 154). Hanna (52) claims the peasant lived in fear of starvation because he could be so arbitrarily expelled from the land. But even if labor was scarce, peasants' leverage did not always increase since landlords often were able to tie them to the land through debt; some landowners actually made a practice of borrowing money from banks at fairly low interest and lending it to their sharecroppers at high interest, thereby increasing their share of the crop and the peasant's dependency (Weulersse 1946:125; Latron 53–56).

Generally, this system, far from giving rise to healthy or productive relations of lord and peasant, was an obstacle to both agricultural development and the integration of society. The landlord played little role in the agricultural cycle; he preferred the sharecropping tenure precisely because it enabled him to derive revenue without making a substantial contribution of investment or management and to put the risk of unstable dry farming on the peasant (Latron 115; Warriner 1948:84–87; 1962:59–60; Klat 52–53). Instead of agricultural investment, the landlord funneled his money into status-maintaining consumption and display (ad-Dahr 113). He rarely visited the estate and, having been raised in the cities, considered farming servile (Weulersse 1946:126–127). The fact that many estates were owned in common by large extended notable families also deterred investment and effective management. Only on medium irrigated holdings, typically of merchants, near the city was there a tradition of investment and innovation. The resulting low levels of productivity tended to relate lord and peasant in a zero-sum game; what one gained could only be at the expense of the other. The landlord regarded the peasant as a mere source of income and power and, always short of cash to meet his growing needs, sought to squeeze the peasant, leaving only enough for bare subsistence. A great cultural gap separated the two. Hanna (72-3) describes, with little exaggeration, the attitude of the lord:

> His "right" created in him a spirit of arrogance, superiority, disdain of work, and profligacy with money he didn't work for. He lived from youth surrounded by servants as if . . . creation was to do his wishes. Becoming lazy, he rides horses and hunts, violates others' women and is presented with the goods of the earth by others who plow it. He despises the world, too: . . . he won't think of public service . . . as long as the "public" is peasants who are lower than beasts. His expenses when living in the city increase while his land is limited: thus he's always insolvent, has no concern for tomorrow: "We're nobles, but broke."

For his part, the peasant, nursing memories of his dispossession, resented landlord power and responded with evasion, theft, indolence negligence, and an occasional jacquerie. His "creativity" went not into work or initiative but ruse and duplicity against the master and his overseer. According to Weulersse, an intense submerged struggle characterized the relation of lord and peasant. Little community of interest bound them: the relation, as Warriner argued, was less an exchange of services or a division of labor in a common enterprise than an appropriation of the producer's small surplus for a scarce monopolized factor of production. The peasant had neither the motive or the means to improve his condition by increasing production. He could accumulate no investment capital by himself and the landlord did not provide it. He had no incentive to improve the land because, given his insecure tenure, improvements would only redound to the benefit of the lord and any increase in output would, at least in part, be taken by the landlord. Reduced to dependency, ignorance and, at best, a subsistence level of existence, the peasant was fatalistic and lacking in any productive initiative; physically undernourished, he had a weak physical capacity for work. The consequences of this system were misery and poverty for the peasant and agricultural stagnation and social malaise in the countryside (Hanna 62–64; Warriner 1962:59; Warriner 1948:86; Klat 53–54; Weulersse 1946:127–129; Latron 49–51; Naaman; Hamide 209; Epstein 598).

Despite all this, a share-cropping tenure was more favorable for peasants than wage labor. The latter was often only seasonal, might require considerable migration or work under a labor boss who took his cut, and at "starvation wages"—of 10 English pounds a year in the early 1940s (Warriner 1948:88). Though capitalist plantations worked with hired labor were the exception in Syria, landless laborers were rapidly growing. Hanna (66–67) reports that in 1939 there were some 800,000 agricultural workers, including women and poor small-holders forced to do seasonal labor. Though, nationwide, agricultural wage laborers amounted to no more than 20% of the peasantry, in two villages which Warriner (1948:87–88) studied in the early forties, they made up 30–60% of all families. Work opportunities varied sharply by season: harvest workers received one-sixth to one-twelfth of the harvest, but in the off-season wages decreased in value 30–50% (Latron 80–90). Only if a laborer worked for a peasant proprietor or petty rural notable might his situation be better; he might then even live as a member of the family.

The position of the small-holding peasant appears to have been better than that of sharecropper or laborer. Peasants themselves had a great desire for landownership (Warriner 1948:85) and there was a palpable gap between living conditions in villages of small proprietors and those on the great estates (Naaman, Weulersse 1946:19). Warriner (1962:94), for example, contrasted the destitution and disease in the landlord villages of Hama with the "relative prosperity" of one of the few peasant owned villages; a study by Ihsan al-Jabiri cited in Hanna (60) indicated that the income of "free peasants" was around 50% higher than that of those "under feudalism." Another observer contrasted two villages in the Ma'arrat-an-Nu'man area: the small-holding villagers of Kafr Nabel, though poor, were characterized by their activity, zeal, work, links to the land, and honesty; although material conditions in the villages on the surrounding estate differed little, there peasants had all the opposite qualities (Hanna 63–64).

But peasant proprietorship did not, on the whole, translate into prosperity. In most cases, small peasant proprietorship survived only on the least desirable land or in mountainous areas where life was often harsh; thus the Druze mountains suffered from an acute scarcity of potable water, Hauran peasants were frequently driven from their land by drought (Epstein 609), and the peasants of the Alawite mountains lived at the most primitive level. Peasant proprietorships, squeezed by the expansion of the big estates and fragmented by Islamic inheritance laws, were frequently too small to provide more than bare survival. In many peasant villages under musha' tenure, a peasant's holdings were fragmented into a number of separate strips which, moreover, were periodically redistributed, discouraging conservation and improvement of the land (Hanna 37); significantly, where it gave way to individual holdings, crop diversification and land improvement sometimes followed (Hamide 193–194).

Equally important, however, was the fact that land ownership did not necessarily confer access to other requisites of production or to an equitable market. In an arid country like Syria, land was often useless without irrigation water. In some places, land and water rights customarily went together and in limited areas, notably the Kalamoun mountains, water works were collectively built, owned, and regulated by peasants enjoying equality of access. But in the many places where water rights were not well defined, the door was opened for "rich peasants" and "great families" to use political power to establish unequal and arbitrary control over water; or villages upstream might acquire monopolistic control of water at the expense of small-holders downstream. As the need for water was separated from access to it, those with privileged access could sell their surplus at high prices or use it as a lever to acquire the land of those who, deprived of it, could not carry on cultivation (Hanna 300; Thoumin 100–123).

Having, for the most part, no access to bank credit (IBRD:89) and normally unable to accumulate much reserve for bad years, small-holding peasants were also dependent on money-lenders—landlords or more typically a merchant—for other requisites of production. Merchants provided credit to peasant clients and bought the peasant's surplus at harvest time, recovering their loans and interest from the proceeds. Once peasants fell into debt, they could seldom extract themselves from it; for example, in the thirties, each Haurani peasant owed an average of thirty gold pounds to Damascene merchants (Epstein 611). Peasants had no choice but to pay the often exorbitant interest demanded: typically 30–50%, but varying from 9–20% in good times, to 150% in an arid season (Hanna 56; IBRD 89). In addition to high interest rates, the peasant was further disadvantaged in these relations because he was forced to buy his production requisites at planting time when their prices were highest and sell his crops at harvest time when their prices were lowest. For example, in Idlib and the Kurdish mountains, small proprietors had to sell their olive oil at 50% below "normal" market prices (Hamide 199). The peasant's grain, seed, houses and cattle were often seized for debts (Hanna 312–313). Yet, though the peasant could seldom repay his debts, merchants often preferred not to foreclose on the land because the indebted peasant was a permanent source of supply at below market prices; in this way, big merchants built "empires of debtors" to service their marketing operations. Grain merchants made fortunes at the expense of both producer and consumer, especially in times of scarcity such as World War II when they sold wheat for triple the purchase price (Hanna 324). In addition to lack of alternative sources of credit, the rudimentary means of transport and the generally primitive organization of the market, especially the absence of storage facilities, kept peasants dependent on merchants to sell their products and supply them—at excessive cost—with the rudimentary goods they could not provide themselves. From the village to the city, there typically stretched chains of middlemen, each taking his share of the product, reducing to very little the return of the actual cultivator (Hanna 312; Hamide 275; IBRD 40, 401; Weulersse 1946:140–141; Latron 124–126; Epstein 600–601). Finally, the rural crafts which had supplemented agricultural income in some small-holder villages declined with Western capitalist penetration. For example, the destruction of the village dye industry by the introduction of artificial dyes was known as the "Kalamoun sickness" for its devastating impact on the viability of these peasant communities (Hanna 30); in rural Aleppo, too, once flourishing rural industries declined as manufactured products flooded the market (Hamide 302). Some, however, survived and in 1954 8.2% of the population was still reported employed in rural industries (IBRD 358).

The system of agricultural production relations translated into a very unequal distribution of income. Estimating from data reported in Ihsan al-Jabiri's study of income distribution in 1937, it appears that peasants "under feudalism" and agricultural laborers, together amounting to about 50% of the total population, received around 19% of total national income. "Free peasants," amounting to 14.5% of the population, received 7.7% of total income; thus the peasants, about two-thirds of the population, got only around a quarter of total income, while 15% of the population—big landlords, high officials, merchants and medium-sized landed proprietors—received about 57% of it, the remainder going to various urban strata (Hanna 59–60; Orgels 44–45; Zakariya 5–6). According to Hilan's (1969:225) figures on *agricultural* revenue just before the agrarian reform took hold (1960), while the top 2% of the rural population—"feudalists," together with urban absentee proprietors and intermediaries—took at least 50–60% and medium proprietors and rural merchants, making up 18% of the population, claimed another 20–25%, the mass of the peasantry, 80% of the rural population, received only about a quarter of the total revenue; while the peasant earned less than 100 L.S./capita, the upper stratum enjoyed an average income in excess of 1,000.

The Stagnation of the Traditional Agricultural Economy

The agrarian system was associated with agricultural stagnation which lasted well into independence. There are many indicators of the exceptional underdevelopment of Syria's rural economy. As late as the forties and fifties, observers were struck by the rudimentary technological level of the countryside: the primitive instruments, the near absence of crop rotation practices, pest control, seed selection, and fertilizer use. Two percent of cultivators used chemical fertilizer and natural manure tended to be burned for fuel in this tree-less land (IBRD 38–39, 73; Warriner 1962:57–58; Za'im 70). Weulersse remarked on the absence in places of so rudimentary an invention as the wheel. As late as 1946, only 284,000 ha. were irrigated although enough water and hydrologically suitable land was potentially available (physically, not necessarily economically), given the right technology, to irrigate 1.2 million ha. (Victorov 144). Although much of the land was held in large estates, none of the supposed advantages of scale were derived from it because the unit of production remained the small plot worked by the tenant. The rudimentary transportation system, as well as the low purchasing power of the population, restrained the market and hence the demand which might have encouraged agriculture. Of six million ha. suitable for agriculture, only one million were cultivated as late as 1922, 1.75 million in 1938 and 2.3 million in 1945 (Hanna 29; IBRD 19). In those areas which were planted, the cultivator produced only enough for 2–3 persons (Arudki 170), a very mediocre surplus. Animal husbandry, still largely in nomadic hands, wholly dependent on natural grazing, and lacking reserve food stocks, veterinary care or good breeding practices, was highly vulnerable to drought and disease; the lack of integration of livestock into the farming cycle meant the waste of fallow land which could have been used for pasture crops, lack of soil enrichment from such crops, and the limited viability of the peasant economy for which livestock is elsewhere a source of security and investment (IBRD 40, 79–88; Bonne 167–168).

In short, under the traditional regime, Syrian agricultural production and productivity remained very low. By the twentieth century agriculture constituted Syria's main productive base, the largest source of national revenue and employment, its products the basis of trade and industry. But its underdevelopment condemned rural life to backwardness and poverty; more than half the population, Warriner concluded, lived in extreme poverty and no significant stratum of prosperous independent peasants could develop (Warriner 1948:91; 1962:58). Moreover, the meager agrarian surplus provided no strong impetus to the development of domestic trade and industry in the cities and the backwardness of "human resources" in the countryside was an immovable anchor on social progress everywhere. The root cause of Syria's underdevelopment was thus the underdevelopment of its agriculture.

In Warriner's (1962:58, 61) view, the lack of responsiveness of the land, the unreliability of rainfall and the absence of irrigation meant agriculture produced a too meager and unreliable return to encourage much investment or development effort, but it was a vicious circle because the lack of the latter contributed significantly to the former. The system of production relations, itself partly an outgrowth of an unpromising ecology, was also a principle obstacle to the motivation, investment and social organization needed to spark sustained development. To break the vicious circles into which agriculture had fallen, Warriner (1948:97), writing in the mid-1940s, thought it would take an intrusion from "outside the system"—a new innovating leadership, modern technology (irrigation and mechanization), a reform of land tenure. But she could not see from where the motive power for such changes might come. Nevertheless, in the next two decades, all were to come about.

The Class Structure of the Traditional Regime

On the twin pillars of agricultural land-ownership and credit/marketing operations, was raised the class structure of Syrian society. At the top were the big landowners, some three thousand notable families, less than 1% of the population, owning half of all the land, and, for all intents and purposes, the peasants on it; the bulk of their income was derived from the land, a surplus extracted from peasant labor. They also dominated government and their educated sons filled the ranks of the country's lawyers, doctors and other professional occupations. Just below, but interlocked with the landed class, were the great merchants—grain speculators and wholesalers, hoarding or releasing the accumulated crop as market advantage dictated, big money-lenders, compradors, exporting agricultural products and importing from the West. There was no clear distinction in traditional Syria between the landed "aristocracy" and the commercial bourgeoisie, both deriving from the urban notability; branches of landed families engaged in commerce, while wealthy merchants invested their profits in land and became gentlemen. To be sure, a more entrepreneurial wing of the bourgeoisie oriented to the possibilities of agricultural modernization and industrialization was emerging, but it only became a leading element after independence and even then there was no real conflict between it and the more traditional wing. The conflict of landed aristocracy and bourgeoisie which led to democratic-capitalist revolution in the West was not replicated in Syria (Safadi 59; Hourani 1946:91–92; Dawn 158; Khoury 518–519; Hanna 71).

Downward from the agrarian-commercial upper class reached business ties linking it to the middle merchants, many of whom were also middle landowners in the areas around the cities, living off both commerce and rents rooted in agriculture. Their educated sons filled the middle ranks of the bureaucracy and the lesser professions. Like the big merchants, this traditional middle stratum failed to constitute an autonomous class able to challenge the landlords' power or yet conscious of a sharp difference of interests from them (Hourani 1946:91–92). Below it sprawled the commercial petty bourgeoisie of shopkeepers and artisans. All these commercial strata were linked by ties of clientage reaching down through the traditional quarters from big notable to petty one; by shared traditional values, above all, Sunni Islam incarnated in the ulama, recruited in its various ranks from the *suq*; and by their shared interest in the agricultural surplus—whether in the form of rents, interest or profits. Even the petty vendors, beggars, domestics, and laborers at the bottom of urban society were, to an extent, dependent on this surplus (Khoury 520–521).

Between the dominant city and the village was a thin stratum of rural notables. Some were rich peasants going into petty commerce and money-lending on the side; there were also the zu'ama, both political leaders and landowners, one face turned to village clients, one to urban patrons or the nearby landed magnate. Below the petty rural notability, were the peasant proprietor-cultivators and larger share-croppers, making up as much as 30% of the agricultural population; while some of these were relatively prosperous, many more were exploited by merchants, and, unable to support their families on their small-holdings, dependent on supplementary seasonal labor on the landlords' estates. The rest of the peasantry, at least 60% of the agricultural population, was landless. Close to the bottom of the social structure and making up the biggest single population category, around 40–50% of the agricultural population, were the sharecroppers on the great estates. A notch below them were the landless agricultural workers and the dispossessed tribesmen forced to migrate in search of a wage, making up around 10–20% of the agricultural population. According to Hanna (48–49) at a time (1938) when the "normal" living standard required an income of 50 piasters a day, peasants received less than 22 per day. Judging by Warriner's data (1948:87–89), the two landless categories were about equally wretched, except for the slightly greater security of the sharecroppers; neither lived at the minimum level of consumption in the mid–1940s (defined as 25 kg. of wheat, 1 kg. of meat, and 40 kg. of olive oil/month, 210 kg. of samn, 4 tins of kerosene and a small quantity of clothing per year) or had access to the most basic commodities.

Altogether, in 1937, peasants, workers, and the lower petite bourgeoisie, making up 74.5% of the population, received about 32% of national income, the middle strata of professionals, officials and prosperous craftsmen, making up 10% received about 11% of the income and the top 15.5% of the population, embracing the landed aristocracy, the middle and upper bourgeoisie, and perhaps part of the idle petty bourgeoisie, received 57% (Hilan 1969:221; Orgels 44–45; Zakariya 5–6).

Rural Politics Under the Traditional Regime

Political power in Syria grew directly out of its social structure. The enormous disparity in political resources the class system dictated deterred any challenge by those at the bottom to the ruling elites. Segmental divisions—clan, sect, locale—determined political competition, retarding the development of class consciousness among the masses. Clientalism constituted the political cement with which coalitions, "vertical" in nature, were built. Together, segmentalism and clientelism linked the masses, however precariously, to the ruling elites: each individual was part of a clan, quarter, or tribe whose patriarchal leaders, seeking protection or advantage for themselves and their communities, sought the patronage of a bigger notable with connections in the central governing power.

At base, clientelism was a function of the great economic scarcities and inequalities which made the masses dependent for land, credit or employment on the few with resources. It was reinforced by the insecurity of a society with a weak and unresponsive state for only through the protection of a powerful patron could common people get their rights respected (Latron 230). Clientalism was also a natural institution in a society with a strong kinship culture in which local personal face-to-face relations were the customary mode of social interaction. Big and little patrons existed everywhere, wrote Latron, linked in unstable alliances from the village up; clientelism was the connective tissue of this otherwise fragmented society (Sweet 45).

From the point of view of the patron, clients were essential political support for power struggles in arenas both small (the village) and large (parliamentary elections) and made up the followings of the proto-parties which began to form after the 19th century. For the state as a whole, clientelist ties between great and lesser patrons advanced the incorporation of tribal, sectarian and local patriarchal leaders, through parties and parliament, into the dominant urban notable class, generating a feeling of shared class interest among these elements. In so diluting intra-elite segmental cleavages, clientelism provided a fragmented society with a certain integrating force at the top. But below the elite level, the system preserved traditional fragmentation and, indeed, the power of the core elite, as in Ottoman times, rested on the mass *dis-integration* which allowed it to "keep each in its place" (Hreib 94).

There was however a basic distinction between the political weight of city and village in post-Ottoman Syria. In the city where the notables' "blocs" and parties were strongest and the masses more politicized and susceptible to mobilization, political leaders were relatively closely linked to their followings through personal leadership, kinship, residence, patronage and their *qabadayat*—quarter strong men (Khoury 1984). Many city people had, therefore, a certain real access to government.

In the countryside, the linkage of landlord and peasant-client was much more asymmetrical, rooted far less in patronage than passive submission and economic dependency. On the great estate, the landowner was natural lord and the sharecroppers, often facing him as atomized families or, at most, clans, were so much at his mercy that little scope for political exchange could have existed (Klat 57–58; Latron 216). Class consciousness was at its weakest, too, among many of the more depressed rural strata. This could be seen at its extreme among the bedouin: as Hanna (87) observes, although they were objectively being reduced to the most exploited and depressed part of society, the tribesmen had, owing to their tribal culture, almost no class feeling and remained subservient to shaikhly leaders.

Among the more independent peasantry, politics was somewhat more complicated. In the minority communities, religious solidarity and loyalty to patriarchal shaikhs was the dominant political feeling. Here, shaikh, za'im, muqaddam, amir, each leading peasant or tribal followings by virtue of lineage loyalty, personal strength, and charisma, linked their communities through clientage or alliance to the ruling establishment, but in a less direct and effective way than in the cities; some of them, turning into landlords, were also starting to identify more with the urban elite than their constituents.

Among the small holding peasantry elsewhere, the penetration of capitalism appears to have both split and stratified the village, opening the door to local political conflict and clientelism. As private ownership was legitimized, collective musha' tenures, often with government encouragement, began to break down, giving way to individual property. As this happened, villages split into family factions, their councils of elders enervated by rivalries. In a society of intense kinship consciousness and scarcity, there were plenty of occasions of conflict: over access to water and pasturage, over the boundaries of fragmented fields, village office, or the chastity of women; conflicts might erupt if the "shaikh al-addan" elected to control the flow of water abused this power, a common occurrence reflected in the peasant saying "no shaikh al-addan starts poor and doesn't end rich." When such conflicts turned into blood feuds, kinship solidarity, the very principle of village social life, became a threat to its existence (Hannoyer 280). Once village solidarity was shattered, internal differentiation and outside intervention followed. As individual property emerged, some peasants were enriched, some impoverished. When village rivals sought dominance through alliance with outside patrons, they opened the village to these stronger forces. A nearby landlord might buy up parcels of land or loan money to get a foothold in the village, and by supporting one village faction against another, establish himself as arbiter and patron; this was one way clientage bases useful in electoral contests were formed. Frequently, as a result of these processes, village political leadership, once based on kinship consensus, courage, force, or generosity was transformed into a petty notability based on economic inequalities and control of clientelist connections to the outside world. But this gave little real access to national-level power. (Latron 217, 220–239; Hannoyer 280–282).

Indeed, the clientelist system, confining the peasants' political horizons to the "little community," dividing them among themselves by local conflicts and solidarities, and linking them upward instead of horizontally, translated into passivity and powerlessness in the national political arena where the major decisions were made—or more often avoided—as it served the interest of the ruling class (Lerner 270; Ziadeh 205; Klat 57–59). Powerlessness produced a profoundly conservative political culture in the village which only reinforced the very regime which kept the peasantry in submission. Unable to control his environment and extremely insecure, the peasant feared change, believing from experience that it would be for the worse and, looking backward to some better age, clung tenaciously to tradition. This, combined with physical disease and debilitation led to quietism and resignation: "everything has its remedy in patience." Inured to the sudden turns of the wheel of fortune, the peasants did not question the why of things: "God provides and disposes" (Koury 46–49). Illiteracy and ignorance crippled their "capacity of . . . political combination" (Hourani 1946:91). Thus, the peasant normally confined himself to a bounded local life: the daily struggle to survive, a "family politics" detached from the macro-political arena.

Yet, the beginnings of the peasant politicization which would change this are evident at least from the time of the French occupation. Peasants and tribesmen made up the shock troops of the major nationalist risings against the French in the 1920s. Significantly, it was largely more independent peasants under tribal-like patriarchal leadership, not the atomized peasants of the great estates, who were mobilized in this struggle. At least initially, they were fighting more for local autonomy or for their chiefs than for a national cause and these chieftains frequently diverted the revolt into raids for plunder or struggles with rivals. Peasants, still very localistic in outlook, tended, once they won a local victory, to disperse to their villages, permitting the French to regroup and reverse their gains. These were all symptoms of the bounded outlook and limited associational capacity of a segmentalized society. But, to the significant extent the revolt took on the character of an Islamic jihad against the infidel, it began to approximate a wider national revolt and the very experience of revolt started to generate national—and hence political—consciousness. While the national struggle at first submerged social cleavages and conflicts, it soon threatened to spill over into social protest against notables aligned with the French and, to the extent the revolts resulted in a vacuum of government power, peasants sometimes turned violently against landlords. It was the mass uprisings of 1925–1926, linking city and *rief,* which forced the French to offer concessions to the urban notable elite leading the nationalist movement. But, alarmed at the anti-feudal character peasant revolt tended to assume, the traditional nationalist leadership never thereafter attempted to mobilize the peasantry in national revolt, and contented itself with largely peaceful protest in the cities. The countryside therefore remained relatively quiescent for the remainder of the French occupation, and as such, it was great power rivalries as much as local struggle which finally forced the French out of Syria in 1946 (Hanna 89–94, 220–225, 368–380, 409–418).

In the 1930s and 40s, symptoms of a submerged social struggle nevertheless occasionally broke through. Hanna (58) argues that the sharecroppers were normally kept passive and fatalistic; but to the extent "the stick and the whip," were removed, their suppressed class hated showed through and landlords realized they would lose control of their estates unless they maintained a "despotic hand." Indeed, where the governmental or landlord grip was weakened, peasant revolts often broke out. There is a record of such sporadic, usually small scale, but continuous peasant resistance to the landlord, especially in the Hama area. For example, when the French separation of Latakia from Damascus removed villages of Hama landowners from the sway of supportive government power, peasants immediately refused to hand over the landlord's share of the crop at harvest. When Alawi peasants in one of his villages so revolted, Muhammad Bek al-Azm had to give in and sell the land to them at half its value. The same happened to Abdu Agha al-Barazi. An armed conflict between the Barudi family and their sharecroppers over harvest division in the Hama village of Kurtaz ended in injuries and in 1935 peasants in the Hama village of Barin attacked guards of the Kaylani family (Hanna 382–385). Hamide reports that in Aleppo, too, peasant victims of landlord encroachment nourished a lively consciousness of their dispossession and the weakening of French power during World War II was the occasion for limited revolts aimed at recovering "usurped" land (Hamide 207, 213). As for small-holders, some, such as the Hauranis had a history of submission (Epstein 607–608). But, generally speaking, small-holders were more politically conscious and disposed to activism than the mass of sharecroppers and tribesmen especially if, taking temporary work in the cities, they came into contact with more class conscious workers (Hanna 67). Landlord encroachment on the land of small-holders or their competition over state land touched off many landlord-peasant conflicts with an increasing class content (Hanna 47, 65, 93, 221). Something akin to class consciousness also appeared among the mountain peasantry, whether sharecroppers or small owners. Kurdish peasants rebelled against their Aghas in the 1930s; a thousand were killed and though defeated, the remnants of the movement became active elements of the Left in the fifties (Hamide 148–150). In the 1940s, Druze sharecroppers calling themselves the *sha'biyun* ("Populars") revolted against the Atrash and although defeated by the latter's retainers, subsequently used the ballot box to sweep them out of local government (Seale 133; Hannoyer 280). In places, intra-village conflicts pitted small peasants against rich village elders who were more disposed to and favored by authority; in Deir Atieh, for example, there was a full scale rebellion against the dominant clans (Hanna 67). Nevertheless these revolts, sporadic or localized, and seldom challenging the nature of the system, only outcomes in specific cases, cannot be considered revolutionary. As Allush (14) put it, despite their deprivations, the peasants, "hating their submissiveness but ignorant of the secret of their own power . . . remained far from revolutionary consciousness or organization."

With the formation of a national parliament, peasants began to awake to the possible use of democratic procedures as channels of protest and redress. Peasants in conflict with landlords petitioned parliament; when it was against the landed family which held the local seat, their protest was naturally pigeon-holed. More often, villagers petitioned for roads, schools, and clinics, for exemption from taxes in bad years, for redress against tax-collectors who seized plows and seed for back taxes, for the right to fetch firewood from forests, and for wells to be drilled; that these petitions were seldom successful raised both the level of peasant political consciousness and alienation from the system. Peasants carried so little clout in parliament because, until middle class radicals began to challenge the landlords in elections, there were no alternatives to landlord candidates and hence peasants lacked much opportunity to use the electoral process to advance their interests: so little was there meaningful electoral competition in rural areas that campaigning was almost entirely confined to the cities (Jabbur 73–74). Peasants also lacked the basic resources—literacy, organizational skills—needed to make an impact on the national political arena; and, urban intellectuals who might have provided them leadership were still too attached to the establishment or engrossed in the urban fight for liberal political rights for themselves. For the great mass of the peasantry, government remained a threatening power to be evaded or submitted to, not a system on which demands could be made or support given. Until peasants produced their own leadership from educated sons of the village, rural politics was not to take on a significant sustained class dimension and national politics remained an urban game largely isolated from village needs and wishes.

State and Power Elite Under the Old Regime

Starting under the French and emerging full-blown after Syria's 1946 independence, an indigenous governing elite and a new constitutional state took form at the apex of society, marking a major break with Syria's history of foreign autocratic rule. Yet, despite the legitimacy which might have been expected to accrue to the leaders of the independence struggle, they never consolidated their rule. And, though liberal in form, the state, profoundly traditional in content and social roots, largely continued, in the first years after independence, the notable politics of the pre-modern era.

The landlord-merchant upper class made up the natural political elite: descended from the Ottoman and urban notability, it led the independence struggle against the French and easily took over the reins of the post-independence state. Landlords overwhelmingly dominated parliament and the same small group of landlord politicians made up the recruitment pool of presidents and cabinet ministers for decades (Winder; Dawn). Even after the introduction of a formally liberal election system, given the economic dependency of the peasant and the absence of alternatives and of the secret ballot, control of great estates gave control of the votes of the men on them. Parties were mere parliamentary blocs of landlords, tribal chiefs and their clients, without ideology or organization, for, secure in their local power bases, landlord-politicians had no incentive to draw the masses into participation or seek their active support.

Politics centered on the rivalry of landlord coalitions over office and spoils. The big divide between them was largely regional, that is, between cities, especially Damascus and Aleppo; after independence the dominant National Bloc (*al-kutla al-wataniya*) would, in fact, split into two main factions, the National Party (hizb al-watani) largely based in Damascus and the People's Party (hizb al-sha'b), based in Homs and Aleppo. An urban-rural split was also dimly visible, and, indeed, a "Farmer's Party" of reactionary feudal lords and rich peasants briefly opposed the National Bloc in the thirties. But, symptomatic of the landlord-dominated state, when parliament dealt with agrarian issues, it did so almost exclusively from the point of view of landlord, not peasant interests. Deputies gave lip service to demands for spending on rural clinics, roads, and development, but, at the same time, routinely called on government for tax relief, chiefly for themselves. Landed interests made repeated drives, often successful, to lower agricultural taxes and interest on their debts to state banks; they also demanded the salaries of urban officials be slashed in order to cut the land tax or finance agricultural "projects." These moves were naturally resisted by leading elements of the urban bourgeoisie in government posts. When, in 1937, 41 landlord deputies asked for renewed tax exemptions, urban deputies opposed it, declaring that landlords had previously been exempted because so many were deputies and that if anyone should be exempted at the expense of the treasury, it should be the poor, who often suffered confiscations for unpaid taxes; landlord deputies would nevertheless have prevailed, having a big majority of votes, if the speaker, Faris al-Khuri, a scion of the merchant bourgeoisie, had not contrived to pigeon-hole the proposal. In a similar case, a committee recommended exemption of tractors from import taxes (having at the same time to explain to deputies just what they were), but was challenged by a populist deputy who pointed out parliament had denied a similar exemption for the simple plows used by peasants (Hanna 71, 88, 210, 394–397).

No sharp cleavages among the elite over basic socio-economic policy were apparent, though there were shades of difference. Many of the great landlords were reactionaries by any standard, such as those in Homs who opposed the opening of schools in their villages for fear it would stimulate demands for change or the Hama landlords who opposed settling peasants on reclaimed state land since it would drive up the price of labor (Shakra 14; Klat 58–59; Hanna 62–63). They professed to see social life as a natural order preordained by God which could not be improved, an attitude which sanctioned venality and irresponsibility (Koury 45–49). Viewing themselves as an enlightened aristocracy superior to the ignorant masses, they saw no role for the latter in politics, except deference and obedience (Warriner 1962:96–97). There was a deafening silence of ministry and parliament alike on the question of land reform, perhaps the major issue of modern Syria. After independence when all social strata expected a better deal, workers, in fact, won a labor code, but landlords would make no concessions, fearing any reform would open the door to challenges to the whole contested legitimacy of their private property in land (Hanna 430–431). Parliament obstructed the mildest proposals for agrarian reform, even the distribution of state land which notables controlled or coveted (Hamide 184), and only later under pressure from the army and the streets was this issue raised. Because merchants feared it would hurt their control of the market, the government even turned aside proposals to build crop storage facilities (IBRD 100). Even the progressive wing of the national bourgeoisie, which might have been expected to view land reform as essential to creation of a market for industrialization, being linked by family and business ties to the landed elite, viewed landed property rights as sacred. Za'im (71–72) argues that Syrian capital was simply too usurious and commercial-oriented to lead reform and that even the nascent industrial bourgeoisie was content to monopolize a small market rather than seek an expanded one. The few progressives in parliament advocated only the distribution of state land or the raising up of the peasants through schools and health clinics.

Government was, thus, not generally seen as an instrument of change or development: this was the laissez-faire state so congenial to the early bourgeoisie, its main functions to provide patronage for notable-politicians and security for the property rights of the "haves." Politicians were preoccupied with filling offices with clients and servicing clientage networks. As Walid Khalidi (1958) put it, after independence the old politicians assumed they had fulfilled their duties to the people and could start attending to themselves; the notables of the quarters, wrote Jundi (43–44), streamed into government offices, each expecting his reward for the independence struggle, and "[President Shukri] al-Quwatli was generous with them." At the same time, though peasant petitions for roads, water, schools, and clinics had bombarded parliament since the thirties, with some exceptions, little was done in response (Hanna 391–409). Far from leading, the government lagged behind rural demands for development: villages appealed for assistance in creating cooperatives in the fifties, but in vain for officials distrusted such experiments (IBRD 93–94). The little interest this elite had in the development of agriculture, the very base of the economy, can be seen in the fact that while it was quick to open a college of law, establishment of a faculty of agronomy had to wait for the formation of the UAR. This was a function of a long history in which power rather than production was the key to agrarian wealth: a law career gave access to government office and the spoils that came with it while agronomists had to work for their living in a primitive countryside (Victorov 156; ad-Dahr 110). The sole major government irrigation project completed, that on the Orontes between Hama and Homs, chiefly benefited large landowners (Warriner 1962:79). The government spent only 2.1% of its tiny budget on health in the thirties and in 1937 there was only 1 doctor available for each 10,000 persons. As a result, peasants suffered from wretched health conditions: forty percent of children died before the age of five and the great majority of peasants had diseases of the eyes and blood, or malaria (Hanna 239; IBRD 158). In Warriner's dry 1948 (97–98) understatement: "Present day Syria is not a welfare state, nor is peasant welfare a present concern." Of critical importance, however, was the one major exception to the government's record of neglect: Syria, under the influence of an outstanding progressive nationalist, Sati al-Husri, invested major resources in the development of primary and secondary education. Ironically, this one major progressive act of the *ancien regime* would be the single most important factor in its undoing: it would create the educated middle class which would bring the regime down.

The Interior Ministry which controlled local administration and its police arm, the gendarmerie, was the major link between government and village (Torrey 1964:38). It still barely penetrated local society; government offices did not extend below the district level, except for roving gendarmes charged with keeping order. The gendarme tended to be hand in glove with the landlord or shaikh; when a new commander was appointed, he would be invited to dine with the local notable and he had neither motive or means to contest the "natural social order." Sometimes notable and gendarme combined to inflict beatings, arbitrary imprisonment or maltreatment on peasants (Hanna 314, 329). When the gendarmes visited the village, the mukhtar made sure to appease them with hospitality and other amenities. Ironically, the peasants, from long tradition, often looked to the notables to "protect" them from the government and notables, in order to build clientage networks, might pay the fines levied on peasants, often as a result of the endemic intra-village conflicts of a segmental society (Sweet 40; Seale 40, 172–173).

The control of state and society by the great notable families and the fragmentation, low political consciousness, and economic dependency of the rural masses all seemed to constitute a stable base for the continuation of semi-traditional rule in the years after independence. But the costs of this system turned out to be too high and brought on its ultimate ruin. Under it, domination of the government by great societal interests, the centrifugal segmented social structure, the great class gaps dividing society, and the political passivity of the masses, made the state a fragile entity deprived of the loyalties and active energies of the great bulk of the population. As such, it would prove incapable of mobilizing the support and power needed to respond to the social crisis and national threat it would soon face. Indeed, hardly had the new state achieved political independence when it encountered, totally unprepared, formidable challenges to its very survival.

Notes

1. The Land Code initiated a long process by which private property was established, but for a long time a certain fluidity remained in land rights. Because land registration under the Ottomans was done poorly, much legal uncertainty over rights continued. A proper cadastral was lacking and while it made headway under the French, by 1943 only a bit more than half the cultivated land had been surveyed. Uncertainty in land rights favored the powerful and facilitated their encroachment on state land and small holdings.

3

The Crisis of the Traditional Order: Social Change and Conflict

By the late forties an accumulation of social changes going back a century was beginning to undermine the structure of traditional society. The penetration of Western technology, ideology, and capitalism precipitated a growing social mobilization which undermined its social bases and created new social forces. Increasingly politicized, these forces mounted a challenge that within two decades brought the old order crashing down.

Capitalist Penetration, State Formation, and Social Mobilization

The acceleration of social change was driven by a multi-pronged post-independence economic expansion. World War II had provided special conditions for capital accumulation and local entreprenuership. Forced savings from restrictions on imports and demand caused by the spending of the allied armies in Syria created unusual opportunities for investors in industry and agriculture and for blackmarketers in scarce commodities; a new "war rich" arose, partly at the expense of the mass standard of living (Safadi 58–59; Petran 82; Arudki 21–24; IBRD 104; Ziadeh 214). This accumulation of capital and a new entrepreneurial spirit among a wing of the bourgeoisie sparked a post-independence economic boom. Agricultural expansion led the way, initially spurred by high war-time demand for food and the machinery introduced by the allied powers. After the war, it accelerated as Syrian agriculture was increasingly commercialized and integrated into the world market: merchant capital, much of it Christian Aleppine or provided by refugees from Turkey settled in Qamishli, introduced mechanized farming on the vast virgin plains of the Jazirah, turning this formerly uncultivated area into a new granary. In older areas some landlords, shedding their absentee habits, began to invest in mechanization (Hamide 207–210). There was a tremendous expansion in extensive grain cultivation for export: annual wheat and barley harvests increased from around 748,000 pre-war (1934–1938) metric tons to around 1,225,000 in 1950–1954. A parallel ten-fold expansion (from 5,000 to 50,000 metric tons per year) in cotton cultivation, also largely exported, was led by landlords and merchants who introduced motorized pump irrigation in response to high Korean wartime prices (IBRD 19; Warriner 1962:72). As security was re-established, long-disused irrigation networks on the desert fringe were rehabilitated and the government began to undertake a limited number of irrigation projects on the rivers. By 1952, the irrigated area had increased almost a third over the pre-war period (Hamide 432–436; Petran 83; Ziadeh 219). The total cultivated area grew from 1.75 million hectares in 1938 to 2.3 million in 1945 and 3.65 million in 1953 while that actually under crops doubled from 1.51 million ha. in 1945 to 3.148 million in 1957 (IBRD 18; Hansen 344; Warriner 1962:72, 75, 89–93). This was accompanied by a major growth in light agricultural-processing industries, almost entirely based on indigenous capital (Hilan 1969:166–167; Ziadeh 214, 220; Petran 83). From 1945–1954 thirty-seven new companies were established; the 25 million L.S. of capital accumulated in industrial joint stock companies in 1945 reached 100 million by 1950 and 1.63 million by 1957. The value of industrial output grew about 12% yearly in the first half of the fifties (Hilan 1969:168–170; Ziadeh 220–221; Arudki 249–250). Expansion of industry spurred the production of agricultural raw materials and growth of the productive sectors stimulated trade. Increased trade was accompanied by the growth of paved roads and motorized vehicles, which increased three and a half times from 1937 to 1953, widening the agricultural market and encouraging urban investment in and penetration of the countryside. A new port was established at Latakia to facilitate export of commercial agriculture and the overland transit trade on which Syria again was profiting. National income almost doubled from the pre–war period to 1954. New wealth increased at a rate of 5–6% per year and a substantial 13–14% of GNP was reinvested in the early fifties (IBRD 20–22, 104). The emergence of an entrepreneurial wing of the agrarian-commercial bourgeoisie prepared to invest in industry seemed to indicate that despite its late start Syria was embarking on a "national-capitalist" road to development (Keilany 1973:61–62; Porter).

The establishment and expansion of the new Syrian state also set off social changes. Government command of resources, one measure of this state formation, grew 13% per year from 1949–1953, raising its share of the national income from 11% to 13.5% while expenditures quadrupled from 1946–1956 (IBRD 176; Makdisi 163). Much of this governmental expansion was financed by taxes on growing agricultural exports, consumer imports, and the overland transit trade between Arabia and the Mediterranean, and by oil pipeline fees—that is, by Syria's growing integration into the global capitalist market. A large portion of government revenue was funneled into salaries for the expanding bureaucracy, but the biggest increases in expenditures were for education and the army, making these the two largest items in the budget. From 1945 to 1957 military expenditures increased nine times; from 1946 to 1960 educational spending increased at nearly the same rate, rising from 17 million to 145 million L.S. (Crow 115; IBRD 255, 455; Torrey 1964:28). The size of the bureaucracy roughly doubled from 1945 to 1957, growing especially in its lower ranks which went from one quarter to one-half of total government employment; by 1952 total numbers stood at 24,000 (Crow 115–126; IBRD 193, 256). Following the Palestine war, the army also rapidly expanded from a mere 5,000 in 1946 to 25,000 in 1953 (Daoud Agha 388; Nyrop 289). In the early fifties the state apparatus—military and bureaucracy together—amounted to only about 5% of the work force, but it carried great weight in the capital, the center of political action, and it grew constantly throughout the fifties. A parallel expansion in the new national education system doubled the number of schools from 1945 to 1950, more than doubled the ranks of primary school students and quadrupled those of secondary students (IBRD 23, 149); intermediate and secondary students, concentrated in the cities, but increasingly recruited from rural families, too, became a weighty social force: a mere 12,000 in 1946, there were 47,000 in 1953 and over 100,000 by 1963. The Syrian university, which in thirty-five years had graduated less than 5,000 students, had that number enrolled in 1955 alone; by 1961 about 19,400 and by 1964 31,500 students had graduated. Thus, beginning during the French occupation and at an ever accelerating rate, modern secular education increasingly became available to strata below the upper class. In 1936 a bare 16% of the 6–12 year old primary school age group were in school; by 1945, about 25% and by 1961 around 50–60% were enrolled. As a result, the literacy rate, which was about 25% in 1950 had reached 35% by the end of the decade (Ziadeh 248–250; Hilan 1969:290; Zoubi 40–41; Daoud Agha 156; United Nations 9–10, 124; IBRD 457).

Population growth was also reshaping society. Improved security, hygiene and medical care reduced mortality rates and the growth of irrigation permitted increased agricultural density. Population, which had reached a low point of around 2.8 million in 1850, began to grow again, reaching a rapid rate in excess of 3% yearly in the 1950s and pushing total numbers to about 3.65 million by 1953 (IBRD 4; Daoud Agha 53). This produced pressure on the land in places and an eastward expansion of population and cultivation. Population in the Jazirah grew by one-third to one-half between 1949 and 1953 (Petran 83). It also set off the beginnings of rural migration to the cities. And, the rural towns were rejuvenated by population growth, the new agricultural wealth, state penetration, and the growth of the road network. They served as intermediate collection centers for crops, administrative centers, tractor repair stations, seats of new cotton-based industries, and residences not only for the rural bourgeoisie of merchants, moneylenders, and rich peasantry but for the new rural intelligentsia and for agricultural workers displaced from the villages. A town like Ma'arrat an-Nu'man, reduced by constant sacking to 5,000 by 1930, had tripled in population by 1956; Manbij, abandoned during the centuries of agrarian decline, then settled by Circassians as part of Sultan Abdul Hamid's drive to hold back the nomad, now became a new cotton center. These towns, links between city and village, agents and symptoms of capitalist penetration and social mobilization of the countryside, were bridging the urban-rural gap (Hamide 353–357, 500–502). In general, economic growth and social mobilization were setting the static old society in motion, creating both new opportunities and new insecurities.

These objective changes set off socio-psychological ones which tended to increase receptivity to further change and yet reflected the imbalances and disruptions which inevitably accompanied rapid development. A study by Lerner of Syrian attitudes in the early fifties (Marsh; Lerner 1958:264–302) found advances in the various objective measures of "social mobilization," that is, in higher literacy, urbanization, media exposure, income, and non-traditional occupations, to be correlated with "empathy"—receptivity to change, awareness of and opinions about a wider "public" world, increases in universalistic and achievement attitudes. About a half of Syrians remained traditional and only a fifth were modern and "empathic." But semi-empathic "transitionals" made up a third of the population and were rapidly growing; moreover youths, increasingly exposed to education, were almost three times as likely to be empathic as those over 50 years old.

But if these trends pointed to the gradual "modernization" of Syrian attitudes, there were other indicators that the transition process was also generating tensions and frustrations. Traditionals felt powerless in the face of change, were unreceptive to it, and, unconvinced that they could control their lives, remained fatalistic. Transitionals "no longer responded unquestioningly to the old ways," and sought integration into the modern world, but being "marginal" men caught between the old and new worlds, lacked resources to satisfactorily achieve it; thus 92% felt powerless and 40% declared themselves unhappy. The breakdown of older ties caused by growth and social-mobilization, unaccompanied by integration into a new order, threatened a certain anomie (Torrey 1964:20); certainly literacy and the formation of opinions outpaced the development of any new consensus replacing the traditional world view. As early as 1950, Lerner found that the frustrations of transitionals were making them susceptible to anti-system ideologies—nativist reaction or leftwing radicalism. Moreover, the erosion of the self-contained segments and certainties of traditional life, opening minds to the wider society or releasing individuals into it, produced a psychological need for some larger unit of identification; particularly among "transitionals," rising nationalism seemed to fill this void. Even "traditionals," typically peasants, reacting to the threats posed by the outside world, had become "xenophobic." Significantly, this common nationalism would become a link between the newly educated radicals and the more traditional masses. As "traditionals" inexorably declined, and frustrated "transitionals" grew more rapidly than integrated "moderns," growing radicalism, nationalism, and instability seemed likely to Lerner. In fact, Syria's uneven social change was producing the objective conditions for just this scenario.

Uneven Development, Class Formation, and the Rise of a New Middle Class Challenge to the Agrarian Bourgeoisie

The forces of social change—capitalist expansion, social-mobilization, state formation—eroded the bases of the traditional social structure. They generated new social forces—occupational groups and classes—in the womb of the old society which gradually transformed it, affecting first the cities, but spreading inexorably outward to the periphery. Independent Syria inherited an enormously unequal social structure full of latent class contradictions, but it took this postwar acceleration of modernization to activate them. The inherited social structure could not integrate or satisfy the needs of the new social forces; the outcomes of development were sharply uneven, some gaining, others losing, generating new inequalities and a heightened consciousness of both old and new ones. Ironically, therefore, its successful initiation of state formation and capitalist transformation would generate the conflicts which would bring the old regime down.

In Syria's major urban centers the dominant classes were making themselves over, while two new classes were emerging between them and the urban mass. The agrarian-commercial upper class was developing a more dynamic industrial and agrarian entrepreneurial wing. Moreover the new wealth fueled an explosion in imports and a proliferation of Syrian agents for foreign firms, stimulating the growth of the commercial bourgeoisie and a stratum of big compradors (Safadi 59). It also fueled a building boom and a new stratum of construction contractors. The bourgeoisie made enormous profits from these developments and paid almost no taxes. Moving out of the old quarters of the cities into new modern neighborhoods, buying cars and living a life of conspicuous consumption, it stimulated the envy of those below it (Petran 85). In addition, upper class command of the offices of state remained complete.

But the more significant change in the urban social structure was the rapid development of a modernizing "new middle class," fueled by the spread of modern education and professional and state employment. Traditionally, the "modern" intelligentsia had come predominately from the landed upper classes and the traditional middle class of urban merchant, middle landowning and middle-rank bureaucratic families. They usually pursued careers in the more prestigious professions, especially medicine and law, and often also had income from landed or commercial property. With the post-independence expansion of education, however, widening numbers of children of yet lower classes found access to modern occupations, forming a new lower strata of the middle class almost exclusively dependent on salaries and hence with interests quite different from those of the property-owning elite. As this stratum grew, the modern middle class increasingly took on the character of a salaried class. Because their nominal tuition opened the teachers' college and the military academy to ambitious youth of even the lowest strata, the lower ranks of the middle class tended to concentrate in these two professions. Of decisive importance was the emergence of a contingent of "rural intellectuals," men who came from the village but had moved up into modern careers.

While before WWII the small middle class had been dependent on the imperialist dominated administration or traditional patrons (Hanna 390), its post-independence growth was driven by the development of a national administration and officer corps increasingly autonomous of foreign or dominant class interests; thus the salaried middle class developed relatively apart from the system of clientage and family loyalties controlled by the notability, and, indeed, was bound together by similar educational, occupational and generational experiences which separated it from the old establishment (Safadi 60). Although of varied sectarian, regional, and class origins, the modern middle class was increasingly the product of a nationalized education system which integrated its various elements through shared common experience and personal interaction (Lerner 274; Akhrass 14). By contrast to previous generations educated in private minority schools or abroad in foreign languages, hence divided or ambivilant in their political identities, the new generation was exposed to a common Arabization which attenuated both sectarian loyalties and attachment to Western thought: among this generation a national identity would establish deeper roots than heretofore (Jabbur 251–253). The new professional associations and modern institutions into which the middle class was recruited integrated elements of diverse origin, generating loyalties increasingly to profession, class and nation rather than exclusively to family, sect, or quarter (Akhrass 144; Khoury 527). The rise of ideological parties among the new middle class signified that, mobilized out of the isolated segments of traditional society, it was capable of political association which reached beyond purely personal and parochial loyalties and addressed issues of wide societal import.

By the fifties, a growing conflict of manifestly class character was separating the agrarian-commercial upper class and the new middle class as the latter came to perceive its opportunities blocked by the system over which the old elite presided. Educational expansion produced a growing number of graduates with high expectations and new tastes but limited opportunities. Top positions in government and business were dominated by the sons of the notability. In spite of the economic expansion, industrial and agrarian capital was highly concentrated in a few family run firms which provided few jobs for outsiders (Ziadeh 288; Hilan 1969:175–176; Daoud Agha 111). An educational system geared to liberal arts and law, rather than agronomy and engineering, did not provide graduates with appropriate skills. Many dropped out of school early, acquiring enough education to stimulate their ambitions but not to acquire a marketable skill; symptomatic of this phenomenon was the rapid growth in the law faculty enrollment, considered a preparation for government jobs, from 1,039 in 1950 to 2,199 in 1956, and, because many admitted without an entrance exam were poorly prepared, a parallel drop in graduates from 304 to 134 (Torrey 1964:27; Van Dusen 1972:126–127; Crow 37). Many graduates had to settle for government clerical jobs, of low status and pay and slow advancement—unless, as they perceived it, one had good family connections. Most government employees were dissatisfied with their pay which was generally insufficient for a "modern" life style, such as nuclear family housing, and with the lack of career mobility, security and job challenge; some dozen civil service strikes from 1945–1958 expressed their frustration. Critical to understanding the alignment of big segments of the white collar lower middle class against the establishment was the fact that the pay of top bureaucrats was ten times that of lower ranking ones whose incomes were close to or even inferior to those of skilled manual workers. In short, the formation of the middle class was outrunning the expansion of the modern economy needed to satisfy its ambitions for income and mobility. Many middle class "moderns" were also culturally alienated: though shut out of the establishment, they also felt cut off from the traditional illiterate masses, too. Low paid white collar employees or "small" professionals posted to or forced to work in the rural peripheries were most susceptible to such alienation. And, among the politically ambitious and the ideologically minded elements of the middle class, discontent was fanned by the little political opportunity which a state so thoroughly dominated by the traditional elite could provide (Lerner 264, 276–279; Daoud Agha 95; Atasi; IBRD 155, 194, 372; Crow 69–70, 124–126, 167–168).

The frustrations of the middle class translated relatively rapidly into political discontent with the establishment and a rising challenge to its supremacy. In Allush's view (139–142), the political alienation of the middle class was directly proportional to its relative economic situation: its upper strata, having property of its own or lucrative professional practices in the big cities, initially identified with the establishment and was only radicalized as the ruling class refused to share political power; the middle strata of the middle class was oriented to democratic reformist ideology and the lower, least well off stratum, recruited from worker and peasant families, to radical ideologies like socialism. Teachers, because of the greater accessibility of the profession to the lower classes, low salaries which hardly met their needs, and their frequent preoccupation, as intellectuals, with the issues of the day, were most often radicalized. The political discontent of the middle class was manifest in street demonstrations, anti-regime plots among middle class army officers, and the growth of radical opposition political parties, including the Syrian Social Nationalists (SSNP), the Communists, the Arab Socialist Party, the Ba'th, and among more traditional elements, the Muslim Brotherhood.

It was among students, representative for the most part of the new middle class-in-formation, that its grievances appeared in the purest, most overtly politicized form. Dissatisfied with their family and sex lives in a constricted traditional society, with uncertain job prospects, as yet unintegrated into the established order, hence less susceptible to the traditional techniques of co-optation, and exposed by their teachers to conflicting ideological currents, students made up the bulk of activists in the forefront of anti-system movements. The enormous gap between the ideals to which their teachers exposed them and the reality of society radicalized them (Hilan 1969:325–326). A product of the national education system designed by Sati al-Husri extolling nationalism and repudiating imperialism and sectarianism, the student body, especially as it incorporated growing numbers from the deprived classes, became intensely nationalist and "socialist;" idealistic, yet having no detailed knowledge or experience, students wanted fast radical solutions to the country's problems. So strong was radical sentiment in some schools that the desire for acceptance pushed even youth from wealthy families into the ranks of ideological parties. Inevitably, in a society with a constricted political arena confined to the capital, their concentrated numbers there translated into disproportionate power; in a regime in which the middle class was largely frozen out of political institutions, students, with their family links to nearly all sectors of society mirrored—albeit in a radicalized way—a broader spectrum of public opinion than parliament. They would become a major tool and advocate of middle class political opposition, student-led protest demonstrations a central means of political expression, and students a "formidable extra-parliamentary pressure group" (Seale 38; Jundi 44; Sayyid 29–32; Jabbur 116–117). And, once they entered careers, they would begin to infect the whole social order with radical dissent.

Ultimately most important, was a particularly alienated but developing social force, the "ex-peasant" educated youth from the villages and rural towns. These ambitious young men were largely frozen out of the patronage network which determined many opportunities in urban Syria, but their modern education had alienated them from work on the land, patriarchal authority, and traditional village life without always providing them with the proper skills to make it in the city; they were classic "marginal men." (Koury 61–75; Van Dusen 1975:139–147) Yet, only recently removed from the village, many carried the grievances of the peasantry against the *iqta'iun* (feudalists) who also made up the city establishment. Their marginality and alienation was reinforced when, as was often the case, they came from minority communal groups. They represented a new and strategic social force, an educated and dissatisfied stratum, able to articulate rural grievances in the wider political arena and linking the discontent of the salaried middle class concentrated in the cities with that of the peasantry; they would constitute the backbone of an emergent middle-class–peasant alliance which was forming against the old regime.

Finally, a wage proletariat was developing at the bottom of the urban social structure which would, for the most part, constitute a junior ally of the new middle class in its challenge to the ruling elite. It emerged partly from displaced urban artisans and partly from the expulsion of sharecroppers and the decline of rural industries which produced a rural proletariat on the move in search of seasonal or permanent work. There were about 35–40,000 workers in industry in the early fifties, and if handicraft workers and artisans are included, more than 100,000 (IBRD 10–11). Though still small, the working class was beginning to make its presence felt. It won a labor code and the right to strike. Only about 27% of urban labor was organized in some 200 small fragmented unions, but progressively, bigger firms, such as the Khumasiya complex in Damascus, became centers of strikes and proseltization by the Communists and the Ba'th (Allouni; Petran 87). The concentration and relative organization of the proletariat gave it a greater political weight than its still limited size would have otherwise warranted. Those who could not find wage work swelled the ranks of the urban lumpenproletariat—petty vendors, peddlers and beggars eking out a living at the margins of society; while this bottom urban stratum supplied manpower for many of the demonstrations which shook the hold of the old regime, especially after the Palestine war, it had no organization and little self-consciousness (Jabbur 96–97).

By 1962, salaried employees and wage workers together made up 58% of the urban labor force (Hilan 1969:350), a major transformation in a social structure previously dominated by independent merchants, artisans, and family and clientelist workers—and one providing a more fertile terrain for the growth of radical opposition.

Social Change and Conflict in the Countryside

While the development of an urban-centered middle class challenge to the traditional establishment was the most visible manifestation of the social conflict being unleashed in post-independence Syria, less apparent to observers then and since, were the effects of social change and landlord-peasant conflict in the rural periphery. These developments were of decisive importance not only because in the early fifties the majority of the population was still rural and perhaps three-fourths of the work force was in agriculture (IBRD 9), but because increasingly it was the disruption and mobilization of rural society which was fueling the development of the new urban forces—the educated middle class, the urban proletariat—which were in the vanguard of change. Moreover, in a real sense, the ferment at the center was the most exposed, advanced tip of deeper more gradual changes in the rural periphery, and without rural transformation urban developments would have remained of limited consequence, a mere tempest in a teapot.

Erosion of the Traditional Rural Bases of the Old Regime

Social change—capitalist expansion, social mobilization—initiated major developments in the periphery of incalculable consequence, namely a gradual erosion in Syria's segmental structure, the self-sufficient solidarity of kin, village, tribe, ethnic and sectarian group which constituted the social base of the old regime and a breakdown in the patriarchal authority and clientelism on which the power structure was erected. As these ties were loosened, rurals began to be pulled into alternative social formations often incompatible with the stability of the old regime. These changes were a pre-requisite of the political mobilization and conflict of the fifties.

The solidarity and sometimes the viability of the traditional rural community was threatened by the erosion of its economic base under the impact of technology and capitalism. Communal land tenures (musha') which had concretized village solidarity were rapidly giving way in hundreds of villages to individual ownership under pressure of capitalism and government initiatives, weakening the tight-knit fabric of village life. In many places the penetration of capitalist norms was manifested in the replacement of traditional mutual exchange of labor by payment in cash (Sweet 196). In the Ghouta, where village life had centered around the collective management of the water flow, the introduction of motor-pumps fueled peasant individualism (Bianquis 1979:293–294). The economic base of the village, particularly in mountainous or extensively cultivated areas, was undermined by population growth on fixed land resources. Capitalism and mechanization, replacing sharecroppers with wage labor and destroying rural industries, such as home textile industries in the Alawite mountains or the handicrafts of Yabroud, put people out of work and undermined local self-sufficiency (Hamide 545, 558–562). In the Hauran, small peasants were damaged by declining prices of wheat caused by the expansion of production in the Jazirah. Such dislocations, as well as periodic drought and population growth, everywhere led to migrations in search of work, weakening local ties, and dealing a blow to tribal organization among peoples like the Alawites (Akhrass 91–97). Among the bedouin, the establishment of security and spread of motor transport, depriving them of opportunities for plunder and caravaning, undermined the economic props of nomadic life (Warriner 1962:56, 88). One observer describes the situation between the wars in grim terms: thrown into a state of "hopeless confusion" and driven by hunger, the bedouin flocked to the towns where they depressed wages; in the countryside "only force of arms keeps the hungry and embittered nomads in check . . ." (Epstein 607).

At the same time, capitalist penetration gave rise to new relationships linking city and village. Thus, in the new irrigated cotton areas innovative kinds of "partnerships" sprang up. Landowners turned their land over to capitalists who installed irrigation pumps and took on a peasant "partner," with half the crop going to the capitalist and the rest split by owner and peasant. With the spread of machinery in the hands of city capitalists and largely inaccessible to villagers, such partnerships proliferated, bringing capitalist influence into the heart of the village (Metral and Sanlaville 1979; Hamide 217, 449–454). Some peasants were able to adapt to and benefit from the new technology and capital, becoming small entrepreneurs in their own right; thus Sweet (156) reports on peasants who acquired a waterwheel by finding a city partner who provided the cash and was paid off in a few years with 1/3–1/2 of the crop. But many others did not and such differential adaptability created new rich and new poor in the village.

The decline of village solidarity, urban penetration, and the growth in inequality which often accompanied these changes, was illustrated by a Deir ez-Zor village analyzed by Hannoyer (295). Before the coming of the cotton boom, this relatively homogeneous village lived on irrigated wheat and sheep raising and had a strong collective life expressed in such practices as collective harvesting. City entrepreneurs used kin connections in the village to introduce irrigated cotton, soon dispossessing and reducing most peasants to share-cropper status: by 1958, four city families owned most of the village. But some peasants adapted, prospered on cotton, bought pumps and tractors, and as the threat of land reform loomed, bought land the city families wished to dispose of. By the end of the process, collective village solidarity had been replaced by "familism," and the village common room, former center of its political life, had fallen into disuse.

State formation and social-mobilization also undermined the solidarity and patriarchal values of traditional kin and communal groups. The expansion of transport and communications broke down the isolation on which segmentalism had thrived. With the growing establishment of security, segmental solidarity, previously a critical means of self-protection from violent attack, became less essential; indeed as the growth in state penetration reduced the viability of isolation and individuals were propelled into the wider social arena, kin and communal loyalties became inadequate as a basis of association, protection and advancement. The rapid growth in education had a profound impact on the old society. Through it peasant youth were exposed to agents of socialization which weakened the father to son transmission of traditional values, including respect for patriarchal authority. This introduced an unprecedented generational cleavage into society. Some youth sought education, in fact, to escape traditional authority. Where peasant fathers could no longer economically provide for their sons on limited holdings and youth sought employment outside agriculture, economic links reinforcing patriarchal authority were weakened. This was accompanied by a gradual decline in endogamous marriage as educated youth began to seek educated wives rather than marrying within the kin-group, thus weakening the tightly knit clans which were the building blocs of traditional society and giving rise to wider ties between individuals and families. Generally, while elders stayed behind, youth were more likely to migrate from the village—for education, military service or ambition—and, interacting with the wider society, to develop loyalties to class and nation. A striking sign of this was the gradual Arabization and hence assimilation of parts of the younger generation of rural communities such as the Kurds, Circassians, and Syriac speaking Christians into the wider society (Daoud-Agha 16; Sweet 77). The radio and the village teacher began to compete with the village elders and the headman's common room as sources of values and knowledge; as secular schools spread, the prestige and demand for Quranic teachers declined (Akhrass 12–16; Van Dusen 1972:104–106, 127; Marsh; Hamide 498).

Clientage ties reaching up from the base of society were also eroded. Growing security lessened the need for a patron's protection. As new sources of wealth and opportunity, such as education, grew, easing the dependence of some peasants, clientelism tended to become less asymmetrical. Clientage ties also lost some of their personal dimension as mobility and the cash nexus expanded. Thus, patriarchal tribal leaders often acquired new tastes, moved to the cities and sent their sons into the professions, differentiating their life style from that of tribesmen; they replaced tribal followers with wage laborers on tribal lands or sold hereditary lands to investors, all undermining the personal loyalties and economic interchanges on which their authority was based. Landowners began to replace sharecropper-clients with tractors and hired labor. As clan and clientelist loyalties weakened and the number of participants in the social and political system widened, the large notable family's ability to dominate local socio-political life declined (Akhrass 125). In all these ways, the primordial and economic bases of clientage were weakened (Jabbur 70–71).

To be sure, traditional ties and authority did not disappear all at once. They often adapted to new circumstances and could even mediate change. Thus, when a peasant family kept one son on the land and sent others to school and into non-agricultural careers, it was seeking to diversify its resources and, for the most part, educated youth returned money to their family, making it a more viable economic unit; but with sons so contributing, patriarchal authority was no longer unquestioned. The traditional institution of *wisata*—personal mediation—often provided a bridge between city and village for migrants and helped facilitate the wider marriage and commercial links being developed. In the larger city environment or within new institutions being created there, kin and fellow sectarians still sought mutual protection and advancement and village migrants tended to settle in the same regions, reproducing small community life in the bigger setting. The introduction of new "modern" forms of association such as political parties or professional organizations often seemed, in its earlier stages, to fill new bottles with old wine, e.g. in Saydnaya where Catholic families sought to join the Syrian Social National Party en-masse because the Orthodox had gravitated to the Communists. But as social mobilization advanced and links diversified, traditional ties became more conditional, less hierarchical and predictable and narrower loyalties were diluted by competing broader ones.

Two local studies give snapshot views of the kinds of changes that were engulfing Syrian villages. A study of the Isma'ilis of Salamiya by Lewis shows how the penetration of the state, modern education, and capitalist agriculture undermined the patriarchal authority of the Isma'ili amirs and created new forces for change. The introduction of commercial irrigated cotton into the village increased wealth, needs, and the demand for education. As the amirs' need for cash increased, they sold parts of their land and tributary relations between them and their peasant/followers were replaced by wage relations. The stature of the amirs as leaders in the defense of the community against the bedouin and the Sunni establishment was undermined by the pacification of the desert and the decline of sectarian conflicts; as the hierarchy of appointed state officials extended into the countryside, the amirs' role as sole brokers between state and peasant weakened. As schooling spread, patriarchal authority and religious belief declined among youth, some of whom left the community for professional or military careers. The survival of bride price kept most young men dependent on their father to marry, but fathers began to give their daughters to educated men without it. Despite the disapproval of their fathers, youth, made independent by their education, joined political parties like the Ba'th and gradually the elders were in part won over to the political views of their educated sons. But sectarian loyalties did not suddenly disappear: Ali Khan continued to be welcomed as leader of the community, an Isma'ili religious brotherhood had formed among youth, and when a Sunni teacher tried to win children to orthodox practices, riots erupted (Lewis 1952; interviews, Isma'ili intellectuals, 1973).

The village of Tell Toqaan in Eastern Aleppo studied by Sweet (1957) reflects in miniature how modernization was associated with both growing inequality and the erosion of traditional bonds. The village was a product of larger developments such as the expansion of security, population growth and sedentarization. It was founded in late Ottoman times by de-mobilized Turkish soldiers who were later joined by a tribe, the Bu Layl, which made it the center of the villages its tribesmen were settling. Ownership of most of the land was divided between the descendants of the Turks who now called themselves Aghas and lived in Aleppo but were represented in the village by a rural cousin, and Shaikh Nuri of the Bu Layl; the land was cultivated by sharecroppers and wage laborers. As security was established and other tribal factions and peasants from the West also settled, population grew quickly. Agriculture developed as irrigated cotton and summer vegetables were introduced into a formerly pastoral and extensive grain economy, spurring growing attachment to a peasant lifestyle and a decline of pastoralism. Like many newly settled villages, Tell Toqaan was fragmented between the non-tribal and tribal population and by intra-tribal rivalries. State and urban influences were rapidly penetrating this formerly isolated community. New roads increased interaction with the city: peasants now traveled to Aleppo, while the gendarmes visited the village weekly, stopping at Shaikh Nuri's house. As the power of the state penetrated, it assumed growing responsibility for security: tribal law still applied within tribes (hence was in the shaikh's hands), but state law applied in relations between the tribe and others; moreover although blood money was still expected in cases of murder, the blood feud had been rendered inactive. Villagers listened to national radio and were starting to think of themselves as "Syrians." No state school had yet been established but an educated Aleppine imam had been brought in to teach in a Quranic school, thus bringing established Islam into the village, with mixed effect: older small-holding peasants became pious, but youth and tribesmen did not. Interestingly, the imam was also an agent of nationalism: he taught his students the oath of allegiance to the state.

The inegalitarian and dis-integrative effects of capitalist penetration and modernization were clearly apparent in this village. Roads opened the village to urban merchants who sold commodities on credit, which doubled their prices. While peasants who had sharecropping contracts clung to the greater independence they allowed, the landowners were trying to replace them with hired labor and, given their ownership of tractors and ability to import Alawite laborers, their leverage over peasants was growing. There were twice as many households of laborers as sharecroppers and the proportion of the former was increasing. This widening inequality was replacing lineage rivalry with a three-layered economic stratification—landowners, sharecroppers, wage laborers—as the main cleavage in the village; indeed, a half of marriages were across lineage lines but none crossed economic stratification lines. While lineages remained units of solidarity, traditional bonds and attitudes were weakening. Cooperative exchange of labor among lineages in house building and plowing was giving way to work for money. Traditions of mutual generosity were declining as some families sought to accumulate wealth and others to protect themselves against destitution. As share-cropping was replaced by wage labor and household heads lost control over land and farming decisions, the extended peasant family and its patriarchal authority declined. But enough of traditional authority persisted that, when combined with growing economic inequality, power relations were, in the short run, actually becoming *more* asymmetrical: the landlords and Shaikh Nuri, whose right to command his tribe was "absolute and feudal," ran everything in the village. But the fact that they considered the imam a disturbing influence suggests that the introduction of even religious education into this milieu could begin to undermine these established power relations.

The Mobilization of Peasant Youth: Social Change and Politicization Among the Minority and Small-Holding Peasantry

One of the most politically consequential changes sweeping in the Syrian countryside was the social mobilization and politicization taking place among village youth, largely through their acquisition of education. These youth would become spokesmen for village grievances and a major force leading the spread of agrarian radicalism challenging the old order. Peasant politicization was strongest among the small-holding peasantry who, outside the direct grip of landlords, retained enough independence and resources to send their children for schooling. The minority mountain peasants made up a main contingent of the small-holding peasantry and one which, socially deprived and peripheral to the ruling regime, would, as they were drawn into political life, put themselves in the vanguard of agrarian radicalism.

The Alawites of Latakia, making up the most important of the minority mountain communities, were traditionally the most deprived and backward community in Syria. Protected by their mountain fastnesses, they had retained some independence of urban domination, but agriculture in the mountain was precarious, providing little base for ease or wealth. Though Arab and so identifying themselves historically, they were separated from the Sunni establishment—which regarded them as inferior and less than Muslims—by a history of communal conflict; their mistrust of the Sunni Ottoman state derived from attempts at forceable conversion to orthodoxy and the appropriation of hundreds of Alawite villages on the mountain slopes which were turned over to Sunni and Christian landlords. Tribally organized mountain peasants, the Alawis were less submissive than the plains peasantry, but, physically scattered into small villages and divided into feuding tribal confederations, they were fragmented and hence politically weak. Except for occasional outbreaks of intercommunal fighting, the Alawites remained isolated from the wider society (Hreib 25–30, 46; Faksh 134; Weulersse 1940).

This began to change after the fall of the Ottomans. Under Shaikh Salah al-Ali they first revolted against the short-lived Faysal government's attempt to control the mountain, but later rebelled against French occupation and demanded union with the nationalist government in Damascus. The French, in divide-and-rule fashion, sponsored separatist feeling, setting up a separate administration in Latakia and distributing some Sunni held villages to Alawis (Hreib 68–79; Hourani 1946:140).

By the third decade of the twentieth century, the Alawis were being drawn into wider society but, for the most part, at the bottom of the social ladder. On the coastal plains and in the foothills of the mountains most Alawi villages were under Sunni feudal control and a population explosion in the mountains created a rural proletariat which provided labor for the great Sunni landlords of Hama and Homs and the lesser notables of the Latakia coastal cities; "here," Fedden (207) wrote of Alawi subordination to Sunni landlords, "the system of exploitation is at its worst." Those who stayed in their mountains raised tobacco which they sold to Latakia merchants at low prices; impoverished, they long sold their daughters as indentured domestic servants to Latakia Sunni households.

Yet, although Alawis started behind the rest of the country, once social mobilization began among them, it accelerated rapidly. The access of Alawi youth to education was facilitated by the concentration of Christian missionary schools in Latakia (where there was also a large Christian community), the Syrian government's effort to combat particularism by integrating the minorities into public schools, and the schools which competing political parties opened in the area. Alawite youth also took advantage of the French practice of recruiting military levies from the minorities to pursue careers outside of agriculture—largely as non-commissioned officers—and after independence this military tradition continued. Unlike many Sunni urban youth who looked on compulsory military service as a hardship and bought their way out of it, Alawi youth saw it as an escape from poverty; moreover after independence they got access to the military academy and hence the officer corps. Thus, the Alawites developed a rural intelligentsia, many of whom followed military careers.

Gradually, politicized youth came to challenge and in part displace the traditional sectarian leadership of the Alawi community. This happened relatively easily and imperceptibly. The traditional political leadership, intensely fragmented and controlling little material base in land, rested on personal qualities and traditional values which were undermined by the spread of education; the traditional religious leadership, in keeping Alawi doctrine and rites the secrets of an "elect," abdicated the religious socialization of the community, resulting in a decline of faith among educated youth. The 1946 crushing of Sulayman Murshid's messianic Alawi religious movement by the army of the infant Syrian state was a turning point, signaling the futility of traditional separatism. Together, the historic fragmentation of the Alawis, the decline of traditional leadership and religiosity, and the social mobilization of Alawi youth eroded Alawi communal solidarity and prepared the conditions for Alawi integration into the wider community (Hreib: 112, 128–129, 139; Faksh 136–138; Van Dusen 1975:132–133; Jabbur 71).

As the outside world inexorably penetrated the mountain, and Alawi youth were drawn into wider society, they had to decide on a political identity. They flocked to radical middle class parties, notably the Syrian Social

Nationalist Party and the Ba'th, which were challenging the Sunni establishment with secular nationalist and reformist ideologies. That Greek Orthodox Christians, with whom Alawites lived on relatively equal terms in
southern Latakia provided leadership in these two parties, probably facilitated
their recruitment. After a brief flirtation with the SSNP's more minority-
oriented "Syrianism," most Alawis opted for Ba'thi Arabism and socialism.
Alawi refugees from Iskanderun, such as Zaki al-Arsuzi, whose Arabism had
been sharpened in the struggle with the Turks, played a key role in bringing
Alawi youth into the orbit of Arabism. But the Alawi adhesion to the Ba'th
and Arabism expressed a natural and powerful drive for acceptance as equals
in the dominant Arab culture. The backwardness of the Alawi community
no doubt facilitated the choice of assimilation and may be contrasted with
that of the Maronites who, more advanced than their neighbors, saw themselves
as a culturally superior elite; thus, although these two mountain minority
communities had similar pre-modern histories, with the dawn of nationalism,
they were to take opposite ways, one toward anti-Arab separatism, the other
toward integration and Arab nationalism. The Alawi attraction to Ba'th
"socialism" was also natural: a community with limited land resources, a
bursting population, and little commercial tradition, could only hope to
pull itself out of poverty through state aid and reform. It is perhaps not
surprising that of Syria's four minorities, the agrarian radicalism of the Alawis
ran the deepest for far more than the others, they were victims of Syria's
"feudal" order. All these factors turned the Alawis, in Hreib's (139–140)
words, from a historical fossil into a dynamic element in Syrian society.

The Druzes of southern Syria were, like the Alawites, martial and independent mountaineers traditionally hostile to the Sunni establishment,
although they never suffered the same deprivation. They, too, at first wavered
between separatism and integration. When the French arrived, the dominant
al-Atrash clan at first collaborated to buttress their position against rival
clans. But in 1925 Sultan al-Atrash led a rebellion against the French, which,
linking up with Damascene nationalists, was made in the name of Arabism.
They later returned to separatism, ousting a Damascene governor. Moreover,
after independence the Atrashes looked to the Jordanian monarchy for political
support against Damascus and were involved in several conspiracies with
"outside" powers against the Syrian government. In 1947, the government
under Quwatli tried to curb the Atrash by encouraging the Sha'biyun revolt
of the poorer peasants under the rival Abu Asali clan. But it did not dare
send the army into the mountain to help its clients when they were defeated
and stood by as government officials were driven out (Hreib 79–86, 127–
128, 142–156; Seale 133; Hourani 1946:139, 147).

But the isolation of a closed cultic society was increasingly inviable and
unattractive to younger Druzes. The hold of traditional chieftains over the
peasants was breaking down; the Sha'biyun revolt was only one sign of this.
As with the Alawis, agriculture had reached a limit: the Druze suffered from
population pressure on a limited land base, from a market on which they
could not get decent prices for their fruits and grapes, and from a lack of

water in their mountain. They exhibited a similar drive for education which drew them into the wider society; the Jabal Druze stood out in the 1950s for its high ratio of children in primary school (IBRD:6, 294, 458) and as early as 1947, 15,000 Druze had migrated to Damascus, chiefly for secondary schooling (Daoud Agha 27). Also like the Alawis, Druze youth sought escape and mobility through military careers and Druze officers were among the first to be politicized. At first they joined the SSNP, which channeled minority resentment against the Sunni establishment, while others were drawn to Akram al-Hawrani's Arab Socialist Party. Both encouraged their participation in the 1949 military coups which challenged the notable elite: they helped colonels Za'im and Shishakli to power and helped overthrow them when they appeared to threaten the mountain. But the increasing power and penetration of the state discredited separatism: while in 1946, Quwatli's forces could not control the mountain, in 1954 Shishakli's much more powerful army inflicted a direct defeat on Druze rebels, marking an end to the immunity of the mountain to central power and affirming that assimilation was the key to future survival (Ma'oz 1972:399; Seale 133–136). Young Druzes had already began to identify with the dominant Arab nationalism, and as the SSNP lacked such a stance, they gravitated toward the Ba'th. Some attended secondary school in Damascus where Ba'th founders Aflaq and Bitar taught and were among the first disciples of the two professors (Van Dusen 1972:129–130). Among the Ba'th's Druze converts was counted Mansur al-Atrash, son of the paramount Druze chieftain. The Ba'th, being both Arab nationalist and secular, appeared a vehicle through which they could enter main-stream society on an equal basis; being populist as well, it also channeled Druze peasant grievances against the city establishment.

Two other rural minority groups were similarly being drawn into middle class nationalist and reformist movements. The Greek Orthodox Christian small peasantry of southern Latakia and Homs, and to a smaller extent, Dera and Suwayda, shared many of the grievances of the Alawi and Druze with whom they lived, against the Sunni city: having developed commercial crops, they were increasingly dependent on and exploited by city merchants. This community had long been socially mobilized by its contact with the West, through early access to education, missionaries, and migration. By the forties the educated sons of this peasantry were being ideologically mobilized through political parties like the Syrian Nationalists, Communists and the Ba'th. As Arabic speaking "Eastern" Christians unalienated from their cultural environment, they were readily assimilated to the dominant Arab nationalist currents. Finally, the youth of yet a fourth peasant minority, the Isma'ilis, were similarly drawn by education, military careers and radical parties into the wider political arena in opposition to the established order. Although the main center of the Isma'ili community shifted from Masyaf in the Latakia mountains to Salamiya on the desert fringe, the spirit of hardiness, cohesion and independence nurtured in the mountains was carried with them to Salamiya.

That the political mobilization of minority peasant youth became part of a broader class challenge to the dominant order was hardly inevitable. The location of these "compact" minorities on the peripheries of the state and concentrated in particular regions could well have given their mobilization a separatist form. So long as the state remained weak and the economy a subsistence one, separatism was an option and as long as the religious and political orders at the center were fused, the minorities were excluded. But with the growing penetration and secularization of the state after independence and the minorities' growing dependence on the wider economy, integration made more sense. In the army, the most secular of state institutions, and through radical ideological parties challenging the old order, they found vehicles of integration which did not require submission to the urban Sunni establishment. As the educated sons of minority peasantry achieved political consciousness, their sectarian loyalties, though never fully effaced, were subsumed in a broader nationalism and agrarian populism. Their special attraction to radical movements is understandable. The minorities certainly had especially intense grievances against the old order. Sectarian differences were crucial to their rejection of the legitimacy of the ruling elite, but the age-old urban-rural conflict between landlord or merchant and peasant also ran deep and, as their sons joined the new middle class, the minorities were drawn into the class conflict between the latter and the traditional establishment. Such overlapping cleavages are the stuff of intense political conflict. But their greater access to education and their greater independence of the landlords and nomads who retarded the social development of the peasantry elsewhere also translated into greater opportunities for mobilization and politicization than other peasants enjoyed. Thus, a combination of overlapping cleavages and uneven mobilization put the peasant minorities in the vanguard of the political movements challenging the old regime. But rather than communal separatism, they sought a radical new social order which purported to address the national and social problems of the whole society.

Somewhat similar peasant mobilization was notable in several Sunni small holding areas. In Dera, the hold of Damascene merchants was especially repressive and the economic viability of the village was threatened by competition from the Jazirah and growing population pressure on an impoverished land base. But there was no great landlord presence to keep the peasantry down. Peasants had thus both grievances and opportunities for mobilization (Warriner 1962:94, 106). Here as among the minorities, mobilization basically took the form of a drive for education and careers outside of agriculture and hence the formation of a rural intelligentsia from the ranks of the peasantry itself. Its politicization turned Dera into a stronghold of the Ba'th Party. Similarly, in the Kalamoun mountains, small-holding peasants, exposed to education and under economic pressure, flocked to radical parties, notably the Ba'th and Akram al-Hawrani's Arab Socialist Party (Jabbur 75–76). Because of their relatively early and intense mobilization, these areas would contribute a large proportion of the Sunni contingent of the Ba'th elite after 1963.

Agrarian Crisis and Landlord-Peasant Conflict

At the same time that traditional ties were being loosened, peasant youth mobilizing, and broader forms of consciousness and association growing in the countryside, the spread of capitalist agriculture was generating the conditions for widened landlord-peasant class conflict.

Capitalist development generated new inequalities. The benefits of the agrarian expansion were pretty much monopolized by a small group of entrepreneurs and landlords. The big growth in grain output, concentrated in the underpopulated Jazirah and highly mechanized, generated little new employment or prosperity among the peasant population; though handfuls of enterprising peasants captured a share of the new cotton wealth, it also was generally monopolized by landlords and urban capital (Warriner 1962:91). Modernization also widened the gap between city and village. Culturally, the dominant classes in the city were engulfed by an obsession with the material attributes of Western civilization and in part alienated from Arab culture, while the countryside, still relatively untouched by material improvement, was exploited to pay for the imported culture (Allush 141–142; Hamide 561–562). Indeed, the burden of change was being laid on the peasantry: as capitalist commercial agriculture encroached on a subsistence economy, the control of landlords and investors tightened over the village and the security and income of the peasant, already low, deteriorated.

Capitalist penetration multiplied the occasions of landlord-peasant conflict. A submerged conflict between them went back at least a century when land concentration began, reducing small holders to the status of sharecroppers and making sharecropping the dominant form of production relation. This system has a built-in conflict of interest between owner and sharecropper which can easily generate revolt under the right conditions. As peasant class consciousness spread in the fifties, overt landlord-sharecropper conflict also widened.

In addition, however, the spread of more overtly capitalist agriculture in the early fifties, intensified this conflict. The biggest single occasion of conflict was the effort of landlords to replace sharecropping tenures with hired labor and sometimes mechanization (Za'im 70). The impetus for this innovation came partly from the landlords' drive for increased revenue as their perceived needs grew with the advance of "modernization"; more entrepreneurial-minded landlords sought to replace a low surplus tenure with a more productive and profitable one. The growing resistance of sharecroppers to their masters also led many landlords to expel them in retaliation and, in a labor surplus economy, replace them with less intractable wage labor. Dozens of villages in the Aleppo, Homs, and Hama area were deserted and a whole peasant subsistence economy destroyed as landlords expelled sharecroppers. Where sharecroppers were still tolerated, the terms of their contracts worsened. For example, in the Idlib and Salkine areas, mechanization of olive cultivation led proprietors to replace tenants having desirable *mugharasa* contracts with wage labor; this so increased their leverage over remaining tenants that the latters' share of the crop was halved. The process fed on itself: as northern Syria became "supercharged" with landless sharecroppers, swelled by an overflow of surplus labor from the densely populated Alawite mountains, driving down the price of labor, other landlords took to expelling their sharecroppers and using wage labor or bringing in more submissive landless peasants. Dispossessed peasants crowed into the cities, driving down urban wage rates, fueling the lumpenproletariat, and setting off riots by workers demanding protection from the influx (Hamide 211–218, 222, 226–230, 454, 457; Lerner 267).

At the same time, the small-holding peasantry was under pressure too. Pushed back into the least fertile overcrowded areas, still laboring under debt, dependent on city merchants, and afflicted by growing numbers, small peasant cultivation was increasingly less viable and peasants forced more than ever to find new work outside of agriculture. Moreover, small holders still suffered from landlord encroachment. In a new round of urban expansion against the small peasantry, the "war-rich" bought up the land of economically precarious peasants, particularly around the cities, at low prices (Arudki 24); in the Homs area such land concentration at the expense of poor small-holders was still going on as late as 1950 (Naaman; Warriner 57: 102–105). Other conflicts arose as capitalists used new technology to extend control over small-holders. Thus, the introduction of pump irrigation in the new cotton-growing areas gave investors who could provide the machinery great leverage; control of water alone allowed them to take more than half the crop and often led to the passage of land to them and the reduction of the peasant to tenancy (Warriner 1948:76; Hannoyer 292, 295; IBRD 37, 69; Hamide 449–452). As a result, small-holders were generally no less hostile to the ruling elite than the peasants more directly under "feudal" control.

As capitalist-minded farmers continued to extend their control where land rights were poorly defined, usually over state-owned land, conflict with both small-holding peasants and the landless grew (Mourad 23; ad-Dahr 79–83). Growing peasant land hunger put pressure on the government which under Shishakli promised the distribution of state lands to landless peasants. But Decree 96 of 1952 merely aimed to prevent further landlord encroachment on state land and to recover unused land which landlords held by affirming falsely that they were cultivating it; under landlord pressures, even this innocuous measure was amended by Decree 135 of 1952 which allowed every landlord, his wives and children title to as much as 200 rain-fed and 50 irrigated hectares of state land; thus, in fact, the law—which became popularly known as the "law for the plunder of state land"—dashed peasant hopes by actually advancing landlords' control of state land. Peasant land hunger was also stimulated by the beginnings of the Ghab project which was supposed to provide openings for the landless but instead became a major issue of conflict: as the swamps were drained, fishing and buffalo raising peasants already established there were hurt, while landlords and merchants from Hama and Jisr ash-Shughur quickly began to stake their claims to the land for cotton growing (Naaman; Hanna 433–434; Hamide 244–252).

Finally, in a somewhat different process in the Jazirah, tribal shaikhs expelled tribesmen from common land to rent it to the new "merchant-tractorists" (Hamide 200, 213); the tribesmen swelled the agrarian proletariat. The large scale mechanized dry farming the new entrepreneurs undertook was periodically devastated by drought, but while they weathered the bad years on the large profits reaped in good ones, the rural workers dependent on them were left to fend for themselves.

Even as the occasions of landlord-peasant conflict multiplied, a creeping political transformation was overtaking the village, namely a growing unwillingness of peasants to accept the landlord dominated rural order. The spread of transportation and communication, tying formerly isolated villages together, the spread of education to peasant youth, and the growing penetration of the village by radical parties, all contributed to development of a peasant class consciousness. The Egyptian land reform of 1952 had an electrifying effect on Syrian peasants, awakening them to the possibility of radical change (Warriner 1962:55). The major manifestation of peasant unrest was the overt, often violent confrontations between landlords and sharecroppers which swept the great plains of central and northern Syria in the early fifties. Unrest was particularly intense in Hama which stood out for its high population concentration and the great estates on which the condition of the peasant was widely recognized as the worst in Syria (Warriner 1962:84, 93; Torrey 1964:167). A tradition of peasant resistance to landlord dispossession going back decades, aggravated by the newer post-war drive by landlords to replace sharecropping tenures with mechanization and wage labor, created a festering sense of peasant grievance. The plains peasantry, kept down by the crushing dominance of the landlords, had not, however, produced the educated leadership which might have transformed sporadic rebellion into a broad based movement; as such, it was the anti-feudal middle class leadership of Akram al-Hawrani's Arab Socialist Party which activated peasant mobilization. But once this began, profound peasant unrest rapidly billowed outward from its core at Hama, southward to Homs, northward to Ma'arrat an-Nu'man and Aleppo, taking the form of violent conflict with landlords on their estates, protest marches for land reform in the cities, and an electoral movement which in 1954 swept Hawrani's partisans into parliament for Hama. On a separate track, in the Kurdish mountains to the north, the Communist Party was also mobilizing a significant peasant movement against the local Aghas and the city merchants.

The case of Ma'arrat an-Nu'man where the severity of the landlords' grip was as intense as in Hama itself and unrest particularly pervasive, illustrates how the agrarian crisis which was coming to a head in the fifties typically had its roots in changes in land control going back nearly a century. One Nuras Pasha al-Haraki, on the strength of a marriage connection to a favorite of Sultan Abdul Hamid, was appointed governor in the region and proceeded to use his power to take control, together with the Azm family, of fifty local villages. The development of the conflict in two villages, Habiet and Kafr Sukhne, is known in some detail. Through intimidation of peasants by "toughs," and false witness before the land registration authority, some land was acquired. Nuras Pasha then stimulated a conflict between the two villages, in which some peasants were jailed and others wounded; they then sold him their land at low prices to buy weapons and pay lawyer's fees; this was a typical example of how notables manipulated the segmental character of peasant society to assert control over it, turning independent small-holders into sharecroppers. In 1937, peasants began refusing to pay rent in kind; the Haraki and Azm families, with a hundred armed police attacked the villages, beat the peasants, destroyed houses and prevented peasants from plowing the land. The peasants appealed in vain to parliament, where a Haraki held the local seat, for redress. The conflict broke out yet again in 1952 when Bahjat al-Azm, with the agreement of the district governor, expelled the peasant sharecroppers from the land and brought in displaced and submissive tribesmen in their place. This time, youth of the local Arab Socialist Party took up their cause and, for awhile at least, got the peasants restored to their land. But the conflict continued and the issue was not settled until land reform (Hanna 386–389, 452–454). A conflict in 1950 between the Barazi family and the village of Tel Bisa illustrates the extent to which rural unrest was erupting in violence. There a dispute over a fertilizer shipment which the Barazis tried to appropriate from peasants, brought out crowds of village youth with sticks and rocks. When they were met by the pistols of the landlord's men, the villagers attacked the manor house with old shotguns, forcing the Barazis to flee; it was this kind of spontaneous outbreak of revolt long festering below the surface, that Akram al-Hawrani was able to channel into a broader peasant movement (Hanna 451).

In conclusion, the political mobilization of the peasantry was taking essentially two forms: one thrust, that among the more independent but economically precarious small peasantry, including the Alawis, Druzes and other minorities, was manifested in a drive for education and recruitment of educated peasant youth into opposition political parties. The second thrust, among the broader sharecropping peasantry on the great estates and to an extent among small-holders under threat of dispossession, took the more classic form of peasant agitation or revolt. This peasant mobilization never acquired the dimensions of mass revolution. It was too regionally uneven, intense in certain areas such as northcentral Syria but, in other areas, where relative peasant prosperity or tribal values dominated, of limited significance. Even where peasant hostility to the old order ran deep, it never took on the form of a sustained organized mass movement; instead sporadic middle class-led challenges such as Hawrani's petered out once they helped catapult their leaders to the center of power. Similarly, the political activism of educated village youth generated factions hostile to landlords in many villages, but was essentially focused on the struggle for power and reform in the capital. Yet although focused on the capital, and only sporadically in the village, the chronic unrest and spreading agrarian radicalism in the countryside undermined the local political bases of the notability and gave limited numbers of middle class radicals the social and moral depth to challenge, and ultimately end, the old regime. The two forms of rural politicization, producing on the one hand an educated ex-peasant leadership and, on the other, a mass peasant constituency for it, would also provide the stuff for the Ba'th-led middle-class–peasant alliance which would challenge the old order and on which after 1963 the new Ba'th regime would be erected.

Regime De-Legitimation and the Crisis of the Liberal-Capitalist Order

Social change and conflict at the heart of society produced forces which challenged the old order from below; but all changing societies experience social stress and these might have been localized or contained. Another crucial ingredient in the crumbling of the old regime was political: a loss of legitimacy by the elite, the political institutions over which it presided, and the strategy of development it advocated. This happened with startling rapidity, unfolding in little more than a decade.

The legitimacy of the liberal order was precarious from the outset. To be sure, the governing elite had won independent statehood after a long history of Ottoman and French rule, an achievement which endowed it with a certain nationalist credit. But the formally democratic regime at the apex of the new state was lacking in supportive traditions and the social roots of the elite were, except in the traditional urban quarters, shallow. Moreover, the imperialist imposition of a truncated "little Syrian" state cut off from the other parts of historic Syria—Jordan, Lebanon and Palestine—and embracing but one corner of the potential nation to which most politically conscious Syrians aspired, deprived the new state of the legitimacy which accrues to those corresponding to a unit of felt nationhood. Lacking much accumulated political capital, the governing elite was vulnerable to a precipitous de-legitimation should it fail to deal with the challenges of governing. In fact, it failed on two major grounds and was, in consequence, nearly totally discredited.

First, the elite, in the eyes of the attentive public, failed to provide effective national leadership in containing or reversing the effects of imperialism and Zionism in the region (Van Dusen 1975:129; Jundi 48, 50–51). Public expectations that the dismemberment of historic Syria would be reversed and Syria linked to the wider Arab world once the imperialists departed were dashed. As al-Jundi (44) puts it: "Syria began to go astray on the seas of large hopes and small capacity; she took on herself the responsibility of Arab nationalism and unity. Independence raised hopes which could not be fulfilled." Yet more damaging, however, was the failure of the Arab regimes to forestall the establishment of the state of Israel in Palestine, a former southern province of Syria. The government was totally discredited, not only for its share in this failure but also by revelations of profiteering with army supplies in ruling circles. There was a near breakdown of civil order for nearly two weeks after the Zionist victory. The feeling of betrayal among young officers was the decisive factor in propelling the army into politics in opposition to the old order. Thus, a bare three years after independence, regime legitimacy suffered a mortal blow. As al-Jundi (42) argues, the creation of Israel had the most profound effect on Syrian politics: "We go astray constantly concerning causes and effects if we eliminate this issue. . . . When we go deeper we find this issue penetrates even in the smallest political and economic details."

The alienation from the old order and radical nationalist sentiment generated by the Palestine disaster were continually reinforced in the following years by recurrent clashes with both Israel and the Western powers. The West's drive to pull Syria into its anti-Soviet security pacts, perceived by nationalists as a form of "neo-imperialism," its support for Israel and its refusal to sell arms to the Arab states at a time when Israel was probing Syria's borders, fueled the flames of nationalist opinion. The rise of Nasir as a Arab nationalist hero who broke the arms embargo and defied the security pacts, electrified Syrian opinion. The middle class parties insisted on neutralism in the East-West struggle, militancy against Israel, and Pan-Arabism but much of the old elite remained pro-Western or ambivilant. The Suez invasion in which Western powers and Israel combined in an attack on the leading Arab nationalist state made radical Arab nationalism a mass sentiment and was a watershed in discrediting the Western ties of the old politicians. Several attempts by the West and its local allies, notably Iraq under Nuri, to intervene in Syrian politics on behalf of pro-Western conservatives only put more nails in their political coffins. Much of the rising middle class, the product of a school system designed to inculcate Arab nationalism, could not accept the compromises of the older Ottoman or Western trained generation. But nationalist sentiment was spreading rapidly among the peasantry too: Lerner's 1951 survey found illiterate peasants to be "xenophobic," extremely hostile to the Western powers and Israel (292–293). In the end, the nationalist legitimacy of the traditional elite was shattered by both its weakness and its pro-Western sympathies and connections. Having failed the critical test of national defense, the elites' monopoly of power and wealth seemed to lose all justification.

The second major factor behind regime de-legitimation was a growing disillusionment with the hybrid road to development resulting from the imposition of a liberal-capitalist model on a semi-"feudal" social structure. In the years immediately after independence, free-enterprise-led economic expansion, building on Syria's indigenous commercial tradition, had made this the unchallenged ideology within the urban establishment: for the first generation ruling elite modernization meant Westernization and capitalist development. But by the mid-fifties, this model was, for various reasons, under challenge by a socialist ideology which was capturing the loyalties of strategic sectors of the new middle class, peasantry, and workers.

The starting point—the system of great landed wealth—out of which capitalism was developing never enjoyed legitimacy: most estates were of recent origin, created by the dispossession of the peasantry, unaccompanied by the local leadership role of the landlord typical of European feudalism, and sanctioned by Western concepts of absolute private property in land which went against Islamic traditions of ultimate community ownership (Nasser 38–39).

Dissatisfaction with the capitalist model was also fueled by the economic instability—inflation, unemployment—accompanying Syria's integration into the world market and by the uneven nature of capitalist economic growth, the costs of which were carried by the poor while the benefits chiefly accrued to the haves. Haddad (192) observed: "jealousies and resentments were aggravated when the wave of economic prosperity . . . gave certain people wealth and power while certain others were relatively less successful and were left behind." The bulk of the benefits of industry, marked by a very high level of capital concentration, were monopolized by a tiny portion of the population (Keilany 1968:30; Keilany 1973:61–63). Workers benefited little from the industrial expansion: in 1956, the profits of industry were 2-1/2 times its wage bill and the decline of artisanship and periods of industrial contraction afflicted workers with unemployment. A combination of inflation and unemployment decreased the real purchasing power of the lower urban strata by about 25% between the pre- and post-WWII periods and another 6% from 1954 to 1964 (Hilan 1969:226–227). Capitalist development in agriculture meant the transformation of peasants into migratory wage laborers on great estates or massive unemployment, shattering peasant communities and placing the heaviest burden of development on the part of the population which could least carry it. Increasingly, however, public opinion expected some relief for the peasantry: "the problem of the land," wrote Naaman (1950), "more and more occupies the spirits of this exclusively agrarian country and constitutes the number one problem of modern Syria." Finally, as has been seen, middle class aspirations outpaced opportunities in an economy dominated by the agrarian-commercial bourgeoisie. Hilan's (1969:227–230) estimate of the distribution of income in the late fifties suggests, when compared to that for 1937 (see page 40), that the upper classes continued to take at least as disproportionate a share as before the war: the top 3% of the population reportedly received 33% of the national income and the top 10% received 50%. The middle class had advanced somewhat, but the share of the bottom 75% had declined from 32% to 25%. In short, a capitalist road to development seemed to promise no major expansion of opportunities for the salaried middle class and certainly no relief for the masses of peasants and workers.

As long, however, as the economy, albeit it with stops and starts, generally continued to expand, generating new opportunities for upward mobility and raising expectations of future improvement, the capitalist model was not seriously challenged. But beginning in the mid-fifties, the boom appeared to come to an end: 1955 was a turning point when simultaneous massive crop failure and overproduction in local industry created a sudden sense of economic crisis (Ziadeh 160–161, 279). According to Hansen (335, 338–341) the growth rate began to decline around this time because resources, opportunities, capital investment and markets were all coming up against limits inherent in the very structure of the economy.

> The decade of relatively high growth from 1946 to 1956 represented a stage in Syrian development that [could not] be repeated [being] . . . based on special circumstances and on the exploitation of natural advantages that [had been] exhausted. . . . a marked decline in the growth rate took place around 1956 largely because of decline in the agricultural growth rate from 4–5% before this date to as low as 0.5% thereafter . . . reducing growth in per capital income from about 3% a year to 1%.

As this happened, expectations were frustrated and consciousness of the cumulative costs of capitalism were heightened. When a period of sustained economic expansion, mobilizing new social forces and raising expectations, is followed by an abrupt turndown or crisis, modern history suggests that a period of political turmoil, even a "revolutionary situation," may ensue; Syria was no exception to this generalization (Davis; Walton: 151–153).

The economic turndown was rooted in the limited base of agricultural development under the mixed "feudal-capitalist" agrarian order. By the mid-fifties the limits of easy capitalist agricultural expansion had been reached. The expansion in grain production was based on the opening up of previously unexploited lands in the East which yielded relatively quick returns on modest capital investment. The limits of extensive dry farming were soon reached, as most cultivable land was brought under cultivation, and probably overreached, judging by the astounding 50% drop in production in the dry years of 1958–1960. As less and less fertile land with a lower average rainfall was brought under the plow, costs rose while yields stagnated, and because fallow increased as the cultivated area expanded, actual area cropped per year stagnated after 1957. There was thus a fall in net value added per hectacre by almost a half from 1950 to 1963 (Hansen 343–346). The weakness of the means of transport between the eastern producing areas and export ports, driving up the cost of transport and tractor fuel at a time when grain prices began to fall, also squeezed output per hectacre between rising costs and falling prices. Moreover, mechanized farming for quick profit was leading to dangerous soil erosion and encroachment on the steppe threatened the base of the animal husbandry industry. The part of the agricultural expansion based on the introduction of simple motor pumps for irrigation in cotton culture encountered similar limits: as marginal productivity from their further expansion declined and cotton prices plunged as well, no further easy advance in cotton farming seemed likely. Here, too, entrepreneurs, seeking quick profits and eschewing the big investments in drainage, contributed to the spread of a ruinous salinity. Many of the new capitalist farmers had little experience in agriculture, especially intensive farming, and as late as 1957 there were only 150 agronomists in the whole country to provide the proper advice. They did not know how to treat the land, saw the import of machinery and exploitation of cheap labor as the key to quick profits, and showed little concern for long term development.

After 1957 investment in agriculture yielded only slow and small returns compared to the boom years (though years of very good rainfall could still produce dramatic but temporary increases in production). Finally, not only was agricultural growth slowing but the form that the big expansion had taken was proving unhealthy: the tendency toward monoculture was making Syria dependent on the export of a few key crops which, subject to great fluctuations in both output and prices (able to double or cancel a real increase in national income), plagued the country with economic instability (Keilany 1968:30–31).

A point had, thus, been reached where, simply to sustain the viability of the existing agrarian base, major investments in land improvement and drainage were needed. *Further* growth required massive investment in irrigation, reclamation and population re-settlement. It would also require a change from extensive to intensive development: improved methods of cultivation, reduction of fallow, improved fertilizer and seed use, integration of animal husbandry into the crop cycle. The vulnerabilities of monoculture could only be eased by agricultural diversification (as well as industrialization) and diversification also required intensification. But intensification entailed a basic socio-economic re-organization of the villages in the vast majority of which technology remained primitive. In short, further development seemed to literally require an agrarian revolution.

There was, however, no sign that the great landowners and merchants could or would lead the massive process of investment and social re-organization necessary for such a revolution. Many remained content with a more exploitative use of the traditional sharecropping system which provided income without risk or, at most, were prepared for modest investment in tractors and pumps. Indeed, according to one source, commercial capital began to desert agriculture after 1956. As it became apparent that profitability and prices alone could no longer drive agricultural development, many became convinced that the initiative would have to come from government without which, Hansen (350) wrote "the general outlook for the Syrian economy will be rather gloomy." A need for state regulation to protect the agrarian ecology was widely recognized: as early as 1951, the disastrous failure of the cotton harvest under an invasion of pests due to the reckless expansion of acreage and lack of pesticide use, brought the first government intervention in agriculture, the establishing of licensing, seed treatment, dusting and spraying by the Cotton Bureau. But more direct government investment in irrigation, land reclamation, agricultural education, marketing and credit facilities, and in infrastructure, also appeared needed: in 1954 the World Bank's minimum program called for five times more government spending than the laissez-faire state devoted to agriculture (Warriner 1962: 77–78, 85, 89, 95, 102, 105, 219; Lewis 1955:60; Hamide 457; Keilany 1968:47–62; IBRD 23–25, 74, 76, 135–136, 300; Porter; Arudki 28; Za'im 70; Hansen 339–350; Metral and Sanlaville 229–235).

On top of this, many Syrian intellectuals, backed by international experts, argued that the whole land tenure system was an obstacle to rational exploitation and modernization: the concentration of agricultural revenue in the hands of big landlords who engaged in conspicuous consumption kept investment low, while absentee control of vast estates and the separation between ownership and labor resulted in mismanagement and inefficiency. No village re-organization promoting agricultural intensification could come about under such a tenure system. The appearance of some improving landlords was too little, too late to alter perceptions that a radical change in land tenure was needed to unblock Syria's agricultural development. Many also argued that land reform was essential to create a rural market and generate an agrarian surplus, without which industrialization would come to a halt and the backward agrarian sector become a drag on the whole economy (Za'im, Nasser, Shakra).

Indeed, the limits of industrialization were also becoming apparent by the mid-fifties. Industry still contributed only 1/5 to 1/4 of agriculture to the national income (IBRD:10). It was dependent on tax exemptions and heavy protection which kept prices high (IBRD 108–109, 380, 391). According to Arudki (27–28), the mentality of Syrian industrialists remained that of the merchant: seeking quick profits through the maximum exploitation of labor, evasion of taxes, and a neglect of quality made possible by their market monopoly. The industrial advance was still confined to the "natural" agrarian-based light processing industries, but as these were established, the period of rapid expansion was ending (IBRD 395). Industry was also constrained and costs kept high by power bottlenecks and a primitive infrastructure (IBRD 123–124, 369; Hansen 342, 353). The low social standards of the mass of the population, largely the product of the backward agrarian system, also represented a major constraint on industrialization. An unskilled socially depressed labor force raised the costs of production; in 1955 only 13.6% of the work force had primary education. The very low incomes of the bulk of the population, especially the impoverished peasantry, provided little market for industry (IBRD:401). Thus, industrialization was, indeed, being constrained, in great part, by agriculture: the World Bank (IBRD 400–401) warned in 1954 that without a substantial modernization of agriculture and rise in agricultural income, industrial expansion could not continue. Moreover, further sustained industrialization required a totally new order of investment. Syria's investment rate had been impressive but wartime capital accumulation was exhausted and new accumulation was insufficient for an industrial transformation (IBRD 399; Ziadeh 245). A "preference for large and quick returns for which there were . . . ample opportunities outside industry," channeled the bulk of profits into luxury housing, construction, land, importing, franchises of foreign firms, foreign bank accounts and consumption for the new bourgeoisie (IBRD 373). The classic extroverted dependent capitalist economy in which foreign exchange from agricultural exports is spent on manufactured imports, dissipating local profits or funneling them abroad, limited both industrial investment and markets (ad-Dahr 200; Arudki 30; Zakariya 31–32; IBRD 16–18; Hilan 1969:227–250; Hilan 1973:163–165; Shakra 75; Makdisi 167). Moreover, rising nationalism and radicalism after the mid-fifties began to sour the investment climate. For all these reasons, from 1956 to 1958 total investment stagnated (Kabbarah; Zakariya 42; Hansen 340–341). The double-digit rate of industrial development in the early fifties slowed to 4.5% from 1954–1958 (Hilan 1973:165). By the late fifties, it was widely believed (Jabbur 89–90) that Syrian industrialists could not or would not make the much bigger investments needed for the next stages of medium and heavy industrialization and hence that without massive government intervention and investment that the road to industrial diversification was blocked.

Syria's capitalist development thus seemed snagged in contradictions. Slowing growth demonstrated the need for a much increased state role in investment and regulation to sustain capitalist development (IBRD 199). Moreover, according to the widely accepted view among Syrian intellectuals, in a mature capitalist world where industrial competition requires huge investments and where late industrializers are unable to exploit colonies and, in an era of militant labor movements, their own work force—as did the early industrializers—national capitalism cannot hope to succeed without a major role for the state. The "progressive wing" of the bourgeoisie (e.g. Khalid al-Azm) recognized, by the late fifties, that further capitalist development required state intervention, but the bulk of the upper class continued to resist any such role (Nassar 68). As long as the private bourgeoisie controlled the major sources of wealth and was entrenched in government, no strong developmental role for the state seemed possible. Agrarian reform, too, appeared unavoidable to raise the social standard of the population and to provide the right conditions for agricultural development and industrialization; but landlord control of the state blocked it and such an assault on private property was likely to discourage the private investment on which development had so far depended. Even if sufficient private investment was forthcoming, many Syrians believed the high profits needed to elicit it implied a continuing concentration of resources in the hands of an economic oligarchy.

Perhaps in part because the bourgeoisie failed to take the lead in reform of the capitalist model, leadership of Syrian opinion increasingly fell to petty bourgeois intellectuals who argued that the "national bourgeoisie" had exhausted itself and that only a socialist course could overcome the contradictions blocking Syria's development. This, they argued, would allow a transformation of the agrarian structure to the benefit of the peasantry, admit of a large role for state-led development bound to open new opportunities for the workers and salaried middle class, and allow a better distribution of the national wealth. In short "socialism" would, they believed, better meet the demands of social justice and development and better satisfy the interests of the majority of the population (Jabbur 90–93; Zakariya 38–39; Hilan 1973:43, 158–168).

The uncertainties and perceived costs of capitalism and the promise of socialism soon convinced a majority of politically conscious Syrians outside the establishment that Syria's model of development would have to be altered. While in the 1940s socialism was widely regarded as an alien ideology and the virtues of free enterprise as self-evident, by 1950 the incorporation of a battery of social reformist demands into the constitution signified a sea-change in opinion (Ziadeh 181, 247–248; Torrey 1964:179). By the late fifties, opinion was much more radicalized. To be an intellectual was to embrace opposition to feudalism and capitalism, but radical opinion had spread to big parts of the lower classes as well; indeed, so changed was the climate of opinion that even the traditional right was obliged to give lip service to some sort of "socialism" (Petran 80; Jabbur 339–350, 400, 434–435). The belief in the bankruptcy of capitalism and the attendant political challenge to the established order became, in a way, a self-fulfilling prophecy since, as the upper classes lost confidence that they could control political events, they lost the incentive to make the investments that might have made capitalism viable (Shakra 78; Petran 113; Akhrass 1).

Rising nationalism reinforced the growing suspicion of capitalism. The hatred for imperialism, stemming from the Palestine debacle, transformed itself into a certain hatred for all institutions of Western inspiration, especially capitalism (Saab; Sayyid 150–153). As conflict with the West and Israel intensified, the lack of stomach for it among the upper classes was widely attributed to the economic connections to the West fostered under capitalism. Many Syrians became convinced that capitalism meant economic dependency incompatible with true national independence; there is no doubt that export-led development was indeed making Syria greatly dependent on Western markets and on foreign imports, the value of the latter amounting to 30% of national income in the fifties (IBRD 11–13). The older generation of elites had wanted political independence, but, this being won, were prepared for political alliances with the West and had little concern for cultural or economic independence; but for the generation socialized in the fifties, the cumulative effects of Palestine, the rise of the Third World, Suez, Algeria and Western pressures against Syria had transformed the political climate, displacing the West as a desirable economic model or alliance partner and putting a premium on economic independence (Jabbur 309).

Simultaneously, Soviet support for Syria in its growing conflicts with the West and Israel opened the country to Marxist ideas on an entirely new order of magnitude, shaping the views of a whole generation being educated at this time—including the future rulers of Syria (Ziadeh 253; Lerner 287). To the middle class intellectuals who led public opinion, the Marxist message was increasingly compelling. With the fall of Stalinism and the emergence of national communism, Marxism-Leninism no longer appeared incompatible with nationalism. Indeed, its claim of an organic link between imperialism and capitalism accorded with the experience of nationalists who also viewed Israel as part of this unholy alliance: it became a fixed belief among Syrian intellectuals that imperialism aimed to keep Syria a backward dependency of the world capitalist system and that Israel was its local outpost and gendarme. It required but a short step from this to argue that only socialism provided a viable road to national independence.

The identification of the capitalism with imperialism and a consequent receptivity to socialist alternatives was also widespread among the mass public. It was remarkable for a Muslim country long under Western influence that as early as 1951 30–40% of the population expressed pro-Soviet sentiments (Lerner 289), chiefly owing to Western support for Israel. One of Syria's greatest feudal lords told Warriner (1962:97) that the cause of the social unrest which threatened his class was the victory of Zionism which had pervaded the country, including the army, with "communism." So influential was the leftwing press in the late fifties, Sayyid (150) complains, that "half the intellectuals and even illiterates knew Marx and Lenin better than the leaders of Arab nationalism and Islam." In this climate it was hardly surprising that Syrian advocates of capitalism would be suspect to nationalist opinion; Sayyid (151–153) reports that by the late fifties, conservatives were so much on the defensive for their Western ties that "if you weren't leftist . . . you were labeled an agent of reaction and imperialism conspiring against the country."

As disenchantment with the ruling elite and the capitalist model spread, support for the formally democratic-constitutional order also eroded. During the independence struggle nationalism and democracy had gone together since the latter facilitated the fight for the former. But support for democracy, too identified with the hated West and lacking indigenous traditions, was nevertheless slim from the start of independence. The elites' own frequent violations of the constitutional principles on which its claim to legitimacy rested, appeared to many Syrians to make a mockery of democratic procedure; as soon as they were challenged by dissent, they responded with campaigns of arrest, intimidations, press censorship, and electoral manipulation. Democracy was also associated with the elite's liberal use of public resources to service the patronage networks needed to ensure electoral victory and with the bankrolling of candidates by foreign powers. The military coups of 1949 shattered what modicum of legitimacy and prestige constitutional procedure had been able to develop (Jabbur 279–283; Akhrass 127; Jundi 43–45; Torrey 1964:36; Petran 93–94).

Social conditions also undermined democracy. Because "feudalism," which kept the mass majority economically dependent, politically passive, or encapsulated in clientage networks, largely shut the door to any quick electoral breakthrough by opposition reform parties, the demands of the middle class could not be satisfied through established constitutional institutions and its loyalties thereby attached to this order. Indeed, the social structure, filling parliament with conservative landlords, made parliamentarianism an obstacle to, rather than a vehicle of social reform. Allush (132) declared that progressive opinion wanted a regime which met the people's needs, not one "giving them the right to vote in order to deny them the right to bread." The middle class was much less interested in democratic procedures than in a government which in substance pursued national and middle class interests (Seale 116); much less did Western democracy have a support base in the masses for whom liberal freedoms meant little. Democracy seemed unworkable without social reforms (Khadduri 132–133) which could provide the minimal social equality to make political rights meaningful, but the constitutional order was used to obstruct those very reforms. Warriner (1962:110–111), writing in the late-fifties, thought it unlikely Syria's parliamentary regime could solve Syria's profound rural problems or contain the polarization unleashed by capitalist development; in observing, too, that change in the political system, still expressive of the old order of wealth and feudal power, lagged behind these social dynamics, she put her finger on its weakness.

Thus, support for parliamentary democracy generally declined as the fifties unfolded. The polarization of society worked against it: as early as 1951 only 18% of Lerner's (289–290) respondents were liberals advocating moderate change, opinion being sharply split between a stubbornly conservative right, concentrated in the urban upper classes and a radical nationalist-left associated with "transitionals" such as rural youth acquiring education. By the end of the decade the balance had decisively tilted toward the radicals. The steady decline in electoral turnout, from 65% in 1947, to 35.5% in 1949 and 40% in 1954 to 27.6% in 1961, was a good indicator of the declining legitimacy of the liberal state and of the disintegration of the clientage networks on which it rested. The regime, riven by intra-elite rivalries and lacking mobilized mass support, appeared incapable of coping with mounting external threat and internal social crisis. Syrians, more and more contemptuous of it and yearning for strong leadership, welcomed the military interventions of the early fifties; by the late fifties, increasingly disillusioned by military politics, they were looking for something else yet and in the following years many would turn to the charismatic leadership of Nasir, others to Leninist formulas, but few to liberalism. As Lerner observed, there was no more poignant testimony to the fragility of Syrian democracy than "the longing of the most Westernized and enlightened elements for its termination" (Lerner 279–281; Jundi 38; Torrey 1964:115; Khadduri 1970:132–133).

The desire among big parts of the frustrated middle class for the violent overthrow of the old order in favor of a dictatorship capable of pursuing social reform and national power was represented by the words of a typical figure which Lerner called a "Syrian Tito:" "I would like to make Syria a really socialistic state and approach Russia in order to get rid of the influence of the Western powers. I would make a second Yugoslavia of Syria and would be its Tito." He expressed contempt for "our so-called aristocracy," wanted to "evenly distribute the national wealth," and "build up a new Arab world, renewing its past glories." Democracy, for him, meant educating the public in the "proper" political and social attitudes. Without forced radical change many young Syrians feared "we will stay 100 years dragging" (Lerner 282–286). Thus, many Syrians, frustrated in their private lives and demoralized by the weakness and backwardness of their country, came to see radical politics as the road to personal and national salvation.

4

The Genesis of a Counterelite
and the Struggle for Power

The Vehicles of System Challenge:
The Army and the Ba'th Party

It was the emergence of two political forces, the army and the Ba'th Party, providing leadership, ideology, a support base, and organized power, which translated socio-economic contradictions and the political discontents of the new middle class and peasantry into a formidable challenge to the old regime. Through these institutions, partly working in tandem, ultimately interlocked, a counter-elite took form and a radical coalition of enough brains, guns, and numbers was put together to make a populist breakthrough. How did the army, which began as mere organization, become a vehicle of radical ideology, and how did the Ba'th Party which began as pure ideology, develop the organization to back its goals?

The Radicalization of the Syrian Army

The transformation of the Syrian army from a pillar of the state into a vehicle of radical challenge to the establishment—hardly a usual outcome—requires some explanation. A necessary condition for the radicalization of the army was its predominately middle class, and later rural ex-peasant, social composition. A major explanation for this composition was the little attraction of a military career for the sons of the upper class notability. In late Ottoman times when a modern army was being created, educated Syrians, by contrast to Iraqis, tended to join the civil service rather than the military (Van Dusen 1975:124). Under the French, who deliberately recruited from minority groups—Kurds, Christians and Armenians, Druzes and Alawites—presumably less vulnerable to Arab nationalism, a military career was seen by many politically conscious upper class families as serving imperialism. The origin of the post-independence army in a French-officered auxiliary, the Troupes Speciales du Levant, recruited from minority groups, deprived the military of the prestige it has elsewhere and the sons of the Sunni upper classes, even after independence, preferred more remunerative and prestigious professions such as law and medicine (Haddad:193). On the other hand, a tradition of military service was early established among the minority groups and it continued after independence. While Kurds, Christians and Druzes filled the officer corps, poorer and less educated Alawites, gravitated into the ranks of NCOs and only later became junior officers. While a minority composition, at first glance, would hardly appear to be a prescription for a radical and nationalist politicization of the military, for reasons already considered, minorities, especially the Alawites and Druzes, would become strong advocates of secular Arab nationalism and populism in the fifties. After independence, the army was "nationalized" and in the wake of the Palestine defeat, rapidly expanded; the military academy was not only opened to all classes but provided scholarships to bright underprivileged applicants; as a result, the Sunni lower middle class, particularly its rural branch, as well as sons of peasants, were increasingly recruited into the army. Indeed, by 1952, a majority of graduates were rurals (Devlin 1976:204; Petran 89; Akhrass 117). This growing ruralization made the officer corps susceptible to both peasant nationalism and an agrarian populism hostile to the landlord regime. As a result of the purges which accompanied military intervention in politics beginning in 1949, older more traditional officers were increasingly replaced by younger middle class nationalist-reformist ones; the small contingent of urban upper class officers was particularly decimated as a result of the purges following Western conspiracies against the nationalist government in the late fifties (Seale 37, 48, 119). The upper class component of the military was definitely far weaker in Syria than in other Arab countries such as Egypt and Iraq and, conversely, recruitment to the officer corps reached further down in the stratification system. In general, the rapid expansion of the military and the relative openness and equality of opportunity in the institution by comparison to the closed civilian social structure, made the military into a channel of upward mobility for middle class and peasant youth (Perlmutter 1969:835).

Modest social composition of the officer corps is, however, an insufficient condition for its radicalization. If recruits can be socialized into a elitist military subculture stressing professional discipline, segregation from civilian society, and an ideology of order and conservative nationalism, they may become faithful praetorians of an upper class regime. But, for this to happen a long military tradition, founded under "aristocratic" or colonial leadership must probably have been established and a good measure of nationalist legitimacy attach to the established order. Neither condition existed in Syria. The Syrian army, beginning as a mere gendarmerie, enjoyed almost no military traditions at independence into which recruits could be socialized. Moreover, a professional military sub-culture, sharply differentiated from civilian society, did not develop. Many recruits joined the army not out of affinity for the military life but as a route out of the village. Many officers had been politicized by their participation in the independence struggle in secondary school and retained ties with political comrades who went into civilian careers (Daoud Agha 390–391). Particularly under the influence of the radical politician, Akram al-Hawrani, youth entered the military academy with political motives: an army career began to be seen as a vehicle of political activism. Almost from the outset of independence, radical middle class parties began to proselytize among officers with growing success: scores of officers joined the SSNP, and later hundreds flocked to the Ba'th. As a result, the loyalties of younger officers often lay less with their hierarchical superiors than with civilian partisans in the middle class political movements (al-Jundi 50). The army did, of course, develop some sense of its special role and mission, but this actually redounded to the disadvantage of the traditional elite. Charged with the defense of the country's independence against outside forces, it tended to become ever more militantly nationalistic. That tradition which did gradually take root in the military did so under the tutelage of radical nationalist officers—such as Jamal Faysal, the Arab nationalist commandant of the Homs military academy who politicized a generation of officers (Torrey 1964:289, 361). The military's awareness that national power sprang from modernization made it an advocate of social reform and rapid economic development, and hence impatient of the old regime.

Equally important in explaining military radicalization, was the national de-legitimation of the governing elite. The fiasco in Palestine, taken by the officer corps as a professional as well as a national humiliation, and blamed on the corruption and incompetence of the traditional civilian elites was, without doubt, the watershed event in the radical politicization of the officer corps and the direct catalyst of its intervention in politics (al-Jundi 50–51). The officers came to see themselves as the only competent champions of the national interest, a sentiment encouraged by widespread public longing for strong leadership in the face of foreign threat. Thus, the military assumed a permanent "guardian" role in Syrian politics after 1949. Subsequent developments, such as the emergence of a nationalist army in Egypt, the fight with the West over arms, Israeli provocations and attacks on army positions at the front, and the Suez war, reinforced and accelerated the radical politicization of the officer corps.

After the first military coup in 1949 the officer corps became increasingly conscious of its own power, the inability of the old order to resist it, and hence of its capacity to force changes the middle class and peasantry wanted and could not get through established political institutions. This politicization of the officer corps made it, in a very real sense, the "vanguard" of the new middle class, and even, to an extent of the peasantry. Similar class background and common profession and institutional affiliation molded the officer corps into a force with a shared hostility to the notability. On the other hand, the military's politicization and the heterogeneity of its regional and sectarian background also fragmented it. Whatever the costs of this politicization for the efficacy of the military as a fighting force, these developments kept the ruling class from using it as an instrument of repression at home.

The radicalization and politicization of the army was, of course a gradual cumulative process and the growing dominance of radical officers suffered several reverses before the Ba'th achieved unchallenged ascendence after 1963. The first wave of politically active officers is well represented by two military politicians who made coups in 1949, Husni al-Zaʿim and Adib al-Shishakli. Both were Sunni, urban and middle class in origin, and modernizing in orientation. The first, al-Zaʿim, was representative of an older generation hardly yet touched by radicalism. An Arabized Kurd with Ottoman training who had served the French, he was pro-Turkish, pro-Western and innocent of Arab nationalism: he signed the armistice with Israel and endorsed the Western security pacts. Motivated by a certain military contempt for the old politicians, he, nevertheless, made a scion of the feudal Barazi family his prime minister; significantly, Muhsin al-Barazi, too, was of Arabized Kurdish descent. Beside personal ambition, Zaʿim was moved by a certain commitment to secularist modernization inspired by Ataturk (al-Jundi 52–53; Petran 96, 98, 102).

Adib al-Shishakli, who followed Zaʿim to power, was far closer to the middle class Arab mainstream. Although recruited under the French, he deserted the Troupes Speciales, joined nationalist revolts in Syria and in support of Rashid Ali Gaylani in Iraq, and later joined the irregular *Jaysh al-Inqath* (Army of Salvation) which fought in Palestine. He was moved by "disgust and restlessness" at the loss of Palestine. His contempt for the old elite ran deep, a feeling captured in his remark that the notable-dominated Shaʿb Party could not run a whorehouse but could govern Syrians because they were stupid (Jundi 59–61). He collaborated with middle class opposition politicians such as the Baʿth leaders and Akram al-Hawrani who was leading an anti-feudal struggle in Hama, Shishakli's hometown. As Chief of Staff he presided over the expansion and nationalist indoctrination of the officer corps and promoted young Sunni nationalist officers to positions of responsibility. After taking power, his nationalism was manifest in the pursuit of state centralization and cultural Arabization against minority separatism and particularism; he crushed separatist movements in both the Druze and Alawi mountains (Perlmutter 1969:831). Yet, his nationalism did not keep him from cooperation with France and the U.S., largely to balance threats to Syrian independence from the pro-British Hashemite monarchies. Despite disdain for the traditional elite, once assuming power he broke with the radical parties, promoted the interests of the industrial bourgeoisie, and eschewed land reform.

Both Zaʿim and Shishakli were anti-feudal reformists who sought to strengthen the state, but they were not revolutionaries; they can be seen as the military advocates of the "national bourgeoisie" (Jabbur:150–151). Complicating yet further the complexion of the early coups which brought them to power is the fact that many of the officers behind Zaʿim and Shishakli had ties to the Syrian Social National Party (SSNP), a secular, middle class, yet minority-based party devoted to a Syrian nation; several Druze officers, in particular, who played major roles in these events seem to have been motivated by a complex mixture of reformism and secular nationalism, sectarian resentment of the Sunni landlord elite which dominated the state and defense of particular Druze interests against it; significantly, many turned against both Zaʿim and Shishakli for similar mixed motives: Zaʿim for his hand in the murder of the SSNP leader, Antun Sa'adih, and Shishakli for his military repression of Druze separatism.

The fall of Za'im and Shishakli opened the way for the emergence in the mid-fifties of a younger generation of yet more nationalist, politicized and radical officers. A decisive development in the ideological coloration of military radicalism at this time was the decline of the SSNP. Nationalist officers who were earlier attracted to it deserted it as its hostility to Arabism became apparent, and most of those who remained loyal were purged after the assassination of the pro–Ba'thi deputy Chief of Staff, Col. Adnan al-Malki, by an SSNP partisan. Its place as the main progressive force in the military was taken by young nationalist officers, often Sunnis from Hama, recruited by Hawrani and by officers sympathetic to the Ba'th. By the late fifties Ba'thi and pro-Ba'th officers, who came to be led by Colonel Abd al-Hamid Sarraj, were the dominant force and the backing they gave the party and the nationalist Left crucial to their success at this time. They, however, shared power with two other factions. A group of rural Sunnis, formerly pro-Shishakli, later aligned with Khalid al-Azm, a representative of the progressive national bourgeoisie, was led by Amin al-Nafuri from the village of Nebek. A third group of "rightists" was of Damascene bourgeois background. When the latter, in alliance with President al-Quwatli, tried to purge some 100 pro-Ba'this from Sarraj on down, the latter joined forces with the Shishakliites and purged the Damascenes instead, further shifting the balance of power inside the army toward the Left (Salamah 11; Torrey 1964:350–361). This paved the way for the first major step in the destruction of the old regime, the formation of the UAR, a process guided by Ba'thi politicians and supported by mass opinion, but which, most directly, was decided and imposed by a nationalist officer corps.

The UAR period, however, had the paradoxical effect of shifting the ideological balance in the military back toward the Right because of Nasir's quarrel with the Ba'th and purge or transfer to Cairo of large numbers of Ba'thi officers (Salamah 16). This opened the door for the 1961 coup against the union led by two Damascene officers, Colonel Haidar al-Kuzbari, a scion of the industrial bourgeoisie who reflected its opposition to Nasir's nationalizations and Colonel Abd al-Karim al-Nahlawi who expressed the resentment of middle class officers against Egyptian domination of the army but also had ties to the anti-Nasirite Muslim Brethren. The separatist coup was thus chiefly a "Damascene affair" and the resultant dominance of top commands by this group was unacceptable to most of the largely rural and provincial officer corps, making it impossible to restore a reliable chain of command and inviting constant military instability (Daoud Agha 393–394). When the *infisal* ("separatist") government began to roll back UAR social reforms, several military uprisings, one by Nahlawi, another by progressive unionists in the provinces, took place. There followed a military conference at Homs in which the officer corps tried to solve its divisions by consultation; this led to the purge of both leading Damascenes and rebel progressives, but also forced a new less reactionary government on the old elite. In general, however, because the bulk of the officer corps remained sympathetic to the nationalist Left, this did little to restore the stability of the "separatist" regime. Moreover, scores of dismissed Ba'thi officers were scheming to return to the army and once they struck the necessary alliances with sympathizers still in the ranks, they were poised for the coup which would restore their lost dominance over the army and put an end to the old regime (al-Jundi 88–112).

Thus, by the sixties, the Syrian officer corps had become intensely politicized. In a real sense, this reflected the fact that, open to popular recruitment, it had become the most widely representative national institution in Syrian society, indeed a better mirror of public opinion than parliament (Perlmutter 1969:835). As Jabbur pointed out, the changing balance of political opinion in Syria was registered at this time through two main processes, coups and elections. While the latter lagged behind in registering it, the coup or army intrigue tended to register it ahead of time since the army was more directly in touch with the "attentive public" and able quickly to translate opinion into direct action. In this sense, the army was truly a "vanguard," its gradual radicalization registering the growing radicalization of the middle class and mobilization of the peasantry. Military politics was, thus, by no means a mere isolated struggle for power among small groups of officers. In the absence of responsive, mass-incorporating political institutions, it was an alternative "armed" parliament. But, of course, an armed parliament is a prescription for praetorianism, for coup and counter-coup, and this was indeed the cost Syria paid for the politicization of its officer corps. The fragmentation of the army also precluded the possibility of successful military rule in its classic "pure" sense. Both Za'im and Shishakli failed to consolidate personal military rule and were brought down when their military base— pulled apart by civilian political forces—fragmented beneath them. Thereafter, an officer corps intensely divided along regional, personal, ideological and sectarian grounds, could veto civilian initiatives but could not govern Syria. Not until after 1963 when the army was decisively captured by one political force, Ba'thism, would it, albeit in partnership with the party, acquire the minimal cohesion to govern.

The Ba'th Party: Development of a System-Challenging Party

Although the Ba'th Party was not the only radical opposition force in post-independence Syria, it was the most important if only because it became the vehicle of system transformation. As such, its history is most typical of the process by which a populist alliance capable of forcing a political transformation of Syria was forged.

Leadership and Ideology: The Ba'th rose out of the twin national and social crises which were engulfing Syria. Its founding leaders were middle class intellectuals whose political world view was shaped, above all, by the Arab East's struggle against imperialism. Many were involved in the various Syrian revolts against the French, the fight against the Turkish annexation of Iskanderun, the Rashid Ali al-Gaylani revolt in Iraq, and the fight to prevent Zionist victory in Palestine, each of which agitated nationalist opinion and spawned new deposits of nationalist activism (Allush 36). Increasingly dissatisfied with the compromises and ineffectiveness of the traditional nationalist leaders, the early Ba'thists made it their mission to lead a movement of national regeneration (Ba'th) to rid the Arab world of imperialism and traditional decadence. At the same time, they sought a progressive alternative to the rising communist movement in Syria which, in denying nationalism, seemed irrelevant to the country's concerns. Michel Aflaq and Salah ad-Din al-Bitar, the party's leading co-founders, were Damascene school teachers from commercial families with a history of nationalist ardor; Aflaq was a Greek Orthodox Christian and Bitar a Sunni Muslim. They studied in France where they were exposed to nationalist, democratic, and socialist thought and returned convinced that these ideas held the key to their mission. Indeed, they would make "Unity, Freedom, and Socialism" the slogan and trinity of their party.

Aflaq was an intensely intellectual, shy, philosopher whose elegant romantic nationalist writings inspired a generation of youth with Arabism and whose integrity, unconcern for riches and comforts, and devotion to the cause drew many of the earlier youthful members to the party. Although his ideas are pre-figured in the writings of Syrian intellectuals such as Zurayq, Rabbath and al-Husri, his achievement was to infuse them into a political movement (Khadduri 1970:154; Sayyid 77, 84–85; Abu Jaber 10; Torrey 1969:446). The more practical Bitar put his aptitude for administration and political journalism in the service of the fledgling Ba'th and for a long time ran its organization and edited its newspaper. Neither men, however, were forceful leaders or politicians. They were ineffective in electoral politics and although Bitar would serve competently in several governments, Aflaq shied away from political responsibility. Nor, despite their radical ideas, were they revolutionaries conspiring to overthrow the social order: scions of the Damascene minor notability, they were essentially liberal reformers. They were intellectuals, men whose ideas would inspire, be seized and reshaped, and then applied by other "men of action" (Abu Jaber 14–15, 187; Devlin 1976:13, 24, 58, 74).

Operating on a parallel tangent at about the same time, was Zaki al-Arsuzi; never a party member, but a brooding presence on its fringes, many of his followers would join the Ba'th. From a prominent Alawite family of Iskanderun, he proved himself, at the head of the Arab nationalist resistance to the Turks, to be a leader of tenacity and combativeness, capable of building a movement transcending localistic and sectarian divisions. Thereafter, an uprooted intellectual teaching in Damascus and an embittered victim of imperialism, he imparted to his youthful followers a virulent Arab nationalism and a contempt for the compromise and corruption of the traditional elite. Disillusioned, he now remained largely aloof from organized activism but was instrumental in drawing Alawis into the orbit of Arab nationalism and the Ba'th (Safadi 63–67; Van Dusen 1972:133; Sayyid 19; Rouleau 159, 164). Two other early founding leaders were Wahib al-Ghanim, an Alawi doctor from Latakia and Jallal al-Sayyid, a Sunni notable from Deir ez-Zor.

Around these men gathered others like them: of the 150 delegates to the party's 1947 founding Congress, the great majority were professionals or intellectuals, notably teachers and students from middle class or well-off peasant families. There was only a sprinkling of sons of the upper classes among them and these, moreover, tended to drop out as the party later radicalized. Roughly half were from urban and half rural background (MacIntyre; Devlin 1976:39, 41–42). They represented a social force quite distinct from and of lesser social status than the great notability which dominated the traditional establishment, an origin to which al-Sayyid (25) attributes the "social resentment" typical of the party. Educated and Westernized, they were initially equally isolated from the traditional masses. But they were already looking to the masses as the natural support for their challenge to the ruling elite (al-Jundi 21–36; Sayyid 15–55; Salamah 5–12; ABSP 1963 v. 1).

On a separate track which in 1953 would merge with the Ba'th, was Akram al-Hawrani, a Sunni lawyer and politician who founded the Arab Socialist Party in his native Hama. An intense nationalist, he volunteered to fight in Palestine and joined groups going to the aid of Rashid Ali al-Gaylani in Iraq; through these ventures he developed strategic connections with young army officers. An agrarian populist, from the late forties, he led the youth and peasants of Hama in a fight against the great feudal lords of the city. Ambitious and bold, effective at both parliamentary intrigue and peasant agitation, he was the politician Aflaq would never be. Not a man of ideas but of sentiments and action, he borrowed the program of his party almost word for word from the Ba'th and, of course, later merged it with the Ba'th (Jundi 62–64; Abu Jaber 33–34). He was regarded by many as an opportunist for his willingness to ally with all and sundry in his drive for power, but his career shows a consistent commitment to core beliefs—secular republicanism, land redistribution, and neutralism in foreign policy. It was he, too, who brought to the Ba'th's top leadership a practical orientation to mass recruitment and mobilization. Hawrani has been considered perhaps the single most powerful politician of pre-1963 Syria, but, in spite of that, he never achieved the broad personal stature among either intellectuals or masses that would have allowed him to emerge as the Ba'th's paramount leader (Devlin 1976:57; Rouleau 167). The Ba'th would, thus, retain a collective leadership.

The ideology of the Ba'th Party combined radical Arab nationalism and democratic populism. The thought of Michel Aflaq, the party philosopher, imparted an enduring direction to the party's world view. Aflaq's preoccupation was the nationalist struggle and particularly with the need to awaken national consciousness and sentiment among the Arabs. Nationalism was, in his view, the motivating force which alone would allow the Arabs to overcome the passivity, fragmentation, decadence and inferiority complex which plagued them and turn them into responsible citizens. This national feeling was, for Aflaq, properly Pan-Arab, embracing all Arabs regardless of religion or the "region" (state) of the Arab world in which they lived. "We represent Arabism," he declared, as against those (communists) who rejected it and those (the traditional politicians) who gave it lip service but were content with governing the truncated Syrian state to the neglect of the wider national interest. Aflaq insisted that all policy-making in Syria had to depart from consideration of the wider Pan-Arab interest and tried to practice what he preached by encouraging the formation of Ba'th branches in all Arab countries. The Ba'th's nationalism was also secular; Islam was considered a leading part of the Arab national heritage and Aflaq urged Christians to accept it as a part of their own Arabness. Aflaq's ideas of the political community, far from being a mere imitation of Western ideology, had roots in Islamic tradition (Babikian). But as a bond of political community Islam was, for him, superseded by Arabism. Most Ba'thists were religiously indifferent and the party opposed and was opposed by religious and sectarian leaders. As the re-birth of national consciousness took place, Aflaq believed the Arab peoples could be mobilized in the struggle to expel imperialism and Zionism and unify the Arab statelets in a single Arab national state. The drive for Pan-Arab unity was perhaps Aflaq's central aim for without it he believed the Arabs would never be able to resist imperialism or build a new society.

Although Aflaq's social thought contained only the barest of blueprints for the new Arab society he sought, it imparted a durable bias to Ba'thist social orientation. There was a strong statist and collectivist strain of romantic nationalism in his thought: the nation and service to it were exalted above "petty material" private interests and individual self-realization was thought to derive from participation in the general will of the community. All rival attachments to family, sect, locale, or class which divided the nation had to be subordinated to national loyalty. In this, Aflaq was no doubt reacting against a profoundly fragmented society, but unwittingly he contributed to a tradition unfriendly to pluralism despite the strong defense of individual freedom from political and cultural constraints which also runs through his thinking.

Aflaq's thought was also populist. The social injustice and exploitation existent in Arab society was a principle face of its decadence. No authentic national community could be created between exploiter and exploited or the masses nationally mobilized until they were given a stake in the nation; nor, without social equality, could individuals be freed from the dominance-submissive relations of a "feudal" society. A "socialist" socio-economic order was therefore needed to ensure social justice and equality and a life free of deprivation for all citizens. It was also needed to replace the selfish search for private gain as the motive force of the economy with the urge to community service. The success of the Ba'th movement depended on a populist alliance between nationalists and the "working masses" who Aflaq saw as least corrupted by vested interests and foreign influences detrimental to the nation. Aflaq was careful, however, to distinguish his nativist Arab socialism from communism, believing the latter's internationalism incompatible with his Arab mission, its restrictions on individual liberty oppressive, its abolition of small scale private property repressive of initiative and independence, and its class struggle incompatible with national unity.

Alongside Arab unity and socialism in the Ba'th trinity is "freedom." While this meant, in the first place, freedom from imperialism and traditional constrictions, Aflaq clearly also wanted to combine his moderate socialism with parliamentary democracy and political liberties. Indeed, much of the political activity of the early Ba'th focused on the struggle for democratic liberties. On the other hand, there was also in Aflaq a certain elitist disdain for the unenlightened masses who needed to be led by an intellectual vanguard—the Ba'thist leaders—along the right path.

The road to the new order is, however, never clearly specified in early Ba'th thinking. Aflaq rejected the military coup as a route to power and the class struggle as antithetical to national solidarity. He insisted that regeneration required an *inqilab*—overthrow—of the old society, but he seems to have had in mind a moral transformation rather than a violent seizure of power; his followers, however, were to take him much more literally. In practice, Aflaq advocated a peaceful struggle to democratize the oligarchic state and to impose an Arab nationalist foreign policy on the regime as the immediate road to the Ba'th's goals; otherwise, he saw his own task as raising consciousness of the need for change which subsequent generations would implement. Aflaq's thought can be considered social-democratic, a Jacobin nationalism which imparted a progressive social content to Arab nationalism for the following generations (Aflaq 1959; Binder 1959; 1964; Kerr 1963; Torrey 1969:446–454; Abu Jaber 97–138; Kannan; T. Khalidi; Suleiman 121–155).

This social content was given a more programmatic form in the "constitution" drafted by the party's 1947 founding congress. While this congress concretized a formal ideology inspired by Aflaq's thought, it also revealed a significant heterogeneity of viewpoints among the party's early leaders. Jallal al-Sayyid was an Islamic conservative, even pro-Hashemite, opposed to all but the mildest social reforms, while the young Alawi followers of Arsuzi were intensely secular and anti-Islamic. The biggest debate was over socialism: Sayyid and a group of Damascene republicans blocked inclusion of the word in the party's name (until the fifties), but Wahib al-Ghanim, leading a group influenced by Marxism, put a certain socialist stamp on the actual provisions of the constitution. The thing that held them all together was their intense Arabism. But the document they produced was remarkably socially radical for its time (Jabbur 336–338; Sayyid 33–38, 41–42; Rouleau 164–165).

The political community was, to be sure, defined in Arab national, not class terms, and only those collaborating with imperialism were considered outside the people. Western style democracy was also adopted as the most suitable political system. However, Syria's highly unequal distribution of wealth was denounced as unjust and its great class gaps had, it was held, to be bridged. Socialism was the social order best able to do this. Thus, a major role for the state was prescribed in society. It was to plan development, pursue industrialization, and control public utilities, natural resources, big industry and transport; a national bank would eliminate usury, renting of houses would be forbidden, and trade would be state-regulated in the interest of the nation and social equity. Private property and inheritance were guaranteed, but state regulation would insure private interests were pursued within the national interest and that property was not used for exploitation. The state would fix a fair wage, promulgate a labor code, and ensure work for all. Trade unions would be established to protect workers, workers would share in the management and profits of firms, and state labor tribunals would settle labor disputes. The state would provide essential social services for all, including free medical care, social security and old age support. Finally, in what was for an agrarian society undoubtedly the most radical provision of the program, the Ba'th called for a land reform which would limit landed property to a size "in proportion to the means of the proprietor to exploit . . . without exploitation of the efforts of others" (ABSP 1962:233–242).

The Ba'th's ideology would have a powerful and broad appeal to a multitude of social forces. The contention that imperialism and fragmentation were the causes of the Arab world's weakness and decadence and had to be overcome before Arab society could be regenerated held widening plausibility as the high hopes of independence were dashed and Syria came under growing external pressures: the time was ripe, as Devlin put it, for the rise of a Pan-Arab nationalist movement (1976:5, 42). The secular modernizing character of the Ba'th's Arab nationalism attracted educated youth seeking an alternative to traditionalism as well as the rising minority groups who were seeking integration into the nation. But the Ba'th's enthusiastic embrace of the dominant Pan-Arab conception of political community, putting it in the mainstream of Arab-Islamic tradition, held wide appeal to the Sunni masses as well (Devlin 1976:25). The Ba'th's social formula was an authentic reflection of the interests of the petit bourgeois salaried middle class which was becoming a leading force in Syrian politics and compatible with those of the peasantry and working classes from which some of the founders came and to whom they were addressing their appeal. In a society dominated by a landed-commercial elite with the barest interest in social change and with limited opportunities for those with modern education, the salaried middle class was bound to be attracted to an ideology calling for a large role for the state as modernizing entrepreneur and employer and for measures against large concentrations of wealth. The appeal of land reform to a land hungry peasantry and of labor law and social security to workers is obvious. But both the petite bourgeoisie and the peasantry either had or aspired to own small private property and the Ba'th's legitimation of such property reflects this, too (Rouleau 162; Ben-Tzur 1965). The Ba'th's moderate "socialism" was by no means a mere foreign import incompatible with local traditions. On the contrary, it had some sanction in historic Islam: in the recognition of private property rights, but as a trust from the community and limited by the good of the whole, in Islam's egalitarian hostility to great wealth and aristocracy, and in its stress on the role of the state in ensuring the welfare of the *umma* (Sayyid 47). In Seale's judgment, Ba'thism provided Syria with a dynamic homegrown ideology at a time when it was buffeted by foreign imports such as communism and liberalism. "Its achievement was to marry radical ideas of social justice and democratic political procedures to the fifty year old dream of Arab unity which . . . is perhaps the only political idea to which the Syrian public will always remain faithful" (157–158). In linking national resurgence to radical social change, Ba'thism gave the latter the legitimation of national sentiment, thereby depriving the conservative right of this customary weapon.

But traditional Ba'th ideology also had its vulnerabilities. The mix of nationalism, populism and democracy which gave it such a broad appeal also attracted an ideologically disparate following and raised difficult issues regarding priorities and means of implementation which were never satisfactorily resolved. For Aflaq and many of the older Ba'thists, Arab nationalism was the overriding priority (Jabbur 421–422; Hanna 256) and commitments to democracy and especially "socialism" were distinctly secondary; but even among those who put Pan-Arabism first, there were divisions as to whether the party should seek union with any Arab state regardless of its internal regime or foreign alignments (e.g. Hashemite pro–British Iraq) or only with nationalist republics, and then on what terms (e.g. unitary or federal). Despite its preoccupation with union, the party, as Abu Jaber (42) points out, had no real design or plan for its implementation and, as such, was rushed into accepting Nasir's demands in 1958. For some early Ba'thists, such as Jallal al-Sayyid (46), socialism meant little more than a vague "social justice;" on the other hand, the incorporation of youth of worker and peasant origin and the merger with Hawrani's Arab Socialist Party in the fifties induced a gradual radicalization of party orientation and Aflaq himself, in Jabbur's words, moved from fearing that social struggle would split the nation to the belief that winning the masses to the nation required such struggle. This change alienated the party's conservative wing, much of which drifted away (Jabbur: 359–363, 417–418). There were also difficult issues concerning the means to the party's social goals which the ideology did not adequately address. The road to power was a major dilemma: the Ba'th was committed to democracy but even the more liberal founders of the party, having had little success at electoral politics, disdainful of its "corruption," and having little confidence in the political consciousness of the illiterate masses, were ambivilant about the utility of elections for achieving Ba'thism. For many Ba'thists who took "socialism" more seriously, acceptance of such a route to power in a society where elections inevitably reproduced the status quo, seemed to doom the party to interminable impotence except perhaps in controversial alliances with other parties which would compromise its program. Thus the party wavered between playing the electoral game to which the older Ba'thists were more committed and intrigue with sympathetic factions in the army, attractive to younger members more concerned with substantial change than procedural democracy (Devlin 1976:29–32). Even if the party managed to take power in elections, preservation of a "liberal-democratic" regime appeared incompatible with the radical social transformation implicit in the party program (Allush 163, 167–169). These deficiencies can all be considered symptoms of the "idealistic" character of Ba'th thought, its preoccupation with ideal goals to the neglect of the practical means for reaching them.

Finally, significant sectors of society remained impervious to Ba'th ideology. It obviously had no appeal to the "feudal-bourgeois" elite, but its etatism, suspicion of private enterprise, and secularism were also of very limited appeal to the pious commercial and artisan communities of the traditional urban quarters for whom Islamic fundamentalism became the preferred ideology of protest. The resistance of the "traditional" urban middle and lower strata to Ba'thism was to be its main weakness. In a deeper sense, one can indeed question whether Syria's historical tradition and the political culture it shaped were compatible with a socialist ideology: the particularism, individualism, and commercial spirit generated by the urban commercial and tribal milieu which long dominated Syria certainly had deeper cultural roots than the agrarian populism and middle class reformism on which the Ba'th rose to power.

Recruitment of a Party Cadre: The Ba'th Party first took form in the mid-forties as groups of small loosely linked *halaqat* ("circles") of teachers and their student disciples. Aflaq and Bitar first began activity in Damascus at the *tajhiz* preparatory school, the main center of public education in the city and a political hub (Khoury 529), recruiting from their students and leading them in leafletting and demonstrating against the French and later the Quwatli government (Seale 151; ABSP 1963, v. 1). In various other parts of Syria a similar process took place, e.g. around Wahib al-Ghanim in Latakia, Sami al-Jundi in Salamiya, Jallal al-Sayyid in Deir ez-Zor, Jamal al-Atasi, Hafiz al-Jamali and Sami al-Durubi in Homs, Abd al-Halim Qaddur in the Kalamoun mountains, and on his own separate track, Akram al-Hawrani in Hama. As the students themselves became teachers or professionals, they also formed *halaqat* in provincial towns and villages.

In this early period, Aflaq's Ba'thists viewed themselves not as a party after power but as a movement seeking to arouse the public, yet remain apart from the corruption and opportunism of the political arena. They would shape a new generation "pure" and Arab, infused with activism and national commitment, and freed of traditional bonds which would, in time, lead the country. Thus, the party began to forge the cadre of activists needed to take its message to the masses.

The Ba'th was able as no other movement to harness the intense political energies of students in the formation of this cadre. The secondary schools and college campuses became breeding grounds of Ba'thism, indeed, the catapults from which the whole movement was launched for through students the Ba'thi message could be carried to their families, hence into the very base of society, and, as they moved into careers, into its strategic heights (Sayyid 31–32). In 1949, in recognition of the party's special strength among students, Aflaq was made Minister of Education in a national unity government and as early as 1951 the Ba'th could mobilize large student demonstrations in Damascus, Homs, Hama, Dera, and Deir ez-Zor (Seale 77, 103); somewhat later and to a lesser extent it developed a student following in Aleppo, too (Van Dusen 1972:134). From at least the mid-fifties, the Ba'th largely controlled the student unions. Student recruitment often began as an expression of rebellion against the patriarchal family and the social constrictions of tradition, for the Ba'thi teachers who recruited students treated them as if their opinions counted and opened their houses to them; the outcome, as Seale (148, 151) argues, was the radicalization of a whole generation.

In addition to its special appeal to youthful rebellion, the Ba'th recruited its core cadre, not uniformly, but—even among students—disproportionately from distinctive sectors of society: from plebeian elements lacking a stake in the dominant order and from those who were alienated from or marginal to the traditional networks of kin and clientage on which the city-based establishment was raised. Uprooted refugees, seeking both change and integration, and, as victims of imperialism, intensely nationalistic, were attracted to the Ba'th: notably Alawites from Iskanderun and Palestinians. Rural students who left their villages to get secondary education in the city were particularly drawn to the Ba'th. This was in part because many Ba'th leaders were teachers in schools they attended: Aflaq, for example, came from a family with traditional ties to the south and long taught in schools where Hauran and Druze youth came for education and Arsuzi indoctrinated many Alawi students in Ba'thism (Safadi 68–69, Van Dusen 1975:129–130). But such rural youth, uprooted from family and village, yet unintegrated into urban society, were generally more susceptible to recruitment than urban ones and more likely to develop strong personal bonds to their party cell (Safadi 68, 202–203; Sayyid 6, 29; al-Jundi 38–39; Van Dusen 1975:140–141). So were students of the typically rural minority sects, alone and cut off from their own communities in the Sunni dominated cities, who found in the party a refuge and a crucible of the new Arab national identities which, as they were mobilized out of their communal environment, they began to acquire. Although some minority recruits were of relatively high social status—Mansur al-Atrash was a son of the paramount Druze leader—most were either youth of the minor notability or mainstream peasant families who were revolting against the traditional zu'ama of their own communities (Safadi 70). Increasingly, Ba'th recruitment spread downward to village youth in the provinces and it appears to have been strongest in areas where small peasant ownership persisted since only such peasants had the means to send their children for schooling and sufficient independence of the landlords's grip to make education and politicization possible. Thus, it was areas such as the Hauran or the independent villages between Damascus and Homs like Nebek and Yabroud and, of course, Suwayda and Latakia which became strongholds of Ba'thist recruitment.

Occasionally, scions of large aristocratic Sunni families could be found in the Ba'th, but even those—such as Nur ad-Din al-Atasi—tended to be either "black sheep" or from poorer branches of these families (Sayyid 8). There were, of course, exceptions to the rule of recruitment from plebeian and "marginal elements." Jallal al-Sayyid, the early Ba'th leader from Deir ez-Zor and its first parliamentary deputy, was from a bedouin shaikhly family and other Deir ez-Zor Ba'thists were middle landowners and professionals; still, they were on the peripheries of the establishment and, according to Sayyid (24–25), such provincial middle class families were long considered ineligible for cooptation into ruling ranks.

The parallel development of Akram al-Hawrani's Arab Socialist Party (ASP) in Hama followed a somewhat different pattern. On the face of it, Hama, a citadel of feudalism, would appear immune to a radical party: it was dominated as no other city by four great feudal families who owned scores of villages in the surrounding countryside. It was also the most powerful center of Islamic belief and tradition, a meeting ground between a mercantile community with a strong Islamic missionary tradition and the bedouin, its population notoriously hostile to all ideas or persons unfamiliar. It was perhaps the very weight of traditional forces, leaving less social space to the educated middle class than elsewhere, which stimulated an especially intense anti-traditional revolt. Radical forces penetrated the city through the revolt of its own educated youth—from middle class families such as the Hawranis, Sarrajes, Kallases and Alwanis—against the dominant "aristocratic" families. First, the alignment of the great notables with the French sparked a pro-Nationalist challenge to them in the thirties by second rank landowning families and, as these old nationalists themselves lost their militancy, they were then challenged by the rising petite bourgeoisie under Uthman al-Hawrani. Akram al-Hawrani, after a brief flirtation with the SSNP, inherited and developed the leadership of the lower middle class youth of the city and, backed by this following, took the challenge to Hama's feudal families into the surrounding villages of the central plains, capturing the imagination of rural youth from Homs to Aleppo. They flocked to his party, giving it roots in the villages, too. Even before the merger of the ASP and the Ba'th, the village youth of the two parties were developing close ties which would give impetus to their union (Jundi 62–64; Hanna 258–260; Petran 88; Sayyid 97–98; Van Dusen 1972:131).

By contrast to its success in the schools and villages, where the traditional establishment remained strong, its primordial or clientage links intact, the Ba'th found its recruitment efforts largely blocked. The city of Damascus, the very center of political life, remained, for a long time, largely resistant to Ba'th recruitment. Although long a focus of Arab nationalism and political fervor (Fedden 21), the obstinate traditionalism of the city, the continuing vitality of Islamic values and practices, the dense tissue of personal and commercial ties reaching down from the great families into the back alleys of the *suq*—all made the traditional quarters immune to Ba'thi penetration and, to the extent they were susceptible at all to political protest, this took the form of Islamic fundamentalism. The leadership of the Ba'th by a Christian made it immediately suspect to the ulama' and pious notability who led public opinion in the old quarters (Aflaq himself proposed resigning from his position for this reason), and the ulama' launched periodic protests against the fledgling Ba'th presence, concentrated in the schools, in both Damascus and Aleppo (Sayyid 84–85; Jundi 38–39; Ziadeh 148). The new modern quarters were dominated by the wealthiest of the bourgeois or "feudal" families whose sons joined the traditional parties. According to al-Jundi (38), the Ba'th, believing Damascus would never be a Ba'thist city, neglected recruitment there, concentrating instead on the rural areas where traditional power was weaker and to which rural student partisans had access; the disproportionate numbers of rural and minority elements so recruited then further diminished the attraction of the Ba'th in urban Sunni circles (Safadi 69). Those Damascenes who joined the party in its early days tended to be conservatives who dropped out early (Sayyid 34–39). Traditional Aleppo seemed even less vulnerable to the appeal of the Ba'th for in the late fifties when the levers of governmental and military power and the streets of Damascus had fallen into the hands of the nationalist-left, Aleppo, where the government-dependent new middle class had a far lesser presence, was still under the control of Sha'b Party notables who made the city the last bastion of the pro-Western right.

Even when the Ba'th established a foothold in traditional areas, it tended, at least at first, to take on the color of the local social milieu—and yet, in the longer run, to alter it. The evolution of the party branch founded by Jallal al-Sayyid in Deir ez-Zor, a city where the tribal ethos remained powerful, illustrates the special character of party development in this type of setting. The party first got its start there because of its sponsorship by Sayyid who, a middle landowner and tribal notable with good personal links to the tribal elites, gave Ba'thism a special Arab nationalist—as opposed to "socialist"— color. Yet, as education grew in the city, the new generation of Ba'thist recruits, influenced by Marxist ideas, began to reject traditional bonds and identities. Sayyid describes how party identity and radical ideas appeared to replace tribal affiliation and mores to the extent that these youth rejected the "Arab values" of loyalty, generosity, bravery and revenge. Yet, the tribal ethos remained below the surface and in 1955 rivalries with local SSNP youth deteriorated into killings which threatened to plunge the city into a blood feud between the families of the opposing party youth. When Sayyid tried to expel the Ba'thi youth involved in the conflict from the party, they accused him of being a feudalist and when he failed to get the support he wanted from Aflaq, Sayyid quit the party; others of his social status followed him while lower status radical elements "rushed in to fill the gap." Symptomatic of their attitudes, was their rejection of the membership application of a "nationalist" tribal shaikh solely because of his social status (Sayyid 128–146). In most tribal areas, however, youth, still largely untouched by education, remained loyal to tribal leadership and beyond the reach of the Ba'th.

In summary, as the Ba'th cadre developed beyond the immediate circles of its urban founders, it took on a distinctive social color. In essence, to mount its challenge to the notability, the Ba'th recruited from further down in the stratification system than the former's clientage networks reached.

The Ba'th therefore became a party of youth, predominately from rural, provincial, petit bourgeois, minority, and peasant backgrounds. These elements formed the hard core of the party to which later comers would adhere and from which, after the 1963 power seizure, Syria's political elite would be drawn.

Although Ba'th activists originated on the peripheries of the power structure, they did not long remain on the outside. As cohorts of Ba'thi students went into the professions, they began to move into strategic positions at the middle levels of the socio-political structure. The Ba'th, as the only major party which was both Arab nationalist and progressive, was the natural political home for young military officers (Perlmutter 1969:835). Both Hawrani and the Ba'th leaders had personal ties to young officers from the late forties. Some of these officers who attained high rank and strategic position, such as Adnan al-Malki and Abd al-Hamid Sarraj, were instrumental in swinging the military behind the nationalist-left and creating the political conditions in which the Ba'th could challenge the notability without fear of repression. But it was the next generation of officers who would actually join the party. Some were Hama youth who Hawrani deliberately encouraged to follow a military careers as a way of building a base in the army: men such as Mustafa Hamdun and Abd al-Ghani Qannut. Others, yet a later cohort, the men who would lead the Ba'th to power in 1963, were Haurani, Druze, Isma'ili and Alawite students, followers of Aflaq, Arsuzi, al-Ghanim and other Ba'thist elders who followed a military career partly from communal tradition and as a road to social mobility, partly for political reasons (Seale 48; Van Dusen 1975:130–134; Sayyid 43). In the 1954 rebellion against the Shishakli dictatorship, Hamdun led junior Ba'thi officers such as Muhammed Umran and Amin al-Hafiz on behalf of the party (Salamah 9); according to al-Jundi (73), Ba'th officers nearly carried out a coup in 1956 (the Qatana attempt) to bring the party to power but were discouraged by the party elders. The establishment of this hold over the loyalties of perhaps the major segment of the rising officer corps would be decisive for the Ba'th's political fortunes. Other Ba'thist students went into civilian professions such as law, medicine, academia, and journalism. Others yet went into the bureaucracy or into public school teaching, the other career relatively accessible to poorer strata and of strategic importance for the political socialization of following generations; teachers, in fact, were the largest professional sector in the Ba'th (Jabbur 119). Generally speaking, the Ba'th became the main party of the petit bourgeois intelligentsia in the fifties (Safadi 61). As Seale (179) put it, being the strongest party among the students—tomorrow's intelligentsia— and the military, the future belonged to the Ba'th.

Limited Mass Mobilization: The pre-1963 Ba'th never became a full fledged mass party but neither did it remain exclusively a party of the middle class intelligentsia. Indeed, especially under Hawrani, it took advantage of peasant ferment to establish nuclei of followers in many villages and to challenge the landed elite in the *rief.*

The Ba'th's early linkage to the peasantry typically ran from Ba'thi teachers, through their rural students, to the village. Sami al-Jundi's (36–39, 44–45) account of this linkage in central Syria is archetypical. Ba'thi students, he writes, returning to their villages during summer vacation, attempted to proselytize the peasants: "We started to shake all their customs . . . faced them with their reality." Initially they rejected the message, considering Ba'thi youth deviants from traditional codes or because of prior obligations of clientage. But, he writes, through persistence the Ba'th youth demolished the old values and brought the peasants to envision an end to a society of ignorance and persecution. The Ba'th movement fed on the injustices inflicted by landlords on peasants and on resentment against the backwardness of the village, in short, exploiting the concentration of the severest disabilities of the old regime in the countryside. For example, in Latakia, Wahib al-Ghanim organized a campaign against the Tobacco Regie which exploited peasants there, resulting in its nationalization; he and other party doctors also gave free medical aid to villagers. In the Hauran and Jabal Druze, the party campaigned for the development of these neglected regions. In Homs peasant youth tried to use grievances against "feudalism" to mobilize their villages against landlords in parliamentary elections. At the same time, from Damascus, the party began to publicly voice peasant grievances: a 1950 party council drew up a moderate but innovative program of demands including an agrarian relations law, distribution of state land, cooperatives, and an agrarian bank. As the party began to acquire supporters inside the bureaucracy, it took to representing peasant grievances to officialdom (Jabbur 357–359; Safadi 71; Chamy).

Meanwhile in Hama, Akram al-Hawrani's Arab Socialist Party linked up with peasants in a different way, largely by bringing middle class leadership to the village from the outside and mobilizing peasants in overt anti-landlord struggle. His support for peasants against landlords helped win him a seat in parliament as early as 1943 where he was a major populist opposition figure; he protested the failure to give rights to agricultural workers in the 1946 labor code, demanded the distribution of state-owned land in "feudalist" hands to peasants, called for the reclamation of the Ghab to their benefit, and pushed for free education for their children. In 1949 he established an office in Damascus to lobby for peasant interests. Next, his Arab Socialist Party launched a "land to the peasant" movement in northern Syria, an initiative on a much more significant and unprecedented scale. It was centered on Hama, the heartland of the great landed estates where peasant poverty and oppression were strongest, but where peasants, dependent for their very survival on the feudalists, had to be convinced they could be successfully challenged. He and other progressive lawyers began by defending peasants in the courts. Soon peasant unrest swept the plains: peasants refused to render feudal dues and services, effectively abolishing these practices in most areas, and fought landlords over control of the Ghab. Hawrani encouraged peasant violence against landlords which kept them from their estates and caused them to appeal to the central government for help. This rural unrest made control of the gendarmerie, guardian of rural "order," into a major contest between the Interior Ministry headed by the great landed magnate Rashad Barmada and the army, more sympathetic to peasant grievances, and contributed to Shishakli's coup against the notable government. Once the notable politicians were deposed by Shishakli, Hawrani's peasant mobilization widened from local confrontations with landlord families to a large scale peasant protest movement demanding reform in rural Syria. In 1951 a three-day rally in Aleppo was attended by perhaps 20,000 peasants from across Syria, who paraded through the streets carrying banners demanding land reform, the first event of its kind in the Arab world (Seale 120). This impelled the issuance of Decree no. 96 of 1952 which aimed to protect public land from notable encroachment, but ended up turning it over to them. When Shishakli turned against the movement, it receded until his overthrow in 1954. But as the 1954 elections approached, Hawrani, now united with the Ba'th, reactivated the movement, setting up peasant unions, seeking out cases where landlords had abused their peasants for legal action, and trucking supporters into villages to challenge the landlord's men, sometimes in pitched battles. Again landlords sometimes found it dangerous to enter their own villages—symptomatic of the Ba'th's growing ability to challenge them at the base of society. This show of force helped overcome the reluctance of peasants to risk defying landlord power. Hawrani and his partisans were swept into parliament with peasant votes, upsetting the representatives of "all that was once great and honored" in Hama (Seale 183). These events suggested the precariousness of the rural order in the absence of coercive police support and the potential threat to it from a democratic mobilization of the peasantry. Shortly thereafter, the Ba'th proposed an agrarian relations law in parliament which would have increased the crop share of tenants, prevented their expulsion, and extended labor law and unionization to agricultural workers (Petran 88–89, 101; Van Dusen 1975:131; Daoud-Agha 304–305; al-Jundi 63–64; Seale 105, 120, 177, 183; Warriner 1962:109; Torrey 1964:306).

According to Hanna (270), the anti-feudal propaganda of the Ba'th and the ASP found ready receptivity among the peasants; they no longer had to search for members but found thousands of peasants ready to enter their ranks. Moreover, as they were incorporated, however tenuously, the peasants' spontaneous class feeling against the feudalists infected the parties themselves. Warriner (1962:108–109) judged that the Ba'th Party was "canalizing" a peasant movement which was the natural outcome of conditions in central Syria; party processions, featuring tribal drums, dancing and singing, seemed more an expression of indigenous revolt from below than of urban ideologies. Thus, the Ba'th successfully extended peasant mobilization to the share-croppers who made up the majority of the peasantry.

Significantly, however, even after the merger with the ASP, the Ba'th Party did not incorporate this peasant base into a nation-wide organization capable of the sustained mobilization which might have brought it to power from below. As Safadi (74) put it, peasant mobilization took the form of extreme emotional rebellion rooted in land hunger, but the Ba'th failed to ideologically indoctrinate and organize this base. It also allowed the struggle to remain at the "political level," i.e. centered on electoral and protest politics. The channeling of the peasant movement into electoral politics led to the successful election of some pro-reform candidates but they lacked the power to push reforms through parliament; as such, the actual effect of the enterprise may have been to temporarily take the steam out of peasant protest, diverting it into a contest in which the rules and resources were stacked against it.

A second weakness in the Ba'th's peasant mobilization was its unevenness. While it was strong among small holders under pressure and among the sharecroppers of north and central Syria, where Arabism had no appeal or in areas where peasants were unusually prosperous or tribal, it found limited receptivity. Thus, the Kurdish peasants on the northern fringes of Syria, not identifying with Arabism, were organized by the Communist Party. In the little towns and villages of the Damascus Ghouta, conservative influence kept the Ba'th weak. Here a graduated property structure mixing large, medium, and small landownership seemed to keep the patronage networks of the notability intact: landlord power was less repressive and based more on clientelism and anti-feudal sentiment was correspondingly limited. Landowners were more likely to invest in their lands to the benefit of sharecroppers, peasants had better opportunities for direct marketing of cash crops, and new opportunities for work in the city raised living standards. For all these reasons, peasants were more hardworking, prosperous, and receptive to conservative ideology than elsewhere (Warriner 1962:95; Wirth 96–137, 166–202). In much of the Ghouta, conservative religious shaikhs had a strong hold on opinion and when radical sentiment appeared here it responded to a Sunni Muslim leader, Nasir. The case of Douma illustrates many of these factors. Considered one of the richest agricultural areas in Syria, Douma was not only prosperous, but was divided between five large Damascene proprietors owning about one-fourth of the land and a large peasant lineage of about 100 households both of which let out a lot of land to poorer peasants through sharecropping contracts (Tower). Significantly, the dominant ideology was Islamic conservatism and it was only with the opening of factories there that Ba'thist appeals began to penetrate, but through workers, not peasants.

On the other hand, in certain tribal and semi-tribal areas, the Ba'th also found itself frozen out. The impoverished villages on the eastern fringe of the Ghouta, like Dumayr, were under the shadow of the great bedouin Shaikh Nuri al-Sha'alan and his armed retainers and hence inaccessible to it. In many areas of eastern Syria where shaikhs continued to play real leadership roles in the community, observe reciprocal obligations with followers, and where the great caste gaps of the latifundia were absent, tribal solidarity and patriarchal authority remained intact. This, combined with its relative educational and infrastructural backwardness, made the area relatively unfertile ground for oppositionist movements and only after the Ba'th power seizure would tribesmen-peasants, with encouragement from above, challenge local power structures.

The Ba'th Party made some efforts to penetrate the urban masses through support for the emerging industrial working class. In 1951 the Ba'th formed a specialized labor bureau to help workers fight for the implementation of the labor code and to develop a following in the trade unions. It supported discharged workers in Aleppo and strikers in Damascus. The bureau in Damascus reputedly organized the first large scale strike in the city (Safadi 75; Jabbur 352–353). In Douma, pro-Ba'thi workers began to compete with conservative shaikhs for the loyalty of the peasants, polarizing the town. In 1956 protests, the Ba'th forced the government to annul a decree allowing business to withhold a portion of a worker's wages for disciplinary purposes and in the same year mobilized 15,000 workers protesting government efforts to break its power in the unions. According to Khalil (127–128), almost half the unions were "Ba'thist" by this time, although only in the sense that Ba'this led them (there being no organizational link); Petran reports better organized Communists still won a majority of seats (7 of 12) in the peak national labor confederation. In the early 1950s unions were controlled by the right; by the end of the decade Ba'thists and Communists shared their leadership and together could bring out thousands of workers in strikes or demonstrations in Damascus, Homs and Latakia (Petran 120; Chamy 8; Allush 122). Communist and Islamic influence competed with the Ba'th for worker loyalties and the working class remained too small to provide a mass base comparable to the peasantry; but, concentrated and organized, pro-Ba'th workers nevertheless provided a crucial second support base for the party.

Leadership and Organization: While the Ba'th had enough direction and cohesion to become a powerful actor in the Syrian political arena of the late fifties, ultimately, its leadership and organizational capacity could not keep up with its expansion in support. As a result, the Ba'th failed to develop into the mass ideological party which might have allowed it to come to power from below.

The Ba'th suffered from grave deficiencies in political leadership, having neither a charismatic leader, a long range strategist, or an effective organizational boss. Decisions were concentrated in the hands of the "three professors," Aflaq, Bitar, and Hawrani, but they did not constitute a cohesive team able to lay down an effective political strategy. In Aflaq, the party had a pure intellectual, appropriate to inspiring the founding of an ideological movement but incapable of leading a party organization to power. A romantic humanist, he lacked objective analytical skills, "wanting not analysis of goals and strategy but absolute belief, blind confidence in the inevitability of triumph since the Ba'th seed was in every Arab." Convinced he alone had the uncorrupted truth and knew the essence of the Arab nation, he refused to have his views challenged in the party (Devlin 1976:13, 24, 58; al-Jundi 33–35, 69). But, refusing to dirty his hands in the political arena, he did not provide practical leadership; he and those like him, according to Safadi (80–86, 115) operated like sufis, imparting wisdom to followers and pervading the party with an evangelical atmosphere and a tradition of talk about radical change but neglecting the work of organization and mobilization needed to bring it about. Aflaq was also too elitist and aloof from mass political work to lead a popular struggle; Safadi (74–75) claims he viewed the masses as too ignorant to qualify for membership and regarded the work of the party's peasant and worker bureaus with suspicion. In Hawrani, the party had a forceful and practical politician but one too engrossed in the immediate struggle for power in the army or parliament to concern himself with long range strategy or organization and too pragmatic and unconcerned with principle to help forge a disciplined ideological party. Deeply divided by personal rivalries and temperament, Aflaq and Hawrani could not work together as a team, retarding the full amalgamation of their two original organizations. Aflaq was convinced that Hawrani's political maneuvering would corrupt the party's principles and that he was flooding its ranks with opportunists hungry for power, but he could do nothing practical to stop it (Safadi 103–107, 214). Bitar had constantly to mediate between the two rivals. In short, while the two men, with very different strengths and weaknesses, could have complimented each other had they worked together, more often than not they worked at odds, depriving the party of an effective collective leadership and leaving a certain vacuum at the top. As a result, criticism of the leadership by the rank and file steadily built up over the years, undermining their authority (Safadi 103–107, 124–125, 188, 119–200).

The weakness of leadership was paralleled by certain doctrinal and organizational liabilities which obstructed the Ba'th's institutional development. Ba'th ideological doctrine was too lacking in priorities as between its trinity of goals, unity, freedom and socialism, and in a coherent strategy for attaining them to provide the basis for a consensus within which decision-making could take place without fracturing the party. As a result, decisions were often the initiatives of individual leaders taken without consensus, or when there was a majority view, a minority would split off in disagreement. Moreover, in the absence of a practical strategy for attaining goals, the party tended, throughout the fifties, to react to or get carried away by events more than to lead them (Jundi 40, 68–69; Safadi 103–104, 187–188). Nor did party ideology become an effective weapon in forging a disciplined party base. Its broad nationalist-populist appeal drew a ideologically heterogeneous following, and because leaders themselves were divided in their interpretations of Ba'thism, recruits could not be socialized into a ideological consensus; indeed, the rapid increase in membership in the later fifties was accompanied by little ideological indoctrination (Devlin 1976:15; Jundi 68–69). Safadi (83–93) says there was no systematic or uniform political education of recruits and collections of articles by Aflaq or Bitar had to serve for educational materials. Doctrine also failed to lay down proper standards of work, personal conduct, and duty needed for an ideologically disciplined movement. Jundi reports that, far from being the disciplined selfless militants dedicated to a vision of change which Aflaq wanted to forge, "talkativeness" was a basic feature of the Ba'thist and that early on, the party became a vehicle of office seeking for its partisans (Jundi 69, 83–84; Safadi 97, 118). This is not to say the Ba'th had no ideological life. For many members, ideological commitments counted for more than just sloganeering. Doctrine did slowly develop as experience made deficiencies apparent and under criticism from the bases; indeed the constant rounds of criticism and self-criticism through which the party went reflected an ideological vitality (Jundi 69; Safadi 93). It was this which made the Ba'th party the crucible of a political counterelite which, despite its divisions, demonstrated a remarkably tenacious commitment to what may be called a Ba'thi worldview. But this doctrinal development came too little, too late to serve the transformation of the pre-1963 Ba'th into an ideologically disciplined party.

Organizational weaknesses mirrored leadership and ideological ones. The party's initial character as loosely connected *halaqat* of local leaders and their personal followers could not be decisively overcome (Jundi 50–55). To be sure, as the party grew, it was structured into a pyramid of cells and branches culminating in a national congress and an elected executive committee (Devlin 1976:16–18). But although party structure was developed and complex on paper, in practice it tended to lapse into inactivity or shapelessness. There was a lack of clear structural relations between the branches, of effective central institutions for finance, personnel, and education, of methods of discipline and inspection, and of records of dues or membership—indeed members drifted in and out of the party. The "individualistic spirit and personal endeavors" or negligence and inactivity often prevailed instead of systematic team work (Jundi 39, 68, 73; Safadi 190–191).

As a result, the Ba'th failed to forge a truly cohesive movement. The Aflaq and Hawrani wings of the party remained in some ways two parties under one name. Local leaders often went their own way and the fortunes of the party varied regionally according to the capacity and local connections of individual leaders. Strong reciprocal links between leadership and base were lacking. The formal rules of internal democracy were too often ignored by top leaders who resisted systematic party consultations in which they might be held accountable to the party bases. Leaders took decisions alone: Aflaq, regarding the party as his personal property, tried to exercise what his critics called an "eternal tutelage" over it at the expense of its institutions. Hawrani and other senior partisans who got political office after 1954 became pre-occupied with the struggle in government, going their own way to the neglect of the party organization; party deputies in parliament often ignored party discipline. The rank and file alternated between passivity and, when given the chance, vociferous criticism of or intrigue against the leaders. Conflict between leadership and base grew; Bitar observed a "fearful" resistance in the bases to party authority. The bases, as early as the 1954 second party congress, criticized the failure of the leaders to adhere to the internal rules, denied any automatic right of the founders to monopolize leadership positions, insisted Aflaq's writings were not necessarily definitive ideological texts binding on the party, and demanded an end to the "individualistic spirit" and personal initiatives of the leaders. One of the major costs of the failure to deal effectively with these organizational pathologies was splinterism: again and again alienated elements of the party split off, experienced members thereby being lost or turned into enemies

(Allush 76–78; Devlin 1976:20, 67–68, 72–73; Jundi 39, 49–50, 53, 64–65, 67–68, 70–73; Sayyid 105–106, 121–122, 127–128; Seale 158–159; Safadi 86, 190–191).

Leadership and organizational weaknesses also retarded the party's mass mobilizational potential. Because of the disinterest of the leadership and the lack of sufficient organizational impetus, the party failed to incorporate its mass support into sustained political activism and, as such, much of it remained passive or only sporadically active (Jundi 68; Safadi 70; Allush 39, 95, 200). The leaders deliberately restricted formal membership, preferring to keep the mass of party sympathizers, to whom they could not be held accountable, on the margins of the organization; the ratio of members to sympathizers was on the order of one to ten (Khalil 107). Significantly, most of the members were intellectuals, most of the sympathizers, workers and peasants (Chamy). This was one reason the Communists appeared to outstrip the Ba'th in mobilizational capacity in the late fifties (Jabbur 354–355). Moreover, the party never fully developed a propaganda capability able to penetrate mass society. For a long time it took the exclusive form of the printed word or intellectual speeches beyond the grasp of the illiterate masses—by contrast to Nasir's use of simple language and radio to reach them (Jabbur:186–191). And, perhaps because the founding leadership was essentially interested in reform, that is, in forcing a closed political system open to the middle class, not in revolution, its methods—electoral politics, demonstrations, student union politics, leafletting, speeches in defense of political freedoms—were of limited relevance to the mobilization of the masses, especially the peasants, and incapable of forcing radical change (Allush 162–172, 211–215).

As the party grew, outstripping the scope of personal bonds between leaders and followers, pressures from more ideologically-minded activists in closer contact with the masses grew for organizational reform, more systematic mass work, and regular congresses to forge a consensus on party strategy. The party congresses of 1957, 1959, 1960 and 1962 called for implementation of the internal rules, for mass political organization in place of coalitions with old regime politicians, for the institutionalization of democratic-centralism and collective leadership to protect the party from the "gap between the responsibilities and the competence of the leaders," and for ending the "predominance of personal over party opinion" (ABSP 1963b; ABSP 1972a:6–48; ABSP 1972c; Salamah 7–15; Jundi 57–76). Gradually the development of internal rules, authority of office, elections, and consultative processes, shaped the early personalistic tissue into a modern organization. The drive to recruit through ideological commitment rather than clientelism marked an advance in "political technology" and produced a core of Ba'thi militants with remarkably strong attachment to the party, sufficient in many cases to override traditional loyalties (Jundi 36–37, 73; Sayyid 131). It may be that the very absence of strong personal leadership forced the party to develop ideology and organization to a higher level than other Syrian parties, giving it a greater durability than its rivals. But in the persistence of traditional practices and personal loyalties and factions, the Ba'th nevertheless remained a hybrid entity—in Safadi's (89) phrase, "midway between a tribe and a modern party."

The basic weaknesses and contradictions of the pre-1963 Ba'th party can ultimately be traced to the ambivalence of its early leaders whose ideology called for the transformation of society but who, being middle class reformists, lacked the will or ability to forge a revolutionary movement capable of putting ideology into practice. The Ba'th therefore lacked, despite the urgings of its militant rank and file, a coherent strategy and apparatus of mass mobilization which could bring it to power through mass votes or revolution. As a result, the traditional Ba'th leaders would be driven into a dependence on Nasir which would make them fatally vulnerable once they lost his favor. When a more radical second generation leadership which did want to make a revolution began to take over the party, traditions of revolutionary struggle and mass organization were only present in rudimentary form and they were forced to seize power by military coup and lead a mobilization from above. But a revolution in the fullest meaning of the word probably cannot be made this way: the leadership lacks the experience in leading men on the ground, and the party cadre, not having been forged through long periods of personal risk capable of separating out opportunists and waverers, lacks the necessary fighting qualities to impose the revolution in village and quarter.

The Struggle for Power: The Rise of the Ba'th and the Destabilization of the Old Order

The post-independence Syrian state rested on the most rudimentary liberal institutions and a fragile legitimacy. But because politics was at first (1946–1949) limited to a tiny elite arena, the new state appeared manageable and the governing elite free to engross itself in factional rivalries and patronage concerns. In the mid-forties, the Ba'th Party was itself a tiny minority of a few hundred on the fringes of political power, agitating in favor of greater militancy against the French, then against the corruption and repression of political opposition by the Quwatli government, and in favor of preparation for the coming showdown in Palestine. It was almost exclusively concerned with nationalist issues and the defense of political liberties against the regime, the preoccupations which swept the emerging new middle class at this time. Although the Ba'th could be little more than a gadfly, it was enough of an irritant to invite the periodic arrest of its leaders, suppression of its newspaper and falsification of elections to its disadvantage; this repression brought it to public attention and won it sympathy. The critiques of the old regime by the Ba'th and Hawrani's Arab Socialist Party were major factors in its de-legitimation. As the traditional nationalist movement, the National Bloc, lost touch with its base and the dependency of the middle class on the old elite declined, the support of the Ba'th and ASP grew (Devlin 1976:12; Jundi 40–51; Seale 151; ABSP 1963; ABSP 1972c; Safadi 56, 60, 103).

The Palestine disaster, shattering traditional legitimacy, triggering a series of reform coups in 1949, and, precipitating a wave of political mobilization, marked the real entrance of the middle class into the political arena. This set off a seesaw battle with the old elite: even as the power and legitimacy of the old regime was in rapid decline, its wealth, and hence its base of patronage and dependency, remained largely intact and the opposition lacked the power to replace it. Radical middle class political parties penetrated the army and began to adopt the modern ideology and organization needed to mobilize the widened numbers of dissidents which the Palestine debacle made available. But these parties, recent outgrowths of personalistic followings, were often fragmented and though they shared a nationalist reformism and the desire to put an end to *iqtaʿiya*—"feudalism"—they were split on what sort of order should replace it: Islamic fundamentalists, communists and secular nationalists battled each other as much as the ruling elite. As long as the mass of "voters" remained clients or passive dependents of the landed upper class, the parties lacked the mass support to force open the parliamentary-electoral system. Thus, despite its formally liberal structures, the regime failed to absorb middle class political activism into institutionalized participation and it took largely "praetorian" forms—street demonstrations, strikes, and a tug of war between the notability and factions of the army expressed in a series of coups and several years of reformist military dictatorship. The coups marked the loss of control of the traditional elite over the coercive apparatus and opened the door to previously contained mass opposition, notably Hawrani's peasant movement, which soon took on unprecedented scale. Symptomatic of the change in the political balance in the wake of the coups were the temporary appointments of Aflaq and Hawrani as ministers of education, defense, and agriculture in recognition of their growing influence among students, officers and peasants (Jundi 48–51; Sayyid 75; Seale 33–147; Carleton; Petran 94–104; Torrey 1964:121–237; Ziadeh 100, 206).

The period 1954 to 1958 was one of rising pluralism, activism, and radicalism. The political arena widened as the middle class parties began to mobilize support in the countryside and the popular quarters of the cities. The politics of shifting coalitions confined to the divans of the notables, the halls of parliament, and the army barracks broadened to include the streets, campuses, even the villages, breaking down the isolation between the national arena and the local arenas characteristic of traditional politics. The incorporation of new mass actors into the political arena shifted the balance of power against the notability and in favor of the radical forces.

The era began with the 1953 merger of the Baʿth and Hawrani's ASP, a watershed in the formation of a more formidable radical opposition, for the two parties neatly complemented each other: Aflaq's with a more developed ideology, Hawrani's with greater experience in mass agitation and the struggle for power. Aflaq's was stronger among the students and minorities, Hawrani among officers and Sunni peasants, the two parties having largely spread in areas where the other was weak (Jundi 63–64). Battle against Shishakli's dictatorship gave the new united party experience in underground opposition which weeded out less committed elements, strengthened its organization, and widened its popular support (Jundi 66–67). The purge of many Shishakli partisans from the army after his fall made pro-Ba'th officers the strongest single military bloc. In 1954 Syria had its first relatively free parliamentary election, the first with a secret ballot and contested on the basis of issues. The success of significant numbers of middle class candidates, who took about 20% of the seats, was indicative of the eroding control of the notability over its political bases (Petran 106–108; Seale 164–185; Ziadeh 149–150; Torrey 1964:254–263). The elections marked the emergence of the Ba'th party as a major political actor on the Syrian stage. The party stood thirty candidates, sixteen of whom won a parliamentary seat, plus ten sympathizers, giving it a major presence at the institutional center of the regime itself (Khalil 125; Jundi 68); this compared to 1947 when a lone Ba'thist, Jallal as-Sayyid, won, largely on his personal resources. The rival Syrian Social National Party, which ran on an anti-leftist platform, got only two seats compared with nine in 1949 (Torrey 1964:263). In part, the Ba'th's success reflected its appeal among a widening new middle class impatient for change: it alone of the middle class parties combined a coherent program of reform rooted in an Arabism which cut across sectarian, regional and urban-rural cleavages. The election also marked the party's success in forging links to the masses, especially the peasantry. Hawrani's supporters swept five seats in Hama, largely with peasant votes. Wahib al-Ghanim won in Latakia also on peasant votes. In Suwayda, Mansur al-Atrash's victory reflected both his personal status as son of the paramount chieftain and growing support for the party among Druze youth. In Damascus, Bitar won, a breakthrough in this traditionally hostile stronghold. The Ba'th's success was, however, still uneven and limited; traditional notables won the great majority of the 142 seats and the party scarcely penetrated areas such as the city of Aleppo.

The overlap of regional and international conflicts with local ones, intensifying cleavages, further propelled the transformation of politics and the Ba'th's fortunes after 1954. The attempt of the Western powers to draw the Arab states into an anti-Soviet alliance against the opposition of Nasirite Egypt made Syria a battleground over which the issue was fought. The threat of Israel, a Western creation, gave the issue a special intensity and biased Syrian opinion against the alliance. While much of Syria's Westernized notability favored a Western alignment, the Ba'th and the Communists led a nationalist mobilization which gravely weakened them and, in forcing the alignment of Syria with Cairo, tilted the balance in Nasir's favor in the Arab world. So strengthened were the nationalist-left forces—the Ba'th, the Communists and independent leftists such as Khalid al-Azm—that they could no longer be kept from government power and a segment of the notability, in an attempt to ride the nationalist wave, joined with them in the 1956 formation of a "National Front" coalition government committed to a Pan-Arab, "anti-imperialist" course. The Suez invasion galvanized the Syrian public, decisively consolidating public support for the nationalist government. Subsequent Western conspiracies against it resulted in the decimation of remaining pro-Western elements and the rising power of the pro-Ba'th security chief, Colonel Abd al-Hamid Sarraj (Petran 108–126; Seale 186–306; Torrey 1964:267–353).

This was a period of intense nationalist mobilization which the Ba'th helped lead and which it was uniquely situated to profit from. It, of all the forces in the political arena, made most clearly the argument which would sweep Syrian opinion: that imperialism, Zionism and "reaction" were organically linked and that only neutralism, Pan-Arab unity, and social reform could free the Arab world of this threat. The Ba'th was, in al-Jundi's (72–73) words, the "nerve" behind the National Front government in a time when Syria felt threatened from all sides. The Ba'th also benefited enormously as a party associated with Nasir as the latter became an Arab national hero in Syria. Nasir's use of the radio to direct a simple message to the masses marked the beginning of the true age of mass politics in Syria and the newly politicized "Nasirites" were not at this time distinguishable from Ba'thists; in Safadi's words (52–54), the Ba'th, "spoke in the name of Nasir, attacked their enemies with his forces . . . [and] rode the crest of the nationalist tide unleashed by his heroics." Rising Arab nationalism not only undermined the traditional elite but discredited two of the Ba'th's middle class rivals, the Muslim Brethren and the Syrian Social Nationalist Party, both of which opposed it in the name of alternative Islamic and "Syrian" notions of the political community (Allush 33–34; Jabbur 241–242; Seale 67–72, 179, 241–243; Safadi 52–54).

With bases in government, parliament, the army, the streets, campuses, and the village, the Ba'th party was by 1956 an ascendent political power. There was a major expansion in its ranks: it had about 6,000 activists in 1954 (Seale 176) and perhaps as many as 30,000 by 1957 and its support was considerably broader than its actual membership. Creation of Ba'th branches in Lebanon, Jordan, and Iraq gave the party a nearly unique Pan-Arab stature and prestige. A measure of its rising power, it now began to attract not just idealists and dissidents but the politically ambitious (Jundi 68–73). Once it got a foot in the door of power, the Ba'th began to develop patronage resources formerly the monopoly of the notability; short-circuiting the notability, it began to assume a role of mediator between the bureaucracy and workers and peasants: in al-Jundi's words, "the partisans appeared in the lobbies of government offices learning the art of polishing apples and gaining of officials' friendships" (Jundi 58–64). The Ba'th also started to systematically insert its partisans into the bureaucracy, police, and information apparatuses, and to get appointments for them in the military academy, the teacher training college, and in strategic city schools from which demonstrations could be mobilized (Chamy; Torrey 1969:445; Crow 264). The Ministry of Health under Wahib al-Ghanim became a "Ba'thist preserve" (Torrey 1964:287, 295). In 1957 bi-elections in Suwayda and Homs leftwing nationalist candidates defeated conservative notables. In Damascus, the Ba'thist standard-bearer, Riyad al-Malki, narrowly defeated the leader of the Muslim Brotherhood who conducted a campaign of religious anti-leftism; this victory seemed to mark a triumph for the Ba'th over urban suspicion of its secular, rural, minority image, and growing public acceptance of the link it pioneered between the national cause and social radicalism (Jundi 73; Seale 290). But it was the weakening of traditional rivals and its association with Nasir, a Sunni Arab hero, that opened the door of the city to the Ba'th more than its own organizational or mobilizational power. Its urban following, being shallow, was, therefore, to prove relatively ephemeral.

Public opinion was increasingly polarized into two great camps, Left and Right, with the latter very much on the defensive. At the same time, power was diffused as never before—between parliament where the conservative notability still had a majority of seats, the National Front government supported by 65 of 142 deputies, the army, whose middle and lower ranks protected the rising progressive forces, and the leftist intellectuals and activists who shaped and channeled public opinion through press and party competition. Inside the government, a triumvirate representing the Ba'th (Hawrani), other progressives (Khalid al-Azm), and the more nationalist notability (Sabri al-Asali), backed by key military allies, dominated power, as much on the basis of their influence in the army and the streets as in parliament.

The new constellation of power began to shift the conservative logjam which had blocked progressive public policy for two decades. The government, led by Foreign Minister Salah ad-Din Bitar, adopted a firm neutralist, Arab nationalist foreign policy aligned with Nasirite Egypt. The Ba'th put forward an unprecedented legislative project, including a law forbidding the expulsion of tenants, the limitation of agrarian property and the distribution of state domain to peasants, enforcement of the labor code, social security, national planning, reclamation of the Ghab and the building of an oil refinery. The Left had enough power to initiate some of these innovations. Military and economic links to the Soviet Union, opposed by the Right as a first step toward a socialist economy, were established and the state assumed a role in economic development, notably in infrastructure and the building of the Homs oil refinery (Jabbur 91–92 Petran 121). But Right and Left shared no consensus on social reform and the only achievement of the regime was a law prohibiting the expulsion of sharecroppers from their holdings. It was pushed through parliament by the Ba'th, justified on grounds that peasant soldiers could not be expected to fight for their country when their families were being expelled from their land; this episode captures how the radical parties successfully linked nationalism and social reform to their opponent's detriment (Allush 56–57). Indicative of the precarious support for reform in parliament, however, was the fact that when the vote was taken the great majority of the deputies absented themselves in protest, not daring, for fear of the army and the streets, to block it; the Ba'th and its allies won a 36–2 triumph (Hanna 435). But demands for thorough agrarian reform, which alone could resolve the country's social malaise and agrarian crisis, could not be satisfied without the virtual overturning of established society and the Ba'th had neither the strength or, under its moderate reformist leaders, the will to attempt this.

The Ba'th was the dominant force in the ruling coalition, particularly shaping its foreign policy, but its power was out of all proportion to its organized political base and rested on precarious coalitions with others: its power in the streets derived in part from spontaneous mass support for Nasir and its alliance with the Communists, that in the army on an unstable balance between its sympathizers and other officers, its role in government on a coalition with traditional politicians. These alliances could not be sustained indefinitely. Indeed, by 1957 the dominant nationalist-left coalition was breaking up, threatening the precarious stability of the National Front government. The growing power of the Communists alarmed the Ba'th which distrusted their nationalist commitments. More specifically, the Ba'th feared that the Azm-Communist coalition, combining the traditional political assets of the great notability with modern party organization, would squeeze it into a subordinate role in the governing coalition; this is an indication of the continuing weakness of the Ba'th even at its pre-1963 height. The more conservative elements in the government, such as Sabri al-Asali and President Quwatli, alarmed by growing radicalism, were looking for a chance to check the Left, and lacking a base inside Syria, were tempted to turn to outside intervention. Thus, the Ba'th felt threatened from both the Right and the Left. Meanwhile, the army was disintegrating into a dozen or so factions, determined by personal feuds or alignments with rival political forces. These internal divisions, combined with Western pressures on the fragile Syrian state, threatened to tear Syria apart.

This situation was the immediate catalyst which drove the Ba'th and the army to seek union with Egypt. The army was seeking salvation from itself; the Ba'th, the one party which had actively worked for union on the testimony of Egyptian ambassador Mahmud Riyad (Seale 314), saw in it a realization of its principle mission and an opportunity to use Nasir's great popularity to defeat its rivals on both Right and Left and establish itself as the dominant force in Syria (Jundi 74–76; Makhoul). The Ba'th never expected union to be instituted so precipitously or that it would take a highly centralized unitary form, but Nasir's popular stature and the insistence of the army on union put the cards in his hands and the Ba'th had to accept his design for the new state. This included the dissolution of political parties, including the Ba'th, and a Presidency which put all constitutional power in his hands. Exhausted by conflict, Syrians, having no confidence in their leaders, looked to Nasir to save them from themselves. The political system had, in a sense, nearly collapsed amidst the mobilization of new social forces which it could not absorb (Torrey 1964:354–383; Petran 117–126; Seale 307–326; Devlin 1976:79–97; Sayyid 156–158; Chamy).

The new "United Arab Republic" (UAR) into which Syria was incorporated in 1958 began with a great fund of political capital, enormous mass adulation for Nasir, and the support of the political movement mobilized by the Ba'th. But the UAR turned out to be essentially bureaucratic rule from Cairo and hence proved no more able to forge the viable political institutions Syria needed than the liberal order it displaced.

Although Ba'th leaders were initially appointed to high office—Hawrani as a Vice-President, others as ministers—Nasir and the party gradually fell out. As a first step in bringing the fractious Syrian army under his control, Nasir transferred hundreds of Ba'th officers to Egypt and replaced many senior commanders with Egyptians. Next he moved to cut the nationalist-left parties down to size, beginning with the Communists but soon turning on the Ba'th. The Ba'th, expecting that it would rule the UAR together with Nasir, proposed creation of a ruling triumvirate of Nasir, Hawrani and Aflaq, attempted to dominate the political structures of the Syrian region, and insisted that its ideology be the basis of governance. But Nasir, regarding it as no more than one political faction among many, took this as impertinent and viewed the Ba'th, despite its official dissolution, to be a dangerously cohesive and independent-minded bloc within the new state which could threaten his power. He viewed its nationalist goals as extremist and incompatible with his international image and obligations, notably after it opposed his post-1959 rapprochement with the U.S. and criticized his failure to respond to Israeli diversion of the Jordan river waters. Arab nationalism, Nasir announced, was not the property of any party. He disdained the Ba'th's factionalism and the maneuvering of its leaders against each other. In elections to the National Union, the single official political organization under the union, Nasir's agents worked against the Ba'th, while encouraging conservative politicians and Islamic elements and many Ba'this withdrew from the contest: only a handful of them (2.6% of the total) were elected, and the Ba'th, which had expected to make the Union its instrument, was largely excluded from it. Ba'thists had collaborated in the purge of Communists from the trade unions and the student union, turning them into its own "domains," but the regime now turned on them; the Ba'thi leadership of the labor federation resigned in protest against new government controls and the prohibition of strikes. As Nasir moved into detente with the West and the conservative Arab monarchies and quarreled with the USSR and leftist Iraq, Islamic sentiment inside Syria was unleashed against Ba'thi secularism. "No right, no left" became the slogan of the regime. The state gradually took control of the Ba'thi and progressive press. Slowly the powers of the Syrian regional cabinet were narrowed and transferred to the central government in Egypt, Bitar and Hawrani were moved to sinecures in Cairo separated from their power base, and other Ba'th ministers were obstructed in their work; Ba'thi ministers soon resigned. The official line of the party continued to support the union, but corrosive criticism of the regime swept the party rank and file; this "coffee house" ferment was a major factor in eroding support for the UAR (Jundi 85). To calls by the party for democratization of the regime, Nasir responded with denunciation of the Ba'th's pretension to "tutelage" over the people. Colonel Sarraj, deserting the Ba'th for Nasir, became Cairo's henchman in tightening the screws over the party. As Nasir pushed the nationalist-left out of the political arena, he came to rely ever more on Sarraj's intelligence network (Abu Jaber 33–56; Jundi 77–86; Petran 128–135, 140–141; Palmer; Jabbur 198–206, 254–256; 291–296; Allush 86–106, 121–122, 224–225; Sayyid 169; Torrey 1969:457–458; Safadi 251–260).

The UAR did, however, launch major social reforms. State planning and eventually the nationalization of big industries were decreed. Agrarian reform was initiated at the very outset: parts of the great estates began to be distributed to peasants and an agrarian relations law was enacted. The reforming power enjoyed by the UAR government was a result of an alliance between Nasir, enjoying enormous popular support, and the Ba'th party's base among the intelligentsia and peasantry; the initial thrust of land reform, for example, rested on a union between the state power and technical cadres supplied by the Egyptians and an Agrarian Reform Ministry staffed by Ba'thist partisans committed to reform and enjoying support in the villages. The Ba'thist ministers running the Agrarian Reform and Labor ministries attempted to vigorously carry out the reforms, provoking a conservative backlash but winning over to Nasirism groups of land hungry peasants. But, particularly after the split between Nasir and the Ba'th, the reform became a bureaucratic exercise from above, failed to consolidate organized roots in the villages, and was enervated by a ruinous drought which devastated the new peasant holdings. The importance of the agrarian reform decrees was inestimable, however, if only as a symbol of the new autonomy of the state and the rapidly declining political power of the landed elite who before 1958 had successfully obstructed even the mildest reforms.

The basic features of the UAR regime, as Jabbur (287) put it, were the charismatic leader at the top, resting on an apparatus of military/police control and Nasir's vast but unorganized mass support: the UAR became a bureaucratic state with a powerful Arab nationalist legitimation. But it had major liabilities. Nasir alienated or demobilized much of the politicized "middle strata," especially the Ba'thists, leaving a gap between the leader and his mass constituency. In theory, the National Union was to embrace and link all the people to government, regardless of social differences or ideology. In practice, it came to be run by intelligence operatives, non-political government employees, and local notables; ironically, many of the leaders of the separatist movement were to come out of the Union. Broad sectors of the urban middle class remained Nasirist to the end, but were never politically organized to defend the regime. Instead, Nasir co-opted traditional politicians, while at the same time attacking—through land reform and nationalizations—their social interests. In trying to stay above and balance the various social forces and to rule through the bureaucracy and the security police, Nasir failed to give his regime a clear social base. In purging "progressive" Syrian army officers, and alienating the officer corps, he opened the door to a military coup by a handful of conservative officers. In 1961 they brought the regime—and the Syro-Egyptian union—down. Significantly, the two key officers in the separatist coup were linked to the conservative Damascene bourgeoisie and *suq* (Jabbur 286–291; Petran 150).

The union had an enduring effect on Syrian public life. It initiated the major social reforms, above all land reform, widely expected by the mass public, thereby raising the standards of legitimacy. But the UAR and its fall sharply divided Syrians over the wisdom of union, over whether to seek re-union, and if so, on what terms. More specifically, the middle class nationalist-left was deeply divided by the unionist issue, setting Nasirites, Communists, and Ba'thists against each other. Thus, an already fragmented political arena was further divided.

The so-called *infisal* (separatist) regime which replaced the UAR represented an effort to turn back the political clock a decade and restore the rule of the traditional politicians. The traditional elite recaptured parliament and government. The regime's first important act was to roll back the UAR reforms. Banks and industries were de-nationalized. The ceiling on the land reform was raised, all but vitiating it, and large tracts—reportedly 30,000 ha.—were returned to big landlords; in places, landlords drove peasants out of their villages, demolishing their homes and burning their crops (Nasser). Only a military revolt stopped this wave of reaction, bringing in a new moderate government which restored the reform. But even then the regime could never win much support. Pro-unionist sentiment agitated the urban masses. Much of the middle class, both Nasirite and Ba'thist, despised the regime, the peasantry was permanently alienated by the reversal of the agrarian reform and the workers by de-nationalization. Unprecedented praetorian instability—street riots, strikes, and military intrigue—was symptomatic of the infisal's utter bankruptcy (Jundi 99–100, 103; Warriner 1962:229; Khalil 235–236). Public ferment infected the officer corps, manifested in incessant factionalism and the alienation of progressive middle class officers. All confidence in the survival of the regime was lost: "people were expecting communique #1 each morning" (Jundi 99). It was only because of the divisions in the opposition itself that the regime lasted as long as it did. When the Ba'th coup came, a year and a half after the break with Egypt, the total lack of opposition was indicative of the regime's complete demoralization, the utter collapse of established authority in Syria.

Prelude to Power: The Dissolution and Fragmentation of the Ba'th Party

Ultimately, the most important consequence of the UAR and *infisal* periods was their effect on the Ba'th Party: the transformation of the party in this period determined its road to power and the nature of the subsequent regime.

The Ba'th was shattered as a unified political movement by the union. Its party organization was officially dissolved, scattering its militants and snapping the links which bound them to the leadership, although some local branches actually remained in being (Jundi 80). When Nasir shunted the Ba'th aside, purged Ba'thi officers, and tried to exploit traditional forces against the party, he plunged the movement into turmoil. The party leadership split over how to deal with him and, after the UAR collapsed, over whether to seek re-union. Hawrani emerged as leader of an anti-unionist faction, denounced the UAR as "Egyptianization," and challenged Nasir on Arab nationalist grounds for his alleged acquiescence in the liquidation of the

Palestinian cause. The "separatist regime" brought a permanent split between Hawrani and Aflaq; Hawrani welcomed the end of union, decided to work through the regime, stood against the unionist movement and took some—by no means all—of his former Hama partisans with him into his reconstructed Arab Socialist Party (Jabbur 195). Aflaq and the Ba'thist mainstream, ambivalent toward a regime which, despite its faults, still seemed to represent a major triumph for the Arabs, professed loyalty to the UAR but were critical of its undemocratic rule. They could not disown a state which embodied the unionism they had preached for years, but neither would they actively support it. After its fall, they called for a re-union on a more democratic federal basis (Jundi 81).

An equally important consequence of the union was the alienation of much of the second generation of party leadership from the historical leaders. Some Ba'thist activists became Nasirites and served the UAR. After the UAR fell, many of these and others who charged the party with doing too little to defend the union and to advance re-union, founded the Socialist Unionists under the leadership of Sami Sufan; they would become the leftwing of the Nasirite movement (Jabbur 195; Safadi 293; Jundi 89; Petran 151). Many of them were from the Sunni urban middle class whose adhesion to the Ba'th had been propelled by its rise as the standard bearer of Arab nationalism in alliance with Nasir. But some older Ba'thists, too, whose commitment to Ba'thism had centered on unity, when forced to choose between the Ba'th and Nasir, chose the latter.

Other activists, especially rurals and those from minority groups, remained loyal to the Ba'th but not to its historic leaders. They violently disputed the dissolution of the party which seemed to destroy the vehicle of their political and social ambitions. Hundreds of "hizbiyin" became "useless" and resentful "retired militants" itching to reconstruct the party (Jundi 78). Moreover, disillusioned with a unionism which had ended in neither a successful Pan-Arab state or a social revolution in Syria, they questioned Aflaq's pre-occupation with Arab unity, per se, while being equally repulsed by Hawrani's collaboration with the separatist regime. They began to stress the need for mass political mobilization and social revolution as the road to Pan-Arabism. A leading force in this ideological ferment was a group of old Ba'thists and former Communists, including Jamal al-Atasi, Ilyas Murqus and Yasin al-Hafiz, who, writing in *al-Ba'th*, criticized traditional Ba'thism for its emphasis on individual freedom and opposition to class struggle and called for an opening to Marxism and a stress on popular mass organization; these writers were important because their work expressed the ideological mutation going on in the party bases and laid the foundations for the radicalization of Ba'thist ideology after 1963 (Safadi 155–161; Jabbur 375–376). Out of this ferment a younger generation of Ba'thists was emerging, militant intellectuals and leftist officers, who would, after March 1963, seize control of the party and turn it from a reformist unionist party into a vehicle of their own version of socialist revolution. A major consequence of the UAR experience was, thus, a general discrediting of the leadership of the party founders and the emergence of an alternative leadership championing a new radicalized version of Ba'thism.

Finally, the party suffered a big contraction in its popular base as a result of the UAR and its aftermath. Much of the rapid expansion of its popularity in the late fifties was owing to its Pan-Arab leadership and its alignment with Nasir; once it broke with the hero of Arab nationalism it lost much of this support—concentrated among the urban middle and lower classes. Indeed, the very rationale of Ba'thism seemed in question: a decisive element of its mass appeal had been leadership in the fight against foreign interference in the Arab world and for Arab unity. Now those were old battles, the union had failed, and the Ba'th bore some of the responsibility for it, having agreed to a precipitous one-sided arrangement which submerged the rights of Syria, yet later withdrawing its support when the union damaged its partisan interests. Both those ardently committed to Nasir and many of those disillusioned by the union considered the party ideologically bankrupt. Thus, the Ba'th was reduced to its original largely rural base, but even much of this following remained dispersed.

By 1962 the "Ba'th" was divided among at least three distinct factions running on different tangents. Aflaq had a couple of hundred students gathered around him in Damascus and a certain prestige as party founder and philosopher. But he seemed strangely reluctant to reconstruct the old party, perhaps aware of the growing rejection of his tutelage and seemingly content to return to the purer days when the party was but a circle of disciples around their teacher; old members were "sick" of his reluctance and insistent that he take action (Safadi 290; Jundi 97–98). Eventually, he entrusted reconstruction to a team of Iraqi Ba'thists who prepared a congress which met at Homs in 1962 to formally reestablish the party. A document from the congress gives a glimpse of the internal condition of the party-in-construction as the Aflaq leadership saw it: the "divisions and doubts resulting from the dissolution" and the "appearance of doctrinal and political deviations among certain members" who rejected "the party's creed and its spirit of discipline" had made many partisans unsuitable for the "disciplined party work" needed for reorganization (Rabinovich 38). Even within Aflaq's faction, opinion remained highly critical of the dissolution and of the disassociation of union from socialism and democracy under the UAR. Aflaq found his right to lead the party he founded could no longer be taken for granted. Indeed, his tardiness in re-organizing would be damaging to his claims, for, even after the Homs conference, his faction was able to establish few organized links to the provinces or the military; as such, in the wake of the March 1963 coup, it remained a mere rump led by a few old associates like Mansur al-Atrash and Shibli al-Aysami, and only one of many groups with a claim to lead the Ba'th (Safadi 8, 286–287, 290, 375; Jundi 98–99).

On a separate tack was a large grouping of rural intellectuals who controlled the remnants of many provincial party branches, particularly in Dera, Deir az-Zor, Latakia and Suwayda and who would come to be called the *Qutriyun* (Regionalists). They were highly critical of Aflaq for dissolving the party, lacked enthusiasm for re-union with Egypt and were, instead, embracing radical socialism as their central concern (Safadi 294; Jundi 90, 95–96). Under the separatist regime they began, independently of Aflaq, to reorganize the party. Alawi Ba'this were in the forefront of such re-organization and when the Ba'th came to power in 1963, the Latakia branch would be one of the strongest—with incalculable consequences for the sectarian composition of the Ba'th state.

Thirdly, various groups of Ba'thist officers remained politically committed. Close in origin and ideology to the *Qutriyun* was a group of former Ba'thi junior officers discharged under the UAR or *infisal,* mostly rural and disproportionately from the minority Alawi, Druze, and Isma'ili communities. They resented the ineffectualness of the leaders in protecting them, the dissolution of the party and the failure to quickly reconstruct it; they were determined to overthrow the "tutelage" exercised by the founding leaders over the Ba'th and make room for a new leadership. Presiding over the so-called "military committee," they were constructing a secret military party organization. The members of this committee included Muhammed Omran, Salah Jedid, Hafiz al-Asad and Abd al-Karim al-Jundi, all of whom would play key roles in post-1963 Syria. Other older Ba'th officers were closer to Hawrani or the Socialist-Unionists. Significantly, all these groups of officers regarded Aflaq as unreliable (Sayyid 172; Rabinovich 36–48; Jundi 84–89, 95–96). By 1962 the "military committee" was deeply engrossed in conspiracies to infiltrate the army and overthrow the separatist regime in the name of the Ba'th; but it clearly intended to take the leadership of the Ba'th itself.

Thus, on the eve of the party's seizure of power, the "Ba'th" had no widely acknowledged leadership and enjoyed no ideological consensus: indeed, what had begun as an essentially reformist party was well on its way, in spite of its founding leaders, to embracing a revolutionary ideology. It was organizationally dispersed and fragmented, its former mass base either alienated or de-mobilized. It is hard to image a more inauspicious juncture for a party to take power. Nevertheless, dismissed Ba'thist officers, fearing the party's—and their own—chances were slipping away, were determined, (despite opposition from Aflaq) to act. They had never ceased plotting a coup, but being on the outside of the army, they had to find allies still holding commands. A number of "Nasirite" officers had been appointed to key commands in an effort to appease progressive-unionist sentiment in the army ranks. The Ba'thists conspired with them but mutual mistrust still ran strong. By 1963, according to al-Jundi (97), the Ba'th had "penetrated" all officer groups, but the army appeared paralyzed by factional stalemate. It soon became apparent that the "independent" commander of the southern front, Colonel Ziyad al-Hariri, was the one man who could break the stalemate and topple the regime if he could be won over. In February 1963 the Ba'th seized power in Iraq. This was the catalyst that brought Hariri, Nasirite, and Ba'thi officers together and on March 8, 1963 they carried out a bloodless coup that put the "separatist" regime out of its misery. Within a few months, the Ba'th and its partners had fallen out, the latter had been purged, and a purely Ba'thist regime was entrenched at the heights of state power; but it was unclear in a regime divided between various rival factions, all claiming to be Ba'thist, just what this portended (Jundi 99–112; Jabbur 206–212, 372–376; Akhrass 175–176; Petran 150, 155–166).

Thus, the Ba'th party came to power, not as a popular movement, but through a coup by a handful of officers. This particular road to power would shape the regime's whole subsequent development. The reduction of the party to a core of rural officers and intellectuals, many of minority origin, and the loss of most of its urban Sunni cadres would lead to an ideological revision in which the Pan Arabism, of first concern to the urban middle class, would be superseded by an agrarian radicalism which put priority on "revolution in one-country." Indeed, from the time of the power seizure radicals intent on a socialist revolution held the upper hand in the new regime. Consequently, the Ba'th would long face the hostility of much of urban society, not only of the landlord elite and Islamic conservatives but of many middle class Nasirites and liberals as well. The seizure of power on the back of the army, without an organized mass base, and in the face of urban opposition, and the party's attempt, in these conditions, to impose a revolution from above made it certain the regime would be dominated by the military politicians which brought it to power and kept it there. Lacking a "counter-state" prepared to take over at the top, the party would have to construct a new state center from scratch. In these circumstances, the Ba'th would resort to authoritarian rule, attempting to reconcile military dominance with the Leninist political organization needed to carry out its revolution. The result would be a regime with bases of power in the army and the village ruling from the heights of state power over an urban milieu which rejected its legitimacy. This regime, in seeking to forge a new state and carry out a revolution, confronted intractable obstacles: a fragmented mosaic society divided by class and urban-rural gaps and rival ideologies, infected with praetorianism, embraced by a state lacking nationalist legitimacy, threatened by powerful external enemies, and with a lagging Western-dependent economy. The Ba'th was not, however, without resources—ideas, leaders, or supporters—with which to confront this challenge.

That in the end it was the Ba'th which became the vehicle of system change was because, in spite of its own liabilities, it nevertheless had the most balanced and potent political assets. The Ba'th forged the most convincing ideology which, in fusing and propagating nationalism and socialism, shaped the attitudes of a whole generation and created receptivity to the radical project the Ba'th would attempt to carry out after 1963 (Allush 160; N. Kaylani 6–7). The party also built an ideologically committed cadre of intellectuals and officers recruited from the rural masses and from which the political elite of the Ba'th state would be drawn (Jundi 36–37, 69, 73, 101; Jabbur 197–98). In the fifties, the Ba'th developed enough organization to forge the broadest coalition of opposition forces, bridging sectarian, regional, and urban-rural gaps more effectively than any of its rivals; although it began as a mere youth movement, it evolved beyond its original student-teacher core, both "upward," penetrating the state itself, and "downward" to the villages where the mass of the population still lived. Although the Ba'th's coalition disintegrated after 1958, and although the party did not take power at the head of a peasant army or through peasant votes, the Ba'th coup in many ways was an outcome, albeit delayed, of the rural political mobilization of the fifties. The Ba'thist officers who seized power in 1963 were shaped by the agrarian crisis and politicization of that period and they enjoyed a potential, if demobilized, constituency forged at the same time and concentrated in the countryside. The Ba'th had the local presence and the organizational experience which would permit it to reconstruct important parts of its old coalition after the power seizure. In the end, most crucial to the Ba'th's staying power was that it had developed the strongest foothold in the army and the deepest roots in the village. Displaying a remarkable resilience as an ideology and organization, it was now rising from the ashes as a striking force for system change.

By contrast, its rivals all labored under fatal liabilities. The Muslim Brotherhood, rooted in the traditional urban *suq,* could generate little support among the educated new middle class which was embracing Arabism or the minorities who wanted a secular state; it had little following in the army or the village. The Syrian Social National Party was a direct rival of the Ba'th for the loyalties of the educated middle class, the officer corps, and the minorities. But, being minority dominated, it was wedded to militant secularism and its "Syrianism" expressed a rejection of an Arabism considered Islamic; hence it had little Sunni Muslim support. As its opposition to Arabism and its identification with the West became apparent, it lost much of its support in the army and among educated youth to the Ba'th (Jabbur 162; Khadduri 1970:193–194; Perlmutter 1969:835). Both the Ikhwan and SSNP, though anti-feudal, were pro-capitalist at a time when socialism was on the rise. The Communists, viewed as anti-Islamic, were confined to the minorities, especially Kurds, Armenians and Christian Arabs, and to parts of the urban intelligentsia and working class. They gave little attention to peasant organization outside Kurdish and Christian villages and they had little following in the army (Torrey 1964:61; Hanna 306, 337, 355; N. Kaylani 10). Internationalist, they never really embraced Arabism and their support for the partition of Palestine was decisive in limiting their national appeal. Jundi (70) argues that the "failure" of communism was a direct factor contributing to the success of the Ba'th: communism opened the eyes of the people to social problems but since, lacking nationalist legitimacy, it could not be accepted, people turned to the Ba'th as an alternative. Equally important, the uncompromising secularism of the SSNP and the Communists, compared to the Ba'th's lip-service to Islam gave the Ba'th a much greater capacity to reach the Sunni mass base of society without diminishing its appeal to the educated intelligentsia. Finally, Nasirism, after 1960 a rival of the Ba'th, would acquire a broad mass following in the Sunni cities, but its leadership was split into several factions, it lacked a clear ideology and was distrusted by all those, including many radical intellectuals and the politicized minorities, who had been disillusioned by the UAR. It possessed little organization, hence remained a spontaneous urban force which failed to really penetrate the countryside.

5

The Formation of the Ba'th Regime

The Seizure of Power

The March 1963 coup brought to power a diverse coalition of forces united only by their opposition to the "separatist regime": the various Ba'thi factions, including the military committee, Colonel Ziyad al-Hariri and his "independents," and various Nasirite officers. Almost immediately a struggle for power broke out. The Ba'th first quarreled with its Nasirite partners over terms of a new union with Egypt, the Nasirites wanting a re-union which would restore power to Nasir and the Ba'th seeking at most a loose federation which would allow them to rule in Syria. When negotiations in Cairo failed, a protracted power struggle broke out, the Nasirites trying to mobilize the powerful unionist sentiment among the urban masses in large-scale street demonstrations demanding re-union, the Ba'thi military maneuvering against Nasirites to consolidate its control over the army. Ba'thists and Hariri's independent officers combined to purge Nasirite officers, constitute a new Ba'thi dominated government and repress massive Nasirite street rebellions and a major coup attempt. Shortly thereafter Hariri and his followers were purged over their resistance to the Ba'thization of the regime and the radicalization of land reform. In this process, Ba'th officers laid the first crucial foundation for their rule: the Ba'thi military committee, from strategic positions in the high command and crucial coup-making units which they had secured on the morn of the coup, presided over a Ba'thization of the whole armed forces: hundreds of conservative or Nasirite officers, chiefly of the urban Sunni upper-middle and middle classes, were purged. Their places were filled by a wholesale recruitment of Ba'thists of chiefly rural and often minority origin, many, indeed, the kinsmen of leading Ba'th officers. So thoroughly were the military foundations of the regime laid that from this time on military politics took the form of intra-Ba'th rivalries. Out of this struggle for control of the army and the streets, Colonel Amin al-Hafiz emerged as the first Ba'thist military strongman and titular head of the regime's revolutionary council; behind him the leading members of the military committee were entrenching themselves at the strategic levers of military power—Salah Jadid in charge of the critical officer's personnel section and later chief of staff; Muhammad Umran, commander of the key

70th Brigade at Qatana, shield of the regime, Ahmad Suwaydani, chief of military intelligence, Salim Hatoum head of the commandos, and Hafiz al-Asad, commander of the air force. Together with their civilian allies, largely rural radicals, they would also take over the levers of the re-constructing party apparatus. The veteran Ba'th leader Salah ad-Din al-Bitar presided as prime minister over a Ba'th dominated government. Thus, at the outset, from dire necessity, Ba'th power was being rooted in control of state office, coercive military command, and networks of trusted clients.

Within a few months the Ba'th had achieved the first phase in a "primitive accumulation of power," the concentration of state power in its hands and the exclusion of all rivals. For this it paid a high price: the hostility of wide sectors of the politically attentive public committed to other political forces. Some were the Ba'th's natural enemies. The Ba'th had deprived the traditional upper class of political power and was threatening it with socialism; the Ikhwan was a historic rival whose rising political star the Ba'th power seizure cut short. But leading sectors of the nationalist-left which had been aligned with or part of the Ba'th's constituency in the fifties were now also in opposition. Social democrats, including ex-Ba'thist Akram al-Hawrani, rejected the single party rule the Ba'th was fashioning. Historical mistrust, briefly put aside in the late fifties, separated the Communists, representing a portion of the intelligentsia and of the working class, from the Ba'th. Major portions of Arab nationalist opinion were now Nasirite and hence alienated. Syrian Nasirism was, to be sure, a heterogeneous movement, elements of which lacked a mass base. Some Nasirites, such as the cadres of the Arab Nationalist Movement, were traditionally recruited from the urban upper middle class and those grouped in the Arab Socialist Union had mostly attached their careers to Nasir as officials under the UAR and now embraced Nasirism as a counter to the more radical Ba'th. But broad sectors of the urban Sunni middle class, including many students, Palestinians, and the numerous former Ba'thists now grouped in the Socialist Unionist Movement, still viewed Nasir as the only leader of Arab nationalism. A portion of the working class and of the peasants, such as those from the Damascus Ghouta which joined the Nasirite disturbances against the Ba'th, were also part of a broad Nasirite coalition. Only the factional division of the Nasirites and their organizational weaknesses vitiated their capacity to challenge Ba'th rule.

The fact that the Ba'th leadership was by now increasingly minoritarian—Alawi, Druze, and Isma'ili—and predominately rural lower middle class and its rivals were chiefly urban, Sunni, and of higher social status represented a major social cleavage underlying political differences. In essence, the separation of the Ba'th, in the immediate years after the power seizure, from the urban middle class constituency it had won over in the mid-fifties and the rural roots and outlook of its leading cadres gave the conflict between it and the opposition at this time more of a urban-rural than a class character. While the Ba'th's now chiefly rural base was still scattered and de-mobilized, the urban opposition was relatively mobilized and concentrated. As such, in the first two years of its rule the Ba'th found itself virtually isolated in the still largely urban political arena and dependent on the use of military repression to stay in power; it was probably only the fragmentation of its rivals which allowed it to survive. The Ba'th's drive to consolidate its rule began as a matter of turning the institutions of state power into rural strongholds dominating the cities. But its leaders knew that to retain power and carry out their revolution they would have to break out of their isolation and reconstruct the middle class-peasant coalition they had forged in the fifties. Thus, at the outset, the Ba'th faced the formidable challenge of a severe crisis of legitimacy. (Rabinovich 26-74; Kerr 1971:1-95; Devlin 1976:231–253, 281–285; Salamah 29-47; al-Jundi 120–139; Qazzaz)

Ideological Revision—Blueprint for Revolution

At the same time, another power struggle was shaping up inside the party between the older moderate leadership led by Aflaq and Bitar and younger radicals, including most of the Ba'thi military, over power and its purposes. At the definitive Sixth National Congress held in late 1963, the partly reconstructed Ba'th party revised its ideology, laid down a strategy for carrying out its revolution and consolidating power, and formally constituted a new leadership. Younger largely rural radicals, seizing the initiative against the resistance of Aflaq and his followers, led the ideological revision; it, in essence, joined the Ba'th's traditional Arab nationalism to Marxist-Leninist ideas, in effect, radicalizing the party and giving greater priority to its historic commitment to "socialism."

Several dovetailing developments account for this alteration. At the deepest level, the ideological mutation was set off by the rise to power inside the party of leaders from lower social strata than the party founders, chiefly junior officers and intellectuals of rural, often peasant, families. Their modest origins and closeness to village grievances made them much more antagonistic to the traditional urban establishment and determined to carry out a radical revolution than the party's urban middle class leaders. Their attitudes reflected a long gestating rejection of traditional society and a powerful longing for the overthrow of a social order they blamed both for their lack of personal opportunities and for all Syria's ills—its backwardness and inequalities, its weakness in face of Israel and the West. Further, the ideological radicalization reflected the growing perception of many educated Syrians, going back to the mid-fifties, that capitalism not only meant growing inequality, foreign dependence, and continuing agrarian crisis but that it had reached a dead end in Syria. This was reinforced by shifts in the global ideological climate; while the founding generation had been educated in Western thought, the new generation of leaders had been socialized in the fifties when Marxism-Leninism had acquired a new appeal in the Third World. But for most Syrians, Marxism had to be thoroughly nationalized and divorced from subordination to international communism to acquire credibility and that is what the new generation of Ba'thist ideologues were trying to do. To them, a fusion of Ba'thi nationalism and Marxism appeared to be an ideological alternative to all the things they rejected—traditional Islam, Western liberal capitalism, communist internationalism—and a viable blueprint for a socialist but authentically Arab revolution. The receptivity of younger Ba'thists to a radicalization of Ba'thism was also facilitated by their mistrust, as a result of the UAR failure, of the classical Arab unity preached by Aflaq; unity without revolution, many came to feel, offered no solutions to the ills of the Arab world, as the UAR had shown. Finally, the new Ba'thist leaders, now in power, found only a revision of classical Ba'thism would serve to guide and legitimize their rule and the revolution they aimed to carry out. They needed a doctrine of revolutionary transformation which classical Ba'thism did not provide. In particular, there was a need to solve the contradiction between the party's radical social goals and its historic commitment to liberal democracy. Younger radical Ba'thists had already discarded liberalism in principle; now, facing powerful resistance to their rule, only an authoritarian model would serve their needs. Marxism-Leninism, embodying a corpus of experience in authoritarian state-building, mass organization, and statist development, appeared a natural source of guidance for their revolutionary project. Moreover, they required an ideological legitimation of their rule, in particular, one attractive to the progressive nationalist opinion they wished to rally to their side: they needed a program distinguishable from Nasirism which would justify their rejection of union on Nasir's terms and from classical Ba'thism which would justify pushing aside the historic leaders.

Three major revisions in Ba'thism resulted. First, the meaning of Arab unity in the Ba'thist creed was transformed. Arab unity was retained as an ideal goal, desirable not only in itself but because in the long run only a large state could confront imperialism and make socialism work. But it could not be achieved by a mere "piecing together of states" or through "imposition by one region" (i.e. Egypt) and it was no longer viewed (as Aflaq is said to have done) as a nearly automatic solution to the Arabs' problems unless it emerged from a popular revolution and had a socialist content. No concrete strategy for advancing Pan-Arabism was put forward, except a proposal for union with Iraq which would soon be rendered obsolete by the fall of the Ba'th government there, and a call for an "interaction of Arab revolutionary experiments," a "deepening of the socialist and mass bases in each region," and a gradual fusing of them. This meant an effort to end the split with Nasir but also that, until it could be overcome, the Ba'th would concentrate first on the revolutionary transformation of Syria. The new Ba'th did not abandon the ideal of Pan-Arabism which remained the most compelling idea in Syrian political life and the notion soon crystallized that revolutionary Syria could serve as the "Hanoi" of an all-Arab revolution, exporting it to the rest of the Arab world. This implied that, for the new Ba'th, Arab revolution subtly replaced Arab union as the first goal of Pan-Arab nationalism; it also meant that, while the Arab nation remained the desired political community and Arab nationalism the mission of the new state, rather than accepting leadership from outside, Ba'thist Syria was now viewed as the natural leader and vanguard of the Arab world. Gradually, however, and especially after Hafiz al-Asad took power, Ba'thism became the official ideology of a new Syrian establishment with a stake in the survival of the Syrian state, just as communism, theoretically international, was harnessed as a doctrine of state formation in Russia. It is ironic that a movement which began as an embodiment of Pan-Arab unionism should end up being the vehicle for consolidation of a state which, however much it sought to act for the Arab national cause, was, to the very extent it developed the power structure needed for this purpose, an ever more formidable obstacle to Pan-Arab union. The 1963 split with Nasir was to be, in practice, the last gasp of Pan-Arabism as a movement for total union of the Arab states, launching the transformation of Ba'thism into a doctrine of "Arab nationalism in one country."

A second ideological change rejected liberal parliamentarianism as the proper political system of the projected new Ba'thi order. Liberal regimes in countries like Syria were held to reflect the status quo distribution of social power and the feudal, tribal and communal struggle, while keeping the masses backward and passive; they were hence an unfit instrument for carrying out radical change. Instead, the party now considered the ideal political model to be a Leninist-style "popular democracy" with a single "vanguard" party run on democratic-centralist lines and linked to mass popular organizations. The single party would express the "general will" and act as the motor of change in its name; mass organizations and popular councils would allow the party to mobilize the masses against the "reactionary classes," would keep the party in touch with mass sentiment, and would provide a means for the masses to control the bureaucratic apparatus— without which the socialist experiment would degenerate into mere "state capitalism," and the rule of a "new class." This system would provide the necessary balance of strong central leadership to direct radical change and mass participation to carry it out. It was democratic because the single party, enjoying internal democratic procedure, represented and was supported by the masses. In practice, this was a formula for imposing single-party rule on Syria in the face of resistance from the Ba'th's urban rivals. Given its weakness in the cities, the party's strategy, in forging this new party-state, was to recruit a pool of cadres from educated rural youth and active elements of the peasantry; these would spearhead the extension of the new party into the villages where the regime expected to find greatest receptivity to its appeal, where the party had already planted roots in the fifties and where numbers, i.e., the majority of the population, still lay (ABSP 1973).

Third, the congress analyzed the social situation in Syria and the Arab world and delineated a course of revolutionary socialist transformation. The conception of social change held by the old Ba'thist leaders was criticized. They were accused of having allowed their dispute with local communism and their petit bourgeois background to give an unscientific character to their socialism: their denial of the need for class struggle to reach socialism was utopian, their acceptance of an inherent right to private property was a petit bourgeois bias which ignored the principle that labor is the sole source of value and hence private ownership of the means of production, however constrained, necessarily exploitative. In consequence, the party had diluted its mass base with petit bourgeois and even bourgeois elements, had attempted to seek its goals through parliamentary reform, and had failed to define a true blueprint for socialist revolution. An analysis of the situation in Syria concluded that the bourgeoisie was no longer capable of economic leadership or capitalism of developing Syria. In developing countries, it was argued, capitalism is inevitably a foreign-dependent comprador enterprise. What capital is not channeled abroad, is squandered on luxury consumption or invested in speculative real estate, commercial and usurious ventures or, at best, light consumption industries. Dependent capitalism cannot mobilize and invest capital in authentic productive development or break its links with neo-imperialism. Given this analysis, the new credo held that the Ba'th must abandon its earlier idealistic social-reformism for a rigorous scientific-socialist course. The party's social base had therefore to be rooted in the workers, peasants, revolutionary intellectuals and soldiers, and, although small tradesmen would be kept within the fold, bourgeois elements had to be excluded.

The documents of the congress and the more concrete "Staged Program" issued in July 1965, together, provide a blueprint for the "socialist transformation" the party proposed to carry out (ABSP 1965, 1973). The major sectors of the economy—industry, transport, finance, foreign trade—would be nationalized and private enterprise replaced with state planning and investment as the motor of development. Limited nationalizations of banks and a handful of the largest industries had already been decreed, but the party now called for going much further than a "mixed economy." Public control of the economy, it was argued, would snap ties of economic interest and dependency with the West which diluted nationalist commitments, would permit the economic surplus to be invested in development rather than squandered, would eliminate the exploitation of labor for the benefit of private owners, allow rewards to be linked to productivity, permit a more equitable distribution of wealth, and replace private profit with the "real needs" of society as the criterion of economic decision-making. The state would direct resources into the productive agricultural and industrial sectors on which sound development depended. It would lay down the transportation and power infrastructure needed to support industrialization, link fragmented markets, and integrate city and countryside. Industrialization was the top priority; a strategy of import substitution industrialization seeking to break Syria's pattern of dependent extroverted development is clear in the stress on channeling of the agricultural surplus into national industry to "realize self-sufficiency . . . end dependence on exports," and contain the effect of the "continuous decrease in the [world] price of agricultural products in relation to industrial products." But a "balanced" strategy of development would be pursued in which industrialization was closely linked to agricultural modernization. Industry would provide agricultural requisites: phosphate deposits would become the basis of a fertilizer industry and a farm implements industry would supply farmers at reasonable cost and without dependence on foreign imports. Other industries would process agricultural products. Industrialization would also absorb surplus rural labor. Thus, industry would help spur the agricultural revolution on which it, in turn, depended for a surplus—food, raw materials, export earnings—and which was required to raise rural living standards and create an internal market. In agriculture, socialism would transfer "the land to the one who works it" through a radical agrarian reform which had, in principle, already been decreed in April, 1963, and which would deepen and revitalize the reform begun under the UAR. The 6th National Congress argued for collectivization of agriculture, a reflection of the imprint of radical ideologues on its work, on the grounds that collective farms could most effectively modernize technique, induce cooperation needed to facilitate economies of scale, overcome land fragmentation, blunt the rise of rural capitalism, "rescue the peasant from his isolation and historic individualism," and, not least, serve the mobilization of agrarian resources for comprehensive planning and industrialization. Full scale collectivization was well beyond the party's capacity and, as leveler heads soon realized, would require a nationalization of the land which "would not be understood by the people" (Zoubi 1969:25); by 1965 this aim had been modified in order to "avoid ideological rigidity and coercion from above." Agrarian socialism would instead be established gradually: the party would begin with state farms in lightly populated extensively cultivated areas amenable to mechanization (such as the Jazirah). It would also create service and marketing cooperatives among land reform beneficiaries and voluntarily adhering small-holding peasants which would only gradually—perhaps within a decade—evolve toward more advanced production cooperatives. The state would begin to plan agricultural development. An infrastructure to supply peasants with credit, production requisites, and marketing and processing services would be developed to break the hold of merchants and money-lenders; stable state markets and prices would insulate the peasant from radical price fluctuations induced by weather and the market. The state, through large scale investment in irrigation, land reclamation and technical innovation, would stimulate agricultural transformation. While socialization of the entire economy was seen as the ultimate goal, in the interim, a role for private enterprise in internal trade, construction, tourism, and small industry would be preserved under state regulation; the petite bourgeoisie would be socialized only gradually and by persuasion. Finally, the state would provide public services, such as education and health, redirecting them toward the poor and rural parts of the population. Rural discontent with government bias toward the urban areas is expressed in the following passage from the congress report (Rabinovich 95):

> Millions and millions of pounds are spent in the cities on bread to make it cheap, while most of the peasants do not eat flour throughout the year, but eat corn and barley. . . . another form of exploitation is the attention given to some regions but not to others so that the country is divided into two parts, the spoiled and the neglected.

Needless to say, this program was also a strategy in the power struggle. "Socialism" aimed to break the control of the old elite not only over the "heights of the economy"—finance, big industry, etc.—but also over land and markets, and thereby the political control afforded by peasant dependency and patronage. In effecting a more egalitarian distribution of resources in society, notably one in favor of the deprived rural periphery, the Ba'th hoped to win the masses to its side, while expanded state control over economic life would in practice make them more dependent on the new state. Thus, socio-economic transformation would provide the occasion for the political mobilization of a mass constituency, particularly in the countryside. The Leninist strategy of state-building would forge a strong new state center and incorporate this constituency, through party and mass organizations, into the new regime. Thus, the party hoped to break out of its isolation, by-pass and undermine its largely urban rivals, and submerge their hostility in a pro-regime rural mobilization. This was a coherent strategy for creating state power.

As a blueprint for social transformation, the program's combination of state planning, nationalization, and land reform was, in principle, plausible and, indeed, some such formula had become quite fashionable in much of the Third World. To be sure, its radical attack on the principle of private property and the vision of a fully collectivized society was a piece of ideological idealism at odds with the interests and outlook of much of the regime's own constituency, and in the proposal to use state controls to mobilize an agrarian surplus, there existed the seeds of a potential Stalinism which could drive a wedge between regime and peasant. But actual policy sought to subordinate the private sector economy to the state, not to eradicate it, and state control over agriculture was to stop far short of a Stalinist strategy.

Nevertheless, to translate this blueprint into reality required the creation of a powerful ideological party; not only did such a party have to be constructed from above, without benefit of years of disciplined struggle from below needed to sift the ideological true-believers from the uncommitted, but at least part of the new party-in-formation was loyal to the older Ba'th leaders. Aflaq and Bitar were strongly opposed to what they considered to be the ideological "mutilation" of Ba'thist thought perpetuated by the congress: they rejected the subordination of Pan-Arabism to radical socialism, considered moderate socialist measures to be sufficient, wanted a more pluralist and constitutional political system, and wished to reach some accommodation with the party's rivals, especially liberal and Nasirite elements. For the next three years, they would be locked in a rearguard struggle against their loss of influence in the party to the largely radical officer-politicians who were claiming the lion's share of power and to the civilian radicals whose capture of influence over ideology and policy had been registered at the congress. Thus, before the Ba'th could go far in carrying out its revolution it would have to forge internal unity behind it and political structures to implement it (Aflaq 1971:187–254; ABSP 1964; ABSP 1965; ABSP 1973; Devlin 1976:211–230; Lenczowski; Rabinovich 75–96).

The Struggle for Power and Policy (1964–1966)

In the wake of the congress, a see-sawing power struggle unfolded, between radicals and moderates inside the regime and between regime and opposition, focused essentially on the program blueprinted at the congress. This struggle delayed serious implementation of the program for almost two years. At the congress a new party leadership dominated by radicals was elected, and while Aflaq retained the largely figurehead post of secretary-general of the party's Pan-Arab "National Command," Bitar's government was replaced by a radical one under General Amin al-Hafiz. Almost immediately, however, events shifted the balance of power back toward Aflaq and Bitar. After the fall of the Ba'th government in Iraq as a result of a split between civilian radicals and the military, a faction of the Ba'thi Left, led by Syrian Regional Secretary Hamud al-Shufi, attacked the role of Ba'thist officers in politics. The latter joined with Aflaq to purge the Shufi-led radicals and although they were replaced by other civilian leftists, the so-called "regionalists," who enjoyed close ties with the Ba'thi military, the Left as a whole was weakened (ABSP 1972a:92–94; ABSP 1972c:255–274; Kapeliuk 1964:35–43; Devlin 1976:286–289; Torrey 1969:466–467). Then, in the spring of 1964 a major anti-regime rebellion erupted in Syria's cities, especially Hama, in which the whole spectrum of opposition—from Communists, Hawrani's socialists and Nasirites to the Muslim Brothers and the traditional notability—joined hands against the Ba'th. The conservative "Right," which led the rebellion, was chiefly incensed by the unfolding radicalism and secularism of the party, its economic reform decrees, and the rural and minority composition of its leadership, but Nasirites had not given up on union with Egypt or the Left opposition reconciled itself to the Ba'th's monopoly of power. Although the army put down the disturbances, the manifest isolation of the party forced a retreat inside the regime by the Ba'thist Left and permitted the moderates to recover the initiative (Tibawi 415; Abu Jaber 89–91; Rodinson 155–156; Rabinovich 109–117). Bitar formed a new government meant to placate the urban upper and middle classes which promised respect for constitutional liberties and dialogue with Cairo. Affirming that the public sector was now large enough to allow government guidance of the economy, he rejected further nationalizations and invited the cooperation of private capital. Moderate unionists and liberals were coopted into the regime.

As events would show, this alteration of the Ba'th's course was acceptable to neither the opposition or the Ba'thist Left. Most of the political opposition refused to cooperate without a dismantling of Ba'th rule which Bitar could not concede, while the bourgeoisie, lacking confidence in a "socialist" regime it could not control, continued to disinvest, smuggle out capital, and emigrate and without a takeover of the whole heights of the economy, the regime was powerless to stop this hemorrhage. Nor was Bitar's course acceptable to the party Left which argued the bourgeoisie would never be won over without returning power to it and abandoning the mass constituency the party wanted to build. In the power struggle which subsequently took place, the radicals soon recovered the initiative. Still in charge of the party machine, they shifted the balance inside the party through a wholesale recruitment of former rural members still outside the organization and some expulsion of Aflaq partisans, thus further ruralizing and radicalizing the party bases. A parallel struggle in the army, partly ideological, partly over personal power, pitted pro-Aflaq officers led by Muhammed Umran against radicals led by Salah Jedid; when the growing personal rivalry between Amin al-Hafiz, the dominant officer in the regime, and Umran, the senior member of the military committee, led Hafiz to back Jedid, Umran lost out. Bitar was forced to resign, the radicals were restored to government power and in 1965 a drive to carry out socialist transformation was unleashed (Rabinovich 117–145; Devlin 1976:291–296; Razzaz 111–140; Petran 176–179). Massive nationalizations of business and industry brought much of the modern economy into the public sector. Radicalized agrarian reform, already decreed but stalled by the reluctance of the moderates to antagonize the owning classes, was given new impetus. In seeking to curb traditional power in the countryside and win over peasant support, the radicals used the implementation of land reform to begin organizing peasants into a party-controlled peasant union. The nationalizations won the party support among urban labor and enabled it to bring the trade unions under its control. A brief shopkeepers' strike by Muslim activists and merchants was quickly suppressed and grudging support for the "socialist measures" won from Nasirites and the Left. This was a major turning point in the struggle over Syria's future: it marked the breaking of the economic hegemony of the bourgeoisie and the dilution of opposition to the Ba'th regime from the Left.

But the power struggle erupted again inside the party when personal power rivalries split radical officers, giving the moderates one last chance to forestall consolidation of the radical thrust. First Jedid, the military champion of the left, was undermined by a revolt among second rank officers against his growing personal power; then Amin al-Hafiz, in conflict with Jedid over preeminence, and leading a Sunni faction alarmed at minority dominance in the army, joined the moderates and Umran was recalled to high office to further buttress their standing. This shift in the military balance gave the moderates control of enough of the levers of power to undertake the dismissal of the radical government and the radical leadership of the Syrian ("Regional") party organization in the name of the Pan-Arab authority Aflaq still retained. In early 1966, Bitar returned to form a government committed to watering down the radical thrust and, in effect, again proposed a detente with the urban bourgeoisie and liberal and Nasirite middle class. He attacked the Marxist and anti-unionist course dominant in the party since 1963 and proposed to exclude the military from politics: in essence he challenged the dominant faction of the party and its whole conception of the Ba'thi revolution. But the moderates had little base in the ranks of the party and army, and, as they prepared the necessary purges to create one, Jedid and his partisans led a military coup on February 23, 1966 which ousted Hafiz's largely Sunni faction of officers and the historic founders from the party (Petran 180–

182; Aflaq 1971:187–254; Rabinovich 150–208; Devlin 1976:296–303; Razzaz 120–186; MacIntyre 350–387; Kapeliuk 1966).

This final power struggle took the visible form of a personal rivalry between leading officers. It also had a certain civil-military aspect, although in the end officers and politicians were in each opposing camp. Moreover, it had a sectarian dimension: Hafiz, a Sunni, exploited Sunni resentment of minority dominance; Umran, an Alawi, tried to draw Alawites to the moderate camp; and Jedid, an Alawi, used minority fear of Sunni resentment to build his coalition. But there were Sunnis, Alawis, Druzes and Christians on each side. The conflict was, at bottom, over issues—over different views of how radical the Ba'thi revolution should be and how it should deal with the urban opposition; as such, though the struggle took place in a tiny elite arena, it reflected deep class and urban-rural cleavages in Syrian society and was to have major consequences for broad social forces. The party moderates spoke for the urban middle class and sought a reformist road to development in which the state could secure the cooperation of capital and direct it into national development while widening social opportunities for lesser strata. The radicals spoke for the provincial lower middle class and the peasants who sought to demolish the urban establishment in a revolution from above. The power struggle reflected therefore an extension of the urban-rural cleavage into the heart of the party itself and the February coup the transformation of the Ba'th, against the wishes of its founding leaders, into a vehicle of rural revolt. The coup ratified and consolidated the dominant tendency since 1963: the ascendancy of the Ba'thi military over Aflaq's effort to regain control of "his" party, the decisive displacement of the cosmopolitan, Western-educated first generation of party leadership by a second generation of rural and Syrian-educated leaders, and the disproportionate role of minorities in the Ba'th's ruling circles (MacIntyre 205–309). Corresponding to this alteration in elite composition was the death of the liberal-unionist trend in the party and the triumph of social radicalism.

Center-Building: The Obstacles to Institutionalization of a Leninist Party-State

Even as the power struggle was being waged inside the Ba'th, an effort was also going forward to concentrate power and institutionalize authority and decision-making in a set of central party-state organs designed to unite the new elite and direct the revolutionary course. But there were formidable obstacles in the way of regime institution-building.

As a result of the organizational dissolution under the UAR, the "party" came to power, not as a movement bound by an agreed ideology, but as a number of rival factions. Nor were these factions united by an authoritative leadership; elder leaders, such as Aflaq, had some legitimacy but no coercive power at their command while others, such as the relatively unknown officers of the military committee, had power but little legitimacy. At the outset, no "objective" associational ties bound a socially heterogeneous leadership divided by generation, region, and sectarian affiliation. Thus the very conditions under which the regime was born made it exceptionally vulnerable to intra-elite factional conflict. In these circumstances, the use of personal and sectarian kinds of political cement in the building of support was inevitable. Moreover, the assumption of power by coup in the absence of an authoritative party center able to take command, and the leading political roles of active-duty officers in this seizure and in regime governance, made it certain that military force would become a crucial resource in these power struggles.

Establishing institutions able to neutralize factionalism and intra-party use of military force was a major challenge of state formation. The party did have consultative traditions reaching back to the fifties and the 6th National Congress attempted to resurrect them in a Leninist form. "Objective party relations"—that is, the rules of democratic-centralism—were, party doctrine insisted, to govern the political process. Elected congresses would set policy and select and renew the party leadership by majority vote; this leadership was to carry out congress resolutions and all lower party organizations were to be bound by its instructions in the implementation of party policy. The state would be a mere arm of the party and partisans holding state office bound by party discipline. Likewise, Ba'thi officers appointed to the strategic command posts of the military would be subject to party discipline but in return entitled to full participation in party policy-making assemblies. Later, at the 8th National Congress, officers holding active duty commands were forbidden from simultaneously holding high state and party office in an effort to separate military and political authority.

The actual outcome, however, was not institutionalized authority, but a certain duality between authority and power. On the one hand, party institutions acquired some legitimacy and power contenders had to mobilize votes and support in them. The ideological blueprint formulated by the 6th National Congress assumed a definitiveness which could not be readily reversed, and party congresses became important arenas in which factions fought it out and sometimes reached compromises. Without the legitimation acquired through party institutions neither contenders nor their policies could normally prevail. But party legitimacy was undermined by the struggle of factions to use and abuse party procedures for factional advantage. For example, because the party was still re-constructing itself, the admission of new groups could shift the balance of party opinion and, as such, competitors maneuvered to flood party ranks or manipulate elections and pack assemblies with clients and followers, prevent opponents from doing likewise, and purge the latter's clients. Also, the vaguely defined authority relations between the party's all-Arab "National" organs and its subordinate yet autonomous Syrian "Regional" leadership organs—notably the conditions under which the former could "dissolve" the latter—resulted, when the two were controlled by different factions as was often so before 1966, in several "constitutional crises" between these rival institutional bodies. The legitimacy of outcomes of the political process, to the extent they resulted from perceived abuse or bending of the rules, was often contested by losing factions.

Partly because of the fragile institutionalization of procedures and partly because military officers remained key political players (and even when not directly holding army commands, had clients who did) military resources could not be isolated from politics. No credible or decisive hand could be played in party politics without a secure base of military support. Thus, a military politics of transfer, dismissal, appointment, and coalition-building in the army ran parallel to party politics. Because only Ba'thi officers—as opposed to civilian Ba'thists or non-Ba'thi officers—could play a credible hand in *both* party and military arenas, they were uniquely situated as political contenders and every major successful party faction has either been led or championed by an officer-politician. In the end, when disputes could not be resolved in party institutions, the resort to competitive military mobilization proved decisive and the coalition which commanded superior force prevailed: this was so in 1966 and would prove so again in 1970. This, of course, only further undermined the thin layer of institutional legitimacy so painstakingly built up. None of this means that party politics was *reduced* to military politics, but it does mean that a key feature of the Leninist model, the subordination of the gun to the party—to ideology and legality— was never achieved, and hence that a powerful current of praetorianism persisted underneath the fragile shell of institutional legitimacy and procedure built to contain it.

Since procedural legitimacy remained so precarious, the authority of leaders and their bases of support remained very insecure, and opponents were encouraged to constantly work to undermine them. Political rivals were thus driven to build maximum coalitions and to try to minimize those of opponents. In this politics of coalition-formation, survival or victory depended on exploiting every available tie and cleavage: personal, generational, class, regional and, not least, sectarian. In such a situation of insecurity, blocs had a certain natural tendency, in a country were segmentalism and localism were historically deep-rooted, to form among those who, by virtue of personal or primordial ties, felt a greater degree of mutual trust, i.e., often those from the same region and/or sect: hence Alawites, Hauranis, Druzes, etc. often tended to stick together and support each other. This does not mean political factions and conflicts expressed nothing but struggles between regional or sectarian blocs, for rival coalitions were built of a multitude of ties and were fluid, shifting with circumstance and issue, rather than being solid primordial "blocs." There was, in fact, a strong counter-tendency for coalitions to cross-cut sectarian cleavages and to ultimately crystallize along ideological lines. Thus, while in the show-down between the moderates and radicals in 1965–1966, Hafiz, Umran and Jedid all exploited sectarian ties and fears, ideological ties were equally important and the opposing factions were both cross-sectarian, civil-military coalitions. This was to be the case in the next major intra-regime conflict in 1970, too. The evidence suggests that sectarianism was not an end in itself, that is, Ba'thi politics was not essentially a contest for sectarian aggrandizement but was basically over personal power and ideological ends. But the exploitation of personal, regional and, especially sectarian ties and cleavages and, in this climate, the disproportionate representation of sectarian minorities in the elite was inevitably damaging to the cohesion, legitimacy, and institutionalization of the regime. The party was caught in a kind of vicious circle: its initial fragmentation weakened institution-building which, in turn, encouraged further fragmenting behavior. Ultimately, this fragmentation was the obstacle on which the effort to build a Leninist collective leadership foundered (Hinnebusch 1986:74–76).

Dominance of the Radicals:
Revolution from Above (1966–1970)

With the victory of the radicals in 1966, removing the ideological and generational split in the party, a new apparently more cohesive political elite set out to consolidate the regime and the policy orientation of the 6th National Congress. The new regime was presided over by a triumvirate, led by retired Major-General Salah Jedid who became de facto Syrian party secretary, Dr. Nur ad-Din al-Atasi, made head of state and Pan-Arab party secretary, and Dr. Yusuf Zuayyin appointed prime minister. Ending the split between the Pan-Arab and Syrian party organizations, power was concentrated in a combined leadership, a kind of politburo which ran the party and appointed the government and army command along Leninist lines. The new elite legitimized its resort to military force inside the party by accusing the moderates of putting their personal preferences over the decisions of party congresses and of having been turned, by their personal and family connections to the traditional bourgeoisie, against the socialist course. Thus, they had paralyzed the "march of the revolution" for three years.

Leninist political organization now became a major priority. The party apparatus was purged and subjected to increased discipline and recruitment procedures were tightened up to ensure a "popular" class composition; nevertheless by 1968 the party had about 35,000 members. The peasant union and a Ba'thi women's union held their first national congresses and a Ba'th youth federation was under construction. The General Federation of Labor was by now under Ba'thist control and indeed, in several confrontations with the conservative opposition, militant workers mobilized in defense of the "socialist transformation." On the other hand, the party still faced stiff competition from "progressive" rivals in the teacher's and student unions and had made little headway organizing urban artisans and small wage-earners, where opposition movements such as the Ikhwan and Nasirites had their strongholds. Moreover, the major challenge of mobilizing and organizing the peasantry, without which the regime could not hope to consolidate itself, had just begun and no instant breakthrough to the villages was in the cards, as the Ba'thists themselves realized. In fact, Ba'thist writings reveal a certain ambivilance toward the very peasantry they considered their natural constituency:

> The vital field of battle . . . is located in rural areas which are a repository of traditional values which block . . . the development the new state leads.

> Rural society segregates itself, withdraws from participation in the programs
> the state advances . . . because of accumulated [negative] images about gov-
> ernment. . . . Rural society increases its demands on government for services
> . . . as a result of the growing means of communication . . . prior to the
> ability of the state to meet them. In these conditions social strains and political
> clashes happen which the feudalists and capitalists try to exploit. . . . The
> people are now beginning to accept the new state. But some still don't understand
> the socialist system. They [deal with it] in the same [manipulative and mistrustful]
> manner as the traditional system (al-Tal).

The Ba'th had little confidence in the possibility of autonomous development
of this traditional society "from below;" rather development could only
come by state action—agrarian reform, the creation of new rural institutions
and the spread of political awareness through party mobilization.

While in some respects the post-1966 Ba'th regime was more unified than
before and had begun to establish a significant organized base, there were,
nevertheless, early signs that the new edifice was being erected on shaky
grounds. The 1966 "radical" coalition put together by Jedid included elements
which had joined for personal or sectarian reasons rather than out of ideological
commitment. As early as September 1966, the coalition began to seriously
fray when several Druze officers who had participated in the 1966 coup,
feeling themselves excluded from the inner circles of power, joined with
dissidents still loyal to the party elders and Amin al-Hafiz, in an attempted
coup with Jordanian backing. Because elements of the party branch in the
Jabal Druze and of the wider Druze community joined in the rebellion, and
because major Druze partisans were purged in its aftermath and the Druze,
as a major military component of the regime, were largely decimated, the
split took on a clear sectarian dimension, and enhanced Alawi predominance
in the regime (See chapter 8, pp. 244–246 for a more detailed account)
(Be'eri 166–169; Van Dam 67–78).

Despite its precarious grip on power, the regime launched an intensified
drive to put radical ideology into practice in the socio-economic sphere. The
public sector was consolidated, an Economic Penal Code decreed to wipe
out inefficiency and corruption in it, and a state planning apparatus created.
Enforced austerity attempted to put all resources in the service of development.
The Second Five Year Plan (1966–1970) channeled a surge of public
investment into the economy, reversing the economic stagnation from the
continual decline in private investment. It went into basic productive projects:
infrastructure, an oil and petro-chemical industry, and the beginnings of
work on the Euphrates Dam project. The Euphrates project was viewed as
the key to the transformation of agriculture and the development of modern
agro-industry on a large scale. It would, planners believed, double the
irrigated area, absorb excess labor, and provide electricity for agro-industry
(Petran 205–217). Moreover, the party looked forward to constructing a
new socialist society in the reclaimed lands: the Euphrates basin would be
the showcase of Ba'thi agrarian socialism. The decision to build the dam
was to commit Syrian resources, in fact, the lion's share of public investment
in agriculture, to this massive project for years to come.

State reform and control advanced in agriculture in a drive to win over and incorporate the rural sector. The new agrarian reform law halved the amount of land owners could keep, and going beyond the earlier (1958) attack on the greatest magnates, struck at the power of medium landlords. The peasant union identified and secured the dismissal of leftovers from the old regime in the Ministry of Agrarian Reform who had given advance notice of expropriations to landlords, enabling the latter to dispose of excess land. The attitude of the authorities changed from regarding landlords as a respected power to treating them as a class to be broken (Bianquis 1980:81–82); implementation of the land reform, formerly held up by the moderates' fear of antagonizing the landed elite, was de-centralized to local party branches which carried it out in a more radical way. Acceleration of the reform essentially completed land distribution by 1969 (except for areas in the underpopulated Jazirah), clearing the way for cooperatization on a significant scale. In areas where the reform had an impact, it generated a "positive attitude toward the state" (Hammadi). The new agrarian relations law, now for the first time seriously enforced, increased the share going to peasants in sharecropping contracts and strengthened their security of tenure (Atasi 339; Petran 175, 205; Zoubi 1969:50–58). A crisis over farm prices also stimulated new state initiatives: as world agricultural prices, notably for cotton, fell in 1964–1965, state prices also fell, sparking unrest among peasants who blamed it on the regime. In May 1966, the regime decided on a new state marketing system to "stabilize prices and peasant income;" the regime put an effective floor on farm prices and in August cotton prices were actually set above international levels (Hammadi).[1]

The new regime also re-shaped Syria's foreign policy along radical lines, seeking to make Syria the "Hanoi" of an Arab Revolution. The regime helped arm and train Palestinian fedayeen operating against Israel as part of a new determination to support the "liberation of Palestine." It even tried to mobilize and prepare the population for "protracted mass armed struggle" in support of the fedayeen. Propaganda was unleashed against conservative pro-Western states and interests in the region and the Iraq Petroleum Company's pipeline was shut down until it raised transit fees paid to Syria. A close alliance was struck with the Soviet Union which began to give Syria significant military, political and economic support. Finally, in a major diplomatic coup, the regime succeeded in getting Nasir to bury the hatchet and Egypt and Syria drew together in a new "progressive axis" for the first time since the UAR (Jabber 160–173; Rodinson 169–171).

The effect of these policies was to polarize Syrian society. On the one hand, the regime won increased acceptance and legitimacy from the nationalist-left. Major elements of the Communist and Nasirite movements, trade union leaders, and militant nationalist opinion in general were won over, sometimes grudgingly. In the cities "the Ba'th regime, aided by workers' militias, trade unions and communist militants, succeeded in crushing bourgeois resistance to the new order." (Rouleau 170). Sporadic conflict between peasants and landlords in the countryside reflected the extension of land reform and peasant political organization. Peasants were often trucked into the cities, flooding the streets with banners and militant chants to render a sense of legitimacy to the regime and intimidate urban enemies (Khalaf 114). An influx of rural youth arrived in the cities—in "caravans" as Jundi put it— to make their claims on the spoils of the revolution or to take advantage of widening educational opportunities. Enrollment at Damascus University was doubled in the five years after the 1963 coup and by 1968 half of its student body was rural in origin. The cities were being "ruralized" (Devlin 1983:23, 121). According to Hreib (136–137), the regime deliberately encouraged a shift in the demographic balance in the capital; certainly these rural youth, the Ba'th's natural constituency, helped the party entrench itself in Syria's hostile urban environment.

The notability, the merchants, and conservative opinion generally were increasingly alienated by a Ba'th in which the moderate urban founding leaders had been displaced by uncultured heterodox rurals who the urban establishment was used to regarding as inferior; bitter jokes, featuring aggressive and rude villagers, often Alawites, in power, circulated among the Damascene bourgeoisie. Land reform and the drive to substitute a state-cooperative agricultural infrastructure for the old landlord-merchant ones was depriving the city establishment of a traditional source of wealth and influence in the villages. Nationalization of industries, the state takeover of foreign trade and segments of domestic trade, its severe restrictions on imports, and its efforts to fix prices and regulate the market, damaged the whole business community, setting off a kind of covert economic warfare between the government and the merchant community. University students from urban families, fearing political discrimination, were much less optimistic about their future prospects than rural ones (Abyad 1968). Waves of emigration, a sign of a true revolution, decimated the ranks of the bourgeoisie, with thousands going into exile in Beirut (Rouleau 169–170). An "uncompromising secularism which drove religion out of public life" inflamed urban opposition (Tibawi 420). In the spring of 1967, merchants, ulama', and other religious protesters took to the streets in major anti-regime disturbances against radical secularism, deeply embarrassing a regime which could ill afford to stir up broad-based Islamic hostility (Petran 197–198).

Despite the hostility of established society, the Ba'th might well have continued its radical course; but the 1967 defeat by Israel and the loss of Quneitra province, checked and gradually reversed the radicalization of Syrian politics. In their haste to challenge Israel at a time when neither Syria—its army decimated by political purges and engrossed in politics—or a disunited Arab world were prepared for war, the radical Ba'thists invited the massive Israeli onslaught. The regime's dismal military performance and the lower priority it seemed to give to defense of the front than to the regime in Damascus, greatly diminished its nationalist legitimacy. The loss of Quneitra became a permanent reproach to the Ba'th. The defeat demoralized the party rank and file and, gravely weakening the radicals' leadership, provided the conditions for an intra-party challenge to them.

The radical leadership was determined to continue the "revolutionary course," internally mobilizing the population for national resistance, externally making Syria an obstacle to any political settlement of the Arab-Israeli conflict at the expense of Palestinian rights and a bastion of support for the fedayeen in spite of the dangers from Israeli reprisals. The radicals were, however, gradually undermined by several post-war developments. Their course entailed Syrian isolation from much of the Arab world, not only from the oil states which were promising to bankroll the military reconstruction of the front-line states in return for an end to ideological warfare, but from Egypt as well once Nasir accepted a political settlement. The USSR which was urging a political settlement, too, could not be counted on to back a strategy of interminable military confrontation and, indeed, its reluctance to adequately supply the Syrian army undermined radicals identified with the Soviet alliance. When, in 1968, pro-Aflaq Ba'thists seized power in Iraq, their pressures generated tremendous tensions inside the Syrian party. Much of the progressive opposition, which had begun to acquiesce in Ba'th dominance, found in the defeat ample reason to reject its claim to special "leading" status, and challenges by various leftist factions to the regime were repressed; this, as the Ba'th acknowledged, produced a "division in the loyalties of the masses." The shattering of regime legitimacy by the defeat spread like a stain over every undertaking of the party and government. As the 10th National Congress (1968) had to admit, the "mistakes in application" which "beset the march of the revolution . . . exploited by counter-revolution" had "undermined the confidence of the people in their revolutionary leadership." This was producing apathy and cynicism: "it is not easy to free the masses of their historic passiveness or to change their conception of the ruling authority" (ABSP 1968). In the longer run, the defeat of Arab nationalism in 1967 weakened what had been the dominant ideology in Syria, leaving a certain ideological vacuum which in time would give credibility hitherto lacking to an Islamic alternative.

Most immediately important, however, recriminations inside the regime over responsibility for the disaster and the proper strategy for coping with it soon shattered the unity of the ruling elite, dividing more ideologically-minded politicos from the military command which bore most immediate responsibility for coping with the Israeli threat. The first sign of this was an attempted coup by the former chief of staff, Ahmad Suwaydani, who had been dismissed on account of the army's poor performance, and who fled to Iraq with a following of Sunni Haurani officers (Van Dam 78–79). The next was the growth of a faction led by the Defense Minister, General Hafiz al-Asad, which sought to suspend the "revolutionary struggle" because, in dividing Syrians and Arabs, it diverted them from their main enemy, Israel, and the "main challenge of the phase," recovery of the lost territories. Asad first challenged the radical leadership at the 4th Regional Congress in 1968 where he insisted that the buildup of the regular army for a military recovery of the Golan had to be the regime's first priority. This required detente with the conservative Arab monarchies which alone could finance this buildup and with hostile Jordan and Iraq whose armies could contribute to the "Eastern Front." Internally, class conflict had to be subordinated to the national unity needed for total war mobilization. Against this, the radicals argued that all Arab resources could never be mobilized without a Pan-Arab revolution and that concentration on recovery of the Golan would lead to giving up on the liberation of Palestine. Asad also wanted an end to political interference in the army—in essence to party control over his right to rebuild the army and reintegrate officers purged for political reasons as he saw fit. While the congress rejected a change in high policy, Asad was temporarily appeased by giving him some of the military powers he demanded, though such personal control over the army risked making it a separate power base threatening to legitimate party institutions. Neither side, however, really accepted this compromise: the radicals tried to neutralize Asad's supporters in the party organization while he built up his faction in the army at their expense and used it to interfere in party affairs. In early 1969, this struggle intensified as Asad responded to a purge of his supporters in the Latakia branch with an arrest of the branch command and sent tanks into the streets of Damascus. An emergency party congress which met to deal with this "crisis," being divided between supporters of the two camps and fearing a coup, acceded to Asad's demands rather than attempt a counter-mobilization of loyal army units. Asad insisted on reconciliation with the opposition, more serious military preparations, and detente with other Arab states, notably Iraq. A new government was formed in which partisans of the two sides shared authority, but in fact a virtual "duality of power" only intensified, as each faction scrambled to shore up its control over the regime institutions in its hands and to win needed support where it was lacking; thus, the radicals tried to develop the party-sponsored Palestinian organization, *al-Sa'iqa*, into an armed force able to counter Asad's tanks, while he quietly courted second rank party apparatchiki. The result was a vacuum of authority and policy-making: the party appeared as a "body with two heads and two brains and so only able to march in place," party discipline declined, and corruption and clientelist networks proliferated (Petran 195–204, 239–248; Seymour; Gaspard 1969a, 1969b; Kerr 1975; Van Dam 83–97; ABSP 1970; Torrey 1970).

This political crisis was paralleled by failures and gaps in the "socialist transformation," economic malaise, and conflicts over the proper development policy between the two wings of the party. While the radicals insisted on pursuit of their massive development program, General al-Asad had simultaneously won a big increase in defense expenditures, straining the resources of the regime. Foreign exchange shortages, combined with inefficiencies and corruption in state foreign and internal trade bodies and hoarding by black marketers, led to growing scarcities. In agriculture, the completion of land reform had yet to bring major relief to peasants because of dismal weather and since the establishment of cooperatives and a credit and marketing infrastructure to replace landlords and capitalists lagged behind. The latter, fearing another land reform, alienated by the increases in minimum agricultural wages decreed by the regime, low state prices for some crops, and barriers to imports of equipment, were disinvesting from agriculture. Where peasants lacked the means to carry on, they rented their holdings back to landlords and rich peasants or merchants loaned credit under the old conditions. The combined effects of landlord disinvestment, big gaps in the state agrarian infrastructure, and several years of poor rainfall, was agricultural stagnation. All this fueled a conflict between the two party wings over whether to respond to these difficulties by deepening the agrarian revolution or liberalizing agricultural policy. The radicals proposed a third land reform to check the continuing exploitation by landowners, "kulaks," and middlemen of poor peasants and agricultural workers. The Asad faction, however, putting priority, in the name of defense, on the need to maintain production, already disorganized by the incomplete earlier reform, opposed this initiative. It is, in any case, doubtful whether the politically precarious regime could have afforded to thus alienate the "middle forces" in the countryside, from which a portion of its political base had in fact been recruited (ABSP 1972b). The two wings also differed over disposal of the vast state lands expropriated in the Jazirah which the regime lacked the means to organize in cooperatives or state farms. The Asad "liberals" wished to enhance state revenues and agricultural production by renting these territories out to entrepreneurs, but the radicals blocked this for fear of the "social consequences" of such a move, i.e. the resurgence of the power of the agrarian bourgeoisie. Asad pointedly blamed the agrarian stagnation on the radicals, observing that they had turned Syria from a historic exporter into an importer of grain. The duality of power in the party prevented a clear choice of radicalization or liberalization. The decline of party discipline which accompanied it also encouraged corruption which undermined the regime's agrarian policy. In Hama, a corrupted local party leadership did nothing to aid beneficiaries of state land who fell into debt to moneylenders and the agricultural bank until peasant disturbances captured national attention, spurring the establishment of cooperatives. In Hassaka, a corrupt governor who had collaborated with landlords to undermine the agrarian reform, was protected by a clique of friends in the army and only removed with great difficulty. The effort of the radical leadership to activate the peasant union against corrupt or heavy-handed bureaucrats bore little visible fruit in this environment.

The duality of power came to a head during "Black September" of 1970 when the radicals ordered the intervention of army units in defense of Palestinian fedayeen under attack by Jordan. When Asad, deterred by US and Israeli threats, refused to commit air power in their support, and then ordered a series of military transfers neutralizing the last military bases of the radicals, the party leadership called an emergency party congress and dismissed him and Chief of Staff Mustafa Tlas from their posts. This brought the final break in the regime. Asad responded with a military coup deposing the radicals and bringing his own faction to sole power. Despite their control of the party apparatus and its "popular organizations," the radicals could do nothing but mobilize ineffectual demonstrations, no match for the army with its monopoly of the ultimate resort. The fragility of the Ba'th's mobilizational effort was exposed by its failure to offer any real resistance to Asad's military coup: unable to transcend a style of "action from above," its organizations remained, at once, too bureaucratic and too riddled with personalistic cliques to mobilize the intense popular activism which might have made a difference in the internal power struggle. Thus, when the legitimacy of party institutions and the holders of coercive power were confronted in the starkest fashion, the latter triumphed. This marked the failure of the effort to create a Leninist state center in Ba'thist Syria. Nevertheless while the political energies of the radicals had been quickly exhausted, they left a permanent mark on Syria.

The radical Ba'th left behind a stronger more autonomous state center. A set of ruling institutions had been forged which concentrated power as never before. The Ba'th state rested on a larger, nationalist-minded and Ba'thized army. A well-organized ideological party had been erected which was incorporating a popular base and in which a distinctive policy orientation was partially "routinized"—a preference for etatist solutions, a deep distrust of private capital and a residual populism which would not quickly dissipate. It presided over a bureaucracy with a much enlarged scope of functions, enhanced capacity to mobilize societal resources for state goals, a growing tradition of state planning, and a large public sector which had become the main channel of investment in the economy. Thus, the state whose helm Asad inherited was a far sturdier structure than the fragile entity the Ba'th had seized in 1963. But, besides the creation of new structures, the trans-formation in the social composition of the state, the re-orientation of policy to serve its mass base, and the leveling of the social terrain on which it rested were crucial in giving the state a wholly new power, autonomy of the dominant societal forces, and impact on Syrian society.

In a real sense, the radicals made the Ba'th party into a vehicle of rural "uprising" which captured, remade, and used the state against the Sunni establishment in the cities. Its policies expressed the powerful hostility to "feudalism" and "capitalism" out of which the Ba'th grew up and the interests of the largely rural constituency it was trying to organize. The incorporation of the mobilized rural minorities, especially the Alawites, historically the most downtrodden of Syria's social forces, into the state gave Ba'thi socialism a kind of surrogate proletariat with nothing to lose and everything to gain from the transformations the Ba'th was carrying out; the famous assertions attributed to Alawite officers (Be'eri 337) that socialism allowed the rural minorities to "impoverish the town" just as capitalism operated to the advantage of the Sunni city, reflected a very real social reality: a land-poor impoverished community, possessing nothing but its drive for education and careers, had everything to gain by the establishment of a state-dominated economy which would divert control of opportunities from the private bourgeoisie. Similarly, in growing sectors of rural Syria, land reform, rural political organization and the decimation of feudal power were giving the peasantry—the majority of it Sunni—a stake in the new regime. In short, while the base of the Ba'th remained narrow, it was nevertheless deeply rooted, one trunk firmly implanted in the minority communities, a web of smaller but broader roots in hundreds of villages.

To this extent, the radical Ba'th enterprise reflected Syria's urban-rural cleavage, pitting a ruling plebeian coalition of the rural petit bourgeoisie and peasantry against a patrician-led opposition of landlord and suq, with the urban middle class wavering between these poles. The durable result was the demolishing of urban dominance over the state.

In another sense the radical Ba'th enterprise was an expression of class conflict. The urban-rural cleavage was itself shaped by the capitalist class relationships by which landlord and suq had subordinated the village. Moreover, the radical Ba'th launched a social structural transformation of Syria which had a far broader impact than a simple rural displacement of urban elites. Though it would only mature under Asad and though it fell well short of socialist ideals, this structural revolution amounted to a major social leveling. In essence, agrarian reform, nationalizations, and the creation of a large state sector demolished rigid class inequalities rooted in monopolistic control of the means of production and more broadly diffused property and opportunity. Thus, land reform, as Table 5.1 indicates, radically narrowed the scope of latifundia capitalism, checked the forced proletarianization of the peasantry, and created a mixed small peasant and medium capitalist agrarian structure. In eschewing a more thorough equalization of land holdings and permitting the preservation of medium-sized estates, the regime failed to make enough land available to wipe out landlessness and create a prosperous middle peasantry. But it broadened the small holding sector and in the seventies cooperatives and the agrarian bureaucracy channeled the resources into the villages needed to consolidate and link small peasant holdings to the state. In addition, an enormous increase in access to education and in the size and socio-economic role of the bureaucracy and public sector made the state a major channel of upward mobility for modest strata. Between 1964 and 1977, primary school students and teachers more than doubled, raising the proportion of the school age population attending from 58% to 86%, and similar increases happened at the intermediate and secondary level. Enrollment in universities grew from 25,600 in 1964 to 109,000 in 1983. Many graduates were channeled into the state which, by the eighties, employed one in every five persons (Drysdale 1981a:102; SAR 1984:92–94, 385).

TABLE 5.1 Pre- and Post-Reform Agrarian Structure

	Pre-Reform		Post-Reform	
	% Pop.	%Owned land surface	% Pop.	%Owned land surface
Large (100+)	1.0	50.0	0.5	17.7
Medium (10-100)	9.0	37.0	15.3	58.7
Small (<10)	30.0	13.0	48.0	23.6
Landless	60.0	0.0	36.1	0.0

Source: Hinnebusch 1989:110.

TABLE 5.2   Indicators of Change in Syrian Class Structure, 1960 to 1970*

	1960		1970	
	#	%	#	%
Industrial & Commercial Bourgeoisie	19,750	2.2	10,890	0.7
Rural Bourgeoisie	39,640	4.5	8,360	0.6
Salaried Middle Class	132,530	15.0	234,930	16.0
Traditional Petty Bourgeoisie	110,900	12.5	216,090	14.7
Working Class	159,720	17.9	257,380	17.6
Small Peasantry	243,460	27.4	608,540	41.5
Agricultural Proletariat	182,720	20.5	130,400	8.9

*Numbers refer to economically active population.
Source: Adapted from Longuenesse 1979:4.

Increased fluidity of opportunity and diffusion of property gave rise to a significant increase in the middle strata while narrowing the top and very bottom of the social structure. This is captured by the figures in Table 5.2 contrasting social structure before and after radical Baʿth rule. There was a decline in the bourgeoisie, not only in its wealth and power, but even in its numbers through downward mobility or exit from Syria. There was a corresponding expansion in the state-dependent salaried middle and working classes, increasing from 32.9% of the economically active population in 1960 to 33.6% in 1970 and 37.8% in 1975 (World Bank v. 2:90). A significant portion of the landless agricultural proletariat was raised up and transformed into a small holding peasantry. There was also an expansion in the "petite bourgeoisie" of small self-employed artisans and merchants. Finally, hidden behind these statistics is a still more complex social reality; individuals— and even more so families—tended to bridge these various strata. Thus, a public sector worker might "moonlight" as a petty private operator or a peasant work seasonally in a public sector factory. A peasant family might pool resources and one brother work the family land, while another sought government office or public sector work, and a third invested in a petty business. If one considers state employees, small-holding peasants, and blue collar workers with a foot in petty commerce, services or artisanship to fall, in a broad sense, in the petite bourgeoisie, this class appeared to become numerically dominant, and, in the establishment of Baʿthism as the official credo, ideologically ascendant.

These structural changes had enormous political consequences. The leveling of the top, the rise of state-controlled opportunities, and the dispersion of property created or widened strata which were either state dependent or beholden to the state for their advancement or survival and structurally incorporated into it; in this way, social reform helped rebuild and cement a Baʿthist alliance of salaried middle class and peasantry. Moreover, the demolishing of the class control of the landed-mercantile bourgeoisie over the state and the assault on the class structure, together, made for a leveled and fluid socio-economic terrain more compatible with state autonomy of class power and more amenable to control by the state.

But, while the radical Ba'th state was in certain ways deeply rooted in the interests and grievances of rural society, the majority of the population, and was on the way to incorporating much wider middle strata, it had, in addition to the failure to subordinate the military to party rule, two fatal weaknesses. First, it had incurred the unremitting hostility of the dominant urban forces. Not only the landed notability, but merchants of all sizes were made to pay the heaviest costs of Ba'th policies. Generally, the socio-economic policies of the radicals and the austere atmosphere of political repression and egalitarian leveling they imposed on Syria's cities alienated large sectors of the upper and middle classes whose money and skills were needed to develop Syria. And the city remained a formidable power, barely under control of the Ba'thi state, politically concentrated and mobilized as the countryside could not be, and dangerous to any regime which could not satisfy it. The second major weakness was that the radical's strategy of "protracted struggle" for the liberation of Palestine and export of revolution isolated Syria in the Arab world and internationally and invited Israeli reprisals against which Syria could not defend itself. There was an obvious contradiction in the radicals' insistence on an ambitious development drive and a provocative policy toward Israel which imposed permanent heavy defense burdens and was likely to bring on a war which would jeopardize the whole development effort. The radical regime simply failed to develop the power to sustain its course in the face of internal recalcitrance and external threat. It could not make the public sector into an instrument for the extraction of a sufficient economic surplus to decisively displace private capitalism and sustain defense burdens. Nor did it develop the mobilizational capacity for mass armed struggle with Israel. It would be these two vulnerabilities of the radical Ba'th's strategy which Asad's alteration of course would address—in a policy of reconciliation with the city, internally, and a "realist" and more effective foreign policy, externally.

The course of Syria's post-1963 revolution resembled in certain striking ways France's "great revolution." As in France, the revolutionary coalition split, with plebeian "radicals" (Jacobins) seizing the initiative from more socially established and wavering moderates. The radical Ba'thists, armed with revolutionary ideology, turned the state from a patrician dominated arena into a command post of class war over the means of production, issuing in a deliberate class polarization of society and a social structural revolution. This revolution, incorporating a mass base into the state and leveling the power and privilege of the old classes, paved the way for a powerful state above society. But in its excesses, it precipitated a conservative Thermidor, giving rise to a nationalist General who promised an end to internal conflict, defense of the nation against foreign enemies, and a new post-revolutionary order. Thus arose under Asad a kind of "Bonapartist" regime.

The Consolidation of Ba'th Rule Under Asad

The elite faction Asad brought to power was initially indistinguishable in social composition from the radicals: both were cross-sectarian, civil-military coalitions led by Alawi political generals. But each was supported by distinct segments of society: the radicals by leftist intellectuals and trade unionists, Asad by senior army officers and the bourgeoisie. In fact, Asad's rise marked the victory of the military over the radical intelligentsia. There followed a corresponding re-orientation of the state from an instrument of class revolution to a machinery of elite power "above" classes and in the service of *raison d'état*—state consolidation and war mobilization.

At the 1971 Eleventh National Congress, Asad led a ideological and policy revision. He insisted that the regime had no intention of changing the "nationalist socialist line," and characterized his coup as a "corrective movement" within the revolution which would merely restore it to the true path. But, in fact, from this time the regime abandoned the effort to carry the revolution forward either inside or outside Syria. Instead, the objective "for the advancement of which all resources and manpower [would be] mobilized [was] the liberation of the occupied territories" (ABSP 1971); their recovery through some combination of war and diplomacy became the overriding pre-occupation of the regime. From this change flowed a whole series of others: a foreign policy seeking detente with conservative Arab oil states and alignment with Egypt, a necessary partner in any war to recover the Golan, a priority to military buildup which dictated continued close alliance with the Soviet Union, but a willingness to explore diplomatic openings to the United States. In a bid to appease the Syrian bourgeoisie, maximize production, and attract Arab aid and investment, economic policy was liberalized, paring back state controls over foreign trade and imports and encouraging the re-activation of the dormant private sector, although without prejudice to the dominant role of the state (Hinnebusch 1984a:305–308). In agriculture, the policy of the new regime proceeded on two separate tracks: on the one hand, there was no slackening in the effort to put in place a state-cooperative infrastructure incorporating the small peasantry; on the other hand, agricultural investment by the bourgeoisie was now encouraged and state lands in the Jazirah rented out to entrepreneurs. The result of these policies and a break in the bad weather, was an economic boom and a revitalization of the private bourgeoisie.

Asad's policies significantly broadened the base of the Ba'th regime. A purge of radical leaders swept the party, but most rank and file Ba'this chose accommodation with the new leadership which continued to expand the party's organized mass base; Asad thus maintained the core of the regime. At the same time, he permitted relatively free elections to local councils in which opposition victories were tolerated, and to a newly formed Peoples Assembly into which a spectrum of opinion going beyond the regime's core constituency, was coopted. This, economic liberalization, the opening to conservative Arab states, a muting of radical secularism, Asad's public deportment as a pious Muslim, and a palpable political relaxation, all helped win the acquiescence of sections of bourgeois and conservative middle class opinion in Ba'th rule. Important elements of the "progressive opposition"— Nasirites, Communists, "Hawrani socialists"—were coopted into a National Progressive Front in which the dominant Ba'th promised to consult with them and accorded them a share of state office; detente with Egypt went far to win the cooperation of the Nasirite factions. All these measures were designed to appease and accommodate urban society to Ba'th rule (Gaspard 1971; Kerr 1975; Yodfat; Petran 249–257; Howard 1972).

The limits of this accommodation were sharply underlined by major disturbances which broke out at the 1973 unveiling of a new constitution which preserved the "leading" role of the Ba'th Party in the political system and which failed to designate Islam as the religion of the state. Although Asad conceded the designation of Islam as the religion of the president, while insisting on his own disputed credentials as a Muslim, the opposition had to be crushed with force (Donahue; Kelidar). But the souring of state-urban relations was checked by the outbreak of the October 1973 war with Israel which rallied Syrians behind their government and—because of the regime's creditable military performance and the new diplomatic stature achieved by Syria—won the regime a significant fund of nationalist legitimacy. The economic boom sparked, in the aftermath of the war, by the influx of Arab oil money and a wave of migration for high-paying jobs in the Gulf also helped accommodate Syrians, especially those in the best position to profit—merchants, middle class professionals, skilled workers—to the regime.

Presidential Monarchy

Asad used the initiative he seized in 1970 and the political capital accumulated thereafter to reshape the Ba'th state—from a failed experiment in Leninism into a hybrid regime which subordinated the Ba'th Party to an authoritarian "Presidential Monarchy." The new priority put on state consolidation over revolution and awareness of the factional fragility of collegial leadership led the new elite to explicitly opt for a strong presidential regime. Asad succeeded in making the presidency the undisputed command post of the Ba'th state and, through it, concentrating personalized authority in his hands; thus he raised himself above the rest of the elite and the power institutions of the state—party "politburo," army high command, and council of ministers (Dawisha 1978a). Personal replaced collective leadership.

Asad's personality and outlook have, as such, left a special imprint on public policy since then. Asad is, first of all, an intense nationalist, strongly committed to the Arab cause, preoccupied by the military and strategic power balance in the contest with Israel, and determined to harness Syria's resources to it. He would like to be viewed as an Arab nationalist leader comparable in stature to Nasir. But Asad is a realist rather than an ideologue; unconvinced that the balance of forces favored either the creation of a full blown socialist state or a messianic liberation of Palestine, he played the central role in the ascendence of raison d'état over revolutionary zeal in the

Ba'th regime. His cautious style is quite distinct from that of the radicals who challenged powerful interests regardless of the consequences. But, tough and tenacious, Asad is also a ruthless Machiavellian prepared to use any means to attain his more realistic ends. Little touched by Westernization, he shows no interest in political liberalism; but he is nevertheless prepared to conciliate opposition interests where possible. He has sought to accommodate the Syrian commercial tradition, but is unwilling to reverse core Ba'thist reforms or restore the power of the bourgeoisie over the state. Determined, intelligent, energetic, able to learn from mistakes, and with a keen interest in international affairs, he has developed into a statesman of more than local stature and turned Syria from a pawn of stronger states into a credible actor in the regional power game (Ma'oz 1975, 1978).

Asad's dominance has been built on several bases. He enjoys, among regime elites, a unique public stature, respected for his combination of astuteness, conciliatory pragmatism, and ruthlessness. He holds the reins of the three major power institutions, leading the party as its general secretary, and, in his capacity as president, enjoying full powers to appoint and dismiss governments and military commands. He took and preserves his power through alliances with key senior Sunni military officers and party politicos: men such as Abd al-Halim Khaddam, Hikmat al-Shihabi, Naji Jamil, Abdullah al-Ahmar, and Mustafa Tlas. Anxious to placate the urban Sunni center—Damascene society—and the middle class as a whole, he deliberately coopted significant numbers of Damascenes into the top ranks of the party and many non-party technocrats into the government. Finally, he constructed a network of personal Alawite clients dominating the strategic levers of the military-police apparatus, including several praetorian guard units and intelligence organs. It is this personal power base with its formidable coercive assets which has made Asad unchallengable within the elite and which, with its special stake in regime survival, presents an obdurate shield to coups or uprisings. The leaders of this military/security network have included the president's brother Rifat, intelligence chiefs such as Muhammad al-Khuli and Ali Duba, and division commanders like Shafiq Fayyad (Batatu 1981). Finally, as ideology faded as a political cement, Asad made increasing use of patronage/ corruption to bind all elements of the elite to him and give them a stake in the regime.

Asad's strategy of power consolidation has altered the character of the elite. The subordination of the collegial party leadership in which all groups were represented to an Alawi president buttressed by an Alawi coercive apparatus accountable only to him represented a significant increase in Alawi power under Asad. The Alawis' dominance of top military posts and their self-serving use of power have since constituted the major threat to elite cohesion and intra-elite sectarian tensions have displaced ideological divisions as the most overt form of intra-elite cleavage under Asad; but Asad has been careful not to be identified as leader of an Alawite block in the regime, and instead brokers sectarian rivalries to his own advantage. To a considerable extent the top elite under Asad came to be dominated by two groups, the

Alawi officers in the president's inner core and the Damascene Sunnis at the top of the party and state machinery. This altered the former rural domination of the state. But the broader elite has continued to be drawn from a wide range of regions and sectarian groups. Thus, while in the powerful military party leadership Sunnis (43.4%) and Alawites (37.7%) shared dominant power, in the cabinet, the representation of communities was more closely proportional to their population: thus from 1963–1978, Sunnis held 58.2% of positions, Alawites 20%, Druzes 10.6%, Isma'ilis 6.5%, and Christians 4.7% (Van Dam 126–129). Nor have provincial rurals been squeezed out: indeed in the late eighties, many Dera Ba'this emerged at the top of the party and state pyramids.

The levers of state power have given Asad and his associates increasing control over society. Elite power derived from a formidable institutional structure, including a party apparatus incorporating at least a hundred thousand members in the early seventies, a large, well-equipped, increasingly disciplined professional army, and a massive state bureaucracy which controlled the vast public sector. The state enjoyed large concentrated financial resources compared to the fragmented private sector and remained the main engine of investment. Besides its control of much of the means of production (land and factories), the receipt of large quantities of Arab aid and oil revenues— so much "rent" at the disposal of the regime for elite aggrandizement, patronage and development—gave the state a second economic base and made it an engine of distribution. But the emergence of this formidable state was only possible because of the preceding revolution which leveled rival sources of independent social power, incorporated a dependent middle class and peasantry, and eroded class solidarities which could become vehicles for challenging state power.

The resulting state center is a complex structure: a "presidential monarchy" resting on the remnants of Leninist party leadership, bureaucratic authority, and military command. In forging it, Asad employed a mixed strategy of power building. He used "traditional" techniques of rule, with long roots in the political culture: primordial political cement—*asabiya*—to forge a reliable elite core, patronage and cooptation, and the playing off of segments of a divided elite and society. But these means were used to serve the expansion of modernizing state power, not traditionalizing ends. And he also employed "modern" political technology—party ideology and organi- zation, bureaucratic rationality—in consolidating state control over society. Through this combination, he incorporated into the state a broad array of interests—the army, the minorities, sections of the bourgeoisie, much of the peasantry and working class, and large sections of the salaried middle class, all of whom had some stake in the regime. This coalition of urban and rural social forces buttressed a more stable although no more institutionalized center of authority than hitherto. This regime, standing above and balancing both established interests and populist constituency, might appropriately be called "Bonapartist."

Limited Liberalization, Elite Embourgeoisement

In the aftermath of the October war, the Asad regime pursued two potentially contradictory policies, military build-up and economic liberalization, which further altered the state. First, the preoccupation of the President and the military inner core with diplomacy and defense in the struggle with Israel continued after 1973. Particularly as Egypt embarked on a separate peace, Syria became increasingly entangled in efforts to build alternative alliances in the Arab East, embroiling it in Lebanon and with the PLO; Asad was also determined to achieve military parity with Israel. An ever increasing proportion of Syria's resources were channeled into a mushrooming national security state with an enormous proportion of the population under arms and reaching into every corner of the economy (Picard 1979b). The military absorbed a large proportion of public revenues which might otherwise have gone to economic development, although Syria's frontline status made it eligible for massive Arab aid, relieving the regime of a radical choice between development and defense and of the imperative of forced extraction from society. But the political weight of the military inevitably grew with its size.

Economic policy, subordinating socialist ideology to economic pragmatism, sought to stimulate growth and appease the bourgeoisie and the middle class, yet preserve the ability of the regime to control the economy and mobilize resources. Economic liberalization opened Syria to Western imports, fueling a consumption boom and the proliferation of a comprador bourgeoisie. As, after 1974, Arab aid and Western loans poured into Syria, a major industrialization drive was launched. Since much of this revenue was channeled through government, the dominance of the state sector was at least nominally sustained. In some sectors, like internal trade and construction, state firms actually expanded their domains. But the state turned over implementation of much of its development program to foreign firms and local contractors, fueling a growing linkage between the state and private capital.

The class composition of the elite was increasingly altered in the late seventies by the cumulative effects of economic liberalization: a new bourgeoisie was being generated in the "heart" and "shadow" of the state. The channeling of massive external revenues through the state, expended in contracts with and purchases from private and foreign firms, created growing opportunities for outright embezzlement by the elite and webs of shared interests in commissions and kickbacks between high officials, politicians, and business interests. Black market operations, fueled by the virtual incorporation of eastern Lebanon under the control of Syrian military officers, mushroomed. The political and military elite was using its power to enrich itself while the private bourgeoisie was finding opportunities to translate wealth into a certain political influence. Within the elite, the Alawis and the Damascenes were best situated to profit. The enrichment of the Alawi elite turned one of the previously strongest forces for radical change in the regime into a group with privileges to defend and a major obstacle to reform of the abuses enveloping the state. Through the Damascene connection a regime which began as a rebellion against the establishment was becoming a partner with families of old and new business wealth in the capital. A 1978 political "opening to the right" started to relax political controls over the bourgeoisie, coopted conservative figures into government, and, had it continued, might have revitalized the rubber stamp parliament. Thus, the political elite was being embourgeoised and the former sharp antagonism between it and the private bourgeoisie was being bridged; new inequalities were replacing those demolished in the sixties and the political elite, as it acquired a stake in them, was being differentiated from its populist constituency (Picard 1979a).

Elite Politics Under Asad

The consolidation of Presidential Monarchy, resting on a mixture of patrimonial techniques and institution-building, and the advance of elite embourgeoisement changed the face of politics in Ba'thist Syria. The ideological and class politics of the sixties receded. The ideologues who presided over the early Ba'th were eclipsed by technocrats and patronage-driven politicos who ceased to take sides in social conflicts and instead sought to stay above, balance, and play off the various social forces in the political arena. Inside the regime, ideological conflict was superseded by personal, sectarian and bureaucratic rivalries, pragmatic debates over economic management, and above all a preoccupation with foreign policy issues. In this climate, which still persists, politics tends to take three typical forms.

Concentrated at the top is decision-making in matters of *high policy*, that is, defense and foreign affairs, grand economic strategy, and issues of internal security. High policy is shaped in good part by raison d'état, that is, elite determination to protect the legitimacy, resources, capabilities, and territorial integrity of the state. It is made by the President and an inner circle of key military, government, and party leaders. Although these men are not quite mere staff whom Asad can dismiss or ignore at will, neither do most have independent bases of power which could challenge the presidency; hence Asad decides who to include in the consultative process, and, while he often takes pains to lead in a consensual manner, he has the last—and frequently the first—word. Influential groups in the army and party appear to have restrained Asad's initiatives on key occasions, e.g. in the Israeli-Syrian disengagement agreement; he also made sure to commit the whole elite to the intervention in Lebanon (Sheehan; Dawisha 1978b). But no member of the elite has successfully challenged the consensus he leads and remained in power. Rifat al-Asad did try to build an independent base of power and position himself as an advocate of policies to the right of this consensus; but this contributed to his downfall. While, officially, party congresses are still supposed to design or at least approve high policy, in fact, in those key issue areas where Asad has chosen to take an initiative—e.g. economic liberalization, the diplomatic opening to the U.S., the intervention in Lebanon— they merely ratified what were often *faits accomplis*.

The President, however, husbands his power and has allowed many lesser matters to be decided by subordinate elites and in the institutions of the Ba'th state, leaving scope for two other kinds of "politics." *Patrimonial politics* is run from close to the apex of the political establishment where elites preside over *shillas* and clientelist networks which take their cut of public resources and dispense patronage. The struggle over this patronage has become a good part of what elite politics is about: e.g. rivalries between opposing coalitions of high officials and supplier agents over control of the contract tender process and the commissions at stake in it. This process is dominated by senior Ba'th officers, especially Alawis, who, with a foot in both army and party and unparalleled access to the president, are powerful brokers and patrons; second only to them are the Damascene Sunnis politicos with their connections to the Sunni business community.

The tentacles of clientelism reach downward through the structures of the state, incorporating many middle and sub-elites and their clients into the patronage game; the incorporation of a large populist constituency into the regime and the emergence of a massive state bureaucracy controlling much of the economy and distributing oil "rent," greatly widened rivalry for access to state patronage. The struggle for patronage puts a premium on personal connections and, of course, regional and sectarian ties are the route of least resistance in establishing such connections. Thus, the clash of ideology and class has been superseded by the search of individuals and small groups for patronage, privilege and redress through clientelism. This has become the dominant political contest even in the wider political arena, displacing the conflict over the means of production hitherto characteristic (Leca 1988).

In such a climate, sectarian identities have tended to supersede class ones and Alawi sectarianism, in particular, to become a major ingredient and issue of politics. If, in the fifties, the identity of mobilizing Alawi youth appeared to be subsumed in a wider Arab nationalism, each phase since in the Alawis' growing ascendancy at the political center has tended to enhance their communal solidarity. In positions of power, Alawis often followed the code of a kinship society in favoring their kin in elite recruitment, and, most significantly, in admission to the officer corps. The dictates of power concentration led Asad, in relying on kin and tribe, to give a strong Alawi flavor to the elite core he shaped around the presidency. With a national core to provide leadership, Alawi identity and cohesion was enhanced. As Alawi status increasingly conveyed privilege and those left out naturally became, in turn, more conscious of their own, usually Sunni, identity, the Alawi's solidarity in defense of their privileges intensified. In times of sectarian crisis, the interests of "modern" and "traditional" Alawi elites have converged in defense of the whole community and president and shaikh are reputed to meet in communal conclave in Asad's village of Qirdahah (Kramer 1987:251). But it is a mistake to think that patronage politics exclusively takes the form of sectarian rivalry. Indeed, clientage networks often cut across sectarian lines, with rival Alawi brokers each having Sunni allies or followings of Sunni clients. The Alawis are also socially differentiated between a handful of wealthy political brokers, and others—ideological minded intellectuals, village youth—who disdain or fail to benefit from patronage and privilege (Batatu 1981; Faksh 137, 143–147).

Bureaucratic politics takes the form of a struggle between institutions enjoying some sense of corporate interest, whether this be a special mission or control of resources and jurisdictions. One typical example is a certain rivalry between party and state. The party apparatus, which still tends to represent the regime's initial rural constituency and views its mission as the defense of Ba'th ideology, tenaciously resists the diffusion of power to the government bureaucracy, more the preserve of liberal-minded technocrats and the urban middle class. On the other hand, however, sectoral or regional rivalries over budgets and resources often cut across party and state, with, for example, party and state officials in industry pitted against those in agriculture or those from one province against another. Associational interest groups expressive of occupational interests—the worker, peasant and professional syndicates—are also players of bureaucratic politics.

Bureaucratic and clientelist politics intertwine in complex ways. The fall of the president's brother Rifat illustrates some of this complexity. Rifat, using his unequaled connection to the president and his praetorian guard units as a base, tried to extent clientage networks across state and society at the expense of the two main power institutions of the regime, the army and party. This episode was no mere personal bid for power by Rifat; rather he stood for an alternative "rightist"—pro-Western, pro-bourgeois—policy opposed to the dominant Ba'thist thrust and based on a rival coalition embracing his security units, Alawi clients, the bourgeoisie and sections of the professional middle class. The rise of such an alternative power base, outside the formal institutions, led from a wing of the "royal family," so to speak, bears all the marks of a patrimonial polity. The offense taken by the army, and behind it the party, was central to Rifat's undoing. It is true that Alawi officers also close to the president led the anti-Rifat coalition. Still, his failure can be seen as a manifestation of the power of bureaucratic interests in opposition to a most potent clientage network.

How, in fact, do the branches of this complex state come together to settle conflicts? There is an institutional dimension: major regime policies are often worked out in a relationship between the Presidency and the Ba'th party leadership bodies and congresses. Party congresses, bringing together party apparatchiki, senior army commanders, ministers, governors and interest group leaders, are the political elite assembled; they have continued to be arenas in which initiatives from the Presidency are reconciled with these interests and intra-elite conflicts settled (Sadowski). The contests in party congresses often take the form of ideological disputes over policy, but such policy conflicts no longer represent the interests of classes so much as bureaucratic rivalry, e.g. between "socialist" party bureaucrats with a stake in statism and "liberal" technocrats sympathetic to the market or with business connections. It is a special feature of Syria's populist authoritarianism that heads of trade unions and peasant associations have access to these party arenas, while the private sector lacks it except through covert or corrupt means. The leader remains, of course, above the fray and personally unchallengable; the one man who holds the reins of all the various power bases in his hands and can alone unite army, party, Alawi and Sunni, Hafiz al-Asad is the indispensable centerpiece of intra-elite conflict resolution. Several intra-elite power struggles, including Rifat's fall, were ultimately decided by presidential intervention. The centrality of the Presidential Monarchy manifests the patrimonial core of the regime.

The Crisis of Regime Legitimacy and the Forces of Change and Persistence

Even as the Asad regime consolidated itself, the cumulative negative side effects of its power strategy led to a deepening crisis of legitimacy which shrank its base and made it increasingly vulnerable to opposition. Support among its own populist constituency began after 1975 to erode. Its embourgeoisement and corruption differentiated the elite from its base. The inflation which accompanied the influx of oil money, and, when Arab aid dropped off, state deficit financing, eroded the relatively fixed incomes of salaried employees, workers, and the small peasantry dependent on sale of the crop to the state for set prices. The disillusionment of the hopes raised by the 1973 war for a return of the Golan, and the 1976 intervention in Lebanon against Muslims and Palestinians in violation of all the Ba'th's historic commitments, alienated many Ba'this and progressives (Drysdale 1982).

Parallel to the weakening of the the regime's base was the development, from the late seventies through the early eighties, of ever more intense and violent urban opposition which threatened the regime's survival and exposed both its strengths and weaknesses. This opposition took the form of assassinations and insurrections legitimized by Islamic fundamentalist ideology. It was led by historic enemies who had never been reconciled to Ba'th rule: old regime landed, merchant, and religious families, particularly from the northern cities; but they were leavened by the general alienation of wide segments of urban youth and the middle class by the corruption and economic instability unleashed by the mid-seventies boom. Neither the co-opted Damascene bourgeoisie or the countryside joined the rebellion, the massive state bureaucracy, incorporating major elements of the Sunni middle class, remained largely compliant, and rural—chiefly Alawite—military units smashed the revolt. The rebellion greatly exacerbated sectarian tensions inside the regime, dividing the elite between moderates, generally Sunni, who wished to placate the opposition with reform and political liberalization and hard-line Alawis who wished to repress it. However, as the intensity of the rebellion mounted, the elite closed ranks to repress the threat from below; the sectarian fissures which the opposition hoped to exploit to bring the regime down were contained and the Ba'th state proved a more formidable structure and its base deeper rooted than many had anticipated.

It was possible that the opposition challenge might drive the elite to revitalize its populist base. The revolt did check the amalgamation between the political elite and the urban bourgeoisie, cut short liberalizing tendencies, and briefly forced the regime to fall back on and cater to its constituency: there was, thus another, albeit modest, land reform, and a mobilization of the popular organizations to "defend the revolution." The regime embarked on a renewed recruitment drive which swelled the ranks of the party. But elite embourgeoisement precluded any real return to the radical policies of the sixties. Moreover, the regime missed the opportunity to purge itself of corruption, widen participation, and regain the support of the nationalist-left. Indeed, the repressive measures deployed during the Islamic uprising deadened political life inside and outside the party well after it was defeated. Then, in the eighties, economic growth gave way to stagnation. The drying up of Arab aid and the plummeting value of the Syrian pound translated into foreign exchange constraints and inflationary pressures, forcing austerity measures which rippled through the economy: in industry factories closed for lack of parts and materials while in agriculture a growing scarcity and cost of inputs began to squeeze peasant incomes. Inflation made life ever harder for the common man while stagnation shrunk opportunities for social mobility. At the same time, the political elite, enriching itself on smuggled luxuries and currency speculation, undermined the crisis control measures of its own government. Thus, a growing wedge was opening between a self-serving political elite and its own constituency. Despite rising discontent, however, the massive repression of the Islamic rising had so demoralized all opposition that the political arena remained sunk in apathy. Thus, in the late eighties, power remained firmly in the hands of a more autonomous but also more isolated state elite suffering a permanent crisis of legitimacy.

A state such as this which lacks a firm class base is, by definition, "unstable" and vulnerable to recapture by the dominant social forces. In the Syrian case, there are forces pushing toward the recapture of the state by a reconstructed bourgeoisie and the readoption of a capitalist strategy of development; but they have not matured. The embourgeoisement of the power elite tends to push regime ideology is a more pro-capitalist direction. The dissipation of the socialist ideological impulse without the creation of viable institutions which could substitute for private capitalism leaves a certain vacuum which statist strategies cannot wholly fill. Patrimonial tendencies enervate the state's rational and extractive capacities, undermining the etatist road to development. This generates pressures for economic liberalization, and indeed a certain creeping liberalization has been apparent since the early seventies; the recent establishment of joint private-state investment companies in agriculture is only the latest such development.

But there will be no significant private investment without a political liberalization which curbs the arbitrary power of the top elite. Whether some version of the "Liberal Empire"—the opening of the Bonapartist state to power-sharing with the bourgeoisie-in-parliament—will yet emerge as it has in Egypt remains to be seen. But elite embourgeoisement has so far translated into no Egyptian-like renunciation of socialism or political liberalization which would restore bourgeois influence over public policy. The regime continues to sharply control political access on its own terms for nearly all social forces. Indeed much of the private bourgeoisie is fragmented, insecure, and lacking in reliable input into decisions while its more powerful wing, now international, has only a limited stake in Syria.

There are powerful obstacles to liberalization. The highly politicized military is unprepared to withdraw from the center of politics and the Alawis who dominate it would be threatened by any return of power to the Sunni establishment. Ba'th ideology is, to an extent seldom recognized, routinized in the party, a powerful organization which incorporates a wide array of interests—public sector managers, bureaucrats, trade unionists, the cooper-atives—which oppose any wholesale abandonment of statist and populist policies. The continuing recruitment of plebeian rurals through the party and army has kept alive a certain populist tendency in elite circles. Creating an investment climate suitable for a capitalist alternative to statism would require revocation of populist rights and practices on which the regime's legitimacy and the support of its constituency rest. The elite, whether as Alawis or Ba'thists, is loath to concede control of the economy, a source of both wealth and power, to private or foreign enterprise toward which it remains hostile or ambivilant. Agriculture, for example, is a source of resources for the state, a political base the Ba'th cannot afford to cede to its rivals, and a terrain for implementing development strategies in which politicians, officials, and agencies have a stake. Finally, the oil "rent" at the disposal of the state has enhanced its relative autonomy of all sectors of society, including the bourgeoisie.

From the side of the main conservative opposition groups, too, there has only been limited willingness to strike an accommodation with the regime. While elements of the bourgeoisie are happy to enter profitable alliances with regime elites, the bourgeoisie as a class remains split over the regime and a powerful element of it, linked to the traditional petite bourgeoisie of the urban quarters, imbued with a merchant ethos and Islamic sentiment, utterly refuses the legitimacy of Ba'thist rule. The Islamic revolt demonstrated that any political liberalization risks Islam would become a potent vehicle of counter-regime mobilization. Thus the ideological cleavage between regime and opposition has remained too strong, pitting the persistent populist statism and secularism of the regime against the private enterprise and Islamicism of the old elite and the suq.

Finally, the regime's central preoccupation with the struggle against Israel makes continued control over society and its resources indispensable. The continued state of war, in discouraging private investment in productive fields and making Syria ineligible for foreign private investment on a serious scale, closes off the alternative of full-blown capitalist restoration, even were there support for it in the regime. Asad's stubborn patience in pursuit of Arab national goals, an Arabness relatively untouched by Westernization, and an aloofness from the Syrian bourgeoisie make him unresponsive to the

Sadat-like detente with the capitalist forces which could bring on full scale amalgamation of regime and bourgeoisie. Presiding over a strong party which incorporates a loyal military and a big part of the peasant masses, Asad has little immediate need for major economic and political liberalization and much to lose if it got out of hand.

In the short term, therefore, the main direction of regime change appears to be patrimonial decline, not capitalist rationalization.Indeed by the eighties, there was growing evidence that a combination of deepening patrimonialization and resource constraints were palpably enervating both the remaining rational and populist character of the state. The growing power of the military and security forces—"centers of power" increasingly immune from accountability, perhaps even to the presidency—translated into a spreading intervention in and "subversion' of government policymaking. At the very time when economic constraints were pressuring the regime into further opening to capitalist investment, arbitrary rule and corruption were major deterrents to productive investment. The growing subversion of policy rationality by unchecked patrimonialism seemed a symptom of a significant weakening of Asad's state—at the hands, ironically, of its own defensive "arms."

In 1984, when the linchpin of the system, Hafiz al-Asad, fell sick, the vulnerability of a such a patrimonialized regime was brutally exposed. His absence from the helm touched off an open jockeying for power between Rifat al-Asad and his rivals, with military units deployed in the streets. The episode seemed to show that when the inevitable succession crisis comes, praetorianism, suppressed but apparently just below the surface, is likely to break out again (Drysdale 1984). Thus, after a decade and a half of personalization at the top at the expense of the party, font of ideology and legitimate procedure, institutionalization has probably regressed.

The following pages will nevertheless show that, however much the center may be weakening, it is linked to society by a dense network of structures which have incorporated a deep rooted village base.

Notes

1. But in the seventies, as world prices again rose and state prices failed to keep pace, price-fixing would create a new source of rural discontent.

6

The Pillars of State Power: Army, Party, and Bureaucracy

The Ba'th regime rests on three overlapping structures of power—the party apparatus, the military-police establishment, and the ministerial bureaucracy. The top political elite presides over and interlocks their command posts: the President holds the legal or political reins of all three and the party's Regional Command, the top collegial leadership body, is roughly divided between senior military commanders, the most powerful cabinet ministers, and top party apparatchiki. These three institutions are the main instruments through which the political elite seeks to settle intra-elite conflict, design and implement public policy, and mobilize and control society. The party apparatus has a special dual role, that is, to both approve public policy reconciling elite goals and public expectations and to mobilize popular support for this policy. To effectively perform this role it must politically "incorporate" a societal constituency, whether in the sense of providing channels of political participation or merely co-opting various interests into the regime. While the army and bureaucracy are, in principle, chiefly "output agencies" they also may incorporate a constituency—their leaders, personnel, and elements of the public dependent on them for services or vulnerable to the sway of state regulation and control. This chapter will argue that these structures have not only concentrated decision-making, administrative and coercive power but, have also attained a considerable "mass-incorporating" capacity, permitting an expansion of regime power without which the survival of Ba'th rule in so volatile a society as Syria can scarcely be imagined. In particular, this and the subsequent chapter will stress the Ba'th's structural penetration of the village, intimate involvement in agrarian affairs, and consequent incorporation of the peasantry into the regime.

The Army: Leading Force, Regime Shield

The Middle East has a long history of military politics and military rule (Khadduri 1953). In post-independence Syria, the failure of the old elite to build viable political institutions opened the door to military intervention in politics and permanently politicized the officer corps. The only way military rule could be excluded or contained was to build strong mass-incorporating political institutions. As Halpern (1963:277) put it:

> There is likely to be an end to army intervention only when the body politic has achieved a . . . new cohesion which, in organizational terms means a new middle class that has established firm links with workers and peasants. The new middle class by itself will be unable to keep the army out of politics as long as the latter remains its better organized, better trained, better armed self.

But from the moment Ba'thi officers brought the party to power, determined to assume its leadership at the expense of its historic founders, it was likely that the military would be an equal or senior partner in the new military-party state and that institution-building would have to go on in concert with military leadership, not apart from it. The military, in linking itself to the party, clearly understood the centrality of political institutions to governance. The only question was whether the political role of the military could be contained and institutionalized by the civilian components of the political system. The army has not, in fact, been subordinated to civilian rule on either the Western or Communist models but its role has, to a degree, been constrained and regularized within the political system.

The Military in Politics: The Structure of Civil-Military Relations: The role of the army in the political system has evolved considerably over the decades of Ba'th rule. In the first years after the power seizure, the Ba'thi "military committee" acted as a unified body to extend its control over the army and maintain its ascendancy in the regime. Through massive purges and wholesale recruitment of politically loyal new elements, frequently Ba'thist teacher/reserve officers, and the establishment of a Ba'thist network in the army, it achieved the Ba'thization of the army. Through a major presence in party and government it achieved its own ascendancy in the regime: party officers held the top positions in the Revolutionary Council, the formal apex of state power until 1966, occupied roughly half the seats in the party's leadership bodies, and Amin al-Hafiz, the senior party officer, combined, for a time (1964–1965), the positions of head of party (Syrian "Regional Secretary"), state (Chairman of the Revolutionary Council), and government (Prime Minister). Control of military commands was a direct source of political power and several major political showdowns were partly decided by such control, although as Gaspard (1969a) indicates, the use of military force was not always overt:

> military interventions in politics no longer necessarily follow the old pattern of march on the capital. . . . Telephone contact is sufficiently easy . . . to avoid the need of actually calling out tanks and cannons every time [to determine] how much military hardware is ready to intervene on each side. . . .

Decisive in this game was the politics of appointment, dismissal, and transfer and a key to power therefore came to be control of those strategic positions from which officer personnel affairs could be manipulated and monitored—the Chief of Staff, the G-1 (Personnel), G-2 (Military Intelligence), the party officers' affairs committee, and the Military Bureau of the Regional Command. For a period Salah Jedid, the man who, as head of G-1 and then as Chief of Staff, controlled appointments had a unique opportunity to build a base of military support; he was to become the regime's second strongman. Thereafter, as the importance of this power became apparent, it was invested in a collective body, the party officers' affairs committee. Significantly, throughout this early period civilian party leaders lacked power over the party military, while the latter was heavily represented inside the party (Seymour 37–39; Rabinovich 150–153, 157–159; Ma'oz 1976:284–287).

The Ba'thization of the army was to have permanent but ambiguous effects on its cohesion. In bridging the former class and ideological gaps between the military and political elite, Ba'thism transformed the army from a system-challenging force into a pillar of the state and put an end to coups as vehicles of radical swings in regime type and ideology. But it also infected the army with all the Ba'th's internal conflicts, with deleterious consequences. The displacement of professional standards which accompanied the Ba'thization of the army, in which officers were recruited, dismissed, or promoted on the basis of political loyalty—for which origin became a shorthand, rurals and minorities being considered more reliable—and subsequent intra-Ba'th power struggles created strong insecurities and mistrust among officers. The frequent disruptions of the chain of command and discounting of professional rank during political struggles created role uncertainty among officers detrimental to professional discipline. These developments put a high premium on solidarity with those one could trust and gave rise to sectarian and regional factionalism and clientelism, further undermining the chain of command and military discipline (Drysdale 1979; Van Dusen 1971; Van Dam). Subsequently, it became a major challenge for Syria's political leadership to restore both professional discipline, cohesion, and the political subordination of the officer corps to constituted authority; to this day that challenge has not been fully met.

After 1966, a serious effort was made to apply the communist—more precisely, the Cuban or Chinese model—of party-military relations. Military strongman Salah Jedid took over the party apparatus in an effort to make it the center of power. The collegial party Regional Command assumed sovereignty over the military through its Military Bureau (*al-maktab al-askari*) from which a chain of political command ran down through the secretaries of the party's military branches. On the other hand, the military party organization was accorded full rights of participation in party congresses: e.g. at the Second Regional Congress in the mid-sixties 40% of delegates were officers. The army in theory was, by now, an "ideological army"—one committed to Ba'thism and recruited from popular classes rather than a de-politicized professional force, which Ba'th doctrine held inevitably became elitist and isolated from the people. To enhance this popular character, the party resolved to eradicate privilege—"luxury" and "unaccounted over-spending"—which differentiated the officer corps from the people, an intention which did little to endear the radical leadership to the army. The radical Ba'th also created a party militia and a "popular army," formations meant to counter the army's coercive monopoly. However, in the event, the party could not keep political control over the army once, after the 1967 war, it relaxed its grip over appointments and transfers to the man who held the reigns of professional military command, Defense Minister Hafiz al-Asad. Asad used a policy of gradual transfers and appointments, combined with minor *coups de force,* and strategic alliances with other key officers, to by-pass and neutralize the Ba'thi political network in the army and assume command over the armed party formations (Ma'oz 1976:287–288). The relative re-establishment of professional discipline after the 1967 war also buttressed his authority over the regular military chain of command. The failure of the "Chinese model" made it clear that the military, not the party apparatus, would be the dominant force in the regime: in the 1970 showdown when party authority and Asad's military command clashed, the latter triumphed easily. In fact, every major turnover in the very top elite has come by military coup, not party decisions. None of these crises were pure army-party conflicts for there was always a certain overlap or *symbiosis* between the two institutions (Rabinovich 212–214); even in the 1970 case, Asad, a veteran partisan, had his own supporters inside the party organization. Nevertheless, the three top leaders of Syria since the rise of the Ba'th, Hafiz, Jedid, and Asad, have all been senior Ba'thi officers who have enjoyed the preponderance of armed support.

Under Asad, the military, apparently triumphant, paradoxically, seemed, in being subordinated to a dominant presidency, to lose power. To be sure, Asad is an ex-officer, but he is now far more than a champion of military interests and he is the first Syrian leader to maintain firm control over the army. The President has retained direct control over the army as legal commander-in-chief and through personal control of appointments and dismissals of senior and perhaps even middle level officers. Preoccupied with the conflict with Israel, Asad also sought to enhance professionalism and this required that officers be appointed, rewarded and punished on performance, not political grounds; while this could increase military discipline, it also carried risks in so politicized an army as Syria's. As Drysdale points out, Asad pursued a dual policy in seeking to reconcile political control with military professionalism: units primarily charged with regime defense were recruited on the basis of political loyalty and (Alawi) sectarian affiliation. In the larger army charged with external defense a new stress was put on professional competence and discipline and purged non-political officers were reintegrated to enhance combat effectiveness and appease dissatisfaction at the damage done to the army by political purges. This policy was legitimized by the army's vastly improved performance in subsequent confrontations with Israel (Ma'oz 1975:285). The result was "one [branch] whose cohesion depended on discipline and a sense of national mission, the other whose members were closely bound by primordial ties . . . [in order] to compartmentalize and quarantine the regime's Machiavellian excesses" (Drysdale 1979:371). But there is a good deal of overlap: e.g., General Ali Aslan, chief of operations and later deputy chief of staff is at once an Alawi, a Ba'thi, and a respected professional officer.

The result is a military made up of three overlapping but somewhat distinct concentric "circles." Closest to the political nerve center is Asad's contingent of personal Alawi kin and clients (Batatu 1981). They command key guards units and intelligence agencies charged with defense of the regime. In recent years Rifat al-Asad commanded the Defense Detachments, *al-Saraya al-Difa'*, and Adnan al-Asad the Struggle Companies, which controlled access routes to the capital and guarded its command posts, Ali Haydar headed the Special Forces, which have been used to smash Ikhwan concentrations, Adnan Makhluf commanded the Presidential Guard, and Ibrahim al-Ali the militia-like Popular Army. Muhammed al-Khuli headed air force intelligence and the intelligence coordinating committee in the presidency and Ali Duba presided over military intelligence. Alawis also hold a very disproportionate number of top operational commands, especially of coup-making armored units; General Shafiq Fayyad, long commander of the critical Third Division, is a durable Asad loyalist, while two other regime stalwarts, Generals Ibrahim Safi and Adnan Badr Hasan had extended tenure as commanders of the First and Ninth Divisions. Moreover, where Sunnis are commanders, Alawis are appointed deputies and where Alawis are commanders, Sunnis or others are deputy commanders. This Alawi network is a key political cement that links the three main power centers of the regime, presidency, party, and army since these officers have a presence in all three.

Given its centrality, the political orientation of the Alawi military is of great import. As students of the Syrian military have argued, the identities and motivations of these officers are very complex, multiple loyalties may pull in different directions according to the situation, and the assumption that they act exclusively on sectarian grounds is untenable (Drysdale 1979:363–369; Ma'oz 1976:277–278; Van Dusen 1975:141–151). Nevertheless, some generalizations are possible. Initially, Alawi officers appeared the most militantly radical force within the Ba'th, the most intense carriers of peasant grievances against the urban establishment and the spearhead of the regime in its showdowns with the latter. Their strong solidarity, based on divisions from the Sunni establishment on both class and sectarian lines, as opposed to the more regionally and class divided Sunni officers, helps account for the Alawis' more intense political orientation and greater success in establishing political ascendancy. Under Asad, the Alawi military evolved into a conservative force for regime maintenance. It has a strong stake in the survival of the regime and has shown the extremes to which it will go to protect it; it is a formidable bulwark behind which Asad has carried out his strategy of state formation. The cleavage between the Alawi elite and the Sunni bourgeoisie continues to have political significance. Many Alawi officers are wary of economic or political liberalization, for the Sunni bourgeoisie is still better situated to benefit from it. Direct recruitment from Alawi villages continues to fill military ranks with elements having populist roots; tough mountainmen, with little of the culture of the Damascene Sunni, Alawi officers remain apart from, arrogant toward, and disdained by the old notability. This cleavage, a barrier to intermarriage between Alawis and the Sunni bourgeoisie, is a major obstacle to amalgamation of the political elite and the private bourgeoisie. Some Alawi officers, particularly Rifat al-Asad, did assume a more ambivilant stance: on the one hand clannishness and sectarian aggrandizement, on the other hand, alliances, often opportunistic and corrupt, with the most conservative forces—Maronites, Sunni businessmen, Saudi Arabia, even the United States. Rifat actually came to be seen as a champion of the Sunni bourgeoisie inside the regime. In this process, he resorted to the most traditional of power building strategies in the Muslim world, multiple marriages to various powerful families. However, he represented only one stream within the Alawi military and with his fall, other Alawi officers, such as Ali Duba, less amenable to such wide ranging alliances, have grown in power. By the eighties, senior Alawi officers had turned into the major obstacle to reform of the corruption and power abuses of the regime and many of them appeared to be virtually above the law. Moreover, they have become an intensely praetorian incubus in the heart of the state, kept under control only by presidential authority. When that weakens, as the jockeying for power between Alawi commanders—Rifat and Shafiq Fayyad—during the president's illness showed, praetorianism starkly reemerges and abuse of power deepens.

The second ring of the military is the Ba'th party's military organization. Certain senior non-Alawi Ba'thi officers were long part of the president's inner circle—e.g. Mustafa Tlas, Naji Jamil, and Abd al-Rahman al-Khulafawi. The Ba'th military has been a major elite recruitment pool and continues to participate in party collegial bodies: military delegates are a contingent of party congresses and the most senior sit in the central committee and Regional Command (Devlin 1983:59). Apart from this, Asad has, by comparison to previous Ba'th regimes, narrowed the role of political officers in top party and government posts. There is now more of a functional division of labor in which the Ba'thi military is preoccupied with defense and security matters, the party apparatus with mass organization and domestic policy-making, and the government with policy implementation. But top politicized officers still maneuver to insert allies and clients into party and government and ambitious politicians in turn seek their backing. Certain ex-officers continue to be appointed for their leadership and management skills to ministries and public companies and indeed the economic role of military-run companies, per se, has grown. Moreover, military officers have become engrossed, on the side, in corrupt economic ventures such as smuggling rings, import trade, and the plundering of state companies; they have become patron-brokers allocating state goods and services to clients and undermining economic rationality (Picard 1988:139–144; *The Middle East,* Dec. 1987, pp. 11–13). Rifat al-Asad's attempt to extend his power beyond security affairs into the party and government combined with wide-ranging, often illegal business ventures, was the most blatant example of this and, having gone too far, invited a reaction which cut back his influence. But there continues to be a powerful tendency for the military to encroach on civilian domains. And the military, when challenged, can still veto initiatives of civilian authorities. Thus, when Prime Minister Abd al-Ra'uf al-Kasm challenged the smuggling activities of top officers, the senior officer corps combined to help bring him down.

Finally, the wider professional officer corps constitutes the outside rim of the military establishment. It is represented in the president's inner circle by men such as Chief of Staff Hikmat al-Shihabi. It is a powerful corporate interest group in the system concerned with military capabilities and uniquely powerful on issues of war, peace and security and, if its budget is any indicator, on the allocation of resources. It has benefited from lavish defense spending, amounting to one quarter to one-third of total public spending and a "cornucopia of sophisticated modern weapons" (Drysdale 1979:372; Picard 1988). In a country in a state of perpetual war, the political weight of the military "corporate interest" is bound to be very heavy.

In summary, the military clearly plays the pivotal role in the leadership of the Syrian state. The paramount leader has always been a politicized Ba'thi officer and while his power has been equally rooted in the party, military politicians alone can straddle the regime's two main power bases. From 1963–1970, Ba'thi officer-politicians held key roles in the party and state apparatus and under Asad Alawi officers, bridging the inner circle of the presidency, army commands, and party organs, are uniquely situated as political brokers. The military, or at least its dominant faction, has been the ultimate arbiter of power struggles and the most powerful institutional interest group. But this does not mean the military is the "real" power and the party and state its mere instruments; rather, the regime is a military-civil coalition in which decision-making power is shared. Since 1970, the role of the military in the regime has, to a degree, been semi-institutionalized as one of three pillars of state subordinate to the presidency. While the army is certainly the first among equals, army, party apparatus, and state bureaucracy are each mutually dependent, none capable of ruling alone. And while there is a certain overlap, especially of senior personnel at the very top, the three are functionally specialized and partly autonomous partners with real power in their own domains.

The Military as Regime Shield: The army, together with its associated security and intelligence *(mukhabarat)* agencies, is also a major bulwark of regime power. The Ba'th came to power on the back of the army and, given the persistence of strong opposition to the regime and the historic role of the army as a vehicle of regime change, the capabilities and reliability of the military remain decisive factors in the survival of Ba'th rule.

The military has become an ever more formidable instrument of control. The steady expansion in its size and firepower under the Ba'th makes violent opposition to the regime, so long as the military remains loyal, difficult and costly, if not futile. The security organs are multiple, pervasive in surveillance of society, and little tolerant of dissent, though "a certain amount of grumbling is tolerated as long as the grumblers don't organize" (Devlin 1983:63–64). The *mukhabarat* is feared for the arbitrary arrest, imprisonment and torture which it has practiced and the corrupt activities in which it has sometimes been embroiled. Certainly, the security apparatus is a major deterrent to opposition of all kinds and a major explanation for the durability of the regime. Yet, it is equally true that the arbitrary and often corrupt behavior of these same security forces has become a major source of public dissatisfaction which, as Devlin (1983:68) points out, the regime is hard put to remedy: "An authoritarian regime that wants to stay in power is constrained in attempts to deal with dissatisfaction by the requirement that it not do injury to those props that are essential to its survival."

Several factors explain the continuing political reliability of the military. The social cleavage between political and military leadership which was one root of Syria's pre-1963 military instability was ended by the overthrow of the notability and the Ba'thization of the army in which elements of the same social background took over command of both state and army. The army's Ba'thist character has been preserved by the creation of a Ba'thist party organization in the army, the preference given Ba'this and, according to some claims, Alawis, in admission to the military academy, and the political indoctrination presided over by the Political Department of the armed forces. Under Asad, military appointments have been a special preoccupation of the president. The creation of several superbly equipped Alawite-recruited or commanded praetorian guards detachments designed and strategically situated for regime defense, the appointment of Alawites to sensitive "coup-making" units, the creation of several competing intelligence organizations watching each other and the army, the pairing of Alawite deputies with Sunni commanders—all have deterred coup attempts and enhanced the political reliability of the chain of command. The greater professionalization of the officer corps under Asad, the stake it has in maintaining the integrity of the armed forces and of its privileged position in society against the political purges which formerly decimated it, the difficulty of planning and mounting a successful coup in an ever larger army—all work in favor of the regime.

In fact, the military and security forces have largely proved their reliability, although there have been periodic breakdowns in it. Since 1963, the army has repressed no less than seven (1963, 1964, 1965, 1967, 1973, 1980, 1982) major anti-regime urban disturbances, an accumulating record that must be a serious deterrent to violent opposition. There have been many abortive coup attempts, and some mounted by Sunni officers since the mid-seventies have been sectarian motivated, but these have been made in the name of Ba'thism, not the opposition. There have been a few instances of actual defection to the opposition motivated by sectarian animosities, including the attempt on Asad's life by a member of the presidential guard and the 1979 massacre of scores of Alawi cadets by a Sunni officer, Ibrahim Yusuf. Moreover in the late seventies and early eighties, in at least two instances military discipline collapsed, as units ordered into action against

Sunni cities split along sectarian lines. While possibly apocryphal, a story surrounding one of these incidents illustrates the role of the Alawi network in the army. During Islamic-inspired disturbances in Hama, the nearby 40th Brigade, heavily Hamawi in composition, was ordered into action against the city. The Sunni commander called his officers together to "discuss" the appropriateness of the order: immediately his Alawi deputy arrested—some say shot—him for military indiscipline and took command of the unit. Although its insubordination was contained, the unit nevertheless split and had this happened on a wider scale it could have posed a major danger to the regime; clearly the regime had overestimated the power of military discipline in such a delicate situation. Indeed, in recent years sectarian animosity has run deep in the army, seriously exacerbated by the Lebanese intervention, growing Alawi privilege, and Sunni rebellion in the late seventies. But it is a measure of the regime's control over the armed forces and its substantial professional and political discipline that it could be used in an overtly sectarian conflict in Lebanon and that despite the unprecedented massive use of military force against Hama in 1982, the army, overall, remained loyal. Of course, should it have to deal again with massive insurgency, suffer defeat in war, or split in a succession struggle, a part of the military could still turn against the regime—possibly at the cost of civil war.

But it is a mistake to see the army exclusively as an instrument of repression; it is also a channel by which the state incorporates mass society. Not only does the large officer corps link thousands through military discipline and careers to the regime, but tens of thousands of conscript youth and a half-million periodically mobilized reservists are incorporated into a national enterprise, defense of the country against a bitter enemy; in recent years the army accounted for about 20% of Syria's manpower and by the mid-1980s it reputedly had 500,000 men under arms. The emergence of this "citizen army" generates a national consciousness which inevitably bolsters the legitimacy of the state which directs it. In addition to this, the political role of the army has given Ba'th officers a special role in linking the regime to society. For example, they may enjoy influence as brokers between kin and village and the state bureaucracy; in many villages, the military is a preferred prestige career and officers preferred marriage partners. Hence in the rural areas, the army is a channel of access and opportunity between state and village.

The Role of the Military in State and Society: The reasons for the central role of the military in the Syrian state are multiple and mutually reinforcing but the consequences of the military's role are increasingly ambiguous; they can be evaluated along three dimensions, state-building, social change, and national defense (Picard 1988). First, military-politicians took the lead in the founding of the state. Salah Jedid forged the Leninist core of the Ba'th state and Hafiz al-Asad created the powerful presidency at its apex. Yet, the plots of officer-politicians have, at the same time, been and remain major threats to the stability of this state and the ambitions of powerful officers are barely and sometimes not at all restrained by its laws or institutions. In the repressive controls exercised by its security branches and the weight, perhaps amounting to a veto, which the military carries in the political process, it dampens the vitality of political life even inside the regime's own institutions; the military has helped to forge and buttress Ba'thist political institutions but has also enervated the capacity to channel participation which alone can give them strength. But as long as the regime's legitimacy remains precarious, the military will remain the central pillar of state power.

Second, the coercive power with which the military endowed the Ba'th regime gave it the autonomy of the dominant classes necessary to launch the Ba'th revolution and to sustain its statist variant of modernization. But, increasingly, politicized officers have become a conservative obstacle to reform and a burden on development: paying themselves the best salaries in Syria (Picard says 4–10 times the salaries of civilians), and engaging in corrupt business (e.g. smuggling), they drain the treasury and frustrate the rational management of the economy. As the main obstacle to the rule of law needed for sound economic development, they deter both private investment and the rationalization of the public sector.

Third, as a champion of nationalism and the main guardian of the integrity of the state in a dangerous inter-state environment, the military has turned Syria from the plaything of regional forces into a powerful actor. But defense is an ever more weighty burden on the economy and the role of the army in the defense of Arab nationalism has often been less than glorious; the collapse in the 1967 war with Israel and the intervention against Palestinians in Lebanon remain irradicable blots on the army's image. But as long as the conflict with Israel remains the central preoccupation of Syrian politics, the military, the core of a formidable garrison state, is certain to remain at the center of power. The army's revolutionary credentials, its nationalist stance, and its popular and especially rural roots give its central political role a certain legitimacy in parts of Syrian society. But as this is eroded by corruption, privilege, and repression, the de-militarization of the state is bound to become a more pressing issue on the Syrian political agenda.

What, ultimately, is the role of the military in the Syrian state? To say, as many do, that the main feature of Syrian politics is military *domination* is to assume that the main cleavage in Syrian politics is civil-military. It seems clear, however, that the more important and active cleavages have been ideological, urban-rural, state vs. private sector, and rivalries over patronage. In these conflicts it is more correct to say that military politicians *lead* various civil-military factions inside the regime and that the military buttresses the regime against the opposition. Needless to say, such a central role is quite compatible with the long history of the state in the Middle East; but it is equally clear that in an age of mass politics, officers must be politicians or share power with them, and an effective, durable state cannot dispense with mass incorporation, and particularly the modern vehicle of participation, the political party.

The Ba'th Party Apparatus

As its radical architects envisioned it, the Ba'th Party was to be forged into an ideologically disciplined vanguard party, the main pillar of the regime and the motor of revolution from above. The party would replenish the elite with ideologically committed cadres, supervise the submission of the state apparatus to party policy, and mobilize mass support behind this policy. Specifically, it would penetrate society, by-passing traditional rivals, and foster a corps of loyal militants charged with organizing the masses behind the regime.[1] In fact, a great deal of time and energy was invested in building this apparatus and a formidable institution—no mere paper entity—bearing some resemblance to the Leninist model was indisputably in place by the seventies.

Yet the ideal "objective relations" defined by the *nizam* (party rules) have in practice been so distorted that the party has turned out to be but a pale copy of the Leninist prototype. From the outset it has been vulnerable to stultifying bureaucratization: its re-creation from above by a military-dominated center, its subsequent subordination to a dominant Presidency more interested in hierarchical discipline than ideological vitality, the tightening constraints on intra-party democracy, the dominance of the apparatus by paid party officials dependent on the top elite, and the flooding of its ranks with compliant careerists attracted by the benefits of a ruling party have threatened to turn the party into a mere appendage of government. Simultaneously, the party has been subverted by traditionalization "from below." The hasty post-1963 re-construction of the party in which rival politicians raced to recruit fellow sectarians, clients and relatives, the apparent decision under Asad to substitute patronage for ideology as the dominant cement of the regime and make the party a major font of it, and recruitment from a political culture shaped by strong primordial loyalties have all threatened to transform the party into a mere framework for clientelism. In short, the institutionalization of distinctive party rules and roles for channeling participation has been retarded by their manipulation from above and cultural subversion from below.

Yet, in spite of this, the party retains the basic structural features of a modern party and performs political functions central to the political system. It possesses channels and assemblies for the articulation and aggregation of interests and opinion, absent in bureaucracies, which still operate, albeit within tight constraints. It is a channel of recruitment, partially governed by rules, to roles independent, to an extent, of the persons who fill them which is absent in clientelist networks. It has specialized structures for mass mobilization which have organized a constituency at a depth and intensity no mere bureaucracy could achieve and on a scale and durability which no mere clientelist network could match. Some, at least, of its cadres are more than mere paid employees or the deferential dependents of a patron, retaining certain of the characteristics of voluntarist activists, whether in pursuit of private interests or promotion of public goals. The Ba'th still retains some of the features of the ideological movement from which it originated, notably, the stress on popular recruitment and on the indoctrination of members, although it has now evolved from a "vanguard" party mobilizing support for radical change into a party of patronage and integration chiefly concerned with stability and control. The party may be considered a political bureaucracy but it cannot be reduced to a mere branch of the administration; it may be thought of as a modernized clientelist system but it is more than a mere chain of personal patrons and clients. The Ba'th Party is one of those hybrid forms so typical of transitional societies.

Party Organization

The party organization links the political elite to society through a four-layered pyramid erected on "democratic-centralist" lines. The basic level "units" (*firqa*, pl. *firaq*), made up of several cells (*halaqat*), are located in villages, factories, neighborhoods and public institutions. These basic units are grouped into sub-branches or sections (*shu'ba, shu'ab*) at the district (*mantiqa*) or town level and these are combined in branches (*far', furu'*) in the provinces (*muhafazat*), major cities, and dominant institutions (such as a university). This structure is joined with a parallel military organization in the countrywide (*qutri*) party organization. Each level of organization has its own assembly and executive committee—"command" or "leadership" (*qiyada*)—headed by a secretary (*amin*). At the countrywide level, there is a more complex superstructure made up of three institutions: a "Regional Congress" (*al-mu'tamar al-qutri*), and issuing from it, a Central Committee (*al-lajna al-markaziya*), and a sort of politburo, the "Regional Command" (*al-qiyada al-qutriya*), which is the top party authority for governance of Syria. A technically superior Pan-Arab National Congress (*al-mu'tamar al-qaumi*) groups representatives of the dominant Syrian party and the small extra-Syrian branches of the Ba'th and from it issues a "National Command" (*al-qiyada al-qaumiya*), in theory the party's supreme executive organ. In principle, this hierarchy is raised on elections beginning at the bases. Since 1971, the Regional Congress has been elected from general assemblies of all voting members at the sub-branch level and it in turn elects the Regional Command which then appoints lower level commands and secretaries, constituting a line of authority running downward. The National Congress is composed of the Regional Commands of the Ba'th organizations in different countries and of delegates elected from the various Regional Congresses; it elects the National Command.

The Regional Command is the center of power in Syria, grouping, as it does, the most powerful military commanders and ministers and the party apparatchiki closest to the levers of organizational power, many of whom also sit in the National Command; moreover, it officially nominates the President and through him appoints the cabinet. In practice the "National" or Pan-Arab party organization is, since 1966 when the Pan-Arab Ba'th movement fractured, an appendage of the Syrian party. The National Congress is little more than a later session of the Regional Congress which, with the addition of delegates from Ba'thi organizations outside Syria (e.g. Lebanon, Palestinians), deliberates on Arab and foreign policy. The National Command, about a half of whom are Syrians, is in part a symbolic body of party elders and in part a kind of little-active Ba'thist "comintern." But the distinction between the two commands is also partly functional, with the National body chiefly responsible for foreign policy and party doctrine and the Regional one for socio-economic policy and political organization. Thus, attached to the Regional Command are specialized offices responsible for internal party administration (the organization and finance bureaus), and for the direction of "popular organizations" and the supervision of state agencies in various functional domains (bureaus for peasants, economy, education, workers, youth, etc.); they have subordinate functional counterparts at branch and sub-branch levels, constituting a functional line of command running downward through Syria. The National Command has offices in charge of foreign affairs, Palestinian affairs, party ideology and indoctrination, and public information, as well as a party court. The supreme policy-making body in the party appears, at least since 1966, to have been a *joint session* of the National and Regional Commands. Since 1971, President Asad leads both commands, uniting in his hands the powers of General Secretary (*al-amin al-'amm*) and Regional Secretary; he is assisted by an assistant-secretary for each command. Figure 6.1 depicts the party hierarchy as it looked in the 1980s. 11,163 *halaqat* were grouped in 1,395 *firaq*, these into 154 *shu'ab*, and these into 18 *furu'*; from this base was elected a Regional Congress of 771 delegates, a Central Committee of 90, a Regional Command of 21 members and a National Command of twenty; these commands, meeting jointly, made up a 41 member supreme leadership headed by the General Secretary and his two assistants. Manifestly, the Ba'th party possesses the structural features of a Leninist party; but what functions does it actually perform?[2]

Party Functions[3]

Elite Recruitment: A central measure of the importance of the party system in an authoritarian regime is the actual functions it performs and the most critical of these is elite recruitment. In principle the Ba'th Party is the instrument by which the Syrian regime recruits "popular" elements from society to replenish the governing elite.

In fact, the party recruitment system does reach systematically into the local community, drawing plebeian elements from villages and small towns into the elite recruitment pool and eventually into the local and regional power structure. In the districts and provinces the party apparatus is itself the dominant political authority, access to positions in government there depends heavily on party credentials, and it is, thus, through the party that villagers make it to public office. Moreover the party is the dominant recruitment pool for and ladder into the national elite. While the army has typically played the decisive role in the succession struggles which constituted the core national elite, this elite has been chosen from veteran Ba'thists; and though military, bureaucratic, academic and professional careers also

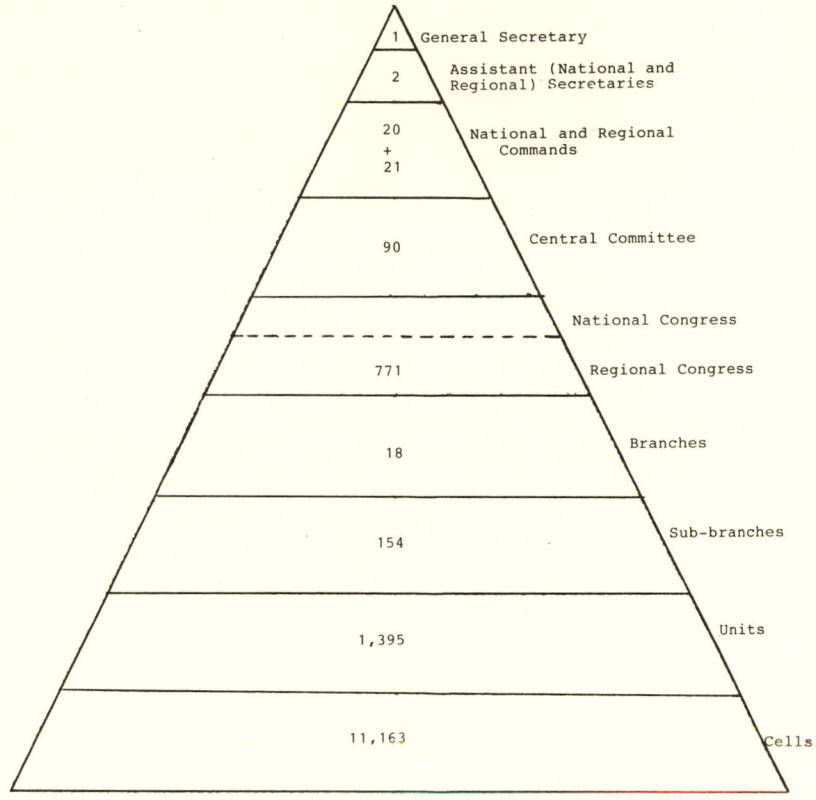

FIGURE 6.1 Structure of the Ba'th Party (Numbers indicate amount of lower organizational units and membership of higher organs.)

give access to the national elite, even those following career routes largely outside the party normally need at least nominal party credentials to go far or last long at the top.

The recruitment process, of course, turns more on cooptation from above than electoral or other support in the party bases. A patron at the top has always been essential to move up in the party and, given the national party leaders' powers of purge over the bases, those below have never been able to use elections to challenge the elite as long as it stayed united. But for a long time, the party's periodic rounds of elections did count for something: ambitious local politicians cultivated followings to win the election to higher assemblies needed to bring them to the attention of higher ups, struggles of elite factions could translate into electoral struggles between their clients below, and elite incumbents who lost party elections often suffered demotion in their political or administrative careers. As long as this was so, lower level party politics counted for something in the recruitment process. The scope of such electoral politics has, however, gradually been narrowed, official candidates now seem to be nominated from above at all levels and alternative candidates ever less tolerated, although this has not effaced the struggle between rival elites to nominate clients for the official list. Asad has also, in practice if not theory, created two privileged pools for cooptation from above, namely Alawis, especially those with kin links to him, and Damascene Sunnis, ascriptive criteria which tend to constrict openings at the top for others, especially the mainstream villagers who have formed the party's political base (Devlin 1983:33–34; Hinnebusch 1980). Nevertheless, party careers remain a major ladder to the top for the Ba'th's constituency.

The role of the party organization in shaping the political elite is illustrated by a 1974 study done by the author of the careers of 22 politicians who held power in the mid-seventies at the province and national level. The results on key party apparatchiki from eight provinces—chiefly secretaries of *shu'ba* and *far'* leaderships and heads of party peasant offices at those levels—indicate the party recruitment process has channeled into power positions a *distinctive socio-political type,* largely village in origin. By family origin about 50% were from small or middle-holding peasant families, 40% were from share-cropper families and 10% from the rural self-employed strata (baker, butcher). All, however, managed to attend school and there, in the 1950s, were attracted to the Ba'th. The most common political events which brought them into the party were peasant struggles against landlords, the anti-Shishakli rebellion and the nationalist struggle against "Western imperialism" in the late fifties. Roughly 30% became lawyers, 30% officials in local government, and 25% teachers but, despite their rural origins, only one became an agronomist and only one—a factory worker—had not made it into a white collar or professional occupation. Most started their ascent at the bottom of the party hierarchy as secretary of their village unit (*amin al-firqa*) moving up to the sub-branch and finally the branch levels, though some were first coopted to staff positions in the central apparatus before being appointed chief executive (*amin al-far'*) at the branch level. There was little variation in their expressed opinions. Though most had been in the Ba'th during the sixties, all were now "moderates" who agreed that class struggle and further land reform could not be a part of the political agenda as long as the national struggle with Israel had precedence and that raising agricultural production was the central priority. But, they held, Syria had no intention of abandoning socialism and would "deepen" it as circumstances allowed, extending state control over the agrarian market, expanding and upgrading cooperatives, etc.

The careers of apparatchiki at the national level are similar. The backgrounds of the Regional Command members in charge of the agrarian sector, that is, the peasant office (*al-maktab al-fallahin*), illustrate this. Taha Kheirat, from a peasant family in Dera, became a school teacher and rose through the party and education bureaucracy before reaching the command. Mahmud al-Zu'bi, also from Dera, was a party member in high school, studied agronomy in Cairo, and entered the agricultural bureaucracy, serving as agricultural director (*mudir al-zira'i*) in Hama, Idlib, and the Ghab. He then became number two man in the central party peasant office, was named head of the General Authority for Development of the Euphrates Basin, and in 1980 was appointed head of the *maktab al-fallahin*. Thereafter, he was appointed speaker of parliament and finally prime minister, bringing a special sympathy for agrarian problems to the halls of government. Ahmad Qabalan, born in a village near Mt. Hermon, studied agronomy and was the official in charge of agriculture in the Damascus university party branch in the sixties; a supporter of Asad in 1970, he was made Minister of State for Front Line Villages (coming from this area), then Minister of Supply and, from 1976–1980, Minister of Agriculture. He was then appointed secretary of the Damascus Rural party branch and finally head of the *maktab al-fallahin* in 1985. In short, for villagers who have been able to get on the education track, the party has opened doors to bureaucratic careers and served as a route to regional and national political power.[4]

The consequences of the elite recruitment system for the village and for the political system are ambiguous. The centrality of the Ba'th party as a vehicle of political recruitment has institutionalized a significant widening of the recruitment pool. Syria's first generation political elite was largely confined to scions of the tiny landed upper class, its power based on land and the men on it and the second generation was dominated by the urban middle class and reached power through professional skills, education, and family property. The current and third ruling generation is recruited from modest rural strata, including the mainstream peasantry, and has risen through education, bureaucratic office and partisan commitment. This transformation marks the growing penetration of the state into society and the growing incorporation of the rural peripheries and the lower levels of the stratification system into the political elite recruitment pool. Thus, the Ba'th party's roots in the rural areas have changed the very face of the political elite.

To the village, this recruitment of its sons gives the regime an image of representativeness and legitimacy it would otherwise lack. The chance to move up in the system may make political participation worthwhile for ordinary villagers. Having villagers in high office is likely, as well, to translate into a greater responsiveness by the state to the *rief* than would otherwise be the case. However, the fact that political recruitment is chiefly a cooptative process means that politicians will seek first to please their superiors in the capital on whom their careers depend. Moreover, the dilution of broad rural recruitment by privileged Alawi and Damascene recruitment at the top, puts particularistic regional and urban bourgeois interests ahead of broader rural and mass interests.

Controlled Interest Articulation and Aggregation: The party and its auxiliaries are supposed to constitute a channel of interaction between elite and mass. But, even in principle, they are not seen, as in liberal theory, as chiefly an instrument for "aggregating" public preferences into policy; rather, as a "vanguard" party, the Ba'th claims it "knows by experience and can crystallize the true aspirations of the masses," and hence cannot be content to merely follow their immediate wishes since they "do not always understanding the meaning of the struggle." On the other hand, to prevent the party from "degenerating into a band exercising tyranny over the masses" and "to develop the state authority and safeguard mass gains," the party must stay in touch with mass opinion and intra-party democracy plays a central role in this (ABSP 1973:84–86).

In theory, intra-party democracy is expressed in the periodic (every 4 year) cycles of party assemblies and elections from base upward in which local partisans pass resolutions and elect delegates charged with articulating them in the national-level policy-making congress. The tight constraints put on this process, however, sharply limit its actual effectiveness as an upward opinion transmission belt. The input of the membership into the congresses is controlled by the ability of centrally appointed local leaderships to set the agenda and manipulate information on which the bases depend, the ideological inertness of many local cells, the fact that participatory rights are only given to "full," not candidate members, and above all by the national leadership's history of intolerance of overt dissent; the few times dissidents have tried to use the process to challenge elite policies in the name of the party's own ideology, they have been purged or arrested. Local activists must have little sense of political efficacy, except the expectation that if they move up in the system their influence may grow; in the meantime they largely confine themselves to local politics where they are movers and shakers. According to local leaders themselves, elections seldom take place over major policy issues and their discussions normally focus on local, not national concerns.

This internal policy process does, however, have a residual life. Delegates to party congresses sometimes do come armed with resolutions reflecting the particular problems or wishes of their constituents. Moreover, the leadership reports which form the basis of debate in the national-level congress are composed by the Regional Command's specialized offices which receive input from lower level derivatives and have intimate connections with government agencies and the "popular organizations" through which mass interests are supposed to be expressed. Thus, the head of the party peasant office, the *maktab al-fallahin*, works closely with agricultural ministry bureaucrats, peasant union leaders, and the lower level (branch, sub-branch) peasant offices in framing the leadership's report and recommendations to the congress on agrarian issues. Local apparatchiki, largely through this chain of functional offices, may call the national leaders attention to local problems or, from consultations with local officials and mass organization leaders, even propose solutions which are adopted at the discretion of national leaders.

But the party apparatchiki who so channel the policy process are neither simply conduits for basic level opinion or mere rubber stamps for the views of the President or the military; rather they appear to express a partly autonomous and distinctive *party* point of view, largely etatist and populist, which leaves a real imprint on policy outcomes. A certain institutionalization of ideology in the Ba'th party apparatus is unmistakable, for example, in the constancy with which, even under Asad, it has continued to pursue "socialist" and etatist solutions in agriculture such as cooperatization, the consolidation of the state planning, marketing and credit infrastructure, and state development investment (Hinnebusch 1989:31–60). The calculus of power and interest, of course, generally reinforces party ideology: the Ba'th has a vital interest in state control over agricultural decisions and resources and in keeping the bourgeoisie—where political opposition is concentrated—from recovering its influence over the sector. Its legitimacy is seen to rest on a state development effort exemplified by hydraulic projects and agro-industrialization and, together with the bureaucracy, the apparatus has a stake in the office, career, and patronage bound up in these projects. The persistence of etatism could be seen as recently as the 1985 8th Regional Congress in which the Peasant Office pushed to have production cooperatives set up on newly reclaimed land, continued to promote the expansion of state marketing into new fields such as fruits and vegetables, and proposed fixing the prices of machine services and transport in agriculture instead of leaving them to the free market.

The reports and recommendations of the party command are, once delivered, debated and approved or altered in the party congress. Historically, the National and Regional Congresses were sovereign legislative bodes of central importance in policy-formation in the Ba'th state: they laid down ideological doctrine and long-range programs, decided between or reconciled competing factions and policy lines (notably the 6th and 8th National Congresses) or legitimized changes of course resulting from major regime splits. Thus, major issues of far-reaching consequence for Syrians were decided or approved in these bodies. For example, questions of rural transformation, i.e. the design of the programs through which the regime sought to carry out its revolution in the village and respond to village expectations, were central to the work of every congress. The 6th National Congress laid down the policy of rural socialism, aiming at collectivization, while the 8th National Congress approved a concrete phased plan of gradual transformation which would begin with service cooperatives and only be upgraded voluntarily to socialist production cooperatives. The 2nd Extraordinary Regional Congress approved a stable price floor for state-marketed crops. These decisions were of momentous importance for agricultural life. However, some resolutions which were pushed through in the absence of a real consensus never seem to have left any real policy impact: e.g. the 3rd Regional Congress's call for party members to go to the villages and organize production cooperatives and the 4th Regional Congress call for lowering the land ownership ceiling.

Since the establishment of Asad's presidential-centered regime, the powers of the national level policy-making congresses are exercised only within the limits of Presidential tolerance. Asad has, however, normally contented himself with defining broad policy lines and has not attempted to dictate a policy from above on all matters; as such, congresses remain arenas of debate and conflict over lesser but still consequential matters. Factions of the elite have battled at each congress and their struggle to win support below suggests that outcomes are not wholly disconnected from rank and file opinion. The thrashing out of congress resolutions continues to constitute a kind of aggregative process through which the various more powerful interests in the regime's constituency get heard and, to an extent, appeased and reconciled. Moreover, congress resolutions have sometimes had a policy bias which has not been on quite the same tangent as the dominant thrust from above. Thus, the resolutions of the 1975 6th Regional Congress incorporated a clear etatist thrust which, while not overtly challenging the emerging economic liberalization, translated into policies potentially at odds with it. This congress approved key developments in agriculture, namely an agricultural intensification program which would deepen state planning, control, and servicing of the agricultural sector and expand the state role in marketing. Subsequent congresses continued to fine-tune the state agrarian system. The 1980 7th Regional Congress directed a crackdown on beneficiaries of land reform who sold or rented it instead of working it themselves and approved priority for establishment of production cooperatives and state farms. At the 1985 8th Regional Congress this statist trend was diluted by the approval of joint state-private agricultural companies, but the congress also approved certain state interventions in the agricultural market. Thus, congresses remain very real arenas of policy consultation.[5]

To be sure, this "public" consultative process has, to a growing extent, been shortcircuited by multiplying webs of clientelist and primordial forms of access to elites by largely privileged interests which have sidetracked and reshaped the policy thrusts issuing from the more broad-based and institutionalized aggregative process. But congresses have also become regularized occasions of vociferous criticism, even revolt of the bases, against elements of the leadership, the president always excepted, chiefly over this corruption and incompetence, in many ways the central issues of Syrian politics today (Devlin 1983:58–59; Sadowski). Is the resultant turnover in the party elite in the elections which follow the congresses a matter of the "bases" holding corrupt leaders accountable, of feuding elite factions using the peccadillos of their rivals to bring them down, or Asad's exploitation of corruption among his subordinates to justify the periodic turnover in their ranks needed to prevent their acquisition of independent bases of power—or all of these? Whatever the case, it suggests that there are certain limits beyond which corrupt practices become a political liability and that party congresses may be functioning as a limited accountability mechanism.

Policy Implementation: The primary initial purpose of the party apparatus was, in theory, to function as a "stable central power" to "steer the process of socialist transformation" and to "control the march of the masses in a democratic manner" (ABSP 1973:84–87). Toward this end, the apparatus was designed to parallel the government bureaucracy and the array of syndicates (*munazzamat sh'abiya*) into which the Ba'th tried to organize the population.

The party apparatus remains a hierarchy through which the Regional Command supervises implementation of its policies by the bureaucracy and mass organizations.

The main line of command in the apparatus runs from the central leadership to branch, sub-branch and local (*firqa*) party committees. More specialized lines run from the central functional offices to their offshoots at lower levels. In the provinces, the branch command, at the apex of a regional political machine, is the primary center of authority, supervising policy implementation and adapting the operations of central ministries to local needs. The branch secretary outranks local officials, including the governor, who is a member of the branch command and in that capacity subordinated to party discipline; because the branch secretary is a local politician and the governor a bureaucrat and normally an outsider they, in principle, check each other.

The actual effectiveness of the party apparatus in implementing party policy is evidently very uneven. As an instrument of political control over government, it seems relatively effective. At times, it has enforced ideological conformity against ministerial initiatives. Without it, the Ba'th leadership would be dependent on orders from above to a sprawling ministerial bureaucracy staffed with many elements of doubtful loyalty. The apparatus has been active and effective in the formation and control of the party's "popular organizations." A few apparatchiki seem active in "problem-solving on a daily basis" for their constituents. But many seem preoccupied with patronage concerns such as placing clients in government office or taking a cut on public contracts.

The party's role in agricultural and rural affairs, probably of greater scope, visibility, and effectiveness than its role in most urban contexts, gives insight into its policy-implementing processes. At the central level, the Peasant Bureau of the Regional Command has wide responsibility for both agricultural and peasant political affairs. It assembles under its authority not only the head of the peasant union, but the Ministers of Agriculture and of Labor, the heads of the Agricultural Bank and of the wheat and cotton marketing agencies etc., to ensure party policy is being implemented; while the head of the Peasant Office has no legal authority over these persons they are normally party members subject to party discipline, an indicator of the political dominance of the party over the state bureaucracy. The Peasant Office draws up a yearly plan, in consultation with its branch offices, on such matters as the expansion of the peasant union, the creation of new cooperatives, recruitment of peasants to the party, supervision of the state agricultural infrastructure, and implementation of the agricultural plan. It also has a hand in drafting agrarian legislation; in the 1980–1985 period, for example, it presided over alterations in the law on agrarian relations, the drafting of the new land reform decree, and the design of the law on the collective organization of reclaimed land. Finally the party apparatus, particularly during the Ikhwan threat to the regime, has assumed policing and control functions. For example, the *maktab al-fallahin* was directed to determine the political persuasion of all agronomists, potentially strategic links between elites and the village. The outcome revealed that 40% considered themselves Ba'thi, 5% were non-Ba'thi "progressives," such as Communists, Nasirites or Arab Socialists, while 5% were "reactionary" or "Ikhwan," and 42% were "politically neutral." The Office also trained and armed 18,308 peasants organized in some sixty "Peasant Detachments" to defend against the Ikhwan (ABSP 1985b:129–130).

At the province level, the *maktab al-fallahin al-far'* (branch peasant bureau) functions analogously, its head regularly presiding over meetings of local peasant union leaders, ministerial field officers (e.g. the province agricultural and labor ministry directors) and heads of the party sub-district peasant committees to tailor the central bureau plan to the province and supervise its implementation. Its responsibilities parallel those of the central peasant bureau. Typically, the branch bureau is divided into 4 or 5 committees. The organizational affairs committee supervises and develops the local peasant unions and runs the province Peasant Cultural Institute which trains peasant leaders; building the peasant union was the first responsibility and the major achievement of the peasant bureaus. The party affairs committee recruits peasants into the party itself: such "cadre formation" is another historic priority. The peasant awareness committee is part of the party's propaganda network, responsible for organizing lectures and meetings in the villages to raise peasant consciousness, e.g. of their rights under the agrarian relations law and of the need to defend the revolution against "reaction and its agents," notably the Ikhwan. Other offices of the branch command take the party message to other sectors of the population, concentrating particularly on teachers and youth as a way of dominating the political formation of the new rural generation. The peasant bureau's agricultural affairs committee deals with "the daily problems of the peasants in their relations to the authorities," following up on peasant complaints over bottlenecks in delivery of credit, seeds, or fertilizer from the agrarian bank, ensuring there is enough machinery for the harvest, intervening on behalf of peasants caught in red tape, and smoothing out conflicts between peasants and state marketing agencies. It also polices crop marketing against efforts by merchants to divert "strategic crops" or subsidized inputs to the black market. In addition to the peasant office, the whole branch command in rural provinces is inevitably involved in rural issues. The branch makes sure to take credit for bringing roads or electricity to villages. It mobilizes party members for the harvest or for road-building, tree planting and literacy campaigns and supervises "popular work" programs which provide funds if peasants contribute labor for agricultural roads, catchment dams, or tertiary canals. In the Jabal Druze, for example, the party's project was to clear stones from the fields to build terraces and to plant seedlings on the hills. Besides these organizational, service, and developmental dimensions of party activity, their control over resources and access points gives local party politicians opportunities to build clientele networks, placing clients in government office or intervening on their behalf with the bureaucracy to get privileges and exceptions; the Dera branch, for example, regarded it as a great coup when it won the right to impose its candidates on local governments. While some local apparatchiki may be satisfied with the influence they thereby build, the growing corruption of the whole political system suggests some extort fees for their services. Whether as a leading force, a center of control, or a clientage machine, the middle-level party apparatus appears to be a powerful force in the provinces.

Below the branch, the party largely ceases to be a full-time apparatus and becomes a voluntary organization. At the sub-branch level, only the secretary is a full-time official. The sub-branch committee members are essentially part-time field agents, linking the province apparatus and village organizations—the *firaq* and smaller *halaqat* into which the latter are divided. The village level party organization is supposed to be the "link between the party and the masses," the main unit of "propaganda, organization, and struggle." The village cadre, being a local, yet, presumably ideologically committed to party goals, was viewed, as the following party document (ABSP 1965b:32–35) indicates, as the key to bringing the party's revolution to the base of society:

> The raising of consciousness . . . is the number one task of the party . . . but it is only possible by collaborating with [the masses] in changing their conditions of life, as much as possible through their own efforts, not by . . . government. The true role of the party [is] in putting an end to the passivism to which the masses of our people were habituated under the feudal-capitalist regime, and to move them with the spirit of invention. The establishment of a co-operative . . . does not depend on the role of the government, and it would fail if it [exclusively] did. . . . the government confines itself to promulgating a law and extending aid to it. The role of the party [is to] incite the peasants to establish at their own initiative a cooperative. The party must prove . . . the advantages it offers to the people. . . . the party encourages the people in the enterprise and eliminates such obstacles as family, tribal and sectarian factionalism. The masses, suffering from the inherited weight of the past, are incapable of taking such an action themselves.

But does the party really have the capacity to penetrate local communities and mobilize the people? An assessment of the quality, quantity, and origins of its cadres provides one measure of this.

Party Mobilizational Performance

Cadre Recruitment: The first task of the party apparatus was, from the outset, the mobilization of a base among the social sectors considered receptive to the party's revolution, namely the "workers, peasants, revolutionary intellectuals and soldiers, and small tradesmen." The first responsibility of basic level organizations was membership recruitment and every member was expected to cultivate another potential candidate for membership. Ideally, recruits were to be shaped into ideologically disciplined militants (*munadilin*) committed to revolutionary change. But, where such ideological cadres have been successfully forged, the effort usually begins during the party's struggle for power when the risks and costs of membership separate "true believers" from the uncommitted. The Ba'th had two decades in opposition when the choice of membership involved an "opportunity cost" and in which remarkably strong party loyalties were generated, but membership never required great self-sacrifice or discipline. Moreover there was a constant attrition of "old" Ba'thists, and the bulk of lower ranking members were recruited subsequent to the power seizure.

To avoid flooding the party with opportunists, a system of screening and indoctrination was established after 1963. At least when the system was most rigorously enforced under the radical leadership (1966–1970), classes judged "hostile" to the party's goals were excluded, commitment had to be demonstrated in lengthy periods of candidacy, and admission to full membership (with voting rights) and advancement in the party were rigorously controlled. But there were many times when these procedures were by-passed. In the period (1963–1965) when the party had to rapidly reconstruct to survive, not only were old members recalled but some party leaders flooded its ranks with kin and clients. In periods of intra-elite conflict (1964–1966, 1968–1970) when the outcome partly depended on building support bases, similar deviations took place, while in the two major splits which followed (1966, 1970) many ideologues on the losing side left the party over principle, leaving it to more malleable and pragmatic types.

It is clear that the membership fell well short of ideal standards even in the early years of party rule when ideology counted the most. One early observer spoke of party members as "high-spirited idealists" who nevertheless lacked initiative or organizational habits. Party documents from the sixties catalog an array of ills afflicting the members. "Idle talk of revolution" and belief in "revolution by magic," without organized daily practical work or concern for the means of implementation, were said characteristic of many of those who sided with the party leftwing. Party reports persistently speak of a "personal style of action," "weakness of organizational habits," lack of initiative and enterprise, and a "spirit of negligence' on the part of members. "Sick relations," i.e. tribal and sectarian factionalism, subverting "objective party relations," has been another constant. "Craving for benefits and posts," "influence-peddling," using party connections to "climb" career ladders, or the use by those who have reached office of bureaucratic authority as a shield against accountability to the party rank and file, reflect the illnesses to which a ruling party is especially vulnerable (ABSP 1965b). Despite these deficiencies, the party had, by the late-sixties, reincorporated much of its scattered former membership and added many younger and lower class members, bringing its strength to about 10,000 full members and 25,000 in various stages of candidacy.

The rise of Asad brought many of the least idealistic elements of the party to power. Internal documents (ABSP 1969) accuse Asad's faction of a "rightist mentality"—at best, "wavering between commitment to the masses and deference to the bourgeoisie," and at its worst, adopting the life style of the rich, indeed becoming a new bourgeoisie "not less greedy and dissolute than the old one." In his effort to dilute the remaining influence of ideological radials and broaden the party beyond its original rural core, Asad accelerated recruitment, lowered admission standards, opened the party to all classes and specially targeted Damascenes for recruitment and promotion. On the other hand, the 1970 establishment of the party youth auxiliary, the Revolutionary Youth Federation, was a major milestone in the regime's effort to regularize recruitment and indoctrination at an early stage in the political formation of the new generation. The evidence suggests that, through it and the party's rural organizations, recruitment under Asad continued to reach down in the stratification system, increasingly recruiting plebeian elements. Thus, a 1974 breakdown of recruits to the Revolutionary Youth Federation between those from Ba'thist families (indicative of the party's initial social base) and non-Ba'thist families (indicative of newly recruited elements) showed the latter to be of lower social status: those from Ba'thist families were 12% upper-middle class and 32% lower class while those from non-Ba'th families were 8.4% upper-middle and 42.4% lower class. By the early seventies, expansion raised party membership to about 100,000, about 4% of the adult population and one of every 13 adult males. By 1974 much of the urgency had gone out of the recruitment drive and the regime abandoned its earlier demand that all partisans cultivate a new member. To shape this membership, the Cultural Bureau of the National Command had established an elaborate system of party indoctrination, including party schools in each province and a Higher Political Institute in Damascus (Hinnebusch 1980:146, 152, 172; Devlin 1983:60).

By 1977–1978, the party had reached at least 200,000 full and candidate members and by 1980 nearly 375,000, but this cadre was apparently of declining "quality." The Asad regime's overt promise of special privileges to members—priority in access to scholarships and to the military academy—not to mention its growing tolerance of the abuse of party position for private ends, inevitably attracted a growing proportion of *intihaziyin* (opportunists); indeed, the 1980 7th Regional Congress admitted that indiscriminate recruitment had opened the party to corruption and opportunism. There is also evidence of attrition in the ranks in the late seventies. There was a falling away of more committed elements disillusioned by the anti-Palestinian intervention in Lebanon and elite corruption. Many "careerist" elements trying to distance themselves from a party under threat of assassination by Islamic militants, had to be forbidden from resigning their membership, an eloquent testimony to their level of ideological commitment.

Yet, despite the costs in ideological dilution of the party, the regime, in the face of the Ikhwan challenge, pushed ahead in the years after 1980 with a crash recruitment drive aimed at broadening its base. By 1984, total membership stood at an unprecedented 537,864, amounting to 8.36% of the population qualified by age for membership. While most of these were candidate members (*ansar*), many of them high school students whose affiliation was probably tenuous, there were 102,000 full members; but to reach this strength it had taken a liberalization of standards for promotion to full membership, raising the proportion of full members from 12% to 19% (ABSP 1985b:51–56).

Social Composition of the Party Bases: There is some empirical data on the social composition of the party bases which give additional insight into the Ba'th's mobilizational performance. First, the data do suggest that the bases have the "popular"—i.e. middle and lower class—social composition the regime in principle has sought. A study (Ben Tzur 1968a) of the 1966 composition of the Quneitra city branch found 77.7% of full members were clerks, teachers or students, 13.9% workers or peasants, and 5.6% employers or merchants (and 2.8% "undefined"). Data on the countrywide composition in 1968 is similar. Of full members, 48% were employees or teachers, 20% students, 16% peasants, 12% workers, and 4% others; but among more recently recruited candidate members, 28% were peasants and 14% workers (Batatu 1981:338). A 1974 study (Hinnebusch 1980:150–152) of the party youth auxiliary in three villages around Damascus was congruent with these findings. Elements from lower middle class families of teachers (15.5%), small merchants and artisans (17.2%), and soldiers (17.2%) made up 49.9% of the sample; lower class elements, from families of peasant small-holders (13.8%), landless agricultural workers (12.1%) and urban workers (15.5%) made up another 41.4% of the sample, while members from higher status families such as merchant-employers (5.2%) and landowner-employers (3.4%) made up only 8.6% and these were from the "middle bourgeoisie," not the Western-educated aristocracy or *haute bourgeoisie* which formerly ruled Syria. The proportion of lower class recruits among those newly affiliated with the party (42.4%) was greater than those from families traditionally aligned to it (32%), again indicative of a widening recruitment further down in the stratification system. All these respondents were from rural towns or villages, but while 29.3% were from farming families (as compared to 43% engaged in agriculture in the Damascus rural region) 70.7% came from families that had moved at least partially out of agriculture and into urban occupations. While this area, being the most urbanized of the rural areas, may not be entirely typical, this *transitional ex-peasant* type historically seems to have made up the core of the Ba'th's active cadres. Finally, meetings by the writer in 1974 with local party organizations in some twenty villages scattered throughout Syria gave the impression that the typical party cell is made up of three groups, local teachers, government employees, and younger peasants. While fragmentary, this evidence suggests that from the late sixties into the mid-seventies, petit-bourgeois elements, many from peasant families, peasants, and workers together dominated the party bases.

More precise and comprehensive data is available on the recent evolution of the party's social composition between 1980 and 1985. Table 6.1 shows the occupational composition of the party.[6] From this data, it seems clear that the party retains its historic character as an alliance of intellectuals, "small" professionals (especially teachers), and government employees (officials) with students, peasants and workers. Although class cannot be directly derived from this data, it seems reasonable to count doctors, pharmacists, engineers, judges and lawyers as *upper to upper-middle class,* nurses, teachers, and public employees as *middle class,* and workers, artisans and peasants as *lower class.* On this basis (excluding students[7] and "others"), Table 6.2

TABLE 6.1 Occupational Composition of Ba`th Party
Membership, 1980 and 1984

Occupation	1980 Number	%	1984 Number	%
Doctors, Pharmacists	298	0.08	1,255	0.23
Engineers	1,104	0.30	3,739	0.69
Lawyers & Judges	401	0.11	688	0.13
Nurses	752	0.20	1,853	0.35
Teachers	19,668	5.27	40,598	7.55
Public Officials	31,390	8.41	48,103	8.94
Workers	51,224	13.70	73,965	13.75
Artisans	3,547	0.95	4,220	0.78
Peasants	65,859	17.63	74,665	13.88
Students	183,355	49.10	267,255	49.70
Other	15,879	4.25	21,523	4.00
Total	373,477	100.00	537,864	100.00

Source: ABSP 1985b:47.

TABLE 6.2 Estimated Class Composition of Ba`th Party
Membership (in percent)

Class	1980	1984
Upper/Upper-Middle	01.04	02.28
Middle/Lower-Middle	29.73	36.35
Lower	69.23	61.36
Total	100.00	99.99

Source: ABSP 1985b:47.
Note: Students and "Other" are excluded.

estimates the class composition of the membership: it clearly retains a distinctively plebeian character, with the lower classes making up 60% to 70% of the membership and the upper strata only about 1–2%. If students are considered to be on their way to middle class status and thus appropriately counted in that category and if the "other" grouping is also included in the middle, in 1980 the proportion in the upper class is lowered to .5% and the middle raised to 67.2% while the lower class drops to 32.3%; were the military party organization included, the middle category would be larger yet. But this still represents a "populist" middle-lower class composition, particularly if it is considered that many in the middle categories have origins and family roots in the village. The party's plebeian social character is also registered in the 1984 educational make-up of the party, indicated in Tables 6.3 and 6.4. (These figures are distorted by the inclusion of the large proportion of students, but it is uncertain in which direction.) Of total membership, 13.8% had not completed primary school and another 57.66%

TABLE 6.3   Education of Ba`th Party Cadres and
Membership, 1984 (in absolute numbers)

| Education Level | Leadership Cadres | | | | Total Membership |
	Fara`	Shu`ba	Firqa	Total	
Illiterate	0	0	0	0	6,807
Some Literacy	0	24	502	526	67,404
Primary	3	53	796	852	136,868
Intermediate	4	59	817	880	173,264
Secondary	21	185	1,891	2,097	100,063
Vocational	12	127	1,173	1,312	26,331
Intermediate Institute	1	22	243	266	9,038
License (College Graduate)	114	325	1,509	1,948	16,203
Masters, Medical Dr., or Ph.D.	18	32	44	94	1,886
Total by rank	173	827	6,975	7,975	537,864

Source: ABSP 1985b:39-42.

TABLE 6.4   Education of Ba`th Cadres and Membership
(by percent)

| Education Level | Leadership Cadres | | | | Total Membership |
	Fara`	Shu`ba	Firqa	Total	
Illiterate	0.00	0.00	0.00	0.00	1.27
Some literacy	0.00	2.90	7.20	6.60	12.53
Total no Ed. credentials	0.00	2.90	7.20	6.60	13.80
Primary	1.73	6.41	11.41	10.68	25.45
Intermediate	2.31	7.13	11.71	11.03	32.21
Total <Secondary Ed.	4.04	13.54	23.12	21.71	57.66
Secondary	12.14	22.37	27.11	26.29	18.60
Vocational	6.94	15.36	16.82	16.45	4.90
Intermediate Institute	0.58	2.66	3.48	3.33	1.68
Total Secondary Ed.+	19.66	40.39	47.41	46.07	25.18
College Graduate	65.90	39.30	21.63	24.43	3.02
Masters, M.D. or Ph.D.	10.40	3.87	0.63	1.18	0.35
Total Higher Ed.	76.30	43.17	22.26	25.61	3.36
Total	100.00	100.00	99.99	99.99	100.00

Source: ABSP 1985b:39-42.

had not completed secondary school; indeed only 25.18% had secondary diplomas and a mere 3.36% had higher education.

However, it seems equally clear that the *leading elements* of this "populist" alliance are, as measured by their educational credentials, of middle class status (though quite possibly of more plebeian origin). Among the *leadership cadres,* a quarter had higher education, (compared to only 3.36% of the overall membership), nearly a half had secondary education and only 28.3% had less education than that. Moreover, the proportion of highly educated elements rises at each level in the party hierarchy: while at the *firqa* level 22.26% had higher education and 23% lacked secondary education, 76.3% of the members of *far'* commands had higher education and only 4% lacked secondary education. The Ba'th is no mere party of the intelligentsia, but intellectuals clearly play the leading role in it. On top of this, a comparison of social composition in 1980 and 1984 indicates a disproportionate increase in professionals and teachers, resulting in a decline in lower class composition from 69% to 61% (or if students are counted from 32% to 28%). Particularly striking is the decline in the proportion of peasant members from 17.63% to 13.88%.[8] This alteration in social composition appears to reflect a drive by the party to widen its presence among independent professionals which has been much too weak to secure Ba'thi control over this stratum, as the rebellion of the professional syndicates against party dictates in the late seventies demonstrated. The large increase in the numbers of teachers in party ranks seems to indicate a renewed determination to control this politically strategic profession.

Closer analysis of the professional composition of the party indicates that even in 1984 the party was overwhelmingly a "state" party—that is, a great proportion of its members were state employed. Teachers, public employees, and most nurses work for state institutions and most worker members are undoubtedly employed in the public sector; if students are excluded, the state-employed made up 61% of the membership in 1984; if the military party organization were included, this figure would, no doubt, significantly increase. This membership certainly gave the party a pivotal presence in state institutions: 31% of state officials and employees, 44.8% of school teachers, and as much as 56.6% of public sector workers appeared to be Ba'thist (assuming the vast majority of Ba'thi workers are in the public sector); of course many of these may be nominal members, having joined to protect or advance their careers (ABSP 1985:47; SAR 1984:109–110, 185, 354–375). By contrast to these "statist" elements, when students are excluded, only 2.1% of the party membership were "free" professionals and many of these are, in fact, probably government employed (this is certainly so of judges and most engineers). The artisan contingent of 4,220 amounted to only 1.6%, and merchants who must be included in the "other" category could have amounted to no more than 8%. This is certainly compatible with strong evidence on the concentration of opposition among independent professionals and the *suq.* The only exception to the "statist" character of the party is its peasant contingent which amounts to about 16% of the peasantry (as measured by the male adult work force in agriculture), well above the national membership average of 8.36% of the total population; this is congruent with the party's historical roots in the village.

Finally, the geographical distribution of membership, indicated in Table 6.5, gives some clues to the sectarian and regional composition of the party

TABLE 6.5 Geographical Distribution of Ba`th Party
Membership, 1984

Province Population	# of Members	% of Province Eligible*	% of Total Membership
Damascus City	51,314	6.13	9.54
Rural Damascus	36,420	5.86	6.77
Dera	21,182	9.23	3.94
Suwayda	23,140	16.53	4.30
Quneitra	19,912	14.12	3.70
Homs	58,114	10.64	10.81
Hama	53,344	9.68	9.91
Tartous	44,851	14.85	8.34
Latakia	58,161	14.91	10.81
Idlib	34,391	8.96	6.40
Aleppo	60,576	4.60	11.26
Raqqa	22,582	9.25	4.20
Deir ez-Zor	18,646	6.36	3.47
Hassaka	35,231	7.52	6.55
Total	537,864	8.36	100.00

Source: ABSP 1985b:56.
* excludes from the calculation those under 14, ineligible
by age

and to countrywide variations in its support. The relatively high proportion of the party recruited from Latakia and Tartous (19.15%) is indicative of the large Alawi presence in the party; the addition of the 4.3% from Suwayda, mostly Druzes, makes these two minorities, about 13% of the overall population, almost 100% "over-represented" in the party; indeed, if Homs, with its large Christian population is added, minorities could make up nearly a third of the party. Certain areas do appear to be somewhat disproportionately represented, too. The south is well, perhaps overly, represented: the Damascus area alone provides 16.31% of the party and if Quneitra, Suwayda and Dera are added to it, southerners make up 28.25% of party ranks. The north (Aleppo, Hama, and Idlib) makes up 27.57%, while the East (Raqqa, Deir ez-Zor and Hassaka) makes up only 14.22%. Nevertheless, all areas are represented by a sizable contingent of the membership.

The figures on membership as a percentage of population in each province demonstrate both that the party does have a nationwide presence and that its support remains uneven. Roughly 15% of the population in Latakia, Tartous, and Suwayda are "hizbiyin" compared to a national average of 8.36%, a fact supporting the greater embrace of Ba'thism among the minorities suggested by historical evidence. By contrast, only 4.6% of Aleppines are Ba'thists, a fact compatible with the intensity of anti-Ba'th dissidence in Aleppo. Still, the figures do not really support the view of the Ba'th as a minoritarian narrow-based party. Around 9% of the population in Sunni

Hama, Dera, and Raqqa is Ba'thi, above the national average, and even underrepresented Aleppo contributes over 60,000 members, 11.26% of the total party membership. The urban-rural distinction is hard to measure from the data, but Damascus city, in spite of the concentration of the political elite and the apex of the party apparatus there, is somewhat underrepresented, while mountainous peasant provinces (Latakia, Tartous, Suwayda) and plains provinces with a history of peasant politicization (Dera, Hama) are over-represented; even the remote Eastern provinces are close to the national average. This suggests the party remains strongest in the historic peasant strongholds from which it originally emerged and that it has done as well in penetrating remote rural peripheries as it has in cracking tough urban nuts like Damascus and Aleppo.

All of this data, quite compatible with the whole historic development of the party, is evidence that the Ba'th regime has not really changed its original social base.

Activist Attitudes and Recruitment Motivations: The writer's (Hinnebusch 1980) 1974 opinion survey of a sample of party youth auxiliary members gives the only empirical evidence currently available on the attitudes and motivations of the new recruits the system has channeled into the party bases and hence on their compatibility with an effective party possessing some ideological muscle.

The political attitudes of the recruits appeared largely congruent with traditional Ba'th doctrine. A high degree of nationalist militancy was indicated by the 83.1% who supported Palestinian commando activity from Syria despite the costs of Israeli reprisals and the 86.1% who believed Syria should boycott goods from nations supporting Israel; indeed, these attitudes appear to support a more militant policy than Syria's government has actually pursued. The sample shows a strong etatist populism hostile to the private sector: 95.4% believed government should take strong measures to ensure an even distribution of wealth and 81.5% believed government should supervise the private sector. A large majority believed people should be allowed to inherit only moderate (44.4%) or little or no property (50.8%), reflective of the party's traditional mistrust of large concentrations of property but also of its tolerance for small and medium property. The biggest differences between recruits were over the role the Quran and Shari'a should play in legislation, with 19.7% saying much, 44.3% some and 36.1% none. Less in line with Ba'th tradition, a majority, 65% of recruits, claimed to be religious practitioners; that 50% of older members and 70% of newer ones were religious suggests either a general decline in secularism or a greater attempt to recruit more religious elements.

Social distinctions among members were associated with some variation in these attitudes. Attitudes of upper-middle class elements (there were no upper class respondents) were less congruent with Ba'thist socialism than those of lower-middle and lower class recruits; they preferred more freedom for the private sector and rights of inheritance, while workers, in particular, opposed all property inheritance. They were also less nationalistic, opposing an economic boycott which apparently would have been bad for business. They were also more religious, a finding congruent with the traditionally Islamic orientation of the middle bourgeoisie in Syria. Religious practitioners, in general, tended to be both less secular and less socialist, but not less nationalist, than those who did not practice their religion. Finally, peasant families tended to be more nationalistic than others.

Recruitment motivations showed a very complex picture. The fact that only 10.7% claimed self-activation (i.e. joined on their own initiative), and that the great majority were brought into the party by friends, classmates, or a party worker, suggests a low level of voluntarist activism. Most respondents did cite political issues or events associated with their adhesion to the party, particularly national issues such as the war with Israel, the Palestine cause and the struggle with imperialism (32.2%), to a lesser extent social ones such as class struggle, commitment to egalitarianism or revolution, and the identification of the Ba'th with the less privileged (17%). But 14.9% cited merely a vague desire for development or the need to overcome backwardness and for a significant minority (25.5%), recruitment was apparently devoid of issue content. Nationalist issues were more likely to be cited by the lower stratum, particularly those from peasant families, 55% of whom claimed activation on such grounds compared to 21% of those in urban occupations. The upper-middle stratum was least likely to associate issues with recruitment. When asked to describe the *rewards of participation*, 46% cited pursuit of national goals or public duty, while 42% cited "solidarity rewards," such as relations with comrades or participation in a group, and 12% claimed no rewards. The upper-middle stratum was least likely to claim rewards from national goal-seeking.

On the basis of responses to items giving reasons for joining the organization, three major *recruitment motivation types* were identified. A *"careerist"* motivation, the desire to "be near those doing important things," or to "make a profession in political work," and associated with "having friends in the party," accounted for 26% of recruit choices; this motivation type reflects joining of the party in search of position, power, and material rewards, often, it seems, through reliance on personal connections. A *"personalist-localist"* motivation type associated with items such as desire for recognition in the village, admiration or trust for party leaders, and local community service, reflects a more traditional form of political tissue in which persons are linked to the party by personal or kinship ties and local loyalties rather than high ambition or ideological commitment; it accounted for 38% of responses. It was associated with measures of low ideological intensity, low scores on nationalist and socialist attitude scales, low feelings of political efficacy, and a low level of participation in the organization and it correlated highly with citation of "solidarity" rewards. Such persons lack much ideological commitment and expect few career or material rewards but find satisfaction as members of a local in-group of relatives and friends. Those from peasant and from landlord and larger merchant families were more likely to display this motivation than those from urban occupations and with greater education. Finally, ideological motivation—the desire to right wrongs, work for national goals, strengthen the country—accounted for 36% of motivational citations. It was correlated with more frequent incidence of nationalist and socialist attitudes, and a higher sense of efficacy and active participation. Indicative of a decline in ideological motivation was the fact that more recent recruits were less ideologically motivated. And an analysis of promotions at the base of the youth auxiliary uncovered no evidence that those favored for advancement were more ideologically motivated.

The Consequences of Party Recruitment: The foregoing evidence suggests a number of conclusions about the outcome of the party recruitment effort. First, the regime appears to have effectively mobilized and incorporated a typical "populist" coalition, that is, an alliance embracing petit bourgeois, worker, and peasant elements. In doing this, it has also bridged the urban-rural gap, embracing educated urban employees, blue collar workers, rurals moving out of agriculture into new occupations, white collar or manual, and peasant recruits. There seems little doubt the regime has built a significant popular consistency. Moreover, the political attitudes of this base appear largely compatible with the regime's historic nationalist and etatist-populist thrust. The nationalist militancy of the bases must be a key to the regime's ability to sustain a costly and apparently endless conflict with Israel. The membership's "socialist" orientation is compatible with the regime's social reforms, with the state planning and public sector which dominate the economy, and may be an obstacle to a restoration of private sector dominance.

The chief effect of the incorporation of this base has been to consolidate the Ba'th state and its initial nationalist-populist policy thrust. But, to a lesser extent, the attitudes of its base may be a constraint on the regime. The need to take account of its nationalist militancy may have limited the foreign policy flexibility of the regime. As the regime's actual practices have deviated from its official ideology, it has met with growing resistance in its own constituency and while it has not hesitated to override this opposition, it has done so at the cost of a dangerous erosion of its own support base. It also appears that the muting of the regime's initially radical secularism after 1970 may have been a concession not just to the opposition but also to its own constituents which expect some role for Islam in the state and two-thirds of whom practice their religion. But the very fact that it has incorporated a large proportion of religious-minded elements suggests that it is not wholly isolated from this part of society and the fact that only a minority of its base expects a large role for Islam suggests that the Ba'th has recruited and shaped a constituency satisfied with a limited role for religion in public life. On the face of it, the attitudes of the party's rank and file appear to be supportive of the main lines of the Ba'thi credo if not always of specific policies of the regime. The social composition of the bases also appears compatible with this credo and the fact that the attitudes of lower middle and lower class recruits are most congruent with it suggests the success and utility of the regime's plebeian recruitment strategy in entrenching Ba'thism in Syria's political terrain. That this base has constituted a major elite recruitment pool probably also imparts a certain durability and stability to the regime's policy orientation.

Second, the data provide some evidence on the complex mix of political association in the party, that is, on the forces behind mobilization and the nature of participation. Ideological commitments play an important role, but are by no means the dominant political cement of the party. Ideology did seem to account for a respectable portion of motivation. That those who claimed ideological motivation appear to have been more ideologically aware, activist, and efficacious, suggests such motivation makes a difference and doubtless gives the party what mobilizational muscle it retains. That ideological commitments were real is suggested by the fact that they were not randomly distributed but, varying by class, were anchored in the social interests of major social strata much as would be expected—i.e. more conservative upper strata and more radical lower strata. The persistent highly disproportionate attraction of the party for the lower strata and its still limited appeal to more well off elements indicates class-shaped ideology continues to shape recruitment. But *nationalism* seems to have been the single most important key to ideological mobilization. Peasant nationalism, in particular, seems to have been a major ingredient in the formation of the regime's rural base; nationalism also looms large in the recruitment of the more religiously pious elements. Clearly, nationalism has been central to the Ba'th's penetration of a still partially traditional mass society.

Yet, other motivations seemed to carry twice as much weight as ideological ones in recruitment. The weight of careerism is hardly surprising in a ruling party which dominates economic and career opportunities and recruits from an economically deprived base. Not all of those who fall in this category are necessarily pure opportunists who would have joined any ruling party. Rather careerism reflects the fact that in the villages and small towns, the advent of the Ba'th to power was widely supported, less because of strong ideological commitments, than because of a perception that it would open doors to government or pathways to career and privilege, hitherto largely monopolized by the urban establishment, for ambitious educated rural youth: the Ba'th was embraced less because it was socialist than because it was rural—it was, for many villagers, "their" party. The increasing transformation of the Ba'th from a vanguard into a patronage party reflects not just the replacement of a radical by a pragmatic leadership in Damascus, but the growing predominance of "careerist" expectations at the village base. Personalist-localist motivation and solidarity rewards also reflect an important side of the party at the local level. There, some rich farmers or merchants will typically join the party not for reasons of Ba'th ideology to which they are lukewarm or even hostile, nor even in the hope for national power, but to protect interests or secure connections to locals who do have power. Many peasants, too, ideologically inert and with little political ambition, may join because of the prominence of relatives in the local party or as a strategy for protecting and diversifying the interests of the family; increasingly, as the state penetrates the countryside and the village is incorporated into the national market, peasants realize that opportunity and protection depend on political access. Such recruitment may provide an inexpensive way of building local party bases, but it is hardly the stuff of which a dynamic local leadership is forged and, indeed, to the extent this type of association prevails, local party organizations may be captured by kinship blocs or fragmented by family rivalries.

On the whole, it would seem that while an ideological dimension continues to help cement and animate the Ba'th, the party has been subtly transformed from an ideological movement into a patronage machine with many of the features of a modernized form of clientelism. This blending of modern forms of association based on ideology, public issues and class interests with more traditional primordial and personal ties, is precisely the hybrid character of political association to be expected in a transitional society in which social mobilization and class formation have diluted exclusively traditional loyalties and provided the basis for political association on a larger "secondary" scale, but where the traditional culture remains very powerful. It is, more specifically, what one would expect where elites have used ideology and party organization—modern political technology—to mobilize a constituency in such a transitional society, but have, in time, exhausted much of their ideological energy and permitted a certain re-traditionalization of their base. In general, while this base has helped to institutionalize Ba'thist nationalism and populism, it probably lacks the ideological intensity to constrain a pragmatic adaptation of Ba'thism to the realities of regional power and the dictates of market forces.

The Role of the Party in the Shaping of the Ba'th State

The Ba'th Party has played a decisive role in the formation of the Ba'th state. Its mobilization drive, in transforming Syria's political arena, was a decisive factor in the consolidation of Ba'th rule. In this process, the Ba'th showed a capacity to use ideology and organization to mobilize thousands of activists in the construction of large scale political associations; this is in striking contrast to the pre-Ba'th era, when intense social fragmentation and political praetorianism precluded the formation of a stable political base for ephemeral governments. Party organization permitted the Ba'th to incorporate a significant political constituency which constituted strongpoints in the cities and gave it roots in thousands of villages across the country, thus linking the regime to the masses and helping to contain opposition access to them. In incorporating the rural periphery, the Ba'th widened the political arena beyond the formerly almost exclusively urban one and bridged Syria's historic urban-rural gulf. Party penetration of society was also a requisite for the social change the regime wished to promote: for example, the party's village presence played a crucial role in the implementation of agrarian reform, from land redistribution to the emplacement of cooperatives and a credit and marketing infrastructure. Finally, in mobilizing previously inactive strata, especially rurals, into the political arena and opening up opportunities for people of modest status to follow political careers—to "live off politics"—while putting up barriers to participation by the high status groups hostile to Ba'thism, the regime in some respects replaced wealth and aristocratic family name as the dominant criteria of political power with party activism and more broadly accessible "connections;" this spelled a certain democratization of participation. The party's incorporation of this plebeian base has helped give a durable populist thrust to government power.

The Ba'th Party suffers, however, from serious weaknesses which have increasingly debilitated its potential to provide the dynamic and legitimate leadership implicit in its claim to be a "vanguard" party. It has had little success in penetrating the traditional urban quarters where hostile notables and Islamic militants have enjoyed the confidence of the masses. The party never developed enough ideological discipline to sustain the mass mobilization needed for the socialist transformation it sought. Moreover, in turning itself into a patronage party, the Ba'th has gradually inverted the ideal of a vanguard party: instead of a party which wins the right to rule by virtue of its greater consciousness, activism, self-discipline—in essence from the greater demands it makes on itself—it has become distinguished by the greater privileges it demands for itself. As a result, a climate of cynicism has been created in which connections, not contribution, are perceived as the basis of rewards. Party networks in state institutions, from ministry to public sector firm and rural cooperative, have in many cases deteriorated from nuclei of leadership and change into mutual protection mafias using party connections for self-aggrandizement and as shields against accountability, bureaucratic discipline, and financial control. The consequences of this for achievement motivation in society as a whole have been negative, discouraging productivity, investment, official morale, and job performance. It also has profoundly negative consequences for the regime's legitimacy and support. Since exceptional performance is not expected of partisans, their privileges are naturally resented. This would be bad enough if partisan privilege was equally accessible, but the growing transformation of Alawis into a specially privileged group within the party itself has narrowed access and opportunities for other elements in the party base, weakening its solidarity and especially the loyalty of its Sunni activists, some of whom may now feel they have lost more than they gained by the rise of the Ba'th to power. Thus, the Ba'th Party has now become as much a burden and a divisive force as a leading and integrating one. It may be, as Sadowski (1985) suggests, that the regime is trying to draw a line between an acceptable level of patronage needed to animate partisanship in a post-ideological era and blatant, excessive corruption. Unless the regime curbs the abuse of power and privilege, the party will lose what still remains of the legitimacy, partisan energy, and cohesion which makes it of value to the political elite.

The Ministerial Bureaucracy

The Political Role of the Bureaucracy

The ministerial bureaucracy, topped by the Council of Ministers (cabinet) and headed by the Prime Minister is a third, but junior power institution.

The cabinet makes the day-to-day decisions needed to implement the high policy defined by the President and the party leadership and supervises the bureaucracy in policy-implementation. The cabinet is appointed by the President on the recommendation of the Regional Command. Ba'thists control about half the ministries, including the strategic ones, and the rest are headed by independent technocrats and a handful of Nasirites, Communists, and Arab Socialists. Cabinet tenure, including that of prime ministers, is, except for a few regime stalwarts who remain in office through turnovers, too short to permit ministers to build power bases. Prime Ministers are always senior Ba'thists, but their competence and power has varied greatly: only a few, notably Yusuf Zu'ayyin and General Abd al-Rahman al-Khulafawi, have combined the competence and party power needed to provide dynamic administrative leadership. Abd al-Ra'uf al-Kasm had exceptionally long tenure (1980–1987), but though personally competent, he lacked strong party backing. The most powerful ministers are so by virtue of their party stature or closeness to the president, and these have often been beyond the prime minister's control. As such, the cabinet often fails to act as a team in the pursuit of common goals. The ministerial bureaucracy is not a major channel of elite recruitment comparable to the army and party. It is subject to lateral control by the party apparatus and vulnerable to military interference. All this limits both the intra-regime political weight and the policy-implementing effectiveness of the cabinet and bureaucracy. Nevertheless, by virtue of expertise or party and personal connections, ministers obviously influence policy-making, especially within their own domains and exercise the practical power over policy that accrues to those charged with its day-to-day implementation.

The bureaucracy has served as a significant instrument of political control. The half of ministerial portfolios reserved for non-Ba'this makes the cabinet an instrument of political cooptation. The wider bureaucracy, having grown enormously under the Ba'th, incorporates thousands of Syrians, making them dependent on the Ba'th elite; public employment has ballooned from around 24,000 in the early fifties to 473,285 in 1983, including public sector workers and teachers but not the enormous military (IBRD 193; SAR 1984:94). While this expansion has been accompanied by a proliferation in bureaucratic functions, it is partly a consequence of a deliberate policy of absorbing unemployment—and hence political discontent—among the educated. While the Ba'th opened the door of education and of the state machine to rurals on a major scale, urban Syria continues to produce better educated graduates at a more rapid rate; thus, the upper levels of the bureaucracy have become, in a very real sense, an instrument of cooptation for the educated urban—largely Sunni—middle class analogous to the role of army and party for the rural areas. Most public officials are incorporated into Ba'th dominated professional or trade unions and many are party members. Many senior officials, even when not well-connected Ba'thists, have access to patrons higher up and thus enjoy privilege and access denied others. At all levels, many of these bureaucrats are, in some respects, a "bought clientele" (Waterbury 1976:435): in return for loyalty, the regime tolerates the petty—and not so petty—corruption and poor job performance for which many are known. Yet, if little is expected of the bureaucrats, little is also given to them, at least at the lower levels. As, in the late seventies, their relatively fixed salaries fell behind the inflation unleashed by economic liberalization and the oil boom, many officials saw the amenities they believed themselves entitled to, notably housing, slip out of reach. Because their aspirations outran incomes and opportunities, many were subject to acute frustration. Many scramble to go into business on the side, moonlight, and otherwise diversify their resources, and to this extent have interests in common with the *suq*. Their subordination to less cultured, frequently Alawite rural politicians and army officers, and the favoritism shown Alawis in personnel matters, also fuels anti-regime resentment among them. Yet, for the most part, bureaucrats have refrained from directly challenging the regime, remaining a pliant administrative tool.

It is as an instrument of reform and development policy, however, that the bureaucracy plays its most crucial political role. As the scope and penetration of state functions has expanded, more and more sectors of life, previously outside the purview of the state, have come under the influence or control of the bureaucracy. Government and the public sector tower over the cities and dominate industry and finance, although the traditional *suq* resists their sway with tenacity. But it is the state penetration of the rural areas which marks the biggest change in the fabric of social life.

Policy Design and Implementation: Bureaucracy and Development in the Countryside

The Ba'th forged the Syrian bureaucracy into a viable instrument for launching a transformation of agriculture which, largely serving the development of village society, has played a central role in incorporating a peasant constituency into the regime.[9]

While agrarian policy is shaped within political parameters laid down by the Ba'th party, the technocrats of the state bureaucracy design the actual programs and projects supposed to put party policy into practice. In doing so they have introduced a palpable rationalizing and development orientation into policy-implementation. The state has assumed a growing role in the planning of agricultural production, the management of resources, the introduction of technical innovation, and in the financing and administration of development projects. The attempt to put plans and projects into practice has translated into a burst of organization-building and rapid growth in the functions, size, penetration, and real impact of state structures on agriculture over the past decades.

The regime achieved several major breakthroughs in the creation of political-administrative technology needed to bring policy to the village. Land reform broke down traditional forces resistant to state penetration and cooperatization institutionalized state linkages to peasants. An array of specialized bureaucratic organizations—an agricultural planning apparatus, a multitude of ministries (Agriculture, Irrigation, Internal Supply, Industry), and a series of specialized "General Organizations" (for cattle, seeds, mechanization, etc.) were deployed to carry out policy tasks. The efficiency of this apparatus failed to keep pace with its structural expansion and it is riddled with "pathologies" which enervate its performance: acute personnel problems, chronic mal-coordination, and a shadowy politics of patronage which often dissipates pubic resources and short-circuits policy-implementation. Despite the resulting waste and inefficiency, the bureaucracy is nevertheless responsible for a long series of reform and rationalizing innovations which amount to a cumulative transformation of the face of Syrian agriculture.

The bureaucracy carried out a successful land reform which checked the proletarianization of the peasantry and replaced the great latifundia of pre-Ba'th times with a mixed small peasant and medium capitalist agrarian structure at the cost of only temporary declines in production. This is a rare accomplishment among Third World regimes. Indeed, the post-reform agrarian economy, in enhancing peasant independence and initiative, increasing the incorporation of the peasant into the market, and forcing greater investment by landlords on their reduced holdings, is more dynamic than the old latifundia structure. The bureaucracy also organized a large portion of the small peasantry into a network of cooperatives crucial to the viability of land reform: they are the framework which channels resources, services, and innovation to the small holding sector, deters land reconcentration, and excludes landlords and merchants from major channels of sectoral interchange. As channels of government control sometimes putting state interests first, the cooperatives have not fully won peasant confidence and they have not become the building blocs of a viable agrarian socialism. But far from being economic failures, cooperatives have upgraded the small peasant sector and fostered much individual peasant development.

The subsequent state intervention in agriculture made possible by the bureaucratic-cooperative link to the village has translated into both greater control and widened state responsibility for agricultural management. The state's planning, credit, and input system has advanced the regime's control over production decisions, while providing peasants with relatively cheap access to the credit and inputs needed to stimulate productivity. State marketing has given the regime reasonably effective control over strategic crops, such as cotton and wheat, essential for export earnings and food security, although it has yet to effectively organize the delivery of produce to processing factories. The state marketing system guarantees producers stable, if not exactly lucrative, markets and has not been systematically used as an instrument of extraction. Indeed, the stable state market and subsidized credit protects peasants from the old threat of debt and expropriation and the ruinous fall in crop prices typical of the free market, providing a basic security which would be rapidly missed if the state withdrew from this role. The bureaucracy has initiated a score of useful innovations, from orchardization, seed and animal improvement to mechanization, and, although in constantly allowing planning and coordination to lag behind its initiatives, it generates ever new kinds of bottlenecks, it has advanced agricultural intensification and mechanization with some success. As a result, there has been, on the average, a general increase in agricultural production since the sixties.

The state has also assumed a new role in expanding Syria's agrarian base. It now plays a massive role in land reclamation and irrigation. The Ghab irrigation project, though long "sick" from incompetent state management, is finally operative and has transformed an area of desolation and urban dominance into a viable peasant community with a certain prosperity. The much more ambitious Euphrates project has so far been a costly drain on the state's limited resources and management capacities. Generally, massive investment in irrigation and reclamation has prevented a backsliding in the irrigated surface, although it has not much advanced Syrian agriculture beyond its crippling dependence on rainfall. But the "hydraulic state" is slowing bringing a growing portion of rural society under its sway.

The public industrial sector has developed some of the crucial sectoral interchanges which stimulate agricultural development. To be sure, agro-industry, the very nexus of the sectoral interchange, is the victim of all the pathologies of the regime: politicized, incompetent, underpaid and under-motivated management, an undisciplined work force, and the subordination of profit to the maximization of employment and consumer price stability. But industry provides inputs, markets, and employment opportunities which benefit agriculture. And the public construction sector provides hydraulic works and the transport infrastructure needed to integrate village and market.

The state, in the form of services, credit, inputs, markets, and investments in irrigation and land reclamation is almost certainly putting more into agriculture than it extracts and has, generally, made village life more viable. The considerable enhancement in the rural standard of living from state-sponsored development is an outcome of both the regime's political need to serve its rural constituency and the development imperatives of the state bureaucracy.

Bureaucracy and Peasant

The bureaucracy is, of course, a burden on as well as a support and stimulant of peasant society. There are, first of all, conflicts of interest between high bureaucrats and the peasant: the former seek control (e.g. in the imposition of crop rotations too often indifferent to the interests of the peasants), while the latter seek to maximize their independence. The pro-liferation of bureaucratic personnel and official corruption are burdens on the rural economy. As the bureaucracy increasingly penetrates the village, peasants are ever more dependent on its services and subjected to its rules and exactions. Local officials find more occasions to exact bribes to overlook regulations or insist on them as the price of the official approvals or services peasants are entitled to. Although the potential for official arbitrariness is diluted by the plurality of local authorities—party, peasant union, ministry officials—who take decisions in committees, peasants are nevertheless often the victims of power exercised in the absence of strong legal or customary checks. The recruitment of many officials from the village itself gives some of them sympathy for village problems, but others are more interested in escaping from their background and dislike having to work in the field. Indeed, there is a gap between the self-interest of the local bureaucrat and that of the peasant: "the peasant is dependent on production; [the bureaucrat's] salary is fixed. He has no need of the people, is not responsible to them, so the quality of his work declines, he lacks a sense of duty and works mechanically" (al-Tal). Inspite of this, the local bureaucrat is not typically part of a new class standing against the peasant and is no longer the instrument of the local landlord. Nor are peasants any longer passive victims; many find ways to evade, even manipulate the state: a son will join the local party, a bribe will sway an official. Indeed, indicative of the new access of the village to the central power are those incidents in which high politicians and bureaucrats use their position to help out kin and village; the case of a strategically-placed aide in the presidency who got the Ministry of Agriculture to drill wells and plant trees in his village is not exceptional. Thus, patronage is "democratized" as public goods are diverted and laws bent to favor locals. In sum, the state has brought opportunities and resources as well as constraints and extractions to the village.

Indeed, in overall socio-economic terms, state intervention in the agrarian economy has increased the options and life-possibilities of peasants even as it has incorporated them into its own networks. Most basically, the state transformed the formerly rigid class structure which kept the village oppressed and encapsulated into a more open, pluralized system. Land reform and the state agricultural infrastructure curbed landlord-merchant control of village agricultural wealth and the regime generally broke the fusion of local wealth and power in their hands by which they had dominated the village. State stimulated development has allowed peasant families to diversify their resources, e.g. by taking advantage of new opportunities for education, off-farm employment and of credit and inputs to intensify production. Cultural and opportunity gaps between city and village have narrowed and a certain peasant prosperity and accumulation has been generated. Generally, the wider dispersion of property, services, and opportunity the Ba'th has brought to the village, and the growing dependency of peasants, once under the thumb of landlords, on the state have all advanced the incorporation of the peasantry into the regime's base.

The Ba'th has, thus, displayed a greater ability to foster positive change in the village than most authoritarian regimes. But it now seems to have reached the limits of its social engineering capacity. The Ba'th exhausted its rural mobilization capacity without having created viable agricultural institutions which could substitute for capitalism. Agro-industry has failed to mobilize the capital for its own reproduction without costly dependence on outside sources and the agricultural marketing system has not become an effective engine of state capital accumulation. As the costs of state intervention exceed benefits in an era of growing patrimonialization, tightening economic constraints are likely to force a certain contraction of the state role in favor of markets and private enterprise. Whether this would open the door to a return of landlord-merchant dominance in the village or give greater scope to the Ba'th's own peasant constituents to prosper from increased autonomy is a question of significant political import.

Notes

1. For the party organizational doctrine which, in a very real sense, constituted the blueprint the architects of the regime aimed to follow, see the following party documents: The National Command, *Some Theoretical Points of Departure*, Damascus, 1973, pp. 57–102; al-qiyada al-qaumiya, *al-manhaj al-marhali*, Damascus, 1965, 27–38; Commandement Nationale, *Programme du Parti*, Damascus, 1965.

2. This analysis of party organization is based on both interviews with party apparatchiki and the published party rules (*nizam*). The party has issued five *nizams* since 1963, each slightly altering its predecessor. The 1971 rules replaced election of local commands by appointments from above and the 1980 one added the central committee to the top leadership organs. See "Statues of the Arab Ba'th Socialist Party," in *Arab Political Documents, 1963* (Beirut 1964) pp. 445–467 and al-qiyada al-qaumiya, *al-nizam al-dakhili* (Damascus, 1968, 1971, 1975, 1980).

3. In addition to the sources cited, this discussion of party functions relies on a program of interviews with party apparatchiki from the central to district level, on various internal party documents, and on discussions with former and current party members.

4. These profiles rely partly on interviews of party leaders at the district, province, and national levels and partly on backgrounds provided by the Syrian press on national level leaders.

5. See the resolutions of these various congresses on agricultural matters in *al-Hizb wal-mas'ala al-zira'iya* [The Party and the Agrarian Question], Damascus 1972; also Regional Command, "Report and Resolutions of the 6th Regional Congress," Damascus 1975; ABSP, 1985b, and Sadowski (1985).

6. No data is available on the military party organization.

7. The reason for excluding students is that their class status cannot be estimated and may be in flux, because they are mere candidate members, and because many, being nominal adherents recruited through pressures in the schools rather than voluntary activists, are unlikely to stay in the party.

8. The vast majority of peasants are, however, incorporated into a party auxiliary, the General Federation of Peasants.

9. This section on the bureaucracy's impact on agriculture is based on the more extensive and documented argument made in my companion volume *Peasant and Bureaucracy in Ba'thist Syria: The Political Economy of Rural Development* (Boulder: Westview, 1989), which looks at the bureaucracy's role in both decision-making and policy-implementation.

7

State-Society Linkage:
The Case of the Peasant Union

The Ba'th state is linked to society through an array of party-controlled "popular organizations" (*munazzamat sha'biya*) and professional associations (*niqabat mihaniya*) which enroll thousands of citizens in every sector of society. Closely associated with the party are the peasant, youth, scouting, artisan, and women's syndicates which it literally created from scratch. The labor movement pre-dates the Ba'th, but Ba'thists, along with Communists and Nasirites, long played a key role in it; today the party shares trade union power with these political forces but maintains a majority in the central labor federation executive committee. The syndicates of higher status professions in which the Ba'th is lightly represented, such as those of the doctors, lawyers, and engineers, have retained a certain independence of the regime, while some other professional bodies such as the teachers' and agronomists' unions are Ba'th dominated.

In doctrine, the role of these organizations is to mobilize the wider portion of the population which cannot be incorporated into the "vanguard" party. They are also to represent the legitimate particular interests of their members, albeit in harmony with the public interest the party claims to speak for. And, they are supposed to be instruments of "self-management" and of "popular control" over the bureaucracy, (ABSP 1973:78–92; ABSP 1965:30–31). In practice, most enjoy only limited autonomy. Party members "lead" most of them, charged with "securing the revolutionary character of voting and elections," in theory by their greater consciousness and activism. On the few occasions syndicate leaderships have proved recalcitrant, they have been removed; the support of the lawyers,' doctors,' and engineers' syndicates during the Islamic disturbances for opposition demands led to the purge of their leaderships. This system, in the enforced articulation of interests through a limited number of government authorized channels and associations, bears all the marks of a particular form of state-society linkage, namely, *corporatism*. But, as will be seen, it is a special "populist" variant of corporatism.

One of the most important syndicates, by virtue of its role in securing the rural base of the Ba'th, is the General Federation of Peasants (*al-ittihad al-amm lil-fallahin*). This chapter will take the peasant union as a case study of the operation of the Ba'th's populist corporatism.

Development of the General Federation of Peasants

The General Federation of Peasants (GFP) was conceived as the major mass auxiliary of the Ba'th Party, fashioned by it almost from scratch. Previous Syrian regimes had discouraged peasant organization. The Ba'th, however, had powerful incentives to mobilize the peasantry. Its leadership, of rural origin and facing intense urban opposition, perceived its base to lie in the villages; the revolution it aimed to carry out was in large part a rural one against the "corrupt feudal social structure;" and the modernization it sought required the mobilization of the human and natural resources locked in Syria's villages.

To bring its revolution to the rural masses, the Ba'th could not rely on a bureaucracy which hardly penetrated the village and had little capacity to win over a passive peasantry traditionally suspicious of government; as it recognized, "an agricultural revolution never happens by government administration" (GFP 1967:73). Nor did the Ba'th expect to work through village notables who had a stake in the status quo, were often clients of the old elite or unreceptive to Ba'thism, and would have turned its political structures into mere disguises for the traditional local power structure; the Ba'th eschewed cooptation of these "gatekeepers," and tried to by-pass them by recruiting and organizing a wholly new village leadership from the mainstream peasantry.

In Ba'thi theory, the function of the union was to "deliver" the peasants from "anarchic individualism, tribalism, sectarianism, and localism" and to create loyalties to the nation and "socialist morality." It would be a vehicle of peasant power, drawing villagers "from the margins to the heart of public life," turning them from a "nebular mist . . . swinging between passivity and temporary surface enthusiasm" into an class-conscious organized force able to defend peasant rights against exploiters and assist in the implementation of an agrarian revolution (GFP 1967:11–12, 65, 73; SAR 1969:3–10). An examination of the actual formation and operation of the peasant union, as measured against these objectives, can throw light on the features and consequences of the Ba'th's effort to mobilize a peasant base.

The peasant union was founded under Law 127 of 1964. A provisional central leadership was appointed and organizational teams of party officials and coopted pro-Ba'thi peasants were set up at the province level. Local party cells began to nominate promising candidates for training as union cadres, by law selected from those who worked and resided on their own land; they were sent to party schools for indoctrination in Ba'thism, peasant class consciousness, and organizational methods, then returned to their villages to organize a union under tutelage of local party authorities (GFP 1967:62–63). These local cadres were the key to penetration of the villages: in principle carefully selected, indoctrinated in regime ideology, and subject to controls from above, they could be trusted to represent the regime in the village, yet, being locals known to villagers on a face-to-face basis and still working their own land, they had a better chance of winning peasant confidence than bureaucratic outsiders. Moreover, once the union was established, local leaders were elected, responsible to and removable by 2/3 vote of the village general assembly.

Backed by the local party, the organization of village unions proceeded at an encouraging pace. Some older peasants who had participated in the struggles against landlords in the fifties were receptive to the union. The ideology of peasant solidarity appealed to educated peasant youth. The union was able to exploit the powerful nationalism of Syrian peasants to win some to Ba'thism. Peasants were also attracted by material benefits. Where reform land was being distributed, the union tried to use it to win over peasants; the fledgling peasant unions were deliberately associated with it and, after 1966 assumed, together with local party cadres and ministerial technicians, a direct role in land distribution. The union funneled credit and production requisites to peasants, represented them in the agrarian courts, and gave access to the bureaucracy. Ambitious younger men were attracted by the chance to build local power in a milieu dominated by elders and by the prospect of office at higher levels. In fact, many peasants who would become union cadres were younger poorer ones who acquired the means to improve themselves through regime programs: Owen (15) noted that two cadres in the Raqqa provincial union were former sharecroppers who got land in the reform and, in time, were farming eight and ten hectares they had partially irrigated. They had become "successful and relatively substantial farmers by local standards." Finally, inserting a member in the emerging new power structure was part of many a family survival strategy. By September 1965, the skeleton of the union hierarchy was in place and the first General Congress was held as a "training session" for the first batch of appointed leaders. By 1967, 546 village unions had been established and the organization held its second congress, this time of elected delegates who, in turn, elected the executive bureau of the national level General Federation (GFP 1967: 14–15, 74–83).

It was soon apparent to the leadership, however, that many local unions were "paper" creations or disguises for traditional factions. The local notability, in principle excluded from membership, often managed to "infiltrate" local unions and take them over for personal benefit. These influentials were sometimes elected to the local union leadership virtually by acclaim (*tazkiya*) because of their status as patriarch of a dominant kin group, their patronage resources, or the respect owing to elders. Rich peasants—even a middle landlord touched by the agrarian reform—dominated some local unions (Petran 229). Some of them reportedly precipitated conflicts with poorer peasants, forcing them out of the union. Even some middle level cadres in the union structure lacked the desired "characteristics of a hard-working peasant" (GFP 1967:82). The warning of the union leadership against attempts to create "gaps" between the union and the local party suggests that some of these elements were resistant to party tutelage (GFP 1967:85–86). Another typical ill was the tendency in some local unions for certain families to take control, use the union for their own ends and exclude rival families, or the latter, seeing the union as a creature of the former, would boycott it; where the balance of power was even, the union might be paralyzed by clan conflict.

In 1968, rectification committees fanned out over the provinces to deal with these pathologies. They undertook to review memberships and expel those unqualified by size of land-holdings or failure to work it personally and those "hidden saboteurs" who exploited the union for personal benefit (GFP 1967:82–83). In 1969 a new union statute tightened the definition of peasant to make it easier to exclude the notability: a "peasant" was one who worked the land personally, without using wage labor or tenants and whose holding did not exceed 8 hectares irrigated or 30 hectares of non-irrigated land. The law also gave the union's central leadership enhanced supervisory powers over lower levels to eliminate the "exaggerated liberty" which had resulted in poor discipline and performance (SAR 1969). So armed, the General Federation began enforcing a policy of "unity of the village," dissolving unions split by family rivalries and permitting creation of a new one only after members—generally younger peasants who accepted that divisive kinship and tribal ties should be superseded by class solidarity—had been recruited from all major kinship groups (GFP 1967:82–83). These reform efforts had a positive effect but there were periodic signs that the ills had not been wholly cured. At the 3rd Congress in 1970, the leadership again had to insist on expulsion of those who violated membership qualifications (GFP 1970:31–32). Reports persist well after this of richer peasants or even landlords who managed to infiltrate the village organizations by registering only a portion of their land. As late as 1981 some local union leaders, mostly household heads who left their farms to their families, worked outside agriculture.

The organizational troubles of the early union were attributed to the fact that the leadership "began with principles" but lacked all organizational experience, to the scarcity of financial and technical resources, and to the "endless problems" generated by the "remnants" of traditional culture. Organizational expansion nevertheless continued, and indeed peasant demand for establishment of unions exceeded the pace of cadre development: by 1970 there were 1823 unions and by 1974, 2984, incorporating about 218,000 members (GFP 1977:19; SAR 1976:793). Those outside the union framework included peasants in areas not yet reached by its organizers, those who were politically hostile or apathetic, and a portion of peasant activists who were loyal to other parties such as Akram al-Hawrani's socialists or the Communists—particularly Kurdish peasants in the north (Petran 228–229).

In 1974, a major transformation took place in the union, its merger with the formerly separate cooperative movement: "the era of struggle against feudalism" which required concentration on largely syndical work had supposedly been superseded by one of "socialist construction" in which the task of agricultural development was paramount. Village cooperatives were brought under the authority of the union hierarchy, where a local union and cooperative coexisted they were merged, and where only one existed, it took on the responsibilities of the other. A new peasant union law was issued to reflect the union's new economic role. It provided for the appointment of experts—agronomists, lawyers, accountants—to the union hierarchy and village cooperatives. It laid down rules for establishment of economic enterprises and to protect the property and finances of the organization, experience having shown such measures needed to "protect the peasants from falling into financial irregularities" (GFP 1974).

The union takeover of the cooperatives from the control of the Ministry of Agriculture has been seen as a union or party victory in a bureaucratic struggle for turf (Bianquis 1980:129). But the merger had a major disruptive effect on the union. It was now charged with many tasks formerly the responsibility of the ministry, notably technical management of the cooperatives. But it lacked sufficient numbers of technical cadres and the ministry, jealous of its own prerogatives, was reluctant to assign its own personnel to the union; a certain duplication of responsibilities between ministry and union also caused conflicts. Many unions rapidly transformed into cooperatives by administrative fiat were unprepared and did not really become economically active entities. The merger between cooperatives of land-owning peasants and unions with their contingents of landless tenants and wage workers introduced a potential class cleavage into the heart of the cooperatives, manifested in such phenomenon as electoral conflicts between the two strata (GFP 1977:21–22; Bakour).

In 1977, the combined organization held its 4th conference of 285 elected delegates. The focus of the congress was the orientation of the union to the tasks of cooperatization and agricultural development. But the organization was still trying to digest the cooperatives. While the agricultural population continued to grow, union expansion had slowed and would make little headway in the late seventies. Pre-occupation with the merger and the much greater difficulty of organizing cooperatives as compared to unions partly accounts for this slowdown (GFP 1977:21). But the movement may also have exhausted much of its energy as the mobilizational impetus of the Ba'th Party itself ran down in the seventies and the community of interest between the regime and the peasantry was threatened, if not superseded, by elite corruption, the growing opening of the state to the agrarian bourgeoisie, and the webs of bureaucratic controls being imposed on the peasant as the scope of state intervention in agriculture widened. The regime now seemed to view the union less as an instrument for a village revolution or the generation of peasant class consciousness against a bourgeoisie it was itself accommodating and more as an instrument of control for the imposition of sometimes unpopular agrarian policies, notably crop planning and state marketing. The peasants' view of the union subtly changed: when it was chiefly a political organization through which they got access to the state and defended their rights against landlords and merchants, peasants had started to see it as *theirs,* but when it was called upon to enforce state policies, union leaders began to be seen as creatures of government. As the gap between regime ideology and corrupt realities widened, engendering a growing cynicism, identification with the Ba'th became as much a liability for local union leaders as an asset.

By the eighties, however, as the regime faced widening urban revolt, it increasingly fell back on its rural base for support. An extraordinary congress of the peasant union was convened in March 1980 in which Asad called on the peasantry to defend the revolution against the "class enemy." The union was charged with "assuring the solidity of the peasants around the party." Armed detachments of some 25,000 peasants were formed to guard against the *Ikhwan* and had a hand in the confiscation of the land of a "feudalist" in Idlib active in the Islamic uprising. The union participated in mass demonstrations in the cities meant to show the opposition that the regime had not lost its support base (GFP 1981: 28, 56–60, 225). In return for union support, Asad told syndicalists that they were henceforth "masters of decision in all matters concerning land and agriculture" (GFP 1981:22); as as token of this, the long-standing union resolution for another land reform was promulgated as Law 31 of 1980, decreeing a modest reduction in land-owning limits. The removal of some members of the union's national council suggests some Islamic dissidence had penetrated the union. But indicative of the regime's apparent trust in the union, the Chambers of Agriculture, a weak vehicle of larger farmers, were put under union control and unionists were appointed to the central committee of the National Progressive Front, the supposedly ruling alliance of the Ba'th and other small progressive parties, thereby diluting the critical influence of the latter. In a speech to the 5th congress of the union in 1981, Asad's tone was reminiscent of the radical rhetoric of the sixties (GFP 1981: 5–22):

> We must remember, if we are to protect our gains, that not so long ago the peasant was exploited, treated as property by feudalists. The peasants never submitted to this oppression, our party flourished from attachment to the peasants, and this brought reaction down. . . . No one can [now] raise his hand over the peasant in the Ba'th state. [But] we haven't reached the ideal state yet. . . . reaction has deep roots we must uproot so it can't regenerate. . . . Reaction forgot the people have a stake in the revolution. . . . You won't allow the turning back of history as they want.

Organizational advance seemed to recover in the eighties and the union has come close to completing its organizational drive, bringing much of Syria's peasantry within its framework. But what significance does the union hold for peasants? Its dual character, instrument of regime control, yet pressure group for peasant interests, obviously puts it in an ambiguous, even contradictory position. An analysis of the union's structure and policy-making process gives some insight into its actual role in the political system.

Syndical Organization and Politics

The union structure, as it has looked since the mid-seventies, is a four-layered pyramid. The village "associations" (*jam'iya*) are grouped into a league (*rabita*) in each of the 55 districts, the leagues are joined at the province level in a federation (*ittihad*) and these are united in the countrywide General Federation. The village level units are now predominately economic in function: the cooperatives with a new name. The leagues are essentially syndical organizations, while the province and central level structures combine both functions.

At the base level association, a general assembly of all members elects a three man council (*majlis*); attached to it is a paid "supervisor" (*muraqib*) appointed by the Federation and charged with carrying out the decisions of the council and managing the work of the association. A three man inspection committee is supposed to exercise financial supervision over the council. At each higher level in the hierarchy there is a congress, a smaller council, and an executive committee. The three-man councils of the base-level associations in each league together make up the congresses of the leagues, each of which elect 17–19 man league councils which, in turn, elect 3–5 man league executive bureaus. The councils of the leagues in each province, plus a delegate elected from each base level association make up the federation level congresses which elect the 17–19 man federation councils from which 5–9 man federation executive bureaus are then elected. Federation level councils come together with the top union leadership to make up the 200–300 delegate general congress of the General Federation which meets every four years to set high policy. The general congress also elects a council (22–26 members) from which the 13-man national executive bureau and union president are elected. The executive bureau presides over a series of specialized offices: secretariat, agricultural affairs, political culture, finance, organization, marketing, animal husbandry, training, rural engineering, production cooperatives, administrative and legal affairs, planning and statistics, and public affairs (GFP 1974).

In principle, the general assemblies of the base level associations are the locus of ultimate authority: they meet twice yearly to approve the cooperative plan, to close the accounts, and to evaluate the performance of their councils; they can, but rarely do, depose members of their councils (GFP 1981:196). On the other hand, higher level executive bodies supposedly acting to implement national congress resolutions, have the power to command lower level executive bodies and councils in the execution of plans and instructions, can nullify lower level decisions against the law or the state plan and can dismiss lower level leaders who break the rules and "harm the interests" of the movement (GFP 1969; GFP 1974). There have been many instances when lower level organizations were simply dissolved and reconstructed by the top leadership. There have also been occasional conflicts between the responsibility of the top union leadership to propose (under state tutelage) the cooperative plan and the ultimate right of the cooperative associations themselves to approve it; in cases where the village level general assembly has refused to approve the plan, the result has been paralysis. Once approved, if a cooperative member violates the plan, the peasant union leadership can take over management of his land for the season (Havens 39–41).

Formally, the union is autonomous, but in practice it is subject to tutelage by the party. Union leaders, especially at higher levels, are party members, hence subject to the discipline of the *maktab al-fallahin* and its offshoots and are expected to keep the union within the party line; they are supposed to do this by their greater consciousness and activism, but they have extensive powers of purge, should these be needed, over lower levels of the organization. The union is also financially dependent on party and government subsidies. In short, although the union hierarchy issues from a village base, it is controlled from above by party authorities.

The peasant union goes through an elaborate internal policy process which, in principle, is supposed to mobilize peasant opinion behind party goals and yet, within these limits, provide for the aggregation of peasant demands into the national policy process. Formally, the policy process begins in the meetings of village level general assemblies which every four years pass resolutions and elect delegates to higher level congresses, culminating in the supreme policymaking General Federation congress. At the beginning, at least, the leadership encouraged competition in elections against the tendency to elect influentials "by acclaim" (GFP 1967:83–84); but it seems likely that the endorsement of a local party leader carried ever greater weight at succeeding levels in the hierarchy, and support from below ever less. In the earlier years, any peasant with primary education could nominate himself for election (GFP 1967:31), but, at least in the last election for higher level offices, a "National Progressive Front List" drawn up from above was presented to voters who duly elected it. There is no record of factionalism based on issues in the electoral process or of any dissident faction ever having challenged the incumbent top leadership or Ba'thist control of it. And, the national-level leadership, with its power of purge over lower levels, control of patronage, monopoly of expertise and information, etc. can generally channel the rounds of elections and assemblies out of which peasant demands and new leadership supposedly emerge. It is questionable how much those elected feel responsible to constituents in a system in which co-optation from above so dominates election from below.

There is still considerable turnover in elections, however. According to the organization report to the Fifth General Congress, the 1981 round began with the meeting of the association general assemblies to elect councils in which about a third of nearly 19,000 incumbent members were replaced. Elections were not held in 170 cooperatives which were inactive or paralyzed by disputes or lack of candidates. At the meetings of the league (district) congresses which followed, about 58% of incumbent council members were replaced and at the federation (province) level 150 out of 230 were new-comers. No data was given on turnover in elections to the national level council and executive bureau, but Mustafa Ayad, the incumbent president since 1971, was re-elected (GFP 1980:195–199).

At the general congress itself, the reports and recommendations of the union leadership form the basis of discussion. The reports are composed under the tutelage of the party *maktab al-fallahin;* thus there can be little doubt that party control over union policy is stronger than any control by the union bases. Nevertheless, the party does not seem to completely dominate the process: it can veto any initiative it dislikes, but otherwise it often only imposes broad guidelines, the details of which are filled in through a consultative process with delegate/cadres from the lower levels of the organization. The union leadership receives "input" from below, through the resolutions passed at lower level assemblies, reports funneled upward through its chain of command, and periodic trips to the bases, and this "input" is, to an extent, incorporated into its reports to the congress. The reports are discussed in committees of delegates who draft resolutions based on them and on the resolutions of the lower assemblies they represent. There is a history of these committees having altered or added to the recommendations of the leadership, but none of major dissidence or factional splits over policy in the congresses. The union simply does not function as a channel of major peasant grievances against the Ba'thi agrarian order. But, the decisions of the congresses probably do incorporate the wishes of union cadres, so long as they do not conflict with the party line, and to the extent these are representative of their constituents, broader village opinion.

But even if the outcome of the union's internal policy process gives some expression to peasant demands or interests, it does not follow that the union has the power to make government decision-makers accept its program. The union does have several partially institutionalized channels of access to decision-makers. The president of the union is a member of the party's central committee and of the Regional Command's *maktab al-fallahin,* and he and other unionists sit in the party's Regional Congress, in parliament, on governorate councils, and on the Higher Agricultural Council which approves the agricultural plan and decides on crucial matters such as prices and subsidies. The union is represented on scores of state committees which make lesser day-to-day decisions affecting peasants: agricultural wage-fixing, grading of agrarian products, rent of government lands, the agricultural arbitration court, the agricultural bank, the supreme council on mills, the cereal office, the tobacco organization, etc. At the province level, unionists meet regularly with party and state officials in the provincial derivatives of the *maktab al-fallahin.* This multifaceted access contrasts with the absence of comparable access for landlords and merchants to the agrarian policy process. The Chambers of Agriculture are very weak and though the Chamber of Commerce is much more potent and has informal access of some weight to the highest levels in the elite, this does not give regularized input into agrarian policy-making. The fact is, the regime's populist ideology institutionalized an unequal system of formal access, but, by contrast to the more common conservative form of corporatism, it is worker and peasant interests which have favored access. Yet the formal privileged access of the peasant union, while a major advance from the pre-Ba'th era, gives only the potential for interest articulation and many other factors determine whether it will be effective.

In an authoritarian regime, the central factor determining the effectiveness of interest articulation is elite responsiveness to the interest. Initially at least, Ba'th leaders had good reasons to take account of peasant interests. Many were sons of the village, saw it as their special constituency, and were naturally more favorably disposed than urban bureaucrats or landlords to peasant needs. To build the rural base they needed, they had to accommodate peasant interests. Yet, there were also contradictions between the interests of state and village: the mobilization of an agricultural surplus for development and defense, not to mention support of a ballooning bureaucratic apparatus, and the securing of cheap food to placate urban masses much more immediately dangerous to the Ba'th than peasant discontent, potentially pulled the regime the other way. If regime and peasant interests overlapped far more than they conflicted in the early years of Ba'th rule, after 1970 this became much more problematic, as the regime was corrupted and money increasingly opened formerly closed doors to decision-makers for the bourgeoisie.

To the extent the union cannot rely on elite responsiveness, it must rely on political leverage. But the union does not carry major stature in the regime, being dependent on the party elite rather than a highly mobilized popular base; as the product of construction from the top down rather than sustained struggle from below, the union simply lacks the organized popular muscle needed to speak with a loud voice in regime councils. Peasant leaders could form alliances with party politicians or military officers when the regime is split. In 1968–1969, Ibrahim Makhous, a radical politician in charge of the *maktab al-fallahin,* tried to make the union a power base in the intra-party conflict with the military wing under Asad. But it was a party, not peasant leader, who took the initiative and peasant union support seemed to count for little against a leader with army backing. The peasant union has otherwise no record of involvement in intra-regime conflicts.

The union's lobbying effort therefore chiefly takes the form of persuasion rather than threats or intrigues; that is, it must argue that responsiveness to peasant interests is ideologically correct and politically and economically expedient. Thus, in its effort to get better crop prices from the state, it points to rising costs and argues that if peasants are to increase production, adhere to the plan, and make crop deliveries to the state, they must be able to make a fair profit. Given the centrality of "reason of state," political arguments carry special weight: in times when the regime has felt threatened from the Right and is in special need of mass support, the demands of the peasant union have been received with greater sympathy—as in 1980 when the regime conceded a lowering of the land reform ceiling.

To be effective in lobbying, the union leadership must be a forceful and energetic advocate of peasant interests. Personal stature and connections inevitably count for a lot in the regime's elite-centered policy process, and the current long-time union president, Mustafa Ayad, is evidently respected and influential in party circles. Union leaders do seem to take their role seriously: one indicator of this is the union's undertaking of its own cost of production studies to challenge those put forth by government agencies. Minutes of discussions on price-setting in the Higher Agricultural Council show clashes between peasant representatives and agencies representing the interests of urban (Ministry of Supply) or industrial (Ministry of Industry) consumers of agricultural goods. The union has recently tried to organize peasant members of parliament and of local councils into a caucus under union leadership (GFP 1981:268). On the other hand, the "sidetracking" of leaders with "personal concerns," admitted by union documents, and their far greater dependency on the party leadership than their own constituency seriously dilutes their motivation to act for peasant interests. The union's very modest command of technical expertise has also hampered it. And, the failure of its internal policy process to go beyond the mere articulation of interests—the typical congress produces nearly a hundred resolutions, only a portion of which could realistically be expected to be implemented—and to aggregate and prioritize them, leaves it to party and government to decide which to ignore.

The Limits of Interest Articulation
in a Corporatist State

Not only structures and access, but outcomes are an indicator of power. Hence, a study of the hundreds of resolutions of the union's five national congresses and of their fate in regime councils, as well as an analysis of the union's overall record in defending peasants within the agrarian bureaucracy can help indicate to what extent the union expresses peasant interests and how much weight it carries in policy-making on their behalf.

A whole series of union positions address high policy issues having to do with the basic organization of the agrarian sector and on these issues the union appears to have wielded only modest influence. Nothing better expresses peasant interests than land reform, and union resolutions in 1967 and 1970 called for further reducing maximum land-ownership to a size "cultivable without the labor of others," in line with the Ba'th's own party constitution. The regime's lack of response was a measure of the union's weakness and the union's sudden silence after 1970 on the issue was clearly dictated by Asad's wish to conciliate the agrarian bourgeoisie. The president of the union explained that when the main contradiction of the stage was with Zionism, neither class conflict or the loss of production could be risked and until the fragmented small-holding sector could be consolidated, further reform made no economic sense. The union pushed with only a little more success to marginally broaden existing land reform laws. Calls (GFP 1965, 1967, 1970, 1977) to implement land reform on waqf lands went unheeded. The union called for the recovery of state land which, it charged, had been sold to or usurped by big owners in Hassaka and for the distribution to peasants of the lands there still in state hands. Though an appropriate decree on recovery of state lands was issued in 1968, in 1977 the union was still asking that it be enforced; some land in Hassaka was distributed to peasants, but in 1981 the union was still pressing the regime to "finish" the job and much of the land was still rented to entrepreneurs. A union demand to limit the size of land holdings which an investor could exploit (GFP 1977) went unheeded. These demands were largely ignored because they clashed with the regime's economic liberalization and the alliance between investors and parts of the state apparatus which had grown up after 1970. But when it suited the regime's immediate political interest, it was willing, as in the 1980 mini-reform, to put these considerations aside.

The union's position on matters of agrarian organization must, in many cases, be seen as reflecting the ideology of the party rather than peasant demands: this is largely so of the union's support for cooperatization and for widening of state agricultural marketing, issues toward which peasants have either been ambivilant or silent. Moreover, the union's support for collective production and compulsory agricultural planning which most peasants oppose, expresses a subordination of peasant wishes to state interests (GFP 1970, 1977). As a result of this, the union was unable to aggressively express peasant resistance to the government's imposition of sugar beet cultivation in the late seventies. It has, however, tried to make planning more responsive to peasants needs, calling, for example, for unification of planning bodies so peasants are not subjected to contradictory demands and for the laying down of a realistic plan.

Whatever the limitations of its influence over high agrarian policy, the union has become a vehicle for the defense of peasant interests within the existing state agrarian system. Demands to increase the prices paid for state-marketed crops have repeatedly been raised, bringing the union into direct conflict with the revenue extraction imperative of the state. This drive appears to have made a positive difference, although not enough to satisfy peasants. The union has pushed, too, to make marketing agencies more accountable and marketing less difficult for peasants. The union began by calling for state marketing centers in the provinces to replace middlemen between state and peasant. As these were established, it demanded they accept responsibility for the value of crops delivered by peasants and pay without delay (GFP 1970), asked for peasant representation on crop grading bodies which had an effect on compensation, and toward the end of the decade, insisted state bodies accept all the crops peasants wanted to sell, that factories expand their capacity if necessary, that the state set up a public transport company to help peasants in crop delivery, and that collection centers be extended to the district (*mantiqa*) level. In 1977 the union itself won an important marketing concession, a 1–2% commission paid by the government on state crop deliveries made through the union; this became an important source of revenue for the union and propelled it into marketing.

Credit has always been a primary peasant preoccupation and the union has also waged many battles, with some success, to make the agricultural bureaucracy more responsive to this need. An early (GFP 1965) demand to give priority in credit access to cooperatives and small peasants was heeded.

Subsequently the union got the agricultural bank to accept a share-cropping contract as a basis for receipt of credit and to extend it to the peasant rather than the landowner (GFP 1970), then (GFP 1977) pushed the bank, against its conservative interest in husbanding its resources against bad risks, to extend credit to cooperatives in the dry "second stability" zone even when they were indebted. The union has repeatedly called for relieving peasants suffering from drought or flood from repayment of loans, and for reducing the interest and extending the period of payment for the cost of irrigation projects. Although the union has won some concessions, the bank's stubborn defense of its resources can be measured by the union's continual demands (GFP 1965, GFP 1977) to exempt cooperatives from paying old debts. At its 1977 conference, the union pushed successfully to get the bank to widen the volume of longer term loans for purchases such as tractors and animals and to give better terms. Generally, the union has succeeded in making the state credit system more responsive to peasant needs, winning an increased volume of loans at subsidized rates, but it seems to take a constant fight to keep it that way.

Union pressure has helped to improve the delivery of agricultural services. In 1967, it called for the "spread of mechanization," and in 1970 for establishment of a tractor factory. As state-sponsored mechanization proceeded, union demands became more concrete, reflective of the need to make the system more responsive to peasant needs. In 1977, the union called for giving peasants title to tractors bought on loan, for state repair shops to be established in each province, for giving the union a monopoly on the distribution of machine spare parts, and for lowering of the state commission on imported machinery; these demands were met. In 1981, it wanted the General Institute for Machinery to improve its mobile repair units and to open sales outlets in the south of the country so peasants need not travel to Aleppo; it also called on the Ministry of Economy to provide foreign exchange for importation of spare parts and kinds of machinery not produced locally. In the field of irrigation and reclamation, early (GFP 1967) calls to "expand irrigation" and to speed up the Ghab project, gave way by the seventies to demands that the state upkeep or refurbish existing systems, reduce peasant irrigation fees, reform the drains in certain irrigation projects to eliminate waterlogging, and unify supervision and maintenance of irrigation facilities in a single agency.

In the field of social services, union demands, evolving from the general to specific, reflected partial satisfaction, but also continuing gaps in delivery. In 1965 the union merely called for the spread of such services to rural areas and an end to illiteracy. In 1967 it called for the opening of rural pharmacies and in 1977 demanded these pharmacies stock veterinary medicines. In 1977 it wanted the number of doctors and clinics in the countryside increased, and electrification of the villages finished. By 1981, it resolved that water, electricity, schools and phones be guaranteed in every village, that broken water pipes be fixed and roads repaired, and that medical graduates be required to perform their compulsory service in the rural areas.

Demands to include peasants in the social security system and to sell milled flour in the rural areas at the same subsidized prices as in the cities expressed authentic peasant demands on the state; peasants remain outside the social security system, but in the 1980s the state began opening retail outlets for basic fixed-price commodities in rural areas.

The union has at various times confronted a whole range of state agencies on behalf of the peasant's fundamental interest in the land. Calls in the sixties for the dismissal of agricultural officials hostile to land reform had party backing. But recent calls to prevent pollution from state factories in the Ghouta, to compensate and settle the peasants displaced by the creation of the lake behind the Euphrates Dam, and for a council to arbitrate disputes between the state and peasants seem to reflect a growing union self-confidence in defending its constituency against bureaucrats. A sign of what the union is up against when powerful interests clash with those of peasants is its fight against the spreading incidence of state expropriation of agricultural land for various "projects." The union protested—apparently without effect—against a plan to cut down orchards on the Latakia coast for a tourist hotel. It has had to petition the Ministry of Defense to compensate peasants whose land was expropriated for military positions—with uncertain effect. In 1981 the union complained that the Ministry of Agriculture sold 80 ha. of cooperative land to a Saudi-Syrian company despite its protests (GFP 1981:204–205). In the case of a Hama village where peasants opposed expropriation of land for an industrial district, the peasant leadership blocked it, despite the provincial party's support for it (GFP 1981:19). But it seems unlikely the union can often prevail where a powerful ministry wants something, especially if the project has a political patron with a personal stake (commission, share) in it. The union seeks to put such seizure of land under the light of public accountability by insisting on a formal commission with peasant representation to rule on such cases.

Another typical category of union resolutions expresses the interests of peasants against landlords, investors, and merchants. Union pressure has helped translate favorable legislation, such as the agrarian relations law, which might otherwise remain mere paper decrees, into reality. Demands to set up an agrarian court and an apparatus to enforce the agrarian relations law were among the earliest (GFP 1967) preoccupations of the union. Later it proposed the government fine owners not registering peasant tenants, make investors who neglected their duties under the law pay damages to peasants, and make grants of licenses for conversion of lands to horticulture contingent on not expelling tenants. It won a decision to prevent seizure of peasant crops to pay debts to money-lenders. By 1981 union demands concentrated on fine-tuning the system, e.g. a proposal to give judges in the agrarian courts adequate salaries. The union also got the law updated to provide compensation not less than 25% of the value of the land for termination of tenancy contracts.

Finally, a number of congress resolutions express a growing "organizational interest." Persistent demands for representation in committees and economic bodies dealing with agriculture express a drive to expand the union's influence. Resolutions to exempt cooperatives from various taxes, for the allocation of a share of agricultural taxes to the union, and for state agencies to contract with the union for harvesting services, seek to benefit the union largely at the expense of the state treasury (GFP 1967, 1970, 1977, 1981).

In general, the union's record as an advocate of peasant interests is a mixed one. It appears that the union has expressed, to a very real extent, genuine peasant interests within state councils. But the limits of the union's power are very clear. When union demands run counter to regime policy or the interests of powerful politicians or private operators with good connections, it is often impotent. Asad's promise to the 1980 union congress that "no longer can there be interference between your decisions and their implementation" (GFP 1981:22) was apparently acknowledging a fact widely recognized by his audience. Equally important, the union has limited power, despite its representation in the planning process, to protect peasants from sweeping decisions by technocrats—such as the imposition of sugarbeet cultivation against their wishes. State agencies operating in agriculture have often proven unresponsive to union demands for better service, less interested in promoting agrarian development than in husbanding or extracting resources. Others appear so mired in bureaucratic lethargy that union complaints have no permanent effect since the union lacks the critical power to get inefficient or corrupt officials dismissed.

Still, the union has succeeded in extracting many concessions from the state, such as more credit and better crop prices, which an unorganized peasantry lacking access to power could hardly have done, as Syria's pre-Ba'th record indisputably shows. Where the interests of peasants and those of landlords and merchants clash, the institutionalized access to agrarian decision-making, which the Ba'th's populist form of corporatism gives, probably enhances the weight of peasant opinion against moneyed interests which would, in the normal course of things, be more potent. Moreover, in hastening the implementation of formally decreed legislation and in calling attention to gaps and oversights in agrarian policy and in the workings of the agrarian infrastructure, the union has become a significant means of redress for its constituents. Indeed, it appears that within the sphere of routine agrarian management, per se, as opposed to wider policy issues and conflicts, the peasant union has become a significant actor often quite able to hold its own against various agencies of the bureaucracy at the central government level (Springborg 1981:202) and with "considerable influence in the decision-making process" at the province level as well (Owen 1980:12). One observer argued that: ". . . the peasant union [has] greatly improved the leverage of [its] members in obtaining services from . . . government agencies [since] the head of the local peasant union and [ministry] agricultural director are [both] invariably party members" (Manzardo 37). For example, in an area of new irrigation and land settlement, the Ghab, peasant union cadres provided local leadership for peasants and gave government critical feedback on the project; peasants were protected from arbitrary official action by the "committee system of making decisions" in which the union was represented (Ratnatunga 23–24, 52). The growing activity and confidence of the union has helped "liberate officials from the residues of the feudal age in their interaction with peasants" (GFP 1981:30); certainly, without the constant pressure of the union, peasants would be even more at their mercy. But this falls far short of "popular control" over the state and indeed the union has been used to muffle some peasant demands and to impose state priorities on peasants. Hence many individual peasants seeking service, redress, or protection from an ever more intrusive state must often have recourse to other means—personal connections to officials, bribery, and evasion of government regulations.

Policy Implementation and Support Mobilization

The peasant union is supposed to mobilize the peasants for the implementation of the regime's agrarian policies and for self-management of their own affairs. A structure of policy implementation does exist: the union's executive bureau translates the resolutions of congresses into a plan of work which is supposedly implemented under the supervision of its various functional offices.

Several of these offices deal with agricultural affairs. The bureau of statistics and planning collects data to monitor production plan implementation and to support the union's lobbying—for example on increased costs of production as part of its case for higher crop prices. The agricultural affairs bureau is preoccupied with ensuring delivery of credit and requisites to peasants. The bureau of rural engineering runs the union's fleet of tractors and harvesters, but not, it seems, very efficiently; in 1980 its mismanagement of this operation became a major scandal. Similarly, the bureau of finance suffered from a lack of technical cadres and was accused of running a disorderly operation. The legal affairs bureau represents peasants in court and in one recent period alone (between 1977 and 1980) claimed to have done so in 610 suits. It also participated in drafting legislation on forests, the agrarian bank, the new land reform, and the law to organize the agronomy profession (GFP 1981:253–254, 259–262).

Central to the political mobilization and "acculturation" of peasants is the Bureau of Cultural and Political affairs. From 1968–1976 its Peasant Institute graduated over 10,000 cadres and from 1977–1980 it gave 705 courses on organizational or technical skills such as accounting, tractor maintenance or driving, horticultural techniques, and insecticide usage to 12,050 cooperative peasants (GFP 1981:220–225). Because of the scarcity of competent staff, however, these courses are of low quality; peasants try to evade demands on their time to attend but since each association must send representatives, the "least influential" peasants are often delegated. The Institute has played a pivotal role in creating a pro-regime peasant cadre, but the union admitted that, twelve years after its founding, it was not training them effectively to lead agricultural development (GFP 1981:220).

The cultural affairs office is also responsible for the peasant newspaper, *Nidal al-Fallahin,* which is also of mixed effectiveness. A 1981 survey of peasant opinion revealed that its technical sections needed much improvement, the cultural pages were incomprehensible to peasants, and the paper arrived late because of the inertia of the union staff. But peasants relished the paper's investigative exposures and thought more space should be devoted to the class struggle, indicative of a considerable political consciousness on their part (GFP 1981:64). The paper "covered" the crucial activities of the *maktab al-fallahin,* but the effort to recruit correspondents in the village associations has not borne much fruit; too few peasants are sufficiently literate or interested.

The machinery of the union has steadily grown from a handful of full-time apparatchiki (*mutafarrag*) to 300 by the seventies, 2–3 in each of the 55 districts, the rest at the province and central level. The number of union technicians grew from 118 agronomists and 483 accountants in 1976 to 251 and 510 in 1979 and 682 and 566 in 1984. Agricultural supervisors, secondary graduates appointed to the cooperatives, increased from 450 to 1020 in the same time but this amounted to less than one for each three cooperatives (GFP 1977:22; GFP 1981:251–252; ABSP 1985b:129). Indicative of the continuing low level of "acculturation" of peasant cadres was the fact that of the nearly 19,000 peasants sitting on village association councils or inspection committees in 1980, only about 300 had even primary school certificates, and 749 were totally illiterate. At the league level, 37% of cadres had some education; at the province level 70% did, but only one-quarter had secondary education or more (GFP 1981:196). Thus the basic organizations were run by barely literate peasants periodically assisted by a "roving" agricultural secondary school graduate and occasional visiting teams of higher level cadres who were themselves short on formal education.

Given the limitations of its cadres, it is hardly surprising that the union has been plagued by what its own leaders consider organizational pathologies. Ideally, the union leadership is to function as a team carrying out general policies in the interests of the peasants as a class, but the "individualistic spirit" damages team work, "personal interests" (doing personal favors for individuals) are often put above "collective general objectives," and "even circles [trained cadres] which have had the opportunity to rid themselves of family, sectarian, and localistic culture [have] remained controlled by personal relations" (GFP 1967:50–51, 66–69). One leader might try to dominate an organizational body while the rest remained passive; sometimes rival factions might split it. Scheduled meetings might not be held or proper procedures followed. There is no detailed planning: the union "plan" is a mere checklist of general objectives. There is a lack of studies and data on which to base decisions. Control, both upwards and downwards, has been weak. Congress resolutions demanding that "failing leaderships" be held accountable suggest a weakness of control from above over subordinate bodies; but assemblies were also ineffective in controlling their executive committees, for while they were often vociferously critical of these committees, the latter found excuses to evade responsibility and were seldom removed. Bureaucratization and negligence were reflected in resolutions against the "bureaucratic attitudes" of leaders toward members, against idleness and avoidance of field work on the part of cadres, and in the continual insistence of congresses on the need to increase interaction between leadership and base. Clientalism was indicated by complaints that when new leaders came into office they threw out lower level cadres and appointed their own personal followers, thus depriving the organization of experienced leaders (Khalaf:199). At the village level, similar pathologies have enervated the capacity of the union to really "mobilize" peasant communities. Many local leaders are ideologically inert: the difficulty the union has had in getting them to attend "cultural courses" shows how little many care about ideology. Some have been engrossed in servicing the interests of their own kin group or faction at the expense of other villagers or in opposition to union goals; thus cooperative board members fail to enforce collection of debts and even see their role as protecting indebted kin or followers, with the result that the agricultural bank stops credit to the whole village. Or, board members rent out cooperatively-owned lands or machines to their families at nominal rents, at the expense of the association treasury. Some leaders have been more concerned with pleasing superiors than representing their constituencies. Others have extorted baksheesh for services or access; hence the call of congresses to eliminate abuse of power for personal interests (GFP 1967:66–68, 82–84; GFP 1970:31–33; GFP 1977:23; GFP 1981:29).

A significant indicator of organizational weakness is the union's failure to become financially self-supporting. Because the cooperative associations have not accumulated much capital from savings or shares, seasonal agricultural financing in the cooperatives basically relies on bank loans and though the cooperatives repay more than 80% of these loans, default has been significant. The leagues depend entirely on a subsidy from the general federation for their syndical work. The province federations have made investments in repair stations, spare parts stores, afforestation, and processing facilities, almost entirely financed by government loans and subsidies. Whether these will become profitable remains to be seen, but the past record is not good: the federations suffered such losses on their machinery that they took to renting them to individuals, defeating their whole mandate to promote cooperative cultivation. There has been a lack of discipline in keeping accounts and stock inventories and scores of investigations have been launched into misman- agement and theft of machinery, fuel, and spare parts. Some of its own cadres seem to view the union as a cow to be milked while the majority of its members demonstrate their lack of confidence in the institution by their unwillingness to commit resources to it. As for the general federation headquarters, its budget grew from 3 million L.S. in 1973 to 11 million in 1980, mostly for salaries, buildings, publishing, training, transportation and administration. It earns a good bit from commissions on cooperative marketing but the organization as a whole remains dependent on a party subsidy of some three million L.S. yearly and, recently, as cooperatives proved unable to pay the salaries of accountants, the government took on this expense. In short, the union hierarchy, incapable of mobilizing significant resources from its base, remains totally dependent on the government (GFP 1967:94–100; GFP 1977:51–73; GFP 1981:233–250, 259–261).

Nevertheless, the peasant union has constructed an organizational network which has steadily incorporated a widening proportion of Syria's villages and peasants. At the end of 1976, 3414 basic level associations existed, embracing 4210 out of 6448 villages or 65%. By 1980, 478 new ones had been founded, although 298 inactive ones outside the rainline were dissolved. At that time, unions embraced nearly all villages in Dera, Damascus and Qamishli and most in Homs, Latakia and Deir ez-Zor; most unorganized villages were in the dryer northern areas of Aleppo, Raqqa and Hassaka, many of them scattered hamlets on the margins of the cultivable area. All land reform beneficiaries had been cooperatized (GFP 1981:189–192). By 1983, 3903 peasant unions existed and about three-quarters of the villages appeared to have been organized (SAR 1984:473). Some 19,000 delegate-cadres manned this organizational structure (GFP 1981:196). Union membership grew from 5,000 in 1965 to 138,803 in 1970 and 210,855 in 1972. In the next decade it nearly doubled, reaching 347,898 in 1981 and 407,558 members in 1983 (SAR 1973:333; SAR 1984:462–463). This amounted to 80% of all agricultural holders (owners, renters or sharecroppers) and at least two-thirds and possibly as much as 85% of all families active in agriculture.[1] By 1985, membership stood at 466,172 (SAR 1986:523). Two-thirds of members were small owner-cultivators, the rest sharecroppers or agricultural laborers (Owen 15). Clearly, insofar as recruitment is concerned, the union has done the job expected of it as the Ba'th party's main mass auxiliary: while the number of peasants incorporated directly into the Ba'th party, in some ways still a selective "vanguard" party, represented only about 16% of peasant families (as measured by the adult male agricultural work force), the union has brought much of the rest of the peasantry into a party-led organizational framework.

The union appears, thus, to have achieved a significant level of rural penetration and peasant incorporation. Traditionally, the party's rural rivals—landlords and zuama—have always been able to keep a portion of the peasant population on their side, but the relative congruity between the proportion of villages embraced by unions and the proportion of peasants organized (75%) suggests that where the peasant union exists, the great majority of peasants join it; if so, it appears to have increasingly marginalized these rivals, a significant achievement. Three groups of peasants remain most likely to be excluded. Older peasants may remain apart, perhaps still clients of the local landlords or notables. Landless workers have less incentive to join than do landed peasants and tenants who need the credit the union delivers. There are also claims that the regime has deliberately excluded the Kurdish peasantry on discriminatory grounds; if so they remain under the influence of traditional leaders, communists, or Kurdish nationalists. Finally, even when their family is included, the virtual exclusion of women (making up a mere 2% of membership), largely due to cultural factors, is not without consequence since, with the growing migration of male heads of household into non-agricultural labor, women assume growing responsibility for farm management.

Organizational expansion has translated into a real but limited union capacity to mobilize peasant support and cooperation in the implementation of agrarian policy. The union has certainly helped advance socio-political change in the villages. It played an auxiliary role in the implementation of land reform; after years of trying to carry it out through the bureaucracy, the regime put the job in the hands of local committees of party, peasant union and ministry officials who finished it quicker, in a way less favorable to landlords, and with fewer conflicts among peasants and greater peasant involvement (Zoubi and Attar). The agrarian relations law was long a dead letter unenforced by an indifferent bureaucracy and of little help to peasants unaware of their rights and unable to take landowners, on whom they were dependent, to court. The union spread awareness of rights among peasants and represents them in court; although it has not systematically policed the law by ensuring registration of written contracts and has neglected to sponsor collective contracts for wage workers, its pressure has helped make the law more effective. By virtue of its policy of unity of the village, the union performs a certain conflict-resolution role, preventing minor village conflicts from escalating into violent feuds. A major responsibility of the union was to prepare cadres and peasant opinion for cooperatization: "every syndicalist a cooperator" was the slogan. Without the union, an organized force preaching the virtues of cooperatives in the villages, the whole cooperative movement would, given the formidable cultural and bureaucratic obstacles to it, probably be dead by now. The current service cooperatives are fairly effective instruments for the delivery of credit and inputs, perform some marketing tasks, facilitate access to services and machinery, and relieve peasants of much of the old dependency on landlords and merchants.[2] In mediating between the cooperatives and the bureaucracy—dealing with the delays and oversights in delivery of requisites, credit, and payment for crops which peasants encounter—the union greases the wheels of the creaky agrarian bureaucracy. But the cooperatives have failed to become institutions of collective cultivation, crop rotation, or investment capable of overcoming the fragmentation of holdings and pooling the modest resources of individual peasants. Their sometimes sickly performance is a major failure which union leaders have acknowledged: "Are we on the road to forming peasants who can work for cooperatization? We find some cooperatives where the most rotten customs and traditions deform cooperative thought and action. . . . it is a sick situation for us" (GFP 1977:22). The union's effort to take the lead in cooperative marketing of crops such as potatoes, onions, fodder, grapes and watermelons has been partially abandoned. Its effort to spread tractor and harvesting services has been plagued by mismanagement. The union has mobilized village labor for "popular work" programs in which the state provides funds and technicians to assist villages willing to contribute labor for roads, utilities, schools and clinic construction, but this has not become an instrument for mobilization of underemployed labor on a significant scale. The union could have been expected to play a major role in fighting illiteracy, at 80% among the poor peasants it serves, but, by its own admission it has done "nothing serious" to spread literacy, an indispensable aspect of peasant mobilization (GFP 1981:65). The union has a hard time discharging its role in "the leadership of production and its guidance according to the state plan." It has offered technical courses to peasants, sponsored demonstration plots and extension work to get peasant acceptance of crop and technical innovations, (Manzardo 32; Havens 42) and has helped make peasants more receptive to such changes, but it has barely scratched the surface in this regard. Peasants continue to evade plan targets. Indeed, as the union has been progressively harnessed into enforcing state planning and marketing, it has lost credibility among many peasants. The union leadership acknowledged the limits of its own performance in 1977: "With 300 *mutafarrag* we should have more influence and a deeper role in the countryside" (GFP: 1977:22).

The Role of the Peasant Union in the Political System

The peasant union has not become a vehicle of broad peasant participation, either in political life or socio-economic development. As a creation of the regime, largely "from above," it is very vulnerable to bureaucratization, its leaders too dependent on the state, its political processes too controlled to admit of widespread peasant activism. On the other hand, in its penetration of and recruitment from a village society still largely traditional it was bound to be infected by clientelism and personalism. It may be that a truly dynamic peasant organization can only be the product of struggle from below in a "revolutionary situation" and neither has really obtained in Syria.

But neither is the union a mere paper organization lacking all power or presence in the corridors of power or the village. In providing channels of access to the power elite for peasant politicians, procedures of interest articulation which express broad peasant interests to decision-makers, ladders of political recruitment, and arenas of local power for limited but significant numbers of activists and potentially for larger numbers of ordinary members, the union is a real political organization, with roots in the villages, not a mere hierarchy of state officials imposed from the outside. Moreover, despite its "traditional" pathologies, the union's modernizing goal orientation and organizational muscle, its plans, offices, procedures, elections, assemblies and syndical and economic functions differentiate it a from a mere network of bosses and their deferent clients. The union marks a real break with the past when the only link between state and peasant was the bureaucracy reaching down no further than the district, and the landlord or zuama dominated clientelist network reaching up to it, essentially short-circuiting any real peasant and state access to each other. Today the link is much more systematic and direct. Without the organizational framework the union provides, the regime's rural base would be much more dispersed and passive.

The consequences of the creation of the union for state and peasant society are two-fold. The union plays a major role in incorporating a rural base into the regime. Although that base is neither highly mobilized or committed to the regime, peasant incorporation enables the Ba'th to systematically bring its message to the village and coopt village leaders. The union, thus, brings a portion of the peasantry to identify with the regime and helps exclude opposition access to the rural masses. It has, moreover, played a decisive role in the waning of the social power of landlords and tribal chiefs in the provinces. It is no coincidence that the countryside, a breeding ground of anti-government hostility before 1963 has, under the Ba'th, proven little receptive to anti-regime activism, even as the cities have become hotbeds of dissidence. Finally, the union-cooperative structure, facilitates receptivity to regime agrarian policies and, in economically buttressing and linking the small peasantry to the state and deterring land concentration, it institutionalizes an organization of agriculture which is compatible with and helps perpetuate an authoritarian-populist regime, just as great capitalist estates provide the social base of conservative authoritarianism (Hinnebusch 1989, Chapter 7).

The role of the union in consolidating the base and control capabilities of the regime does not exclude its utility in servicing peasant interests. In fact, in two crucial ways it can be seen as compatible with peasant interests. First, as the village is ever more incorporated into the state and the market, increasingly dependent on state services and emeshed in its regulations, an organized group to defend peasant interests in the centers of power is ever more important. The form of populist corporatism institutionalized by the union gives the village a certain real access to government which is utterly lacking in the more common forms of conservative authoritarianism found in the Third World. Second, the union has played an effective role in organizing small and middle peasants as a socio-political force able to counter the power of larger proprietors, investors, and middlemen. It has helped put teeth in protective social legislation and has given roots to institutions which buttress peasant independence of these social forces. Finally, the union has helped foster habits of peasant political association which, if regime controls were to be relaxed, could in future acquire greater scope and autonomy.[3]

Notes

1. Exact figures on the proportion of eligible peasants in the peasant union are not available, but estimates can be made. The proportion of the rural population dependent on agriculture which is in the union could be calculated as follows. Usually, though not always, only the head of a family becomes a "member" of the union/ cooperative (GFP 1981:191–192). Since the typical rural family includes 6.6 persons, the membership of 348,000 (mostly family heads) in 1981 could actually incorporate close to 2,296,800 persons or about 48% of the rural population of 4.8 million persons at the time and (assuming 75% of rurals were in agriculture in the eighties, amounting to 3.6 million persons), 64% of the agricultural-dependent rural population (SAR 1984:55, 59); excluding the perhaps 4% ineligible by virtue of larger land-ownership, the union therefore incorporated around two-thirds of the eligible agri-

cultural-dependent population in 1981 and thereafter an even larger proportion. The proportion of land holders incorporated can also be estimated. The 1981 membership of 348,000 was 78.5% of the 449,000 holders existing then; if we assume 4% of holders were larger holders ineligible for cooperative membership, it was equilivant to 80.7% of the 431,000 eligible holders. But since landless workers have also been incorporated into the union membership, they must be excluded from the membership total to find the proportion of holders incorporated. Since no breakdown on membership by such status is available, we will estimate that 15% of members are landless workers— this figure being the proportion of the agricultural population that are agricultural workers. When they are excluded, the holder membership drops to 296,000 or 68.7% of eligible holders. By 1983 membership had reached 407,558, presumably including about 346,425 holders or 80% of holders counted in 1981 (and they, land being constant, are unlikely to have much increased in two years). Finally, recruitment can be measured by estimating the proportion of the agricultural labor force incorporated. 407,558 members in 1983 (SAR 1984:473) compared to an agricultural labor force of about 700,000. A small proportion of this labor force (perhaps 5%) is made up of ineligible larger landowners, renters, or managers. A significant proportion is family labor—women and youth under 18 (probably about 30% according to the population census); few women have joined the union (8,253 in 1980), since normally the head of the household alone registers, and children under 18 cannot join. Since the family is the unit of social significance in the village, the most important indicator of cooperative recruitment is the proportion of peasant families incorporated, as measured by the proportion of heads of households, and for purposes of estimating this, women and children can be excluded from the labor force; when ineligible peasants and unpaid family labor are excluded, the male work force eligible for membership must have been about 465,000 (SAR 1970:306; SAR 1984:91). This can be compared to a male union membership which, excluding perhaps 10,000 women, must have been about 397,560. By this reckoning as many as 85% of eligible peasant families had been incorporated by 1983. Taking these three calculations together, it seems reasonable to think that the union has reached about 3/4 of the peasants.

2. The economic functioning of the cooperatives is examined in detail in chapter seven of the companion study, *Peasant and Bureaucracy in Ba'thist Syria: The Political Economy of Rural Development* (Boulder: Westview Press, 1989).

3. In addition to the internal documentation cited, this analysis benefits from interviews in 1974 and 1977 with union cadres at the central, province, district, and village levels.

8

State and Village:
Rural Politics, Social Change,
and Peasant Incorporation

The Ba'th Party established a core in many villages in the years before the power seizure. Thereafter, consolidating its rule and revolution depended on linking up with, reviving, and spreading its village base. A dense network of party and state structures now links most of Syria's roughly 6,500 villages. A state line of command runs from the Ministry of Local Administration to the province governor, the district *mudir al-mantiqa,* the sub-district *mudir al-nahiya,* and finally to the village mukhtar or, in larger communities, the *rais al-baladiya* (mayor). A party hierarchy runs from the Regional Command to the province-level branch, district-level sub-branch, unit (in larger villages) and cell (in smaller villages), normally paralleled by a supporting array of "popular organizations."

The Ba'th appears to have structurally penetrated rural society, but with what consequence for regime consolidation and state formation? Has the regime politically mobilized peasants, created new village institutions, and implemented programs which have won peasant support? The following village case studies will seek to show to what extent, how, and with what effect the regime established itself in the villages. How has the regime, itself, been shaped by Syria's varied rural milieux? Each of the village cases exemplifies a different configuration of interpenetration between regime and rural society. Three of the cases examine communities of mountain peasant minorities which played a major role in the Ba'th—Alawites, Druzes and Christians. Another is an Alawi coastal village under Sunni dominance, three are Sunni plains villages in the south, center, and north of the country, one is an urbanized village in the irrigated gardens around Damascus, and one is a tribal-dominated settlement in the Euphrates valley. Together, they present a mosaic of the diversity of the Ba'th's rural base.[1]

Homs Village[2]

This is a Christian village of small-holders situated about 20 km. east of Homs city in Tel Kalakh district. The village had experienced a profound social and political mobilization long before the Ba'th took power. In the late thirties, the village was still self-contained, engrossed in traditional rivalries between its three dominant lineages. But, by the late forties, population pressure, land fragmentation, and new opportunities in the cities and overseas had induced migration and a drive for education and jobs outside of agriculture.

Politicization accompanied this social mobilization, leaving a profound imprint on the village. A number of parties appeared, seeking recruits, first the Syrian Social National Party (SSNP), then the Communist Party, the Arab Socialist Party of Akram al-Hawrani, and finally the Ba'th. Politicization helped undermine traditional kinship solidarity and rivalry: the parties recruited across kinship blocs, gradually realigning the village into new party-based blocs. By the early sixties, intermarriage across kinship lines was common and young men remembered the fighting among families in their childhood as a thing of the past. Family name was no longer the focus of identification and status, as education became the key to success.

The Ba'th cell here was founded by a villager who had gone to Damascus for schooling and there met Aflaq, a fellow Orthodox Christian. He returned to the village and opened a free party-affiliated school nearby, attracting many villagers who would have found schooling otherwise impossible: these students filled the ranks of the Ba'th. Others were recruited by ideological appeals: the ideals of Arab unity, nationalist hostility to Israel, socialist demands for a better deal for peasants. Some joined because of friendship or family ties to the ideologically mobilized or—as the power of the Ba'th grew in the fifties—because they saw opportunities in it for careers outside of agriculture; some fathers joined to further their son's prospects. Sometimes revived family feuds affected allegiances: e.g. if the family's enemies were SSNP or Communist, one joined the Ba'th. Whatever the original motivation, party schooling and early recruitment shaped the political views of many young villagers in adolescence, leaving a lasting imprint.

Social conflict in the area reinforced early politicization, making it fertile ground for socialist, anti-feudal and anti-bourgeois appeals. Although the village was not itself owned by a landlord, peasant struggle with landlords in nearby villages sometimes reached the level of violent conflict, spilling out over the entire district. Peasants organized by Akram al-Hawrani seized dozens of villages in the fifties until landlords called in the police to evict them. The village itself was in the grip of urban merchants who lent credit for production requisites at usurious interest, then collected the crop from their clients at below market prices; sometimes peasants destroyed their grape crop rather than accept such prices. In 1954, the party founder in the village challenged the local landlord ticket in parliamentary elections. Since, in this multi-sectarian district, candidates had to run on multi-sectarian lists, he, a Christian, had to find an Alawi partner. It was a measure of sectarian solidarity that no prominent Alawi figure could be recruited to challenge the dominant Alawi family in the area which was aligned with the landlords. But he did find support among the many poorer Alawi youth who had

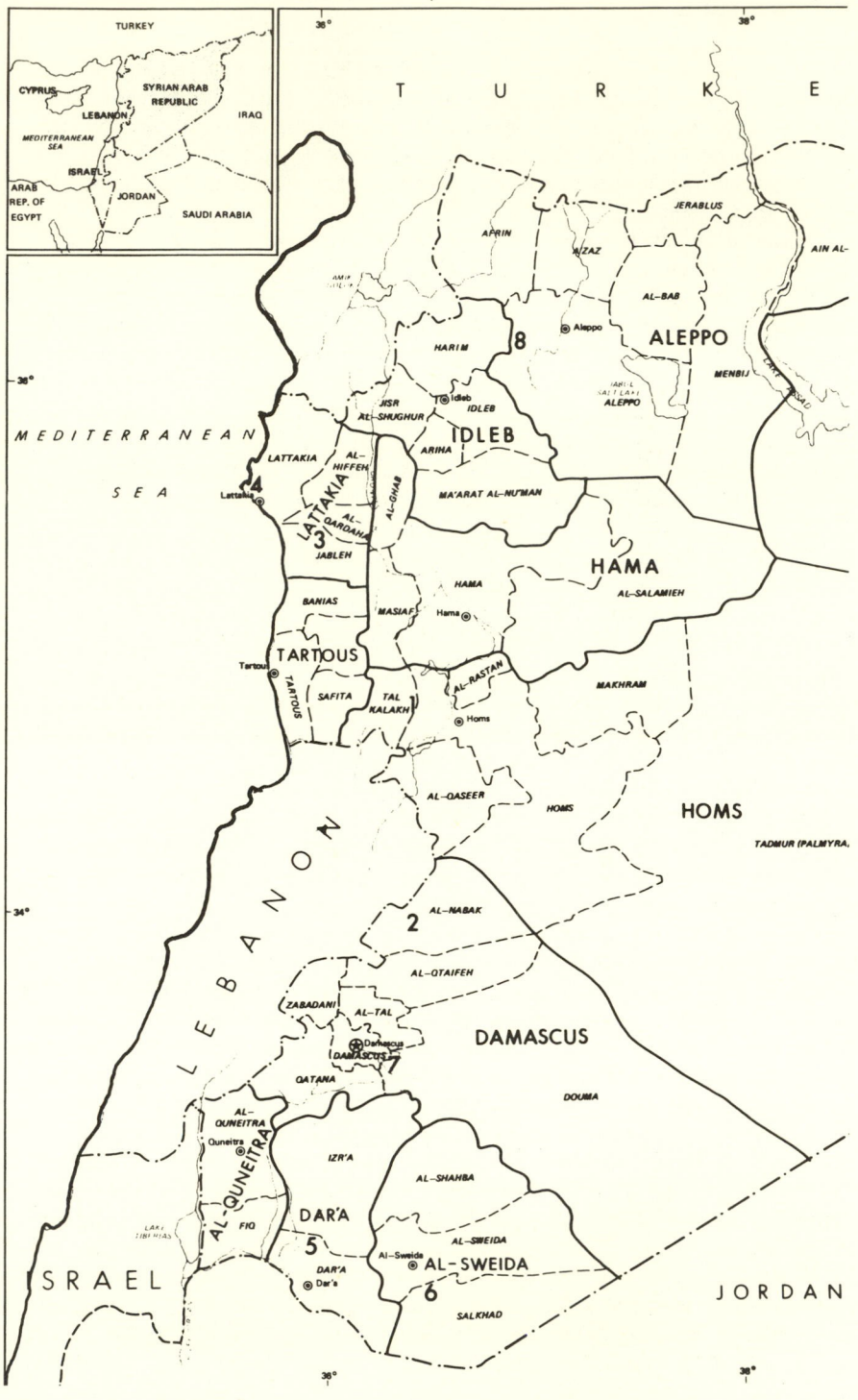

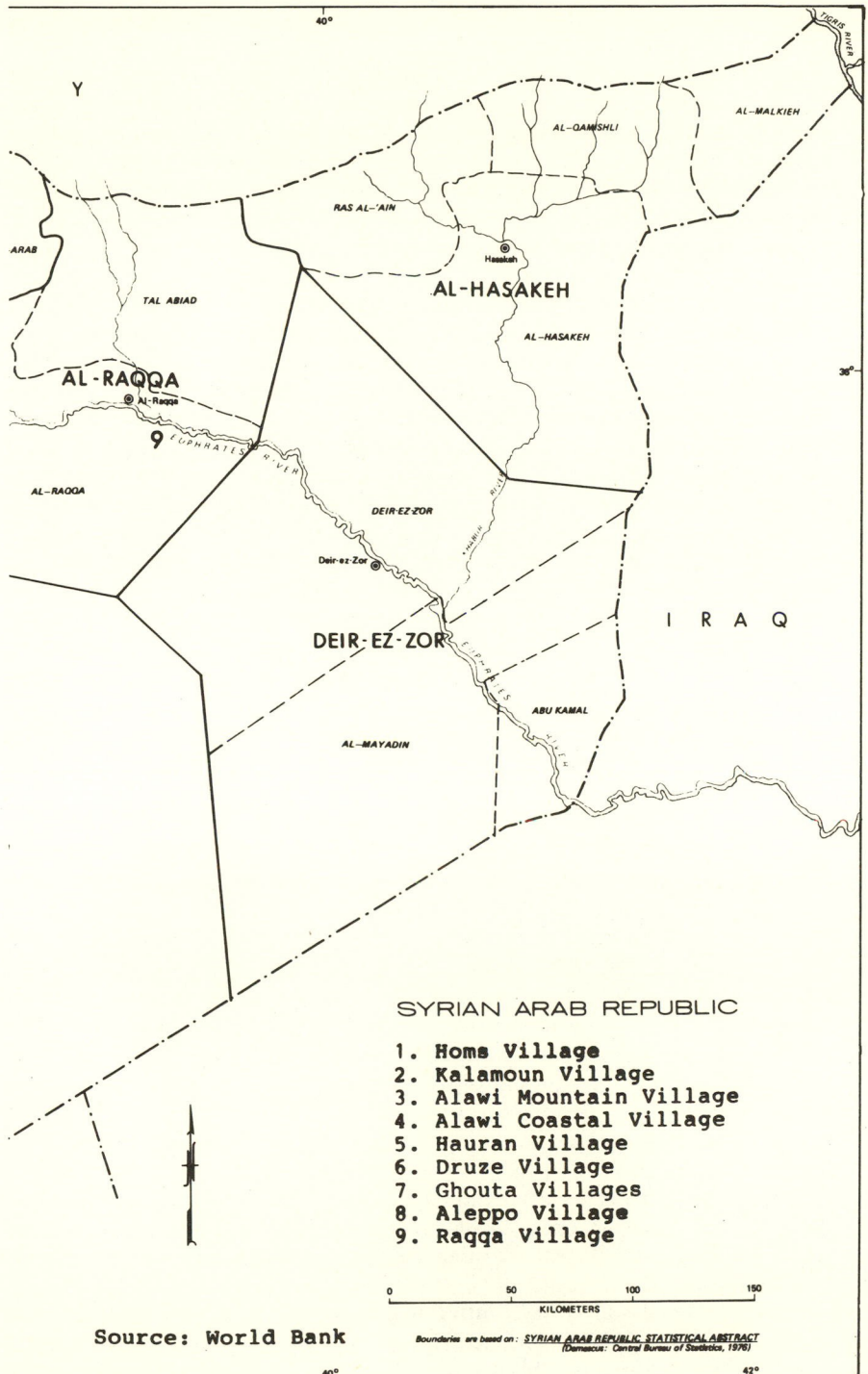

SYRIAN ARAB REPUBLIC

1. Homs Village
2. Kalamoun Village
3. Alawi Mountain Village
4. Alawi Coastal Village
5. Hauran Village
6. Druze Village
7. Ghouta Villages
8. Aleppo Village
9. Raqqa Village

Source: World Bank

0   50   100   150
KILOMETERS

Boundaries are based on: *SYRIAN ARAB REPUBLIC STATISTICAL ABSTRACT*
(Damascus: Central Bureau of Statistics, 1976)

attended his school. They and their Christian comrades fanned out over the area to mobilize support for their candidate. Although the Ba'th lost the election, it made a good showing. The campaign indicated that the grip of landlords and of sectarian leaders on their communities was declining and that politicization was generating new forms of cross-sectarian association; the kind of Alawi-Christian alignment generated here among village youth persists among the ruling Ba'th elite today.

The Ba'th Party, merged with Hawrani's followers and profiting from the smashing of the Syrian Nationalists in the fifties, became the dominant political force in the village by the late fifties. But this did not politically unite the village and, in fact, it is today fragmented. As a village which followed the path of the Ba'th Party, it came itself to reflect the splits that party has suffered. Before 1958, the growing radicalism of the party as well as personal conflicts had caused some of the earliest partisans to drift away, although they continued to consider themselves the true "old Ba'thists." In 1961 Hawrani and Aflaq parted ways over policy toward Nasir; Hawrani had strong support in the village because of his record in the peasant struggle against "feudalism," but others could not stand his anti-unionist support of the "Separatist" regime. Another traumatic experience for village Ba'thists occurred in 1966 when the left-wing of the party chased party founder, Michel Aflaq, from Syria; as most village partisans had joined the Ba'th in the early years when he was undisputed mentor, many left the party with him, regarding the 1966 coup as an undemocratic military putsch against the party. Others, however, had themselves become radicalized, and supported the Jedid regime in Damascus. But in 1970 the radicals themselves fell from power and their supporters in the village were now alienated. In the early seventies, the Asad regime successfully attracted some of the older Ba'thists back to the party, but even after the establishment of the "National Progressive Front" in Damascus, many Hawrani followers still regarded the regime with hostility. Some of these now considered themselves Marxists and were sharply opposed to Asad's tendency after the 1973 war toward political accommodation with Israel, although they did not cooperate with the radical Ba'th when it was in power. Some Aflaqite Ba'thists also put a distance between themselves and the accommodationist trend in Damascus. All these older Ba'thists regarded the incumbent party leaders in the village as opportunists; they spoke of the corruption of the regime, the loss of party internal democracy, and military domination. On top of this, there is a residue of Syrian Nationalist sentiment among villagers who still believe that Syria— not the Arab nation or even the Palestine cause—is what counts, and although they are very hostile to Israel this is because Israel is Syria's enemy. This indicates the enduring effect ideology and early politicization can have on attitudes, for these villagers are otherwise indistinguishable from the various Ba'thi groupings.

As the older Ba'thists have withdrawn from the party, its leadership has gravitated into new hands. The older Ba'thists came from the more prosperous peasantry who were first able to get education for their sons; while a few remain in the party, many of this stratum have left both the party and the village, from political disappointment or in search of economic opportunity. As a result, the lower strata of peasants have emerged as party and peasant union leaders. This indicates a deepening of politicization in the village. Indeed, by the seventies, this was so thorough that political issues were followed no less avidly and discussed with no less sophistication than in the cities. Yet actual political activism seems to have contracted. Party membership certainly has: although a historic center of Ba'thi recruitment, the village now has only one *halaqa* (cell) attached to a *firqa* in a larger neighboring Alawi village. The new group of party leaders appears unable to win the confidence of this intensely politicized and fragmented peasantry. There is a peasant union in the village and a cooperative experiment has sputtered along but, partly because of political rivalries, many older more well-off peasants have remained aloof from it. Politicization and Ba'thi mobilization has brought, not unity for common goals, but fragmentation to this village.

There has been some social change in the village under the Ba'th. One important change is that the old dominance of Homsi merchants over the village has been broken: more well-off peasant families, whose sons have found employment outside agriculture, have their own sources of credit, while poorer ones have access to government credit. The village now markets grapes and potatoes through the cooperative, although abuse of cooperative accounts and equipment led to government intervention against the cooperative council, shaking peasant confidence in it. Services—paved roads, electricity, and water—have arrived and peasants now have access to government marketed construction materials with which many have built improved housing. As amenities reach the village, some of the youth who left are returning. Others permanently employed in government or business in the city are investing in the improvement of their family holdings; a few of them have made a lot of money growing apples for the market and one has a small arak factory processing local grapes. These developments have been accompanied by a certain sharpening of previously minimal income differences between peasants. Families whose sons first got education and now have well paying jobs outside the village are prosperous; since much of the youth are long gone, the improved family property is managed by aging fathers and worked by hired labor recruited from less prosperous villagers and the neighboring Alawi village where, education having become available later and land being scarce, there is a surplus of landless peasants. The political inactivity of the richer peasants and the control of the party and peasant union by poorer ones may give wage earners protection against employers they might otherwise not have. Meanwhile, the careers of two old Ba'thists who have left the village illustrate a curious but by no means untypical transformation: one, a former Aflaq partisan runs an import business in Damascus, while developing orchards in the village; he maintains close connections in the party where some of his old school chums have now reached the very apex of power. The other, a former radical partisan of Jedid, works as the Middle East agent of an American multinational corporation; these men have given up politics, accommodated themselves to the failure of socialism and are joining the dominant mercantile-bourgeois culture of the cities. Yet, in their political attitudes they remain radical nationalists and loyal to Ba'th ideals of socialism and revolution.

Kalamoun Village[3]

This village, situated below the Kalamoun mountains near the Damascus-Homs highway, has a long history of social mobilization which has progressively incorporated it into the urban economy. It is a mixed Muslim-Christian village of small-holders in which property size differentiation does not exceed one to four. Its economy was traditionally based on grain farming and animal husbandry on meager infertile land which had constantly to be de-stoned. It was very vulnerable to natural disasters, not only famine from drought and pests, but flood from a nearby *wadi* which in 1937 destroyed 300 homes and drowned 76 people. Large extended families were typical, putting pressure, as they grew, on limited land resources. The instability of agriculture impelled migration from the land which soon became a tradition; Christians first went to the Americas, then Muslims to the cities and afterwards to the Arab oil states for work. Ever since, families have typically been divided, some at home, some abroad, sending or bringing back money which increases the viability of the village economy. In the 1930s, irrigation was introduced by restoring long disused canals to bring nearby spring water to fields. Crops were diversified: potatoes, legumes, wheat, and orchard trees were now grown. Water rights, detached from land, were bought and sold. Water became more important than land and irrigation water "shares" the major source of village prestige and wealth. Related families worked their lands with mutual self-help to make up for the loss of manpower from migration.

Traditionally, the patriarchs of the richer peasant families dominated the politics of the village—the mukhtarship, the council, the committee on water. Sectarian conflicts were, until recently, a main cleavage in the village: the Christian minority was kept politically inferior, and mutual disdain ran deep. Each confession had separate quarters, inter-marriage was taboo, and Christians had to move aside if a Muslim passed in the streets. But land and water were also major issues of dispute; and irrigation, in particular, introduced another major cleavage into the village, cutting across the religious one. Richer peasants arranged and paid for cleaning of the old canals and developed a cooperative irrigated farm. When those left out—basically poorer peasants—wanted to build a new canal to irrigate another such farm, the village notables tried to block it, wanting to keep limited water resources for themselves: law suits deteriorated into violence. By this time, political parties had started to penetrate the village and local communist youth, championing the poor peasants, made the conflict out as a class struggle. The richer peasants had the upper hand in the courts, but the poor ones in the streets (Hanna 447–449). Eventually a new cooperative farm was established by poorer peasants, though on a smaller scale. As irrigation spread, the "water committees" which supervised the flow of water and the water guards—*al-shaikh al-addan*—became positions of power as disputes over water increased; these guards were widely thought to enrich themselves by selling water secretly.

After Syrian independence, the SSNP, Hawrani's Arab Socialist Party, and the Ba'th arrived in the area competing with the Communists, and when the Ba'th and ASP merged, they established a leading position. The Ba'th flourished on the animosity between the village and the city and on the strong nationalist sentiment among villagers. Together with nearby villages such as Nebek, Yabroud, and al-Qara the village helped elect a Ba'thist deputy, Abd al-Halim Qaddur, to parliament in 1954. After 1958, the Nasirist movement also achieved strong support here. When the Ba'th took power in 1963, it gradually achieved unrivaled dominance. After the radicals took over in 1966, membership requirements were tightened up: candidates had to go to training camps, master ideological texts, and spend eight years in candidacy. But local youth nevertheless rushed to join, attracted by the prestige of a ruling party; they also expected that membership would open doors of opportunity formerly limited to city youth and pressure from both teachers and peers tended to override the objections of some parents to membership. Radical politics was on the ascendence. The nationalist militancy of the Ba'th struck a response in a village where Israel, feared and hated, was an obsession: superstitious opinion held that the Israelis had listening devices in the trees and walls to spy on conversations. When Sadat expelled the Russian advisors, one old woman, speaking for a part of nationalist opinion, denounced him for lack of gratitude: "We have lost our Arab honor!"

The career of the most famous son of the village at the time illustrates the curious way national ideological politics can take unexpected local forms. This man, of a modest family, entered the Orthodox church and led a schism against the great families who dominated it; he established a rival church and was recognized as the legitimate Metropolitan of Homs by the Ba'th government. Having studied in Moscow, he was known as a friend of the Russians, a promoter of agricultural collectivization, a militant for an egalitarian society, and a patriot who detested America.

Since the midseventies, the popularity of the Ba'th among youth has declined as the regime has come to be seen as corrupt and sectarian. One big man in the village is now the Ba'thist mayor, who reputedly is making corrupt money. But alienated opinion has remained Arab nationalist and little receptive to Ikhwan appeals. In recent parliamentary elections, a well-liked local school principal, a Nasirite, rather than a Ba'thist, was nominated to run on the National Progressive Front ticket and was elected to parliament. He is seen as a channel of village access to government. But the most important local "favorite son" is a personal secretary of President Asad and, in that capacity, a man who can do big things for the village.

The village has increasingly been exposed to the winds of social change under Ba'th rule, and while some is government sponsored, the increasing integration of the village into wider markets has had the most profound effect. In 1965, services began to arrive in the village, starting with piped water, then paved roads, later electricity. Mud houses were replaced by larger concrete block ones. In 1968, the government built a dam in the area to contain flooding and store more water for irrigation. A new cooperative was established, capital pooled, successful crops harvested, and profits distributed to share holders; the long tradition of entrepreneurial cooperation here seemed to pave the way for a success which has eluded other villages. The hand of the government here seems particularly light; there is no imposed plan because many peasants, having their own resources, are not dependent on the agricultural bank for credit; the cooperative supervisor is seldom seen, leaving cooperative affairs to the board of elders and the elected manager. But, increasingly, agriculture takes second place to other pursuits. In this land-poor village nobody wants to be fully dependent on it; those who are often have to sell their labor to others to supplement their income and are counted the village poor. Education has changed the values of many youth: they no longer want to work the land and seek jobs in the city. The tradition of overseas work intensified after the post-1973 oil boom, as younger males flocked to the Gulf. Money sent back by emigrants was invested in a multitude of entrepreneurial pursuits which diversified peasant resources. Some peasants invested in tractors and became petty entrepreneurs, renting their services out. There are now thirty tractors in the village, filling the gap left by continuing migration and the needs of surrounding areas. Construction of a new Damascus-Homs highway provided locals employment and some used their earnings to purchase oil trucks and become independent truckers carrying oil from the Homs refinery to Damascus.

But even as the village in some ways boomed, in other ways it seemed to be "dying." The rug industry withered because newly rich peasants did not want their women working for the "low" prices paid by the government for the product—even though the price had been raised ten times in twenty years. Then a disaster hit part of the village: indiscriminate well drilling and pumping in the area led to the fall of the water table and the village's major irrigated farm lost its water supply. The government was well aware of the threat for some years and peasants had had plenty of warning: three hundred springs had dried up in the Kalamoun mountains between 1969 and 1972. The government tried to regulate drilling, but some peasants bribed officials or thought it worthwhile to pay the fines and, as a result, everyone has suffered. This contributed to a loss of confidence in government which was seen as too corrupt to enforce rules to guard the common good. At this juncture, however, the village's connection to the very apex of power served it well. The President's secretary used his connections to get the Ministry of Agriculture to find new underground water sources and a prominent figure in the inner elite who owns a drilling business contributed drilling equipment; the village is now back in business by virtue of its special personal access, but neighboring villages are not so fortunate. As the oil boom has petered out, many villagers are returning from Saudi Arabia. Many have lost the work ethic and are uninterested in agriculture; some have money to invest and have set up green houses or are raising chickens. Some are weekend farmers, while holding down a job in the cities.

Cultural change has accompanied socio-economic transformation. The Muslim-Christian divide is no longer politicized and the two communities are overtly friendly. As late as 1965 there was an attack on the church, but now the Christians are seen as protected by the "Alawite government." Under the surface, some animosity persists. In some households deprecating discussions of "the others" is still common. There is envy: the Christians who got education long before the Muslims, at first forged ahead socially, but now many Muslims have got richer in the Gulf and Saudi Arabia. Cultural change has produced a gap between younger educated "moderns" and the elders, especially elderly women who still believe in spirits and the evil eye and visit the nearby tombs of saints. Women's status has improved. It used to be that women did most of the work, in the fields, carrying water, caring for the animals, white-washing the house, while the men, the bosses, saved their energy so they could be "cocks in the night." Since women were a man's honor, they were otherwise restricted so as not to become the object of gossip which could embarrass the family. They were not educated since this would cause them to develop vices like singing, dancing, or writing love letters. Women inherited one-third to one-half the share of a man. Much of this has changed. Girls are now educated since they can then make money as teachers and become more desirable as marriage partners. A woman wanting a fair inheritance share can find redress with the Ministry of Justice. As women have become educated and have found employment, they are more independent. With many of the men recently away, women lead a freer life.

Alawi Mountain Village[4]

This village, located near the rural town of Shaikh al-Badr in the Alawi mountains, is a small-holding community which has undergone a major social and political mobilization. In this process, traditional leaders have been superseded by new ones and the village incorporated into the wider state and market.

Traditionally, the Alawis were virtually a society apart from the rest of Syria: a heterodox offshoot of Islam regarded as heretical by the majority, they sought refugee in their mountain fastnesses. Alawi society was organized into tribal hierarchies (*ashira*) headed by shaikhs who contested with each other and the outside world in forging petty principalities in the mountain. The shaikh's authority was essentially political, although some originated as religious leaders and many combined religious and political functions: they offered their clients protection in an anarchic environment, represented them to the intermittently present state authorities who sought to collect taxes or conscript peasants, and acted as judges and conflict-mediators. Men of forceful personality surrounded by armed retainers, their strongman rule was legitimized by kinship bonds, real or fictive, to followers, frequently by shaikhly descent, and by a quasi-religious authority; in the last capacity, they collected zakat supposedly for the poor and the building of saintly tombs, the centers of Alawi religious life. They also enjoyed a monopoly of literacy and benefited from the deeply religious character of the peasant who believed in the magic talismans they alone could dispense. Some accumulated wealth from tribute or in land, often as gifts from peasants in return for protection, but scope for large landed property was limited by the mountainous ty-pography. Since tribes often encompassed more than one village, the shaikh assigned leadership of villages to a "saih" and picked a mukhtar as well, usually from a saih family and perhaps the same person. This village was a center of the Bashargha tribe of the Matawirah confederation, led during the mandate period by the famous Shaikh Salah al-Ali who achieved para-mounty over the whole mountain and led a major uprising against the French until coming to terms with them. Although there were also families of the Haddadin and Khayatin tribal groups in the village, it was dominated by Shaikh Salah's tribe, and its saih and mukhtar were from a segment of his clan.

This area, situated on an inhospitable rocky and eroded terrain with an uncertain water supply, was very backward. Agriculture, on fragmented small-holdings, was primitive. A subsistence barter economy prevailed into the period of French rule, an occasional itinerant peddler being the only link to the wider market. Roads running up from the coast deadended on the mountain slopes while Alawites, in frequent conflict with the Muslim and Christian townsmen, were unwelcome in the coastal cities. Unlike Lebanon, wrote Weulersse (1940:312–326), where the mountain was humanized, in the Jabal al-Nusayriya, man was "ensavaged":

> The peasant must eke out his fields against the rock and scrub and yet his work remains superficial: plowing turns up more rocks. It is not worth it to take pains for an earth so ungrateful.To resource feebleness and dispersion, corresponds population feebleness and dispersion—multitudes of little hamlets lost in the mountains without great villages where enough wealth could support civilization. . . . [But] poverty gives independence here. The dominance of urban landed capital doesn't reach the mountain for it is too risky. The local notable's exploitation remains fraternal. . . . The poverty of this dispersed society is reflected in villages that can't support artisans, merchants, or—till the mandate—a single school for Alawites in the whole mountain.

To the natural impoverishment of this society, was added political repression and economic exploitation. The retribution levied by the French for the 1920 rising forced many peasants to sell their sheep, the land, even their daughters into domestic service (Petran 64); tobacco-growing peasants long sold their crop to Sunni merchants at low prices. Of one Alawi village, a observer wrote during World War II (Petran: 71–72):

> the wretched inhabitants were in a deplorable state of misery, dejection and abandon: they were past hope, resigned, their spirit utterly broken. . . . Not

a single week had passed . . . without my seeing an Arab suffering unnecessarily from fever, disease, torture, hunger and poverty. . . .

Several forces, altering the features of life in the mountain, prepared the way for the gradual transformation and incorporation of the village into the wider society. As state pacification and capitalist penetration of the area narrowed the scope for traditional kingdom-building, some tribal leaders, especially those nearer the lowlands, established themselves as landlords and mobilized their clients in elections which put them in parliament; they gradually developed an identification with the ruling agrarian bourgeoisie in Damascus. At the same time, the whole of Alawi society was being put in motion. Rapid population growth was driving Alawites outward from the mountain in search of agricultural work, spilling into both the coastal areas to the West and toward Hama and further East. Restraint in production of large families was rejected in the belief that Allah would bring the bread with the baby. For some time, youth had been taking advantage of the French recruitment of minorities to the "Troupes Speciales" to get out of the village, beginning a tradition of military careers which continues today. Education, which began to penetrate the mountain, was also seized upon as a route to employment outside of agriculture. In the 1950s, educated youth began to join the radical political parties, including the Ba'th and to identify with Arab nationalism and oppose their tribal chiefs. (See Chapter 3, pp. 62–64 for a detailed account of Alawi mobilization).

This wider picture of declining self-sufficiency and social mobilization was reflected in the village of this study. Land was increasingly fragmented by the fifties and no family in the village could support itself on it alone. A French school and a Quranic school for saih families existed in the area, however, and were supplemented by the opening of private and government schools in 1958. Before long, most village families aspired to get education and jobs for their sons outside of agriculture, expecting them to send part of their income back to the village; for youth, too, a job with a steady income became the ideal. By 1970, eighteen sons of this small village were at university. Education and government penetration generated a "new middle class" of employees in the area, outside the traditional framework of shaikh and peasant. Slowly, roads were pushed through the mountains, reaching most villages by 1970; radios appeared in the fifties and by the seventies every family in the village had one. As non-agricultural income and the money economy grew, it fueled the development of petty commercial capitalism in the mountain itself.

Agrarian structure in the seventies remained little differentiated. Two families had somewhat more land because, being larger, they had received more in the days when it was periodically reallocated under *musha'* tenure. Landholdings were too small to be divided among a holder's sons: rather, typically, one son worked the land, while the others became teachers or military officers. Only two families were share-croppers: one peasant who was too old to cultivate his land let it to a "partner" in return for one-third of the crop, and another share-cropper family paid one-third of the corn and 75% of the olive crop for use of the land. It is commerce which became a vehicle of differentiation among peasants. Several families opened profitable shops, selling consumer goods, notably clothes, on credit for 25% interest. In the early seventies, two merchants had large sums loaned out and were partners in the local bus, a thresher, and an olive press. A butcher shop and a bakery opened, catering to the new employee class.

These developments substantially altered the tribal-kinship base of village society. The extended patriarchal family and the larger clan or lineage—of which there were twelve here—persisted; lineage cousins were expected to help each other in dealing with the outside world. But these bonds were being undermined by social change. One reason is the earlier access of men than women to education; educated men wanted to marry educated women who could earn an income, regardless of their family status, rather than the frequently uneducated village cousins who remained unmarried. Thus, the endogamy supportive of lineage solidarity was undermined. When an educated man married an educated woman their incomes allowed them to set up separate nuclear family households and some left the village to escape family constraints. These tendencies and the effects of education and economic independence on attitudes, eroded the patriarchal authority on which the whole kinship superstructure was erected. Tribal identities also declined: tribal endogamy was no longer the rule in the seventies and many youth did not even know to which tribe they belonged. This seems to run counter to claims that tribal rivalry and bonds are a crucial ingredient of politics in the Alawite national elite, but it is possible intra-Alawi politics under Asad has reversed the tendency toward tribal decline: if so this is a curious inversion of the otherwise largely "modernizing" impact the state has had on Alawi society.

In part due to social change, in part due to the rise of the Ba'th to power, local political leadership and the political relations of the mountain villages to the state have been transformed. This village was an early stronghold of the Ba'th Party; in the late fifties, 20–30 students going to high school in Shaikh al-Badr formed a Ba'th cell in the area. They held "political-cultural" meetings in the village, stressing themes such as the revolt of peasants against landlord exploitation; though there were no landlords in this village, many Alawites were sharecroppers or seasonal laborers for Sunni landlords elsewhere and this theme was favorably received even by traditional leaders. In 1957 a mass rally held in the area reportedly attracted 15,000 peasants to denounce feudalism and demand roads and schools. The Ba'th's message of Arab Unity was also received enthusiastically by villagers: the Alawites' historic sense of apartness was being rapidly eroded by absorption into a larger Arab identity. Despite the fears of some Alawis that the UAR would result in Sunni dominance, the union was initially very popular in this village. The dissolution of the Ba'th in favor of Nasir's "National Union" was, however, seen as a step backward, especially by the youth: the union incorporated traditional leaders, including the village mukhtar from a saih family. But party members remained active in spite of the dissolution and when the Ba'th took power in 1963, party cells in the Alawi mountains were among the biggest and best organized, a factor which would contribute to the subsequent Alawi rise to national power. After 1963, the membership of the local party rapidly expanded. The national power of Alawi Ba'thists also widened local access to army careers, building on a tradition in the mountain; in fact, the preferred marriage partner for village girls became an army officer, a career seen as the key to prestige and income. Another indicator of the rapid expansion of military careers here is the fact that one of the first and best circulated newspapers was the army organ, *Jaysh al-Shab*. General Ibrahim al-Ali, recently commander of the People's Army, is an offspring of the Shaikh Salah al-Ali lineage dominant in this village (Gubser 1979b:35); other scions of Shaikh Salah's Matawirah tribe are also to be found in the regime elite. The fact is that through the party and the army, the mountain, including this village, has become something of a privileged elite recruitment pool.

New sub-elites also appeared in the village. The educated young officials who ran the local party assumed the major leadership role largely on the basis of their ability to bring amenities—schools, roads, waterlines, a clinic—to the area and because of the prestige of education: they were seen as having a broader outlook than traditional leaders and able to "lead the way to development." The historic correlation between the shaikhly elite and literacy, between age and knowledge, had been broken. Officials not recruited locally, however, played little political role, an indicator of the importance of local recruitment to the Ba'th's penetration of the village. The rise of new sub-elites was paralleled by a decline of traditional authority in the village. There was still a mukhtar, a seventy-year old patriarch from a saih family who held the post thirty-five years, a saih, and a three-man council representing the three village tribes. But their role had contracted. The mukhtar and the saih families used to be the nearly exclusive gate-keepers between village and state. They interpreted outside events and were the main opinion leaders; outside forces, especially the police, were dependent on them for information and villagers were dependent on the mukhtar to keep the village on the good side of these feared officers with meals, firewood, and deference. The mukhtar now has little to do as the police have directly assumed many of his functions and, being locally recruited, are no longer feared. Moreover, Ba'th partisans and educated government officials give better access to the keys of power. The role of the local saih is increasingly confined to religious ritual. There has been some conflict between the traditional and modern sub-elites. When this has happened, older villagers tend to stand with the former, while not totally opposed to the latter, while the younger generation has sided with the modern officials; the intermediate generation maintains contacts with both, turning to the former for religious guidance and to the latter in secular matters. Yet there is also overlap between "old" and "new" leaders: the youth of saih families have been incorporated into the new sub-elite, but their status rests on their education, occupations, and office, not on family lineage. The saih still receives zakat, even from the youth, but the religious feasts which used to incarnate Alawi community life have declined and the saintly tombs are visited chiefly by women. It is not so much that traditional authority has been overthrown as that competing new sources of power have emerged, pluralizing power and influence and multiplying channels of access to the state. All this is an indicator of a shift in political culture: a breakdown in the traditional isolation and alienation of Alawi society from the state.

One key to the influence of the new party-state sub-elites was their effort to organize villagers into modern institutions. The mixed record of the women's union and of the cooperative gives some insights into the achievements and limits of such state-promoted change here. A branch of the General Federation of Women established in 1968 is devoted to raising the status of women who traditionally ranked very low in Alawi society: according to religious doctrine they were inferior to men, not even acknowledged to have souls, and early marriage, constant maternity, and the burden of work left them old at age thirty. Women did not inherit and their husband's authority was supreme. All women in the village over thirty are illiterate as no girls went to school until the late fifties. The local women's union was founded by unmarried college graduates; three of its leaders are village school teachers. They established a night school to teach older women to read and write and encourage better health practices, sponsored discussions of women's problems, and set up a kindergarten. Parents did not like the union because it violated the tradition that girls should stay home and do housework; but they did not prohibit their daughters from joining, perhaps because the union was sponsored by the Ba'th Party. Many of the illiterate peasant women were passive, quiet during the union's discussions, and content to leave decisions to the educated leaders. The union did not really mobilize deprived peasant women or change many basic male attitudes. Peasant women are still burdened with work, having to work in the fields while the men spend free time in the coffeehouses. But the union helps to support the slow alteration of attitudes being dictated by economic change. Fathers now send their daughters to school because without education they cannot find a suitable husband; nursing and teaching are now considered acceptable occupations. As education spreads, women are no longer forced into arranged marriages.

The village cooperative was founded at the initiative of Ba'th party youth who persuaded their families to join and by 1971 it had 121 members on 241 hectares. It encountered a spate of difficulties. Its primary role was to channel credit and inputs to villagers, but initially many peasants spent the credit on clothes, furniture, to repay old debts, or to build a house, and resented it when they had to repay their loans: some got the money by doing seasonal labor on the side but a few, still indebted, were cut off from future credit. Special corn seeds supposed to improve production were delivered too late to the cooperative and consumed for food. The cooperative owned no machinery, partly because the area is so rugged. The key to development of the village is irrigation and orchardization, but only 8.8 ha. are irrigated and 80 ha. in orchards and the cooperative has not been a force for such development. A basic weakness is leadership. The peasants lacked confidence in the inexperienced agronomist supposed to supervise the cooperative, and he had six other cooperatives to tend to as well. Yet, the cooperative council, composed of illiterate elders, left most of the administration—keeping the books, calling the general assembly—to him. The general assembly did not actively control the cooperative either, only a few younger peasants in it being active. The Ba'th youth who founded the cooperative, being themselves employed outside of farming, gave no sustained leadership. Peasants lacked supportive attitudes: they felt the cooperative should be doing things for them and when matters went awry they blamed it on the institution and accepted no responsibility for its success or failure. Some saw it as exploitative since they had to pay 5% interest on credit, forgetting how much merchants once charged them; indeed, the main success of the experiment has been to lighten their dependence on usurers and merchants. One other success, perhaps indicative of where the villagers' real interest lies, was its project to build a high school.

This land-poor over-populated area has adapted to new opportunities: villagers have been uniquely successful in translating education into income and careers in the state and army. From being one of the most backward, this area has become one of the most socially-mobilized. Once at the bottom of the political hierarchy, it has become a bastion of the ruling party and a privileged recruitment pool for the national elite. The costs have been the neglect of agriculture and the disruption of community life, especially for those unmarried women left behind in the village. Ambition for income and mobility and appetite for new goods have rapidly developed, fueling the growth of petty capitalism and bureaucracy, but if the cooperative experience is any indicator, productive habits of saving and work lag well behind new aspirations.

Alawi Coastal Village[5]

This village, on the outskirts of the city of Latakia, is representative of Alawi villages on the *sahil* (coast). Here, by contrast to the mountains, tribal organization had broken down under the power of government and urban landlords by the time of the French "Mandate." Most property was urban and Sunni owned, large estates in a few places, many medium-sized farms, and even more small ones located close to the city; in Latakia alone there were 5,000 landed proprietors of various sizes. Typically, city folk who accumulated some commercial wealth bought land and contracted it to Alawi sharecroppers. According to Fedden (207), relations between the bigger landlords and peasantry were close to classic serfdom: peasants owed personal service, including in some places a *jus primae noctis*, the landlord's word was law, protection had to be bought, but the overlord recognized no obligations: "Whatever payment is made everything still remains to be paid for. The peasant is the victim of perpetual blackmail." Because the tenants were Alawites, the city's religious and social scorn for them reinforced each other. The Alawis, totally excluded from the city until the Mandate, were conscious of "belonging to a people despised but elect." As late as the thirties, tension between Sunnis and Alawis in the area was "like an atmosphere of pogrom which makes one remember all the past massacres and fear the future ones" (Weulersse 1940:254). Even dress was distinctive. Alawi women unveiled and in white contrasted with black-veiled Sunni women. Although the establishment of stronger government reduced overt conflict, and although some Alawite landowning families emerged and settled in Latakia, class, urban-rural, and religious cleavages tended to overlap and reinforce each other here. Once education began to touch the Alawite community, young Alawis were politicized; youth joined the Communist Party, the SSNP, and later the Ba'th, seeking a vehicle of protection and protest against the Sunni city. An incident in Baniyas, not far down the coast, when the Ba'th took power, gave overt political expression to the historical conflict here: clashes erupted between the Sunnis from the town, some the scions of the old landed families, some flying the banner of Nasirism, and Alawi villagers identified with the Ba'th Party, emboldened by the rise of their comrades to power in Damascus.

This coastal village was owned by four Sunni landlords from Latakia and worked under the sharecropping system. The peasant received 25% of the product if he provided work and animals, and, if only his own labor, 16%; in practice, he received even less, as the landlord, doing the weighing of the harvest, had "a special way of counting," and made extra deductions for sundry services such as transport and credit given at usurious rates. The sharecropper had no security of contract and migration from village to village in search of a sharecropping contract was common. The landowners were absentees with little interest in improvement of their lands. Some sons of these share-croppers joined the Ba'th in the fifties, looking for a way out of a deadend life, and one is now a big man in the Latakia party apparatus. But, while sons of share-croppers now exercise political power over the Sunni landlords of Latakia, this political revolution has translated into no comparable social overturning in this particular village.

To be sure, there is a new leadership in the village presiding over new institutions—party, peasant union, cooperative—and some modest reform has taken place. But landlord power remains very much a fact of life. The key to its persistence is the very limited impact of the land reform here. A poorly drafted land reform law failed to stop extended families from dividing their land among nuclear families and these proprietors did so, thereby diluting much of the impact of the law. Fear of another reform did precipitate the sale of some additional lands to villagers. In 1974, of the 1200 ha. in the village, 200 were owned by small holders before the reform, only 40 was re-distributed in the reform, 160 were thereafter purchased by villagers, but 800—2/3 of the village—remained in landlord hands. However 600 of these hectares are worked by peasants under share-cropping contracts which, now regulated by law, are much more favorable to peasants: they have virtual security of tenure and must give the owner only 20% of the crop for land rent. The final 200 hectares of land is managed directly by a proprietor using hired labor.

The new leadership in the village is headed by the chief of the party cell (*al-amin al-halaqa*), the local school teacher. He is assisted by the head of the peasant union. Here, as is often the case, pro-Ba'thi peasants are small-landowners who benefited from the agrarian reform. The union leader received .3 ha. in the reform, holds 4 ha. under a sharecropping contract and has managed to buy 1.8 ha. Though modest, the agrarian reforms have increased income and security over the old days for peasants and many have been able to build new houses of concrete bloc furnished with simple amenities. But the reform certainly did not create a prosperous yeoman peasantry.

The local party sees its role as largely mediation between state and village: it explains party policy and the state agricultural plan to villagers, and intervenes on their behalf with the bureaucracy when problems of credit, fertilizer delivery, etc., arise: this seems so typical of what other party officials have elsewhere reported that the oil of party influence seems crucial to make the creaky state agrarian machinery run. Peasants are dissatisfied with the land reform and want it extended, especially since some landlords don't cultivate all their land, but the most the local party had been able to secure in 1974 was a promise to see if the reform was evaded or the distribution process distorted by favoritism. The cooperative funnels credit and production requisites to peasants, both landowners and sharecroppers, relieving them of some dependency on merchants and landlords, and markets the crop to various state agencies. A second dairy cooperative has permitted peasants to purchase cows and fodder, apparently adding to their income. The party and peasant union supposedly ensure that peasant rights are respected under the agrarian relations law, but they have not organized a collective contract for the wage-workers working on the big landed estate.

This village appears sharply divided by kinship rivalries. The head of the peasant union is clearly not of a caliber to hold his post and was elected by acclaim (rather than competition as union rules provide) only because, belonging to no major kinship bloc, he can be trusted by all not to show favoritism. The persistent influence of kinship bloc rivalry appears, thus, to have left a gap in local leadership. Perhaps because of this, a third actor, the local agent of the Ministry of Agriculture plays a more salient role than is typical of other villages: it was he who organized the cooperative and continues to supervise it. Generational conflicts also divide peasants. The assumption of local power by young men has not set well with the elders of the big clans. Ideological views divide the generations, too: many elders believe that, God having made some rich and some poor, men must be content with their lot, while younger men are responsive to the party's socialist and modernizing ideology.

Intra-peasant conflicts, combined with the largely intact wealth and status of the landlords which keeps some peasants economically dependent on them, has permitted the landlord families to sustain political influence in the village. The party leaders claim landlords tell the elders that youth are not capable or responsible and that leadership should lie with those having experience; they are said to exploit family rivalries as well. The landlords' social prestige persists to the extent that older peasants who visit the city call on them as part of their clientage obligations. Thus, the landlords appear to maintain an independent system of political influence in the village hostile to the Ba'th-centered one. While this is not unusual in villages where land reform was partial, what is remarkable here is that landlord clientage networks cut across the Sunni-Alawi divide, despite the long history of Sunni-Alawi clashes which have marked the coastal areas. The relative weakness of the pro-regime village leadership must help account for this. It is curious that the powerful Alawi-dominated Latakia party apparatus has not pushed for a revision of the land reform. It would appear that the detente between the Alawi power elite in Damascus and the Sunni bourgeoisie takes precedence over the much-celebrated Alawi communal solidarity. The peasants of this village, no longer a despised minority, enjoy greater income, security, and access to government than hitherto. But political mobilization and social transformation here has been quite limited.

Hauran Village[6]

This large village—almost a rural town—is located seventeen kilometers north of Dera City in the middle of Dera governorate, known as the Hauran. Historically, the Hauran was the granary of Damascus, but over the last century it suffered from growing aridity and agricultural decline. In the 1930s it appeared as a riverless, treeless land of dryness, encroaching desert, and famine, its fields strewn with black basaltic rocks from which the villages themselves were built. Of 300,000 hectares of cultivable land, only 50–70,000 were actually cropped, the balance either abandoned or left fallow in this arid region. Much of this deterioration resulted from human exploitation and neglect. The decline of security under bedouin encroachment in Ottoman times discouraged production; many of the ancient cisterns for collecting water had long fallen into disuse. Even as, under the French, security was re-established, bedouin who had lost their rights of tribute or their grazing land under the land registration campaign, flocked to the towns. Impoverished and bitter, only arms kept them in check: "although [the nomad] is for the present subdued, his presence hangs like a cloud over the farms and is a continual source of danger" (Epstein 607). Owing to nomadic penetration and settlement, the spirit of the area was bedouin, its speech close to that of the tribes, the ethic of family and tribe and of disdain for the land pervasive. But urban exploitation was equally a root of decline. This was not an area of great landed estates, 80–85% of the land was peasant owned, and only one-quarter of the peasantry was landless. But holdings were so small, fragmented, and vulnerable to drought that no truly independent peasantry could establish itself. On the contrary, peasants were in "utter subjection" (Epstein 601) to Damascene merchants to whom they sold their grain and on whom they were completely dependent for credit, loaned at usurious rates of 50–200%; the average debt of each peasant in the thirties was thirty gold Turkish pounds and the average interest on this debt amounted to more than the entire family budget for food and clothing. Through their control of the market and credit, Damascene merchants took the bulk of the peasant's meager surplus. Fragmented holdings and exploitation prevented the peasant from accumulating any surplus for emergencies, making him extremely vulnerable to shifts in the weather. In the thirties, catastrophic droughts caused mass famine and induced widespread migration. Migration at a lesser rate has been constant since then, many going to Palestine until this outlet was closed off. As a result of these factors, the social and economic level of the Hawrani peasant was long among the lowest in Syria. His food was barely enough for subsistence. There was practically no industry, health care, or paved roads. So poor were the villages that few had mosques or churches and peasants were sunk in superstition. Exploited and oppressed for generations on all sides—by the government, the merchants, the bedouin— the Haurani had lost all initiative, and was viewed by other Syrians as lazy, improvident, cowardly, passive, and lacking in self-respect. He was said unwilling to work more than necessary for bare subsistence. "As soon as the Haurani has obtained a morsel of bread with which to satisfy his hunger, he will abandon all work without the slightest care for the morrow. His greatest pleasure is to spend endless hours in the common guest hall of the village, drinking coffee, smoking or listening to gossip" (Epstein 603). All work except ploughing was left to the wife who was treated as a beast of burden. "The husband cares but little either for her or for the children and beats them mercilessly upon the slightest provocation" (Epstein 603).

The leading family of the area was the Hariris. Ismail al-Turk al-Hariri joined the 1925 rebellion against the French, but was the first to give up when the balance of forces turned against the nationalists; thereafter local leaders were known for acquiescence in French rule. In the late thirties about two-thirds of local officials were Damascenes to whom many locals preferred the French. Damascenes even controlled many of the local shops. A strong sense of difference from these richer more powerful outsiders translated into a certain sentiment for provincial autonomy.

After independence, the winds of social change began to sweep the province, contributing to growing political ferment. Resentment of Damascene dominance and of the underdevelopment of the area fueled unrest among peasant youth. In the early fifties, they began to question and rebel against the traditional order in the area. And the loss of Palestine, especially felt here because it closed off opportunities for work there and flooded the province with refugees competing for housing and jobs, stirred up nationalist feelings. The founders of the Ba'th Party had historic family ties to the area and in the forties a few local youth who went to Damascus for schooling came into contact with them. From that time, the Ba'th began to make the Hauran a major center of its recruitment.

The Ba'th arose in this Hauran village as a product of this wider political ferment, and most immediately, as a manifestation of revolt against the traditional local leadership which enforced the old order and tied the area to Damascus. On one side of the struggle was the *za'im* of the Hariri family who had his headquarters here, dominated village life, and wished to preserve the traditional culture and social structure against disturbing influences. On the other side, were youth of the poorer peasant families who wished to acquire modern education as a route to careers outside of a precarious agriculture or as a way of bringing change to the area. The conflict was politicized by the tendency of those who went to school to be recruited by the Ba'th and to openly question traditional practices in the village.

The za'im was not a large landowner since his family's holdings, like those of smaller peasants, had been fragmented by Islamic inheritance practices. By the 1950s, he owned only 150 unirrigated hectares. But as head of a large extended lineage, with traditional prestige, he held the Turkish title of "bek" and was regularly returned to parliament. As a member of parliament, he was able to solidify his position with petty patronage. He had the power to nominate mukhtars in this and other villages. Through alliance with some village notables and the government, which sanctioned his rule, the za'im seemed to be the natural leader of clan and village. According to traditional practice, peasants paid a tribute to maintain the laborers who worked the za'im's land and the assortment of retainers and servants in his household, including a chauffeur and "coffeemaker." It also went to maintain a guest room where government officials were entertained, local disputes arbitrated, and the solidarity of clan ties between the za'im and other families reinforced. It was through the za'im that peasants could hope to mitigate the impact of government in the area or acquire access to it for favors or redress. In order to preserve his status as "gatekeeper" between state and peasant and the traditions on which his leadership was based, the za'im consistently opposed penetration of the village by outside influence. He opposed the introduction of schools and a project to establish the village as a government center for the area.

Inevitably, the za'im's effort to contain the spread of education failed. Government primary and intermediate schools were established in Dera city and some peasants sent their sons there; indicative of the growing perception that education offered a way out of a deadend agricultural economy, is the fact that some peasants sold their land to pay for their sons' education. In Dera, many of the teachers were Alawi refugees from Iskanderun, preaching Arab nationalism and Ba'thism. When the za'im discovered that some youth had been sent to Damascus for secondary education he decided to make it an issue. He called the heads of the offending families to his headquarters and tried to persuade them to recall their sons. They would, he predicted, lose religion and go with girls. But his arguments were rendered less credible by the fact that his own cousin was studying medicine at Damascus University. As such, peasants were following a precedent set by the leading family, and efforts to discourage them were seen as designed to maintain status differentiations. When, in vacation time, the sons returned to the village preaching Ba'thism, the stage was set for a confrontation. The za'im, his clan and retainers prepared the atmosphere in the village against the errant families, assembled them in the guesthouse and administered the "fellika"—a traditional educator's punishment by which the soles of the feet are beaten—against the students: "That's education!" declared the za'im. When the Ba'th's district secretary came to investigate this incident, he was handled roughly by the za'im's retainers. But the confrontation only polarized the village rather than restoring traditional authority. The numbers of educated youth—and the Ba'th nucleus in this village—expanded in the subsequent years and in 1954 the party was strong enough to headquarter one of its Dera sub-branches here. Thus, well before the party's coming to national power, it already had a presence in this area.

Since the establishment of Ba'th rule in Damascus, the balance of power in the village has shifted against the za'im. He still lives in the village, retaining a good measure of support and prestige. But he has lost his former privileges and his power has been undermined by the loss of his patronage connections to the government and the shift of such access points to the local party organization. His relatively modest land-holdings were an insufficient economic base with which to retain village control once traditional authority was undermined.

The party is now the center of an alternative—indeed ascendent—power bloc. In this area of tribal culture, party strategy was to recruit educated youth from all families and clans. A number of new schools were built in the village, staffed by party members who were expected to attract their students to the party and through these youth the party aimed to mobilize their families under its leadership and dilute the effects of clan cleavages. There are now three party units (firqas) headquartered in the village, with 25–30 members in each, two chiefly made up of teachers and one of peasants. One of the three party secretaries is a Hariri, a nephew of the za'im; he joined the party while in school in Damascus and claims to have done so because of his revulsion against tribal divisiveness, the backwardness of the area, and his identification with the "toiling classes." In recent parliamentary elections, he worked to help elect the head of the peasant union against his own uncle, the za'im. In this contest, at least, the village was indeed split into two blocs, the Hariris and the "hizbis" (partisans). But the overlap in membership between the two blocs symbolized by the party's recruitment from the za'im's own family, indicates that this cleavage is on the decline; and indeed since Asad, the national elite has encouraged reconciliation between such blocs instead of the former confrontation.

The new big man in the village in the mid-seventies, in some ways eclipsing the za'im, was the Branch Secretary of the Ba'th Party in Dera city. He is the son of a small butcher from the village, with no family connections to the dominant clans. But he managed to get education by enrolling in the industrial school in Damascus which provided scholarships and free lodging for poor students. In school he was attracted to the party by a popular teacher, met and studied with Zaki al-Arsuzi, and worked himself up in the party hierarchy. Intelligent and dynamic, he made it his business, as party secretary, to extend party control over the local service bureaucracies bringing roads, electricity and water to the villages, and hence over the levers of patronage; through him, thus, local government was controlled by locals, not Damascene appointees, and the area had at least as powerful a connection to the central government as under the za'im. His case is a classic example of the opportunities opened to some rural youth by the Ba'th. Indicative of the extent to which the combination of education and Ba'thi politics had become the major alterative to agriculture for ambitious peasant youth, is the fact that the six members of the Dera province branch executive committee of the party were all school teachers from peasant families. The other leg of party leadership in the area were pro-Ba'th peasants. Typical of these was the head of the peasant union in this village, a prosperous small holder with twelve unirrigated hectares of land planted with wheat and olive trees. This alliance of educated village youth and the small and middle peasantry is entirely typical of the Ba'th axis in most villages.

Despite the shift in political power, the level of party-led ideological mobilization here seems modest. Even educated party activists did not appear very politically conscious: thus, when asked their reaction to certain decisions taken by the government, they said their role was to elect their leaders, not to question decisions taken by them. Also, the number of politically organized peasants was relatively small. In 1974, besides one party branch of twenty-five members, there was a peasant union embracing a hundred families, perhaps a tenth of those eligible, and the cooperative, having just been founded, had only fifteen members. It appears many peasants in the village preferred to avoid aligning themselves with either the party or Hariri bloc. The overall result is not that traditional leadership has been displaced by a new one, but that two rival poles have pluralized power in the village.

Under Ba'th rule, the viability of rural life seems to have been enhanced. The party has presided over a major educational expansion in the village. In the 1950s there was no school there, one primary school in the district, and one intermediate school in the whole province; in 1974 in the village alone there were four primacy schools, two intermediate schools, and one high school. Fifty-five sons of the village were university graduates. Illiteracy, hitherto typical, has been eradicated among the new generation. Another sign of change is the fact that girls attended an integrated high school in the village despite the warning of the za'im that they would only use their new skills to write love letters. Electricity has been installed, paved roads built, sanitation facilities and an infirmary set up. The establishment of four private bakeries in the area is a sign of economic expansion and the generation of a petty capitalism. One of six irrigation projects undertaken in the governorate is located near the village, irrigating 320 of its 7,000 hectares and a reservoir has been excavated to trap rainwater. Orchardization has been pushed to check aridity and diversify the peasant economy: there is a center for the distribution of seedlings at nominal prices which peasant union members took advantage of to plant some 15,000 new olive trees.

The growing penetration of the agrarian bureaucracy and the growth of party-sponsored local peasant organizations appears to have buttressed the position of small owners and tenants. The classic debt dependency on Damascene merchants has been alleviated by the access of peasants to government credit. Indeed the regime has tried to cut these merchants off from the local market: in 1973 the grain trade was nationalized, no grain may now be privately transported across district lines, and peasants are obliged to sell their crop to the state. Government marketing does provide peasants with a price floor and hence security from the ups and downs of the private grain trade, but when free prices exceed state ones, a black market has developed here. In 1973, eighty tons of wheat were confiscated and peasant unionists mobilized to help stamp out grain smuggling, a measure hardly likely to make them popular in the village. In practice, peasants seem to have more choice than before the Ba'th, able to deal with the state or the black market as their interest dictates and hence no longer as dependent. The enforcement of the agrarian relations law has improved the security of tenants and their share of the crop. As a result, rich peasants and landlords, such as the za'im, have taken to either selling their land to tenants or buying tractors and using hired labor instead: in either case reducing a non-productive tenure form which traditionally retarded agricultural development. When owners wish to replace tenants they need approval from the peasant union which ensures the tenant receives his legal compensation. This jurisdiction over agricultural contracts gives the union significant power in the village.

A significant growth in the population of the village reflects the return of prosperity to this once desolate region. The fact that some landless peasants have used earnings from work outside of agriculture to buy land suggests that farming is still a valued and viable way of life. But for many youth in this village, work opportunities in Damascus, the Gulf, or Lebanon have seemed more attractive. The rapid spread of education, seen as an alternative to agriculture, tends to drain farming of its most talented elements; the fact that one of the early Ba'thists who led the fight against the Hariris is now practicing medicine in London shows the danger of a brain drain. The drive for education and the movement off the land may diversify resources and opportunities for local families, but if this rapid social mobilization exceeds—as seems very likely—the pace of national economic development, the result is likely to be the growth of the educated underemployed, and quite possibly, another wave of political discontent which could erode the regime's rural base.

Druze Village

This Druze village is situated some 10 km. from Suwayda in the Jabal Druze mountains. Since the mid-19th century, the Druze of Syria lived as an autonomous community, secure in their mountain fastnesses, professing a heterodox variety of Islam, under their own political and religious leaders, independent and martial of character.

Druze villages were among the few in Syria which escaped urban domination since they lay outside the sphere where the government could make landlord rights respected. Although great notable clans such as the Atrash accumulated relatively large properties, most Druze peasants were small-holders. In an area where individual care and effort were required to clear fields of stones and build terraces and where the surveillance of the master was frustrated by obstacles of terrain not encountered on the plains, the small peasantry could more easily escape reduction to tenancy. Social structure was aristocratic, separating za'im from fallah, but was based less on wealth than personal qualities, force, courage and ruse; social relations were more a question of man to man, gun to gun, than proprietor to sharecropper or creditor to debtor (Weulersse 1946:260–261). On more than one occasion, when Druze chieftains pushed their clients too far, they were met by armed rebellion (e.g. in 1886 and 1947). Besides za'im and fellah, the Druzes had a separate hierarchy of religious shaikhs, a small elect initiated into the esoteric secrets of the cult, of which the majority remained ignorant; but these never became a political or economic elite (Gubser 1979a: 116–118). Druze villages suffered from a shortage of water and from a terrain inhospitable to agriculture, but, to observers, they appeared prosperous and independent by comparison to the poverty and servility of their Hauran neighbors.

The Druze joined Damascene nationalists in the 1925 rebellion against the French, but thereafter tried to keep Damascene officials at bay and even after independence, the authority of the new state in the mountain was often more formal than real. In the late forties and early fifties, however, change was undermining the isolation of the mountain and traditional authority there. Population pressure on the land, a drive for education and entry into the army by Druze youth, and Shishakli's curbing of Druze autonomy, prepared the way for the gradual identification of Druze youth with radical Arab nationalism. The Ba'th party soon made Suwayda province one of its strongholds. (See Chapter 3, pp. 64–65, for a detailed analysis of Druze mobilization).

When the Ba'th took power in 1963, it therefore had a pool of support at the grassroots level in Suwayda. Further, Druze officers such as Hamad Ubayd and Salim Hatoum had played a major role in the military committee and the March coup. They and other Druze militants, notably Hamud al-Shufi who emerged as Syrian (Regional) party secretary in 1963 and helped lead the radicalization of party ideology, appeared among the most prominent members of the new leadership in Damascus. The emergence of significant Druze participation in a centralizing party and government and the penetration of the mountain by this party, marked a major re-ordering of relations between the Druze community and the political center: the rise of a younger generation of national-oriented leadership and the decline of traditional localistic notables. But this process has been marked by strains and even reversals and, as such, remains incomplete today, perhaps in part because major Druze figures in the Ba'th regime have since continuously lost out in factional quarrels at the center. In 1964 al-Shufi was purged as party secretary and in 1966 Mansur al-Atrash was thrown out with Aflaq in the 1966 coup. The most dramatic example of the unevenness of change in political loyalties came in the aftermath of an intra-party struggle in September 1966 when Ubayd and Hatoum broke with the regime in a struggle with leading Alawite officers. They fled to the mountain and sought refuge with the Druze elder, Hassan al-Atrash, took the regime's Alawi strongman, Salah Jedid, prisoner and fled to Jordan when Alawi Defense Minister Hafiz al-Asad threatened to bomb Suwayda. While a handful of Druze politicians stood with Damascus, most of the Suwayda branch party apparatus was subsequently purged. The incident seemed to show that besides the public cleavage between "radical" and "traditional" forces which marked the first decade of Ba'th rule, deep sectarian divisions and solidarities persisted and could, in time of crisis, override the former.[7] Certainly, the fall of so many prominent Druze leaders must have reduced Druze identification with the Ba'th regime. Nevertheless, party authorities here, from the branch level *amin al-fara'* down to the village *halaqa* are all Druzes, not outsiders; thus the Druze enjoy both local self-government and representation in ruling party councils. Younger educated men professing loyalty to the national ideology have largely supplanted the traditional notables from the levers of access to government and patronage (Gubser 1979a:124–125).

Many of the trends and patterns typical of the mountain as a whole can be identified in the village of this study.[8] A traditional za'im used to be unchallenged political leader. Although he only personally owned a quarter of the land, he made many of the decisions of importance for village life, e.g. the selection of harvest guards, control of pasturage and of the agricultural cycle; in return he received tribute from his clients. The community was preserved undisturbed by its isolated location and primitive roads, impassable in bad seasons, although it was roused during the 1925 anti-French revolt.

The Ba'th Party first penetrated the village in 1954 when youth, converted to Ba'thism in Damascus secondary schools, returned in the summer; a son of the za'im was among the first converts. By the late fifties, perhaps fifty villagers were sympathetic to the party. After the Ba'th seizure of power in 1963 many of these formed the nucleus of the local party organization. There has consequently been a shift, although not yet decisive, in the locus of political power. The za'im is no longer politically active and a village council has become the center of decision-making. Behind it stand the party, peasant union, cooperative, and other "popular organizations." As in other villages, the backbone of the party bloc is an alliance of educated youth and a segment of the younger peasantry, apparently on the basis of a greater orientation to national issues and receptivity to social change. The most prominent local partisan, the head of the Suwayda branch Peasant Bureau, associated high school movements against Shishakli, the Baghdad Pact and the Suez invasion with his adhesion to the party. The local *amin al-firqa,* a school teacher, was recruited in high school as well, where students were concerned with Arab history and national causes such as Palestine. He cites the radical coup of 1966 as the occasion of his recruitment and dismisses the subsequent falling out of Druze stalwarts, Hatoum and Ubayd, with this regime as a question of personalities irrelevant to the deeper issues of nation and class. These partisans appear to exemplify a trend of opinion which identifies with national leaders and issues rather than regional influentials and sectarian issues and they, in turn, seek to recruit the upcoming generation. According to them, even the educated sons of the za'im and the religious shaikhs have been won over by national-oriented teachers and textbooks. This spells the end of the old Druze isolation and of the quasi-independent political system which held the loyalties of their fathers.

But if the reins of overt political leadership have passed to new men, alternative centers of influence clearly persist in the village. The za'im, the elders, and religious men make up the leaders of this other bloc. Since the local party and popular organizations embraced only about 30% of the village population in 1974, it is likely that they retained substantial influence over peasants, while yet others remained uncommitted or apathetic. Still, the cleavage between the old and new is probably not that sharp here: no deep or abiding class differences separate the villagers and kinship links, however attenuated, bind most of them. Political differences are certainly overlaid by the Ba'th's recruitment of the offspring of traditional leaders. Party leaders themselves distinguish between "reactionary" religious shaikhs and "progressive" ones, said to be from less well-off families, whose "minds are open to change" and with whom they are on good terms. Moreover, at least according to one Damascene school teacher posted in the mountain, even Ba'this retain a sense of difference and apartness rooted in their special Druze identity, which they share with "traditionals."

State-sponsored social change here has been modest, but peasants have been incorporated into new institutions which link them to the national market. There was no land reform here, as the za'im's holdings were under the land reform limit, but tiny pieces of state land were distributed to two-thirds of village families. There is a prosperous cooperative which possesses two tractors, one a reward from the party for high production levels. Peasants cultivate wheat and grapes, a crop well adapted to the terrain, and have recently introduced fruit trees: thousands of fruit tree seedlings have been planted as part of a governorate level program to turn the mountain into a center of orchard culture. Party-mobilized labor helped lay a fresh water pipeline and push agricultural roads up the mountain. The limits of social change can be seen from the fact that wives of peasants doing military service are "by tradition" not cooperative members and thus those that most need help seem excluded from benefits and services.

In this village, the most-striking changes are the cultural and political shifts which signal the integration of this centrifugal area to the national center. Sectarian identities have certainly not been effaced. Rather, secularization—a broadening of identities resulting from nationalist education—and the linkage of the mountain to a centralizing party-state which forbids overt expression of sectarianism in politics, has pushed them back from the center of public life. They retain a vitality which, as the Hatoum incident shows, can, in times of conflict, re-erupt into politics. But, as compared to a case like Lebanon, such eruptions can be contained; this is the difference between state formation and decay.

Three Ghouta Villages

The Ghouta of Damascus was traditionally a green and desirable world apart from the grain-growing plains where great "feudal" estates dominated. In Ghouta villages, with their relative security and sufficiency of water, a dense diversified orchard culture thrived. In many places, there were three separate harvests of lucrative fruits and vegetables, rather than the single poor grain crop of the Hama or Hauran plains. To be sure, most land was not owned by the cultivators themselves, the larger notable-owned estates and the medium-sized properties of the urban merchant bourgeoisie encompassing the larger part of the cultivated surface. But, relieved of the plague of drought and able to work year around, more small peasant owners could survive than elsewhere. Moreover, because irrigated arboriculture required the skill and motivated cooperation of the cultivator, share-cropping contracts were more favorable to peasants than elsewhere: they might get as much as two-thirds of the crop. This contrasted sharply with conditions just beyond the borders of the Ghouta—in the Mardj—where landlords prohibited their sharecroppers from building houses and planting trees and periodically replaced them with newcomers. Most small-holding peasants in the Ghouta were dependent on urban merchants for credit and the marketing of their crops and were typically indebted, but where they could sell their products directly to the city market, villages prospered. Many of the big landowners in the area had no more interest in developing their estates than elsewhere and most small peasants were too indebted to improve their properties. But the area had reached a relatively intensive level of development centuries ago, the tradition of private ownership (mulk) around the cities had always been more favorable to investment than the state ownership on the plains, and some merchant-proprietors introduced new crops, pumps and tractors; peasants as well as owners benefited from this relatively advanced level of development (Weulersse 1946:129–131, 165; Thoumin 28, 228–231; Latron 170–175; Warriner 1962:94–95).

In sharp contrast to much of the rest of western Syria, the Ghouta was not an area of radical peasant ferment. This was partly because of the relative prosperity and partly because of the more developed relations of lord and peasant which, where great estate and small ownership coexisted, or where share-croppers worked in arboriculture, could take on an authentic patron-client character. Peasants, fearing the government most of all, sometimes looked to landlords for protection. Ghouta villages were the bases for a number of important Damascene politicians—the Quwatlis, al-Azms, Mardam Beys, Ajlanis, al-Hakims, and al-Barudis—organized on the basis of economic dependency, patronage, shared traditional values, and under the Mandate, hostility to the French. Indicative of the strength of landlord influence in this area was the reluctance of some peasants to accept reform land in the belief it violated Islamic precepts or clientage obligations to the lord. As a result, the Ba'th Party did not develop a strong base here and although its appeal did grow with the nationalist politicization in the fifties, most "progressive" Ghouta peasants chose after 1958 to follow Nasirism rather than the Ba'th and the area became a Nasirite stronghold. Muhammad Jarrah, a retired Nasirite officer, used the Ghouta as a base to try to overthrow the Ba'th government in July 1963. Communists and Muslim Brethren also had significant followings in Ghouta villages and towns. More than elsewhere in the Syrian countryside, the conservative cultural and religious influence of the city spilled over into the village; indicative of the continuing power of traditional religious forces is the fact that schools are segregated by sex in a town like Douma while in far less developed Raqqa villages, they are not. This was one of the few rural areas, too, where the party has demonstrated fear of infiltration of its organizations by the Ikhwan.

The Ba'th's rise to power unleashed or accelerated a certain amount of socio-political change in the Ghouta. Agrarian reform here had a limited impact because the great extended notable families who had held their estates as a unit, divided them among the various branches of the families. Thus, only 2,960 hectares out of 40,000 in the area were expropriated. Some villages were untouched; in others there was too little reform land to be distributed among all peasant candidates and where the outsiders brought in by landlords as sharecroppers got it (as the law provided) in preference to locals, reform set off resentments against the party. The middle holdings of the merchant bourgeoisie went untouched. But the holdings of some great proprietors were significantly reduced: e.g. the Quwatli family's holdings were cut from 1,193 hectares to 714. The reform also precipitated the sale by great proprietors of land under the ceiling, although frequently to "outsiders" with money from Mnin, Tell, or Nebek. Land distribution barely broadened the base of small proprietorship in the Ghouta (Bianquis 1980:22–120).

Party-backed cooperatives took root in the Ghouta, some at peasant initiative, a relatively rare phenomenon. They have made seasonal credit relatively available, sharply reducing dependence on merchants. In the seventies, they channeled significant amounts of development credit into the area for the purchase of cows, tractors, green-houses etc., in an effort to give impetus to development among small peasants. But city merchants still dominate crop marketing. State marketing of fruits and vegetables is underdeveloped, the state typically paying a price inferior to merchants, although its presence in the market puts a floor on prices. Those more educated or enterprising peasants who market their own crops save themselves the third of the value of the crop now taken by merchants. Many peasants have also bought little trucks to save the cost of transport (Bianquis 1980:121–174).

The more significant development, however, has been the steady urbanization of the Ghouta. By the late seventies, only one-half of the population was still predominately in agriculture. The sons of peasants were now working in factories, construction, government, commerce, or the Gulf; many villages had been transformed into dormitory communities housing migrants to Damascus unable to find housing there. Agricultural land is threatened by encroachment, pollution, and pressure on water resources. Diversification of income has certainly raised peasant living standards; new houses and little factories and shops have sprung up across the Ghouta. It has also spurred a certain differentiation among the peasantry. Money earned in the Gulf or in non-agricultural employment has purchased small and medium sized farms worked by hired labor and selling on the market—a new burst of agrarian capitalism arising out of the mainstream peasantry itself. But because movement off the land drove up the cost of agricultural labor further here than elsewhere, small proprietors whose sons left could not afford it and had to rent or sell their land or contract with a *damman* (middleman) to harvest their fruits. (Bianquis 1980:175–185).

These forces, together with the rise of Ba'thist power in the city itself, have changed the balance of political power in the villages of the Ghouta. The influence of the great families is greatly diminished because of their reduced economic base, lessened peasant dependence, and the weakening of their political solidarity by the division of their holdings among the branches of the family. Despite its earlier weakness, the Ba'th had established a well-organized presence by the seventies. Party cells exist throughout the Ghouta: for example in Douma district alone, an area of 48 villages and 27,000 families, 137 *halaqat* (cells) of 10-20 members each existed in 1974 (44 in Douma city, 22 in Nashibiyah, 26 in Haran, 16 in Idmir, and 29 in Harasta), embracing about 2,000 members. In addition, peasant unions, cooperatives, and the other array of popular organizations are entrenched and an increasing number of Ghouta youth are being incorporated into employment in government offices and state factories. Three Ghouta village cases give some insight into how and how far the Ba'th has managed to entrench itself here.

Ghouta Village 1 is a major village between Damascus and Douma. The Ba'th appeared well established here in the mid-seventies. The party was quite active and through it younger villagers had assumed political leadership by virtue of their education and connections to the government center. The career of the local party head is typical of many peasant youth who have used education and politics as tickets of upward mobility. The third son of a medium peasant, he was picked by his family to go to university to study law, while his older brothers cared for the land and household; supported by the family, it was expected he would use his skills and resources to diversify and protect its interests in the wider social arena. In school, he joined the Ba'th in the mid-fifties and when it took power received a job in the Ministry of Supply. Later, political connections made him a big man in the village: besides heading the village party unit, he became a senior cadre of the party youth auxiliary, and was elected to the governorate council in which role he had the ear of the governor and could arrange favors and redress problems requiring government action. By village standards, he was doing very well and in the shell of the traditional mud-built family house, he erected a modern one, a symbol of upward mobility and a metaphor of much of what is happening in this village. His house was a center of activity, often filled with villagers seeking assistance in such matters as credit from the agricultural bank, getting government jobs, and disputes over boundaries.

Around the party clustered its peasant, women's, and youth organizations. The local peasant union leader appeared to be a dominant personality and he too was elected to the governorate council. If these elections, which observers believe were left relatively free—and which Ba'th candidates lost in most of the cities—can be taken as an accurate indicator, the balance of local opinion favored the Ba'th and its allies. The other local member of the council was a Nasirite of the Arab Socialist Union who ran on the pro-Ba'th National Progressive Front list. That a part, at least, of the strong Nasirite current in the Ghouta had aligned with the Ba'th was also indicated by the fact that sons of Nasirite families were joining the party youth auxiliary. But other "rightwing" Nasirites, led by the durable Muhammad Jarrah unsuccessfully contested the party ticket in alliance with landlord-notables who were centers of an anti-regime faction.

In this traditionally conservative area, the party had, however, to tread softly and adapt itself to local sentiment in order to establish itself. Its strategy in countering the influence of conservative religious shaikhs who attacked secularism and socialism was to avoid any direct response to them and to insist that the place of religion is in the mosque, not in politics. The head of the local women's union reported the religious conservatism of the area forces her organization to go slow. She gave up on recruiting suspicious older women and concentrated on younger ones. She disliked segregated schools but acquiesced in them, since fathers here preferred no schools to mixed ones. This, she says, can only be changed with the next generation and her union's role is to create a conscious younger generation of mothers. The deportment of the village party chief illustrates the curious combination of traditional and modern here. Possessing modern education and speaking the language of modern politics, his leadership represented the overturning of the rule of traditional elders in the village. But in other respects he observed traditional mores on the grounds of keeping the confidence of the people. Thus he veiled his wife and kept her in traditional seclusion; on the occasion of a wedding in the village, men and women ate and celebrated in segregated areas. His friends from the provinces have never seen his wife and compare this practice unfavorably with their more liberal customs. He was certainly not in conformity with official party policy on women's role in society and seemed to act on separate planes in his private life and in his official work in which he dealt with women in the women's and youth unions in modern fashion. His behavior may have been merely politic. Or it may have been an example of an upwardly mobile peasant adopting the former customs of higher urban classes.

Ba'th political leadership translated into little direct social structural reform here. This village of small-holders was barely touched by the agrarian reform. Villagers were quite active in the formation of cooperatives, however, and created agricultural, milk-marketing, and transportation cooperatives. A school was built and utilities brought in. Urban employment grew rapidly. But the recruitment of villagers to positions of power in the political hierarchy was perhaps the most striking change here, bringing the presence of a government formerly feared and avoided into the heart of the village. The case indicates that the Ba'th is able to establish itself even in villages where the cultural environment is unreceptive and major social reforms are not carried out.[9]

Ghouta Village 2 is a hamlet not far from Village 1, but here social reform cuts deeper and a substantial social experiment has been attempted. Four-fifths of the village land was formerly owned by landed notables, including the Quwatli and Ghazzi families. The land reform distributed less than one irrigated hectare to each of some forty-three peasant families, but it did buttress the position of village small holders and set the stage for an attempt to create an "advanced" form of agricultural cooperative rare in Syria. Fourteen party-affiliated families, taking advantage of the government's desire to promote a dairy industry in the Ghouta, joined together to found a milk production cooperative.

The head of the cooperative, a village elder, and his four sons, all party members, appear to have been the leading force behind the experiment. They are an example of small peasants who have done well under the Ba'th. He used to be a sharecropper for a landlord family and remembers this as a time when the landlords "stole by paper" and "did not believe in God." The family was eventually able to buy some property and received an additional piece in the land reform, but it was not enough for four sons; one who became an air force officer now provides money for the family. But it was the cooperative experiment which promised, with generous government support, to transform these poor peasants into rich ones. In 1974, the cooperative head extolled the work of the party and professed his belief in socialism, despite the injunctions of the shaikhs; although he admitted to knowing little about what the party was doing on the national level, being "too old to learn about such things," the changes in the village had all been to his advantage.

The cooperative was founded by each of the members agreeing to pay in 200 L.S. and provide 5 dunums of land for forage cultivation. A ten year 160,000 L.S. loan was granted by the agricultural bank, 150 cows were collectively purchased, advanced milking facilities installed by the government, and an agronomist provided. The cooperative threatened almost immediately to founder on the novelty of collective ownership when some members insisted the cows should be divided up while the cooperative leaders argued this would be economically inefficient and defeat the cooperative purpose of the experiment; the former withdrew their membership. Initial high costs and inexperience which led to the loss of numerous calves soon put the cooperative in trouble and higher authorities had to intervene to save it. By the mid-seventies it appeared to have recovered. It bought thirty more cows, and received a tractor from the government. Members had learned to work in teams responsible for feeding, maintenance, and provision of forage. By 1974, 162,000 kg. of milk was being produced yearly. It was marketed with the newly established government milk factory and, according to the leadership, earned them 36,000 L.S. a year, permitting them to pay back half their loan. By the late seventies production reached 381,000 kg./year. Membership grew. But in the early eighties, the experiment seemed on the verge of failure again. Half the herd was lost in a year because insufficient fodder was produced by the cooperative's thirty-three fragmented hectares, and it failed to secure supplementary concentrated feed. A government veterinarian was not available when required. The prices paid by the state milk factory did not keep pace with rising costs but the cooperative was not permitted to seek alternative buyers. Finally, feuding between the original families who founded it and others split the cooperative. Thus, failures on both sides of the government-peasant connection put this showpiece project in jeopardy. This episode underlines the regime's general inability to foster advanced "socialist" institutions in the village.[10]

Village 3, on the fringe of the Ghouta near the Mardj, has undergone much more extensive structural change than those in the Ghouta proper. Dominated by a great landed family, it used to be planted in extensive grain and worked by sharecroppers who got one fourth of the harvest, were forbidden to build houses, plant trees or vegetables on the land, and periodically replaced with new-comers. After 1963 this village became a "land reform" village. The reform, virtually wiping out the holdings of the former landlord, transformed a population of sharecroppers into small owners. Unlike most Ghouta villages, this one, lacking independent peasant proprietors or a core of prosperous elders, was immune to the local conservative currents and, on the contrary, had some history of conflict between peasants and the landowning family in which the former were jailed or expelled from the land. Curiously, the ideas of the Ba'th were brought to the village by an imam from Yabroud. The party organization is now well established among the peasants: there are eighty members in addition to a peasant union/cooperative. The party leadership is made up of an employee of the local municipality, a employee at Damascus university, and three peasant members of the cooperative.

But turning the new peasant holders into viable farmers has not been easy. A cooperative was formed, but it vegetated until the state cotton organization stepped in and underwrote village debts, allowing the purchase of pumps for growing irrigated cotton. However, the cooperative fell into dependence on merchants, incurring more debt and a fall in the water table contracted the irrigated area. In 1972, higher cooperative authorities replaced the cooperative leadership. New credits allowed the establishment of a fuel station which made money servicing motorists and tractor-owners. A good harvest allowed the cooperative to start repaying its debts. By 1974 it was reportedly getting 400,000 S.P. yearly in credit and selling 1,250 tons of cotton to the cotton agency. It was "rewarded" with a tractor and a storage facility was built. Over the years urban amenities arrived: a village school, paved roads, water, sewage, and electricity. A significant number of youth—mostly professed Ba'thists—are teachers or army officers.

State promoted reforms, aid, and credit have certainly increased the viability and security of peasant life. But, compared to other Ghouta villages this one remains relatively dry and poor. Whether the village cooperative is really an economically "going operation" or will continue its dependence on the state remains to be seen. Despite the strong party presence in this village and party control of the cooperative, its recurrent debt and dependence on merchants give cause to wonder how politicized or active nominal peasant partisans really are.[11]

Aleppo Village[12]

This village, a cluster of "beehive" houses and narrow alleys, is situated about 20 km. southwest of Aleppo. It is a village of small-holders, averaging 3.3 unirrigated ha., with an excess of population (5,000) to land and little class differentiation. The village was long dependent on urban merchants who provided credit for production requisites at up to 50% annual interest, then returned at harvest time to claim crops at below market prices; merchants built "empires of debtors" to supply their marketing operations and a towering debt structure kept peasants in their grip. Especially as population increased, many peasants had to do seasonal migrant labor in eastern Syria to make ends meet.

This village was plagued by internecine conflict. The basic units of social life were the extended family clans, allied on the basis of lineage proximity into rival factions, and then finally into two larger blocs located in opposing eastern and western halves of the village and symbolized by dual cemeteries, mosques, threshing grounds, and mukhtars. Patriarchal heads of clans controlled family wealth, manpower and marriage arrangements; those who used these resources most efficiently or possessed more emerged as village leaders. They built leadership by virtue of their ability to protect the kin-bloc's honor and goods, reconcile internal bloc conflict, maintain its solidarity by kinship symbols, discipline deviants, and manipulate the feeling of threat from the rival blocs. The principle of political action was that in any conflict one's primary obligation was to support one's nearest kinsman against those less closely related. As such, any individual conflict could escalate into bloc conflict unless mediators could localize it. If so escalated, the village split into two armed rival camps and the issue might be settled only after killings and revenge killings had become prohibitively costly. The *udas* (meeting rooms) of the various clans were the principle locus of clan-politics. The traditional objects of conflict were rivalry over offices such as mukhtarships and harvest guards; disputes over boundaries, commonplace given the division of land into small narrow strips; and face or honor, usually connected with the chastity of women which was believed to reflect on the whole kinship bloc.

Village conflict interlocked with extra-village forces. Rival landlords in nearby villages, seeking to build clientage networks in their bids for parliamentary seats, used and exacerbated village conflicts, for the more the village was divided, the more village factions sought the support of an outside patron. The local government officer appointed mukhtars on the advice of these landlords and the latter could intervene with him in case a village client should get into trouble—perhaps commit a crime in the course of village conflict. Villagers perceived these outside powers as threatening, greedy for their resources and seeking to impose their control on the village; but when village conflicts broke out, alliance with them could be decisive in gaining the upper hand against village rivals. Increasingly, in the fifties, outside powers were penetrating the village. The local gendarme acquired the mobility to intervene in village disputes, sometimes to stop the violence, sometimes as agent of the landlord's purpose. He tended to establish himself as a "little king" in the area based on the support of the landlords, his increasing monopoly of the means of violence, and his right to impose state law on relatively voiceless peasants (e.g. to administer summary punishment such as so many lashes or days in prison). But the growing power of the police did begin to curb intra-village violence. Although on occasion the village could present a solid negative front against the outside, internal conflicts were an obstacle to positive cooperation; thus, the village was unable to constitute a village council giving it some institutional channels to the government because rival blocs could not reach agreement on it.

But as cumulative change penetrated the village itself, traditional attitudes altered. Although it took two years of negotiations, villagers agreed to ask the Land Survey Office to consolidate their fragmented strip holdings. As security was established, one lineage took the lead in developing a prosperous orchard culture. Villagers quickly became aware of the value of education and cooperated on one major all-village project, the construction of a school in the years after independence; by the early sixties there were three state teachers in the village who, on the basis of their education and understanding of the outside world, gained some status as opinion leaders. As the ability to deal with the outside world grew in importance, mukhtars were appointed from the growing number of younger villagers with some literacy. New roads connected the village to Aleppo; frequent visits and even some limited migration for factory work followed. Village youth conscripted for military service or who moved to Aleppo for secondary education became politicized, joining political parties, especially the Ba'th. When the Ba'th seized power nationally, it already possessed a small 6–7 strong nucleus of support inside the village.

The Ba'th cell in the village was charged with establishing itself as a new leadership and creating a new politics based on the Ba'th principle of peasant class unity. Since most of the Ba'this belonged to one kinship bloc, rival clans had turned anti-Ba'th and the first step in rectifying this was to recruit educated youth from the other blocs to establish channels of influence into all clans. Step two, taken in 1966, was the establishment of an all-village peasant union supposed to dilute kinship rivalries and foster cooperation for common village interests. For several reasons, the party youth did have some success in wresting leadership of the village from clan elders socialized in the politics of intra-village conflict. Traditional leadership—based heavily on clan solidarity against threats from other clans—had already begun to decline as growing public security muted inter-clan hostility and fears. The downfall of landlord power in the region after land reform and the loss of the landlords' seat in parliament and influence with the local state apparatus, removed outside influences which had stimulated intra-village disunity. This also snapped the link of traditional village leaders to government. As access to government fell into the hands of the local party, village influence flowed its way. In contrast to the old days of outside dominance, the party connection in the village gave villagers themselves access to the political recruitment ladder and at least one used it to move up in the political world, becoming a cadre in the party's Aleppo branch Peasant Office. By 1974, village "hizbis" were, by outward appearances, in charge: for example, new streets bore the names of party slogans—*wahda, hurriya, ishtirakiya* (unity, freedom, socialism). The peasant union had succeeded in organizing about half the village households. Not only did the organization cross-cut clan divisions but it also seemed to bridge the modest stratification lines which existed: the executive committee was made up of two small-holders and three agricultural workers. Gradually the objects and methods of political action altered, too. As the government consolidated fragmented strip holdings into larger more well-defined blocks, the occasions of boundary conflict declined. Competition for political position no longer took the form of kinship rivalry: indicative of the decline of the old East–West rivalry was the end to the system of dual mukhtars, one having retired and the other of much reduced influence. The functions of the rival headmen were assumed by a village-wide municipal council.

Alternations in the conflictual political culture seemed to be taking place. Attitudes toward women's honor, at least among the younger educated generation, appeared to be changing. The new village leaders defended the right of youth to choose their own mates regardless of kinship politics and declared that persons guilty of murdering women for alleged breaches of chastity should be severely punished, rather than as before, being left off in deference to custom; whether or not they advocate such a message in the village, they do know the attitudes expected of "progressive" partisans. Old ways die slowly: there was recently a double suicide in the village when family elders blocked a marriage between rival families. But the party and peasant union claim some success in establishing themselves as vehicles of intra-village conflict-resolution. They cite a number of cases in which they defused potentially dangerous quarrels: one between brothers disputing over whether to give their sister a full share of the family inheritance decided on the side of the sister, one over boundaries in which property had been destroyed. The petty disputes of everyday life are being solved without escalating into violent conflicts drawing in whole clans and blocs. But a sign that clan social life and politics persists is the fact that the party sends partisans to the various udas when it wishes to inform or mobilize the village.

There is evidence that an enhanced ability of the village to cooperate for common interests has advanced village development. The party and town council have presided over the arrival of paved streets, a clinic, modern bakery, rug factory, electricity, and the erection of a modern market positioning the village as a regional marketing center, and the village has contributed funds and labor for these projects. The new stone houses of a whole new village quarter indicate that some villagers, at least, are prosperous. Income sources have continued to diversify beyond agriculture. New intermediate and secondary schools in the area and forty teachers instead of three have spread education and ended migration to Aleppo for high school. Twenty-two of these teachers are party members, presumably inculcating the new generation with Ba'th ideology. The grip of merchants and money-lenders has eased as alternative sources of government credit have become available through the peasant union; marketing too, now state controlled, shifts peasant dependence from merchants to state bureaucrats. There has been some economic development. The draining of a swamp has reclaimed land, wells have been sunk to spread irrigation to 200 of the village's 1,800 hectares and orchards have been further developed. Nevertheless population growth on village small-holdings cannot be accommodated and youth are increasingly dependent on employment outside of agriculture. Party affiliation gives special access to employment and not surprisingly, many villagers embrace it as a channel up and out of the village. Thus, the party is presiding in many ways over the integration of villagers into larger society; but if, as seems likely, employment opportunities fall behind movement off the land, political dependence could change into political dissent.

Generally speaking, the party presided over no major transformation in this village; but in situating itself to accelerate and consolidate changes already underway, it put itself at the center of village life and established a political base.

Raqqa Village[13]

This is a settled tribal village on the banks of the Euphrates River in Raqqa. The case, recounted in a masterful study by Sulayman Najm Khalaf, shows how the state and market have penetrated and re-shaped the village. But it also shows how villagers, far from being passive objects, have, through the accumulated impact of individual efforts to adapt to outside forces, contributed to the outcome of social and political change.

The first stage in this saga was the undermining of the old tribal order by the penetration of capitalism and the state in the years immediately after independence: all over eastern Syria sedentarization, private appropriation of tribal land and proletarianization of the tribal masses was proceeding. The introduction of tractors, irrigation pumps, and cotton by Aleppine merchants and investors made large scale capitalist agriculture possible where previously only small plots could be cultivated. As the value of land became recognized, tribal chiefs used influence in the government to acquire personal title to what was previously considered common land; sometimes violent quarrels over boundaries broke out among tribal segments, frequently ending in the forceful appropriation of land by the more powerful. In the case of the powerful camel-herding Fed'an tribe, the paramount Muheid shaikhs were, through influence in government, able to appropriate title to thousands of hectares. Their tribesmen were proletarianized as, simultaneously, the pacification of the country put an end to raiding and the truck displaced the camel. This process, plus the migration of surplus peasant population from western Syria, produced a "floating agrarian proletariat" moving from place to place in search of work. In some places tribal elites rented or sold the land to investors. In other places they became cotton farmers themselves, frequently turning tribesmen into sharecroppers on their new estates. To maintain control over the sharecroppers, many landlords redistributed assigned plots yearly and expelled troublemakers; through loans to their sharecroppers, they put many in debt to them, too.

Everywhere the new "cotton shaikhs," their wealth now based on control of private property rather than tribal tribute, were freed of the obligations of patriarchal leadership. As land fell into the hands of a few and calculations of economic gain took precedence over tribal obligations, economic inequality inside the tribes grew rapidly. As their links with tribesmen weakened, the tribal elites began to identify instead with Syria's urban bourgeoisie, bought cadillacs, built houses in the city, employed household servants, assumed a life of affluence, and sent their sons to university for professional education. They saw this life style as legitimizing their continuing political control as wealth slowly replaced patriarchal courage and generosity as the basis of status. At first, the dominant shaikhly "beits" were, indeed, able to combine older forms of political control rooted in lineage loyalties with that based on economic dependency. However, allegiance to the shaikhs steadily weakened: the growing alienation of the tribal population caused by capitalist agriculture was expressed in the saying: "May Allah damn the cotton which has made some folks not recognize others." There were clear signs of the erosion of the traditional political cement which had linked chiefs, subchiefs and tribesmen: for example, a sub-shaikh of one tribe, enriched on cotton, had the temerity to challenge his tribe's paramount shaikh in parliamentary elections and among the tribesmen, votes, no longer automatic, were sold to the highest bidder for cash, forcing the candidates to spend 1.8 million L.S. between them for votes.

A similar, though less overtly exploitative process, led to the establishment of the village under consideration. The tribe that settled this village, the Afadla, was originally a semi-sedentary sheep-herding tribe in the Balikh region. The Afadla were clients of al-Fed'an, paying tribute (*khuwa*) for protection and sometimes sharecropping al-Fed'an land. Pacification in eastern Syria undermined the ability of the Fed'an to coercively control their subordinates, and in 1950, the Meshrif, a lineage of the Afadla, seeking to escape a resented overlordship and aware of the new possibilities of capitalist agriculture, left the Balikh and bought 450 ha. of land along the Euphrates from an Aleppo landowner. This would become the village. Though clients of the Fed'an, the Meshrif—or more exactly the three dominant families which controlled the wealth of the lineage—owned 40–50 camels, and 400–500 head of sheep and paid the 100,000 L.S. for the land from the accumulated wealth of their husbandry operations. At first in association with Aleppine merchants, but later as independent landlords, they installed pumps, built canals, and began to grow irrigated cotton for the market. The Meshrif imported Afadla tribesmen and later outsiders to work the land on a share-cropping basis. Eighty sharecroppers received for their labor 23–30% of the crop—bare subsistence—and the owners typically paid out about 30% for the expenses of tractor plowing, seeds, and irrigation water, and reaped the remaining 40% or so as profit: by the sixties the Meshrif earned a half a million L.S. yearly.

The Meshrif were initially linked to their sharecroppers by tribal and even clan ties, but gradually these were overshadowed by the "cash nexus" between landlord and peasant. Nevertheless, the Meshrif largely continued to combine political control with their economic power. The lineage patriarch, Hajj Khalaf and his son, who he made mukhtar of the village, acted as gatekeepers between the village/tribe and the national government; government approached the village through the *madafa* (guesthouse) of the chief or the mukhtar and the only access of tribal members to it was through these notables who were known locally as "the keys to government." Behind them was the Meshrif clan which made up about 1/5 of the village, for though many of the clan outside the dominant families were only moderately well-off, they did still tend to stick together.

The life histories of the village patriarch, Hajj Khalaf and his son Mukhtar Mahmoud exemplify, in microcosm, the transformation from a tribal to a capitalist society. Hajj Khalaf, though a "traditional" figure was, as founder of the village, a leading innovator of the "first generation" tribal elite after independence. Known for a certain generosity and idealization of tradition, he held strongly to many tribal values such as loyalty to the superior shaikhs of the Afadla and the obligation of sons to marry their *bint 'amm,* thus reinforcing the solidarity of the kin group. Yet Hajj Khalaf was also an exponent of the virtues of free enterprise, idealizing the fifties as a period when government did not interfere, everyone looked to his own welfare, minded his own business and did not ask what others owned. In his relations to his lesser kinsmen, this capitalist ethic prevailed; indeed, the Meshrif's successful adaptation to the capitalist market "functionally required" the disentanglement of personal and kinship relations from economic ones. His hardheaded business views also came out in his belief that peasants could only be made to work by threat and fear of their employer. He saw only the positive side of Syria's capitalist development: cotton brought riches and people lived better.

His son, Mukhtar Mahmoud, representing the further evolution of the second generation Meshrif away from tribal tradition, was much more thoroughly a creature and advocate of the capitalist world view dominant in the early fifties. As a youth, he hobnobbed with the sons of the Aleppo bourgeoisie in nightclubs. His father and brothers put the management of the clan estates in his hands and he proved shrewd and effective in advancing Meshrif prosperity. When his father asked him to make a no-interest loan to a shaikh of the Afadla he refused: an affront to tribal obligation but good business practice. His sharecroppers remembered him as a strict master who overlooked nothing and believed that the fellah would only work under threat. Many of his close kinsmen regarded Mahmoud as efficient and capable but also individualistic, calculating, lacking in loyalty to family and tribe, and pre-occupied with building his personal fortune rather than clan wealth; in fact economic disparities within the Meshrif grew under his stewardship. Mahmoud, by contrast, felt constrained in his personal enterprise by his obligation to manage the clan estates and considered his kinsmen simple, unenterprising, and unwilling to supervise their sharecroppers effectively. But Mahmoud still felt his family obligations and accepted marriage to his *bint 'amm*, an illiterate rural girl with whom this "modernist" felt nothing in common.

The next stage in the transformation of the village resulted from the arrival of Ba'thist power in the region intent on unleashing social conflict, redistributing resources and replacing the tribal leadership of the village with a new pro-Ba'th one. In spite of its seizure of national power, the Ba'th would never have succeeded in penetrating this village were it not for the disintegration of tribal ties under the spread of the capitalist ethos. But equally important was the recruitment strategy adopted by the party in the area: particularly after the seizure of power by the radical Ba'thists in 1966, the regime explicitly focused its recruitment drive on the lower strata in the villages which appeared most responsive to its ideology. In fact, it succeeded in winning a portion of the poorer strata to its side and recruiting a new local leadership from them. For example, in Raqqa, the son of a traveling vegetable vendor ended up as party secretary and the son of a former household slave of the Fed'an shaikhs became head of the party Peasant Bureau. In the village, the party recruited from similar elements. There, the lesser lineages of sharecropping families, notably the "Jhamat," founded the party organization and after 1966 drove the Meshrif and their kinsmen from it. Thus, the Ba'th started to turn the hierarchy of political power in the area upside down.

Then land reform struck a decisive blow at the economic power of the cotton shaikhs. Expropriation committees, controlled by local peasant activists, carried it out in a punitive way: the Fed'an Muheid shaikhs lost all their land and the paramount shaikh of the Afadla most of his. In the village, the Meshrif lost 300 hectares, over half their land, which was distributed to 69 peasant families; it cut their income to one-fifth of that in the early sixties.

At the same time, the Ba'th began to build new organizations in the village, notably a peasant union and cooperative, both of which the lesser lineages controlled by virtue of their numbers and Ba'th connections. A party school opened in the area teaching reading, writing and party ideology. Thus was set in train what one shaikh called the rise to power of the "unionists" in the village, depriving the shaikhs of their old roles as "keys to government." Complained one shaikh: "Everyone has become a unionist, even women want to join unions." After 1966 the shaikhly families were also subject to considerable political repression. At the time of the attempted Salim Hatoum coup—carried out in league with some tribal leaders, Jordan and Saudi Arabia—the shaikhs were rounded up by police and jailed. They remember the Jedid regime as a time when they had no freedom to talk.

Ba'th penetration of the village did, indeed, as the regime intended, unleash a period of class-like intra-village conflict. The village was sharply split between the Meshrif and the pro-Ba'this. The division tended to take geographic lines with the Meshrif concentrated on the remnants of their land in the West while land reform beneficiaries were organized in a cooperative in the East. The "hizbiyin" and Meshrif each tried to harm the other. So intense did feelings become that poorer members of the Meshrif bloc eligible to join the peasant union went armed to union elections in the East. Ba'thi militants tried to close Hajj Khalaf's guest house as a symbol of the defeated old regime. Khalaf al-Abbad, a cooperative leader and local party founder, carried on a campaign against the Meshrif, motivated according to the latter by personal hatred. The so-called incident of the "dust storm and peasant union," though recounted from the point of view of the Meshrif, conveys the atmosphere of social conflict at this time and the challenge to traditional power by formerly subordinate social elements relying on the radical Ba'th regime. When the car of the Meshrif patriarch passed a vehicle of peasant union cadres, showering them with dust, the latter, taking this as a deliberate provocation, called in the police, and according to the Meshrif, falsely accused them of attempted murder. Summoned by the police, the Meshrif mukhtar denied it, saying, "this is the day of the peasant and . . . now justice [the authorities] is with them under all circumstances." He was warned that "the days of the feudalists controlling peasants are gone." Mukhtar Mahmoud replied that "thinking everyone prosperous is a feudalist . . . is wrong since the Meshrif were peasants who worked hard." When the police declined to take further measures against the Meshrif, the peasant union complained to the Interior Minister who ordered the jailing of Hajj Khalaf for a year. The Meshrif petitioned the deputy governor of Raqqa, an old family friend, who got the governor to intercede in Damascus. Though the Interior Minister questioned the motives of the governor, saying "it seems this person is dear to you," the Hajj's sentence was reduced to a month. Access to and the sympathies of the political authorities had clearly shifted radically away from the dominant families. But as the intercession of the deputy governor showed, they retained influence in the bureaucracy from pre-Ba'th days.

The flavor of village politics and the effect of the radical Ba'th on it can also be seen through the eyes of a peasant union activist, Omar al-Hasan. Omar's father was a landless ex-tribesman, forced to move from landowner to landowner in search of work. Because they were related to the Meshrif, the family migrated to the village, thinking they would be taken in, but only received a 2.5 ha. plot to sharecrop. Omar recalls, "I was treated as a fellah among fallahs but somehow I didn't realize they were acting toward me as a feudalist toward a peasant." Impoverished as a youth, girls "fled" from him, knowing he lacked the brideprice. Then the Ba'th Party arrived on the scene. Land was distributed and "everyone got his share"; the party ideology of equality opened his eyes to the injustice of the old social order. He participated in the land distribution committee, received a piece of reform land in addition to his sharecropped holding, and helped found the cooperative in 1968, becoming treasurer. Conflict with the Meshrif followed when they tried to cut off irrigation water to cooperative lands until the head of the Peasant Union in Raqqa intervened. The cooperative built its own canal to irrigate reform lands and had enough to reclaim hitherto unirrigated lands which were distributed to the landless. But when the cooperative pump broke they had to resume buying water from the Meshrif landlord. The landowner tried to oust some sharecroppers from his property and again the president of the peasant union intervened, bringing the police who forced the owner to provide plowing and inputs. These sharecroppers joined the party. The cooperative bought two tractors through the agricultural bank to plow cooperative lands and rented them out to earn money for the cooperative treasury. But before long Omar came into conflict with Khalaf al-Abbad the head of the party *halaqa* (cell). He accused al-Abbad of trying to favor his kinsmen in land distribution and in the use of a cooperative tractor, driven by his brother, "as if it were his private property"; he also suspected al-Abbad of stealing tractor rent money. Omar was elected president of the cooperative against al-Abbad's opposition, but al-Abbad took to holding secret meetings of the party cell which excluded Omar and failed to notify Omar of a job offer in the party hierarchy. After six months, Omar quit as cooperative head, lacking the stomach for internecine fighting. Thus, the effort of the regime to foster peasant class solidarity foundered on the venality of its own cadres and personal and clan rivalries.

The rise of Hafiz al-Asad to power in Damascus marked yet a third stage in the transformation of the village: social conflict came to an end while economic development spilled over into the village. On the political level, the Asad era brought an "opening" to the old elite, including the Meshrif. While veteran party leaders kept power in Raqqa, members of the old elite were co-opted into a governorate council; Feisal al-Haweidi, chief of the Afadla, was even elected to parliament in 1978. Political discrimination against old families was at least partially ended. The educated sons of the Meshrif lineage were allowed into the party and began—with the encouragement of the Mukhtar—to join it; by the eighties they seemed on the way to capturing ascendancy in the village by virtue of their superior professional qualifications and professed loyalty to the Ba'th, though the lesser lineages remained in control of the peasant union. It would be simplistic to say the Meshrif *shabab* (youth) infiltrated the local party to capture it for the Meshrif. Rather, since Asad, they are convinced the regime no longer threatens their families, that their professional careers can best be advanced if they possess political credentials, and that the party stands for a nationalist and modernizing policy which is best for them and the country. They now

seem to represent the regime to the village as much as the interests of their
class and tribe in the regime. Though family loyalties are important to them,
the Meshrif *shabab* do not act as a solid political unit and the attitudes of
the younger generation to the state are much more positive than that of
their elders. The youth seek to present the village to the party hierarchy as
a bastion of progressivism; the elders remain embittered toward the Ba'th.

The views of Hajj Khalaf exemplify the elders' attitudes toward the Ba'th
today. The loss of his land, "the worst thing that ever happened to him,"
has shaped his bitterness toward the state. He does not hide his contempt
for "socialism." The peasants, he says, no longer work as they did when
they feared the landlord would expel them from their land; now they have
freedom with no one to "ride" them. In the state farms, they take their
salaries and do nothing. Today youth all want education to get a government
job and escape manual labor. The Hajj, however, in spite of his idealization
of free-enterprise farming, understood that education was becoming the key
to income and status and made sure his own sons got privileged access to
it. The Hajj also disapproves of the stranglehold youth now have on politics
in the village and of the political participation of simple fallahin: in recent
party elections, he complains, the villagers were active, showing no feeling
for *'ashira* (tribe). His hatred of the Ba'th runs too deep for him to approve
of the affiliation of Meshrif youth with the new powers that be. But even
he acknowledges that, compared to the Jedid period, under Asad one can
talk freely as long as one does not organize against the government.

Mukhtar Mahmoud shares much of his father's attitudes but is more
pragmatic about the new order. Cooperatives, he asserts, haven't worked
because peasants won't work hard without an overseer; accustomed to living
simply, their attitudes pre-capitalist, they care little about accumulation and
consumption. Nor can one today make sharecroppers work by threatening
expulsion because the state will interfere. State farms have failed because "it
is state property and . . . our people still lack civic . . . consciousness.
. . . they put in as little work as possible." He complains of bureaucracy:
now every step you take needs to pass through government-controlled
institutions; he claims that his Meshrif kinsmen are incompetent to cope
with such complicated procedures, but they retort that there is no problem
in dealing with the government and he exaggerates the difficulties in order
to be thought indispensable to the clan. Before, he argues, enterprise was
easy, profits and incentives good, but because this is no longer so agriculture
is in decline; to escape the grip of the government, he is directing family
enterprise back into animal husbandry but, as he puts it, using modern
capitalist methods. Yet, ever the pragmatist, Mahmoud has encouraged Meshrif
youth to join the Ba'th Party.

Two such "third generation" Meshrif who have joined the Ba'th illustrate
the attitudes of these adaptive new elements now penetrating the regime
from below. *Rafiq* (Comrade) Hussein is a son of the dominant Meshrif *beit*
and has always had a comfortable life. His career, perhaps in consequence,
appears to have been driven by a search for power and prestige; it gives

insight into the process of political recruitment and patronage which today links the village and the national elite. Hussein first started in politics in the private high school he attended in Idlib, where, with sons of the urban bourgeoisie, he helped found a branch of the National Union of Syrian Students. From this time he had an "inclination for social relations"—for building personal links to important people higher up in the establishment. He joined the Ba'th under Amin al-Hafiz, when it did not discriminate on grounds of class background; this, according to his cousin, was out of calculation for advancement and at the urging of bourgeois friends who wanted to infiltrate and subvert a party deemed threatening. When Jedid and the Ba'th left-wing took power, Hussein's party activity lapsed. He entered the law school of the University of Damascus, and through the influence of friends, briefly joined the Nasirites, but found them too splintered and weak. In 1970, when Asad came to power, Hussein claims he was one of the first to welcome it. The turning point in Hussein's career was his meeting of another student who was a member of Rifat al-Asad's party faction. He was sponsored for re-newed party membership under Rifat's patronage. After acquiring his law degree he returned to Raqqa and became a lawyer for the peasant union, the very organization in conflict with his own family. In the Raqqa party branch where many partisans were poorly educated workers and peasants or opportunists, Hussein, articulate, well-educated, with developed political skills and powerful friends in Damascus, soon became a big wheel. He founded a local branch of Rifat al-Asad's association of university graduates. Although disappointed when the Raqqa graduates, seeing him as a villager, managed to get a city man appointed association head, he was compensated by being made vice-president and was appointed general director of the state company distributing construction materials in Raqqa. Hussein had made it: he had a plush office, a car and driver, a 1,200 L.S./month salary—"not much" by the standards of the private bourgeoisie, but many times that of a peasant in the village. He values the authority of office and is fond of the intrigues and "swaggering prestige" of political power. He speaks in Ba'thist ideological slogans which seem to run counter to the interests of his family. Socialism is the quickest way to get the development we as nationalists all want, he avers. Under Asad there is no longer discrimination against the old families and the regime is "seeking national development beneficial to all." When he tried to convince Hajj Khalaf of this, the patriarch remained silent. Of the Hajj, he says, "he who owned everything is left to hate everything." But "do those who complain offer anything? No, our people have become used to talking from hate; they cannot forget the loss of the land. It is hard to change the thoughts of the capitalists; it is the children we must train now." Comrade Hussein feels caught in every way between party and family: "people in the tribe think they can get favors from me in the cement and iron company—jobs or supplies—and when I refuse I'm no good—they don't understand as a party member I'm committed to new values." But Hussein has used his connections to get a job for one relative and a scholarship and passport for another. Not for Comrade Hussein an illiterate *bint 'amm*, however; he married an educated girl from Deir az-Zor.

Ustaz Omar, a village teacher, is an example of another Meshrif youth who has adapted to the new order, but at the lower village level. Off-spring of a less prosperous branch of the clan, he was nevertheless sent to school by his family. He was a poor student, flunked out as a troublemaker, gambled, fell into debt, stole money, but finally managed to graduate from teacher training college and was appointed to his home village. At about the same time, he got religion and has since become an advocate of Islamic piety. Omar is "an intense person who relates to things with a passion without developing intellectual depth or harmony." His value system appears a bundle of contradictions but this has allowed him to play a multiplicity of modern and traditional roles which situate him centrally in the village. He was instrumental in mobilizing the village to build a mosque and he acts as its temporary imam. He speaks approvingly of the rapid recruitment of girls to the village school pushed by the government, something which used to be regarded as "shameful." But his real feelings about the role of women in society appear intensely traditional; his attempts to prevent mixing of female and male teachers at the school have driven a number of women teachers from the village. Speaking in Ba'thi slogans, he affirms that "woman is an active and important part of society and we have to give her full rights," but, he goes on: "letting the door swing wide open for women to do as they like, as it is now, is wrong. The woman has deviated morally. She has duties, too, to protect her honor. . . . I begin to feel women are created for the house only, to raise her children, not spending hours making up in front of a mirror. Our society must protect its honor against Western corruption." Omar seems virtually untouched by the liberal views of others of his generation. Paradoxically, while he did marry his illiterate *bint 'amm*, he is now thinking of marrying a second educated wife. Despite his Islamic traditionalism, Omar has hitched his star to the "progressive" political currents and not necessarily entirely from opportunism. He "cried like a baby" when Nasir died, to the disgust of Hajj Khalaf. In 1973 he joined the Ba'th Party "to avoid transfer to another village and to free myself from the lovers of intrigue." Asked how he reconciles conservative Islam and Ba'th ideology, he declares that Islam is all for unity, freedom and socialism. The party's goals, he says, are "above personal interests . . . but it does not neglect benefits for us." In fact, Omar has tried to use party connections to benefit the village: he and his friends were the force behind the establishment of the preparatory school, his lobbying with the governor brought a paved road, and he publicly presented the governor with a list of demands—for a bus, a consumer cooperative and compensation for land expropriated by GADEB, the Euphrates Basin administration. His ambitions for the future seem entirely typical of this money-oriented generation: to build a house in Raqqa, enjoy comfort, work in the government, and start a business.

The reentry of the Meshrif on the political scene has not quite turned back the political clock. The old gatekeeper system with its dominance of a single political hierarchy has not been restored and power remains pluralized in the village. But there is little doubt the Meshrif has recovered some of its old preeminence: indicators of this are the fact that when potable water was brought to the village, the Meshrif elders managed—probably with the help of their offspring—to get control of three of the four taps, crowding the peasants into the use of one. They also got illegal access to the tap "key" which they used to water their orchards at night. Still, a Meshrif youth whose ambition was to "be an eagle to protect the sky of the fatherland" was rejected by the Air Force academy on political grounds; he attributes it to "sick souls that hate us" like Khalaf al-Abbad who still retains influence with the party hierarchy. The persistence of the old tensions was also revealed when a speech to the village by the Raqqa party secretary denouncing "feudalism and tribalism" was poorly received by a segment of village opinion.

Bureaucratization and the extension of services are now integrating the village ever more tightly to the state and market. The nearby state agencies, factories, and farms being established by the Euphrates Basin development project impinge directly on the village. Educated youth have found jobs in the administration, while wage labor on state farms has significantly raised peasant income; peasants say they no longer need be submissive to landlords because such alternative income sources are available. Some have given up sharecrop farming to work on the project; Omar al-Hasan, for example, gave up his contract with the Meshrif and earned enough to get married while working for the state. The state has also brought expanded services to the village. Piped water was installed, although the pipe was soon broken by a tractor and only fixed after long delay. Schools and teachers have all increased, largely at local initiative and there are now two elementary schools and a preparatory school in a village where not long ago there were none. A state decree denying public employment to illiterates filled adult night classes set up to eradicate illiteracy, although the indifference of the teachers resulted in only a quarter of the students completing the program. Electrification in 1979 was received with special delight by villagers and inaugurated with plenty of Ba'thi pomp and a visit by the governor. TVs and over fifty refrigerators now exist in the village, the latter providing much valued cold water in hot summers. Concrete block homes have replaced mud ones. Consumption of purchased commodities has increased significantly, prompting one elder to observe that "people no longer know how to save." Some locals have earned nest eggs in the Gulf which they now invest in the village. All this makes the village a more viable place to live in the eyes of youth who formerly longed to escape to the cities.

Yet the penetration of the state in its extractive and regulative aspect also weighs on the village as never before—especially in the view of those who formerly were lords of the area. The Euphrates project has proved a mixed blessing, for many villagers lost grazing land and husbandry opportunities to the project for which they received little compensation. The Aleppine brokers who used to provide credit and market the cotton crop have been replaced by state agencies mired in inefficiency and determined to impose an agricultural plan on villagers. Regulations constrain the freedom of action—especially of those with resources—at every turn, and take a lot of getting around, as illustrated by the plight of one Meshrif youth. He received a technical degree from an intermediate institute and planned to continue engineering studies abroad but was faced by a new law prohibiting emigration of persons with such degrees. But for those with connections such constraints can be overcome and Comrade Hussein got him a scholarship and visa to study in Rumania. He could not get out of military service so a brother went in his place. Aware of the importance of political connections, he joined the party. For him, family solidarity became a resource in negotiating the growing fabric of opportunity and constraint emanating from government.

Nevertheless, the growing presence and control of the state has stimulated as much as constrained "entreprenuership," licit and illicit. Raised income has meant increased demand, fueling commerce, construction and transport. The contrast with the previous period is that the energies of the ambitious center less on agriculture than on commerce, real estate and the professions where the easy money is to be made and state controls are relatively less dense. As the state presence grows, it is accompanied here, as elsewhere in Syria, by the "corrupt activities" whereby locals try to exploit public property for private benefit. One village youth who worked as an agricultural machinery supervisor for GADEB was so horrified by the theft, intrigue, and lying he couldn't prevent that he left the job.

The careers of two more villagers illustrate the way individuals adapt to and manipulate the constraints and opportunities issuing from the growing impact of state and market on this "little society." Dr. Najm, the village doctor, was the son of a less well-off branch of the Meshrif and his father had to work for the clan patriarch as a sharecropper. Though still living in a tent, his father made sure he went to school in Raqqa, a rarity except for children of the wealthy, and eventually he enrolled in the medical faculty. On his way to becoming an educated professional, Najm bowed to family pressure to marry his illiterate *bint 'amm*, but, ashamed of and unable to communicate with her, he sent her back to the village. Unpolitical, Najm had two ambitions. One was to marry an educated girl and in defiance of family feeling he took such a girl as a second wife. Thus, in his first marriage Najm put the demands of family first but in his second gave priority to modern individual choice. Yet, paradoxically, the vehicle of his self-assertion, polygamy, is a traditional institution, albeit emptied in his case of its traditional rationale, the building of political alliances. This is characteristic of the contrary values to which villagers are now subjected. His second ambition was to make money. He first worked in a government clinic in Raqqa, but opened a private practice on the side and by 1979 reported a 7,000 L.S. monthly salary (almost $1,000), and the purchase of a TV, refrigerator, car, and house. He also wants to take trips abroad. He is untouched by either socialist or traditional ideology, nor does he express any sense of professional duty or call to service. His profession is a mere vehicle to attain the consumerist life-style of the modern bourgeoisie.

A final figure, Nahar, exhibits the continued scope for rags to riches entreprenuership even in the increasingly bureaucratic Syria of today. Nahar's mother died early and his father was a thief and outcast who he left at an early age to work on his own. He is, thus, a man without the web of family support and obligation of which most Syrians are a part. At age eleven, he started work as a tractor driver and then as a mechanic and irrigation supervisor for the Meshrif. In 1964, he joined the village Ba'th cell, but his loyalties were with his employers and he reported party decisions to them "as a matter of friendship and honor;" he opposed seizure of Meshrif land, publicly cursed Amin al-Hafiz over it, and quit the party. Later he stole money, took to gambling and womanizing, and came to be regarded as a reckless adventurer and violator of traditions. He quarreled with his Meshrif employer and was fired; he took his case to the agrarian arbitration committee and tried to get help from the local labor union, but his employer "got to" the union head. "I could not generate or manipulate any serious contacts within the ranks of the Worker's Union"; when he refused dismissal, he was jailed. After this, he went into petty business for himself, buying a traizeina (a three-wheeled motorized vehicle), taking people on trips in them, and doing a little cigarette smuggling along the way. He worked himself very hard to break out of poverty. Soon he accumulated enough to lend money to cotton farmers, took to buying and selling traizeinas, and opened up a spare parts and appliance store. He was jailed for violating price controls, fell into spending in nightclubs, bought a car, ran over a pedestrian, tried to bribe the judge in his case, and went to jail for driving without a license. As the government moved to ban traizeinas for their noise and pollution, he managed to become local representative for the state Aftomachine company and to trade in Japanese pick-up trucks. By the end of the seventies, Nahar was a rich man with a modern house, three wives, and a quarter of a million pounds. But, unable to have children in a culture which highly values them and with little family, he described himself as a "lost soul." Nahar was an individualist and innovator, an outcast driven by the desire for self-improvement. He was adaptable to bureaucratic constraints and opportunities and able to change his strategies as the latter changed.

Nahar illustrates how capitalism still flourishes in the interstices of state and village. Given this climate, the infiltration of the party by formerly dominant forces which are more capitalist than socialist—such as Ustaz Omar—or more interested in privilege than equality—such as Comrade Hussein—suggests that it is only a matter of time before the bourgeoisie re-asserts a commanding influence at the heart of the state. This village may, however, be somewhat exceptional in that the retarded access to education here allowed only the top village strata—the Meshrif—to get it. The more widespread access to education and political mobilization of popular strata elsewhere appear to have had a counter-balancing effect on the resurgence of the village notability in several of the other village cases. But the readiness of an ostensibly pro-socialist activist like Khalaf al-Abbad to manipulate cooperative institutions for individual benefit suggests how tepid is the commitment to "socialism" of even the modest societal elements which used it as a springboard for their emergence in the political arena.

Village Transformation Under the Ba'th

Perhaps the most important generalization supported by the case studies is that national level politics and policies, far from being mere superficial struggles between cliques in a distant capital, are intimately connected with political life in even the farther parts of the rural periphery. Indeed, far from being imposed from the capital, it is clear Ba'thism had extensive roots in the villages even before it came to national power. Significantly, not only in the minority villages—the Alawi, Druze and Christian Homs village, but in the Hauran, Kalamoun, Aleppo and two of the Damascus villages—mainstream Sunni areas—some Ba'th recruitment pre-dated the rise to power. The Ba'th presence does seems to have been earlier and deeper in the first four villages: hence it is not surprising that the national elite is disproportionately composed of men from these areas. In only two of the cases did a pre-1963 Ba'th presence appear to be lacking: in one Ghouta village and in Raqqa—and even there Ba'thist ideology quickly found local resonance. Even where a historical presence was lacking and where the (conservative or tribal) political-cultural climate appeared unfavorable, the Ba'th had no difficulty in establishing itself. But what explains the ability of the Ba'th to link up with villagers?

Social conditions helped pave the way for Ba'thism. In many places land hunger and peasant struggle against "feudalism" and tradition explain receptivity to the Ba'th: this was so in Raqqa and in one Damascus village and some of the deepest and broadest peasant support for the Ba'th was historically concentrated in the latifundia of the Hama-Aleppo plains where Akram al-Hawrani mobilized sharecropper discontent against Syria's greatest landlords. But the cases make it clear that even in small holding villages where there were no large landowners, social mobilization—the drive by peasant youth for education—and the politicization which went with it caused peasants to identify with the struggle against "feudalism" and the urban domination they blamed for rural backwardness and closed opportunities. In the Homs, Kalamoun, Alawi mountain, Aleppo, Druze and Hauran villages this drew them to the Ba'th Party. The Hauran village shows perhaps most clearly how the drive of rural youth for education against the resistance of traditional authority translated into Ba'th political mobilization.

The villages also illustrate that the success of Ba'th penetration owes much to the strategies and instruments deployed by the regime to establish itself. In true Leninist fashion, the regime targeted for recruitment those most receptive to radical change and least attached to the old order the Ba'th wanted to tear down—namely, the less privileged elements of the peasantry and educated youth alienated from traditional authority. Moreover, in some places, it deliberately sought to foster peasant "class struggle" against the traditional elites—a strategy clearest in the Raqqa village. The

Ba'th could not have put down durable roots had it been content to simply make superficial alliances with local traditionals while extending the authority of bureaucratic officials into the periphery, as other reforming authoritarians, such as Nasir and Ataturk, have done. That the Ba'th chose to "by-pass" traditionals and center its local presence in party organization rather than the notability or officialdom, at least initially was part of a conscious design to build a Leninist state and carry out a revolution; but it is probably also true that, unlike these leaders with their unchallenged charisma and nationalist legitimacy, the Ba'th having a much more precarious hold on power and facing a more formidable opposition, was forced to take organization-building more seriously. As a result its presence at the rural bases of society is less superficial than that of many other authoritarian-populist regimes.

The social reforms which accompanied political penetration were equally important to regime consolidation. Land reform not only won peasant beneficiaries to Ba'thism but, in contracting landlord/merchant control over the villages, it shrank the dependency and patronage the latter historically used to build political bases. This is even the case in the Ghouta where Damascene landlords built some of the strongest links to peasants which existed anywhere in Syria but have, under the Ba'th, largely been cut off from these bases. Even where the impact of land reform has been marginal, as in the Alawi coastal village and the Damascus cooperative village, it gave a crucial foothold for the organization of a local party faction. Finally, particularly since Asad, the Ba'th has employed less radical means of entrenching itself. That local Ba'thists now offer access to government and that the regime uses them as funnels of desired services into the villages is certainly an ever more crucial key to their local political influence. In every village, the delivery of credit, roads, water, and electricity was identified with the party. The party also presides over the establishment of education, intensely valued by peasants, staffing the village schools with Ba'thist teachers who indoctrinate the rising generations.

The importance of the Ba'th ability, clearly documented in these cases, to establish a support base inside the village itself, recruiting local elements into its political organizations, cannot be overstated. Without such political penetration, the regime could not have put down roots, spread its message, or established its village institutions with any efficacy. The Aleppo case shows the difference this has made: a village which once viewed government as a hostile power to be avoided has, to all appearances, been totally penetrated, its youth, its schools, even its street signposts thoroughly Ba'thized. This Ba'th penetration of the village has clearly advanced an entirely new magnitude of political integration of the rural areas to the national center: this is most striking in the cases where government was hitherto barely present such as the centrifugal minority areas like the Druze and Alawi mountains or distant tribal areas like Raqqa, but it is evident in every village. That this change has not simply meant the imposition of outside power, but the localization of national power, is clear from these cases, too; here one may merely note the fact that the police, formerly feared outsiders in the Alawi village, are now familiar locals and that in Aleppo the gendarme is no longer an instrument of the local landlord. In village after village, too, it is the recruitment of local youth and a segment of the peasantry which has allowed the establishment of the village institutions meant to replace landlord/ merchant dominance and foster agricultural development: in Aleppo, Hauran, Raqqa, Damascus, and the Druze village, to the extent cooperatives are going institutions, it is local recruitment that has made it possible. The Aleppo case also shows that, to some extent, this recruitment has diluted the segmental fragmentation of the peasantry which traditionally retarded development of peasant class solidarity and opened villages to urban domination: some sense of class consciousness has been fostered in the villages by the party and especially the peasant union and peasants now enjoy rights and an awareness of them hitherto far less developed.

Of course, the intensity of Ba'thist political mobilization in the villages does not compare to that of more authentic Leninist regimes such as China or Vietnam and the outcome is more ambiguous. One sign of the limits of mobilization is the intractability of kinship rivalries which, in a number of cases, particularly the Raqqa and Alawi coastal villages, paralyzed the organization of peasant energies for development and weakened them in the face of landlords. Moreover, while politicization can overcome kinship divisions, as the Aleppo case suggests, it can also create new political and ideological divisions in the village, as the Homs case shows, and indeed, here, where political mobilization has gone furthest, its effect has been to fragment rather than unite the peasantry: the intense political fragmentation long typical of the urban center has here had time to seep down to the base of society. Generally, the Ba'th's local organizations lack the dynamism to carry out a cultural transformation in the villages. In the Alawi coastal village local Ba'th leaders missed the opportunity to use unionization to mobilize workers on the landlords' estates. In no case has traditional power been destroyed. Its durability is particularly striking in cases where social reforms were superficial, as in the Alawi coastal village. But even where it cut deeply, notable families can adapt to the regime and, as the Raqqa case shows, are thereby able to recover some of their old power.

Still, there are many signs that Ba'th mobilization has been quite enough to prevent urban counter-elites—the notables, the Ikhwan—from forging the link with village forces needed to successfully challenge the regime. Pro-regime forces exist in nearly every village and appear to have the upper hand in most of them. Where village dissidence exists, it appears as likely to take a nationalist-left form, as in the Homs village, as a conservative one; whatever their disenchantment with the Ba'th regime, most villagers have no love for the city landlord or merchant who historically dominated them. Moreover, the policy of reconciliation initiated by Asad between the Ba'th and its rivals appears to be much more successful in coopting the notability in the villages than it has in the cities and thereby in blocking any linkup between city and village traditionals: this is clearest in the Raqqa case, where the leading clan has been coopted despite the hostility of the patriarch but there are also signs of it in the Hauran and Druze cases, where a similar tribal like leadership exists. And, indicative of the Ba'th's relative ascendence in the villages is the fact that where traditional leaders wish to recover influence, as in Raqqa, they must adapt to the Ba'th, not the reverse.

It is, of course, problematic to what extent Ba'thi political mobilization has translated into meaningful peasant political participation. In the Homs case, peasant complaints of military dictatorship and lack of democracy showed peasants enjoyed little sense of political efficacy and in the Kalamoun village a similar sense of political alienation at corruption and sectarianism has appeared. In the Hauran village, party cadres seemed politically inert. In the long run, peasant alienation or indifference are probably major threats to the regime's rural base. But, in two senses one can speak of a political opening of the state to peasants which has been crucial to regime legitimation. First, peasants are now included in the recruitment pool to the political elite: in many of the cases—Damascus, the Druze village, Aleppo, in the Hauran and in Raqqa—sons of the village had been incorporated into regional political hierarchies and in the Alawi and Kalamoun village into positions of national power. Second, in the village itself, Ba'th organizations have become arenas for activism and local power: this was clear in every case without exception. As a result, power in the village has been pluralized and the balance, formerly in the hands of landlords, merchants and zuama, has decisively shifted in favor of politicized peasants and rural youth aligned with the Ba'th.

The cases also illustrate how center and village have been tied together in a socio-economic sense under Ba'th rule: both state and market impact on the village as never before. The sixties were a time of "ruralization of the cities" as ex-peasants were catapulted to the seats of power and their followers streamed into the cities to make their claims on the spoils of the revolution; as Khalaf (584) observes, the seventies were, in a sense, a period of "urbanization of the village" as many of the attributes of the city arrived in the village. The bureaucratic presence of the state there grew immeasurably, the gendarme now supplemented by the agronomist, the teacher, the accountant, and the irrigation manager. To some extent, this translated into growing constraints on the village, particularly as the state imposed its crop targets and expanded the scope of state marketing; in two villages, Aleppo and Hauran, there was evidence that the peasant union was being enlisted in efforts to impose unwelcome state grain marketing on the peasantry. In a sense, the old dependency of the peasant on landlord and merchant has been replaced by a new one on state agencies. The Damascus milk cooperative experiment shows how two-sided the effect of even well-intentioned and welcomed government intervention can be. While government provided the opportunity for this experiment, its bureaucratic inefficiencies also enervated it to the cost of peasants who seemed to lack the initiative to save their own enterprise: state dependency can be debilitating. On the other hand, in one of the Damascus villages, in the Druze village, and in the Raqqa one, there is evidence that state sponsored cooperatives have enhanced the viability of small holders.

These villages make clear, too, that "urbanization" has also meant state-delivered services: roads, water, and electricity have made village life more viable in each of the cases. But perhaps the most important things the state has delivered are redistributed land, agricultural credit and education: the first two make it possible for those peasants who want to farm to do so; the second opens doors for those who want out or cannot carry on to seek employment elsewhere. Whether in the long run the infusion of resources into peasant communities and the exit of rural youth will make agriculture more or less viable is not yet clear. But the evidence of growing peasant income was apparent in almost every village: new houses under construction, the growth of commodity consumption, cash income, and petty commerce. Without such revitalization, the villages cannot hope to retain talented youth.

All this has political consequences. The villages have become dependent on and expect the state to deliver services and opportunity. As the integration of the village to the outside grows, peasants need access to the state more and everywhere are trying to build connections to it. But the early-mobilized villages which used politics and education to diversify their resources—notably in Homs and the Kalamoun—are becoming less dependent and more entrepreneurial; thus, even as many peasants need the state more and are likely to be more politically submissive, other villages, needing it less, could become centers of both autonomous economic dynamism and political dissidence. But in the short-run, at least, the socio-economic integration of the village into wider society has largely worked to consolidate the regime in the village.

The cases provide some clues as to the deeper impact of the Ba'th's efforts in the village on socio-cultural change. One excellent indicator of cultural change in this society is the treatment of women. A number of cases—the Hauran, Alawi mountain, and Ghouta villages—have made clear that rural women have been perhaps the most oppressed sector of Syrian society, not only sharing all the disabilities of the peasantry, per se, but oppressed by peasant men, regarded as beasts of burden or as symbols of male honor, kept confined and illiterate. The cases suggest that limited change has taken place. The women's union is present in a number of villages, trying to propagate new values. Women are getting access to education, and as schools are de-segregated and employment opportunities open up, they have won more personal independence and freedom. Yet the persistence of old male attitudes seems more striking. In the Raqqa village so-called educated men did not hesitate to abandon or subordinate illiterate village girls and take a second wife. The women's organization, up against patriarchal hostility and older women's resentment of educated ones, has proceeded very cautiously: significantly, there is no evidence it has tried to introduce birth control to women, a key to liberation from unending child-birth. In the Ghouta village the party chief himself follows rather than challenges traditional customs.

In social structural terms, the regime's leveling reforms did not result in a revolutionary transformation of social structure: indeed the limits of land reform are brought home dramatically in some of the village cases. In the

Damascus milk cooperative village and the Alawi coastal village, peasants got only bits and pieces of reform land while landlords retained major holdings, and in the Druze and Hauran ones the holdings of the resident za'im escaped the reform altogether. On the other hand, in the Raqqa and Damascus Mardj cases, land reform virtually created a small-holding sector from deprived sharecroppers. Moreover, the small peasantry has been buttressed, protected, and politically organized as a social force through the cooperatives and formerly nonexistent routes of political mobility have been opened for its children through the party. In narrowing great class gaps and monopolistic control of resources and broadening opportunities, the Ba'th has created, from the point of view of the village, a more open social structure.

The new state and cooperative "socialist" institutions the regime has established linking center and village are, however, fragile. The cooperatives have gone far to curb landlord/merchant dominance and to protect the historically precarious viability of small peasant cultivation, but they do not represent a viable "socialist" alternative to capitalist development. Collectivist values are not being inculcated in villagers who remain divided by kinship rivalries, lack trust in their cooperatives, and seek to manipulate state and cooperative alike for private benefit, as the Raqqa case showed. Nor have the cooperatives become instruments of peasant capital accumulation and investment on a significant scale. Indeed, the Alawi coastal village suggests they have sometimes been the opposite—channels of consumption; if that case is typical, cooperatives have not produced the peasant work and savings ethic needed for an agrarian revolution. Moreover, far from bringing a strong sense of civic loyalty and public consciousness to the villages, the interpenetration of a bureaucratic state and a society in which pre-capitalist kinship culture and the capitalist ethos mingle, has encouraged patronage and corruption in which political leaders exchange public goods for support or "sell" decisions—privileges, exceptions—to society (Khalaf 543–544). While the immediate effect is perhaps politically functional for the regime, linking rural society to it, and introducing a certain flexibility into the interaction of the two, in the long run it vitiates the capacity of the regime to mobilize resources for investment and to rationally implement policy, jeopardizing its development capability.

To the extent the state-cooperative rural sector lacks the dynamism to propel accumulation, investment, and growth, it encourages peasant resort to the growing petty capitalist informal sector. Indeed, a number of our cases—the Alawi and Raqqa villages, for example, suggest that petty capitalism has been stimulated by social mobilization and village integration into the wider state and market. In the long run, the formerly excluded village might thereby be incorporated into the dominant commercial capitalist networks previously monopolized by the city. But this will not be without costs: for example, as the Raqqa case illustrates, capitalist penetration is accompanied by a breakdown of traditional obligations and the growth of individualism, consumerism, callous calculation, and "a-moral familism." Another effect of the incorporation of the village economy into the wider market, namely migration, may—as in the Kalamoun and Homs villages—bring new resources and enterprise to the village. But it can also, as in these cases and the Hauran, end in a brain drain and the neglect of agriculture, and, as in the Alawi mountain and Raqqa villages, in the marginalization of uneducated village women.

The Ba'thist agrarian model may be preferable to Latin America style latifundia capitalism which degrades and exploits peasants for the sake of landlord consumption and idleness, a route Syria might well have taken under traditional leadership. It may even be preferable for peasants to Stalinist or capitalist routes to development, such as the English, which typically put the heaviest burdens of development on the peasants or shatter the viability of peasant life. But without the ruthless but proven methods of capital mobilization pioneered by these systems, economic growth in Syria may stagnate. Without continued economic growth, the absorption of the socially mobilized and excess peasant population into productive employment is at serious risk. If the result is cities increasingly bloated with an underemployed population, agricultural stagnation, food shortages and growing import dependence, needless to say, the erosion of the Ba'th's rural base will result, with incalculable consequences for political stability.

What is certain is that the penetration of the market and state under the Ba'th have dramatically reshaped attitudes and life prospects for individuals and groups at the village level. To a great extent, they have been the beneficiaries or victims of changes imposed from the outside. The dramatic turnabout in the fortunes of the Alawi mountain villagers made possible by opportunities for military careers reflects not only Alawi power in Damascus but the continuing expansion of the armed forces as a function of Syria's never-ending conflict with Israel—a development beyond the control of village society. Even more striking is the extent to which the value changes and breaks between three generations of Meshrif in the Raqqa village correlate with transformations in the macro-environment—the first generation caught between tribal values and the new capitalist ethos, a second one having almost fully embraced capitalism, a third generation pulled between etatism and capitalism. Yet, locals are not merely passive receptacles of outside forces; rather, the cumulative impact of their efforts to adapt to and manipulate these forces re-shapes the latter and ultimately long-range outcomes. For example, everywhere the infusion of socialist ideology has been bent to local understanding, largely interpreted to mean a mere populist "right" of access to government resources. Traditional values persist and infiltrate the "modern" organizations which penetrate the village: in the Damascus village, so strong are local values that they have forced the party to adapt itself, abandoning some of its ideological tenants in this conservative society. The case of the Raqqa Meshrif shows how dominant village actors, first innovators, then victims of change, can rebound from adversity, adapt, neutralize, and finally turn to advantage formerly threatening outside forces. The Homs and Kalamoun villages show how enterprising peasants can find a multitude of ways to take advantage of outside opportunities to diversify their formerly meager resources through education, migration, and petty capitalism and hence better cope with a changing environment. If the limits of government social engineering have been reached in Syria, it is the dynamism unlocked by the Ba'th in its villages which may propel progress in future.[14]

Notes

1. The cases reflect the diversity of Syria's villages, bridging the sectarian spectrum, embracing all geographical regions and a variety of ecological and land tenure types, including villages of small holding mountaineers, oasis peasants, plains sharecroppers, and settled tribesmen. Picked largely by chance, the cases are not, however, technically "representative;" nor is a systematic uniform comparison attempted. But each village illustrates a typical facet of the regime-village interrelation.

2. Based on the author's visit to the village, 1974.

3. Based on a study by Ikram Antaki, *Deir Atieh,* Paris, 1973, and on personal interviews.

4. The village case study is based on Kamil Ismail's work, *Die Sozialokonomischen Verhaltnisse der Bauerlichen Bevolkerung in Kustengebirge der Syrischen Arabischen Republik,* Berlin 1975; the historical analysis of wider Alawi society is based partly on Jacques Weulersse, *Le Pays Des Alouites,* Institut Francais de Damas, Tours 1940.

5. The account of wider coastal conditions relies on Weulersse (1940: 218–299) and of the specific village conditions on a 1974 visit.

6. Background on the wider area relies on Epstein (1936) and "Syria: L'emigration de paysans menace l'agriculture," *Commerce du Levant,* May 1972; the account of specific village conditions relies on a 1974 visit.

7. Van Dam, 67–78; Be'eri, 159–160; Interviews, Druze party politicians, Beirut, 1974, Damascus, 1977.

8. Based on a 1974 village visit.

9. Based on a 1974 village visit.

10. Based on a 1974 village visit; also Bianquis 1979; 1980:135–139; and GFP 1980:203–204.

11. Based on a 1974 visit.

12. The pre-1963 analysis is based on interviews with village youth and Alan Horton, "A Syrian Village in Its Changing Environment," Ph.D. Dissertation, Harvard University, 1961; the post-1963 analysis is based on a 1974 visit.

13. From the study by Sulayman Najm Khalaf, "Family, Village and the Political Party: Articulation of Social Change in Contemporary Rural Syria," Ph.D. Dissertation, University of California, Los Angeles, 1981; also based on a visit by the writer to the area. All quotations are from Khalaf.

14. The studies of the Alawi coastal village, Homs village, and Aleppo village originally appeared in somewhat different form in the *Middle East Journal,* v. 30, n. 1, Winter, 1976, pp. 1–24.

9

Political Islam: Sectarian Conflict and Urban Opposition Under the Ba'th[1]

The strongest and most durable opposition to Syria's Ba'th state has taken the form of political Islam, and Syria's Islamic movement has been distinctively shaped by its recent character as a reaction against Ba'thism. While in much of the Middle East Islamic fundamentalism expresses nativist populist rebellion against upper class regimes linked to the West, in Syria it is linked to the privileged classes and opposes a regime originating in lower-middle strata and in the front line of struggle with Israel; significantly, it is only as the populist character of the Ba'th regime eroded that the Islamic opposition achieved popular breadth. Syria's Islamic movement and its opposition to the Ba'th is rooted in four basic factors, each of which explains the receptivity of somewhat different segments of the population to its message.

1. Political Islam has, of course, historical roots which predate Ba'th power. It originally grew out of nativist reaction by the most traditional and religiously pious segments of society, notably the ulama', against the threat posed to their way of life by the decline of Islam, Westernization and the post-Ottoman rise of the secular state. Under the Ba'th, a more rigorously secular state than its predecessors, Islamic fundamentalism continues to express the aspirations of pious Muslims for a reunion of political power and Islamic morality. To conciliate pious Muslim opinion, the regime under Asad tried to establish the Muslim credentials of Alawis and the personal Islamic piety of the President, but otherwise its public discourse and policy have made few of the concessions to Islamic law and morality of states like Egypt and Sudan (Humphreys 13–15).

2. In the most immediate sense, the Islamic opposition expresses Sunni resentment of the disproportionate role played by members of the minority communities, particularly Alawis, in the Ba'th leadership. The Ba'th rise to power in which the Sunni establishment was subordinated to a minority-dominated state generated an enduring hostility for which Islamic fundamentalism, denying the legitimacy of rule by other than orthodox Muslims, was a congenial ideological vehicle. As long as Alawis in the regime acted on behalf of Ba'thism, opposition to their dominance remained largely limited to the old establishment, but as they abused their power and favored their

own kind, resentment of sectarian "minority" rule became a powerful force fueling Islamic opposition. Since Sunni Muslims make up perhaps three-quarters of the population compared to the approximately 11% of Alawis, 9% of Christians, 3% of Druze and 1% of Isma'ilis, the growth of alienation among them is a major threat to the regime (Abd al-Salam 391–393).

3. At another level, however, Islamic opposition expresses the reaction of the urban establishment and its mass following in the traditional city against a rural-based regime which has profoundly damaged their interests. In the 1960s, the Ba'th became a vehicle of rural revolt against the city, pursuing land reform and socialist policies challenging the hold of the city over the economy and the village. The historic ties of the ulama' to the merchant community and the concentration of Islamic institutions in the traditional city made Islam, interpreted to exclude socialism, a natural vehicle of protest against this assault on urban interests. The cleavage between the Ba'th and political Islam continues to express the split between the city establishment and the (Sunni as well as non-Sunni) village.

4. Finally, in the seventies, political Islam spread to wider sectors of the population who embraced it, not chiefly from religious, sectarian, or economic motives, but as a means of political protest or as the only viable alternative to the regime. Economic troubles, growing inequality, corruption, elite embourgeoisement, and departures from traditional Arab nationalist policies enervated the precarious legitimacy of the regime, while its relentless authoritarianism gave little legitimate outlet to dissent. That the growing political opposition this generated took an Islamic form was natural. Both liberalism and Marxism lacked credibility beyond limited middle class circles. The populist variant of Arab nationalism which had long dominated Syria was seriously weakened by the 1967 defeat and the inter-Arab fragmentation of the seventies; to the degree it had been pre-empted and institutionalized in the Ba'th regime itself, it was tarnished by the regime's failures and deprived of utility as an ideology of protest. Thus, there was a certain ideological vacuum: if the national state and imported ideologies had failed, Syrians could turn back to the indigenous and familiar, to an Islam deeply rooted in custom and sentiment and with a moral content relevant to individual lives. Finally, the rise in the wealth and prestige of "Islamic" regimes such as Saudi Arabia, and the spectacular success of Iran's Islamic revolution gave political Islam a credibility it hitherto lacked.

The Islamic Movement:
Leadership, Ideology, and Organization

The Islamic movement in Syria embraces a diversity of forces. The Muslim Brethren (*al-Ikhwan al-Muslimin*) have provided the most organized leadership and comprehensive program but other elements more on the peripheries of the political struggle—the ulama', traditional notables, smaller Islamic associations—have contributed leaders, ideas, and support on a more sporadic basis.

The ulama' have long been a political force in Syria, pressing Islamic demands on government and contributing to the Islamic politicization of the population. Traditionally, they have resisted the secularization of the state, demanding Islam be designated the state religion, that the head of state be a Muslim, that the shari'a be the basis of legislation, and that the leaders of government comport themselves as pious Muslims. The assumption of power by the Ba'th which, being a secular party led by a Christian, they held in great suspicion, very much alarmed the ulama' and they have ever since demonstrated their dislike for the Ba'th regime. They led protests against radical secularizing tendencies in the regime in the sixties and shari'a court judges fought to introduce Islamic provisions into the 1973 constitution. Recruited from urban merchant and notable families or, in the case of lesser imams and khatibs, combining their religious functions with petty trade and artisanship, many ulama' have also pressed religion into the defense of private enterprise and property, attacking Ba'th socialism as an alien import, Marxist (hence atheistic) and contrary to Islam (Batatu 1982:14).

While many ulama' are not politically active, a substantial number have been allied with or have even led militant anti-regime political groups or rebellions. Islamic inspired disturbances against the Ba'th have often started with anti-regime sermons in the mosques, then spilled over into protests in nearby streets, and the call to rise has often been proclaimed from the minaret. Shaikh Muhammad al-Hamid led Islamic militants in Hama and was killed in the 1982 uprising. In Aleppo, Shaikh Muhammad Abu al-Nasr al-Bayanuni founded the militant Abi Dharr society. Shaikh Habannakah, president of the ulama' association in the sixties, led anti-regime forces in Damascus from the traditional Midan quarter; despite the sometimes violent demonstrations he headed, his influence seemed to make him virtually immune from arrest. The League of Ulama' long had ties with the Ikhwan and the students of the shari'a faculty were a main recruitment pool for it. The Ikhwan have tried to mobilize the ulama' as a group against the regime. Ikhwan leader Said Hawwa, himself an alim, brought many ulama' into the fight against the 1973 constitution and the Ikhwan sought to enlist them in its jihad in the late seventies; reproachful reminders to them of their duty to join the "lonely" Ikhwan struggle against the regime indicates their success was mixed, but as violence escalated and regime reprisals became more indiscriminate, many inactive ulama' were driven into Ikhwan arms (Abd-Allah 116–118). A few ulama' have been co-opted by the regime, which appoints the imams of the major mosques. Ahmad Kaftaru, the Grand Mufti in the sixties, was a "progressive" supporter of the regime and Shaikh Muhammad al-Shami, a prominent Aleppine *alim* and friend of President Asad, was assassinated by Islamic militants in 1980 for refusing to endorse their anti-regime campaign. But by comparison to other Muslim countries such as Egypt, in Syria there is no powerful "establishment Islam" aligned with the regime.

More on the peripheries of the Islamic coalition were notables—rich landlords and merchants—who had lost wealth and power to the regime.

They supplied money, engaged in conspiracies, and quietly nurtured anti-regime sentiment; some of their educated sons also became activists. Typical of the notables was Ma'ruf al-Dawalibi, a pro-Ikhwan religious shaikh and Aleppine politician in the ranks of the upper class Sha'b Party in the 1950s. He was a staunch foe of the middle class army officers who were challenging notable rule at that time. He also made a name for himself as a radical, advocating land reform and ties with the USSR to thwart the West; called the "Red Shaikh," he declared that Syria would rather become a Soviet Republic than submit to Western pressures to accept Israel. Yet, as prime minister in the "separatist" regime, he presided over reversals of the UAR land reform and nationalizations. He fled Syria after the Ba'th took power and reputedly engineered several conspiracies against it with Saudi help. In the mid-seventies he was briefly back in Syria as part of the conservative opposition. Dawalibi is by no means the only scion of the old aristocracy who speaks the language of political Islam and there is much to the claim that, particularly under the Ba'th, "behind the mask of religion stands the Khumasiya"—the power of capital[2] (*Middle East International,* 13 February 1981).

The main leadership of the Islamic movement has been provided by overtly political organizations. Many such groups have formed and reformed over the years. The Islamic Liberation Party, founded in Jordan by Shaikh Taqi ad-Din al-Nabhani, spread on a modest scale to Syria where it was regarded in the fifties as more militant than the Ikhwan. Some dozen groups were reported active in the late seventies, e.g. al-Jihad, Junud Allah, Kataib al-Haq, al-Khulasah, al-Salafiya (Dekmejian 183–184). But the Muslim Brotherhood is the most durable, largest, and politically significant of them. The divisions among these groups long weakened political Islam in Syria, but in the eighties most joined the Ikhwan-led anti-regime "front," a sign of the Ikhwan's preeminence.

The seeds of the Ikhwan were carried to Syria by shari'a students returning from Egypt where they had contact with the parent organization. A first proto-Ikhwan group was founded in Aleppo, then spread to other provinces. Mustafa al-Siba'i, Muhammad al-Mubarak, and Salah ash-Shash gathered these groups, together with members of older Muslim welfare and education associations which had sprung up opposing Westernization, into the Ikhwan al-Muslimin in 1946. Siba'i became the acknowledged leader—*al-muraqib al-'amm* (General Supervisor)—of the organization which he made a force in Syrian politics. Siba'i was born in Homs of an *alim* family, studied at al-Azhar where he was a follower of Hasan al-Banna and, on his return to Syria, was jailed by the French for anti-imperialist agitation. He then taught at the Syrian University and became Dean of the Faculty of Shari'a, a strategic position for recruiting disciples. The Ikhwan under Siba'i did not develop an elaborate disciplined organization as in Egypt but operated in more traditional fashion through the personal links of its leaders to disciples and to like-minded ulama in the mosques and local Islamic associations. It undertook peaceful proselytization in schools and mosques, appealed to the wider public through its newspaper *al-Manar al-Jadid,* and competed in parliamentary elections. Siba'i fought secularizing tendencies and confronted secular politicians and Christian churchmen in the 1950s over the role of Islam in the constitution. Although the Ikhwan opposed secular nationalists and the Left, it also expressed the nationalist and reformist sentiments of its lower middle class following. Thus, Siba'i denounced feudalism and the old oligarchy for its Westernization and alienation from the people. He was also strongly anti-imperialistic, attacking the Hashemite monarchies for their close Western connections and rejecting foreign economic concessions and Western security pacts as ploys to maintain spheres of influence and divert attention from Israel. Although advocating closer ties with the East to check Western influence, Saba'i viewed the Soviets as equally imperialistic and hence insisted on Syrian neutrality between East and West. He denounced the 1948 truce with Israel and called for armed struggle and an oil embargo to liberate Palestine.

Siba'i advocated an Islamic "third way" for Syria: capitalism was rejected for allowing a small group to dominate the economy and socialism for abolishing private property and individual initiative. The Islamic way would rest on social justice and mutual social responsibility arising out of religious belief and moral activism. Private property would be legitimized within limits but was to be treated as a trust from God and the community to be used for the common good. The rich would pay zakat to support a welfare state for the poor, excessively large private estates would be distributed to the peasants, and free education provided to all. An independent national economy adapting modern technology to Islamic ends would transform Syria from its decadent dependent state. In reality, Siba'i accepted capitalism but sought to limit its inegalitarian and materialistic consequences by religious law and morality (Abd-Allah 116–118).

The writings of Saba'i's colleague, Muhammad al-Mubarak, contain an idea of the Islamic state the Ikhwan wished to establish. The ruler would assume power through a contract in which the people pledged obedience in return for his enforcement of Islamic law. His legitimacy was also contingent on rule by *shura* (consultation) in matters of *ijtihad* not determined by the original sources of the law. The state would fuse, rather than separate, religious morality and political life: thus, freedom of political belief and expression would be limited by the demand for allegiance to Islamic principles and these would penetrate all areas of social life (Jadaane 129–132).

Isam al-Attar, a teacher, replaced the ailing Siba'i as Ikhwan leader in 1957. Al-Attar appears to have been a less populist, more conservative leader than Siba'i; thus, for example, he refused a post in the moderate reformist government of Bashir al-Azmah (1962) on account of the latter's alleged "communist biases" (Mayer 591). Though a dynamic speaker and a durable figure, al-Attar left a lesser imprint on political Islam than the founder, for the Ikhwan was repressed under the UAR and al-Attar exiled by the Ba'th and forced to lead the movement through his lieutenants still in Syria. They included Muwaffaq Da'bul, a professor at Damascus University, Adnan Sa'id in Latakia and Amin Yakin of Aleppo, the deputy supervisor who devoted full time to the organization but often quarreled with al-Attar. Al-Attar's absence and his reliance on personal, often Damascene, followers to the neglect of countrywide organization led to the decline of organized activism and of links between the leadership and the provinces. Nor did he have Siba'i's good relations with the ulama', not being himself an alim and since, as a *salafi*, he condemned both sufism and the four traditional legal schools. Despite the repression of the Ikhwan under Ba'th rule, Attar long rejected demands for violent opposition from younger members on the grounds that it would bring retribution. Thus, the Ikhwan remained fairly quiescent under his leadership; indeed, it supported Asad in his quarrel with Jedid, hoping for accommodation with a less radical Ba'th. In the late seventies Attar rejected all Arab monarchies and republics alike as repressive and reactionary but refrained from calling for violent resistance, condemned the anti-regime assassinations of the seventies, and questioned the political motives of those advocating them. He disavowed the mounting violence in the late seventies and asserted that an end to the regime's police repression would be enough to defuse the tensions in Syria. But although he retained the loyalty of parts of the Ikhwan in Damascus, overall leadership had passed out of his hands by then (Abd-Allah 101–103). As the violent resistance to the regime escalated, Attar finally, in 1980, endorsed jihad against it.

In the sixties, a new militant leader, Marwan Hadid, arose on the fringes of the Ikhwan in Hama. Hadid was an agronomist from a middle class cotton-growing family. He was convinced, by his association with Sayyid Qutb in Egypt, that there could be no compromise with repressive "anti-Islamic" systems like the Ba'th and that only armed struggle could bring them down; hence, he trained in guerrilla warfare and began preaching jihad against the regime. Hadid never joined the Ikhwan leadership: al-Attar rejected his strategy and his open provocation of the regime was seen as dangerous. Hadid ignored organization and proselytization and his following remained small. But he was a charismatic leader and his message and example found receptivity among younger Ikhwan leaders who would eventually replace al-Attar and steer the movement into armed rebellion. Hadid played a leading role in the 1964 anti-Ba'th uprising in Hama, then broadened his activities during the 1973 disturbances and went underground to form a militant fighting faction, *al-tali'a al-muqatila.*[3] In the mid-seventies, Hadid led a campaign of assassinations against the ruling elite, declaring "the regime will disappear only when armed groups . . . kill its members." In 1976 he was caught and died in prison, but his followers in Hama carried on under Abd al-Sattar al-Za'im, a dentist from a merchant family who was himself killed in 1979 (Abd-Allah 103–106; Mayer).

In 1969, a leadership crisis began inside the Ikhwan when al-Attar was challenged by prominent northern leaders such as Amin Yakin and Shaikh Abd al-Fattah Abu Ghuddah of Aleppo, Sa'id Hawwa and Adnan Saad ad-Din of Hama, and Adnan Sa'id of Latakia. Influenced by Hadid, they wished to prepare for jihad against the regime. For awhile, the Ikhwan split into three groups, al-Attar's in Damascus, supported by Deir ez-Zor; Aleppo and Latakia which elected Shaikh Abu Ghuddah, a shari'a teacher from an alim and artisan family, rival *muraqib al-'amm,* and the Hama branch which remained neutral, often collaborating with but distinct from Hadid's followers. By the mid-seventies, a new militant leadership had triumphed in the nationwide Ikhwan, though the Damascus group remained partly loyal to al-Attar. Adnan Saad ad-Din, a middle class educator and writer was made General Supervisor in 1975. Sa'id Hawwa, a shari'a graduate from a middle class family who spent years in prison for his role in the 1973 disturbances, became "chief ideologue" of the movement. He was an exponent of Islamic revolution and jihad well before the mainstream Ikhwan adopted that view. Ali Sadr ad-Din al-Bayanuni, an Aleppine lawyer from an ulama' family, became deputy supervisor. Husni Abu, a teacher from an Aleppine business family and son-in-law of a prominent alim, headed the military branch in Aleppo, *al-tali'a al-muqatila lil-mujahidin,* from the clashes of 1973 until he was killed in 1979. He was succeeded by Adnan Uqla, a son of a baker who became an engineer, served in the army, had close links with Marwan Hadid, and directed the 1979 massacre at the Aleppo artillery academy and the 1982 uprising in Hama. In the mid-seventies Hadid's followers remained on a separate tangent responsible for the assassinations which had not yet been officially endorsed by the national organization. He was occasionally joined by individual Ikhwan, especially from the Hama branch; this forced the hand of the national leadership which set up a wider network of military cells to absorb these individual initiatives. When in 1977 the leadership endorsed jihad, Hadid's followers were largely absorbed into the Ikhwan, although certain factional divisions persisted.

Under Saad ad-Din's direction, a nation-wide Ikhwan organization took form in the late seventies. The personalistic leadership and de-centralized structure hitherto dominant was by now at least partly superseded by a collective leadership presiding over a formal organization with bureaucratic offices, chains of command, and representative bodies. The General Supervisor and his deputy (*na'ib*) were elected from a *majlis al-shura* composed of representatives of the provincial branches. They presided over an executive bureau with specialized sections for training, finance, publicity, etc. The military branch (al-tali'a al-muqatila) was divided into three-man cells each headed by an *amin;* they developed sophisticated techniques, including false identities, to evade the security forces. As the struggle with the regime escalated, further steps were taken in the consolidation of a unified Islamic leadership. In 1980 the "Islamic Front in Syria" was formed under the leadership of Shaikh Bayanuni, joining independent militant groups, such as the Jama'at Abi Dharr and the Islamic Liberation Party, parts of the League of Ulama and other groups hitherto less politicized with the Ikhwan organization. The scale and durability of the rebellion the Ikhwan mounted in the early eighties indicated a substantial advance in organizational capabilities (Abd-Allah 107–128; ABSP 1985a:37–48; Dekmejian 119–123).

In order to broaden its base and define the goals for which it was fighting, the Islamic Front issued a manifesto and program in 1980 (Abd Allah 201–

267). It begins with a call to jihad against the regime—a sectarian dictatorship led by unbelievers—which, incapable of reform, had to be destroyed. The core of the manifesto is an attack on what is seen as the essence of the regime: Alawite and military rule. The Alawis' Islamic credentials are denied: they have rejected the finality of the message of Muhammad, and are *batinis,* subordinating the literal meaning of the Koran and shari'a to an esoteric one and coating a mixture of paganism, Christianity, and Mazdakism with a thin Islamic veneer. They are also accused of collaboration with French imperialism, are warned that a minority cannot indefinitely rule the majority, and are urged to rid themselves of the Asad brothers before it is too late. The experience of the Ikhwan under military rule is reflected in strong anti-military sentiment. The military is accused of having been a tool of foreign interests from the time of Husni al-Za'im, who settled with Israel, to the Ba'th officers who abandoned the Golan, and Hafiz al-Asad who is accused of serving both U.S. and Soviet interests. The Alawite dominated army is an instrument of internal repression controlling the people's lives and a burden on society; riddled with intrigue and corruption and purged of competent officers, it is incapable of fighting Zionism. It should be replaced by a "people's army"—the whole people armed for popular war.

The Islamic program called for the replacement of the Ba'th by a true Islamic state in which Islamic morality and law is restored in every branch of social life. Key to this is the moral re-generation of the citizen through a return to the way of the prophet. The vices which infect society—corruption, gambling, extravagance, alcohol, prostitution, nightclubs—must be eradicated. The integrity of the family is the key to societal health and women's role in nurturing it must not be jeopardized by female employment outside the home. Modern technology is not rejected, but only by incorporating it into an Islamic value system can the ills of materialism which plague the developed world be avoided. For many Islamic activists, only a new ideology, synthesizing a revitalized Islamic morality and a modern scientific worldview, could cure the "sickness" which afflicted Syria.

In place of the Ba'th's single party regime of partisan favoritism and corruption, the Islamic program advocated a relatively liberal political system. The Islamic Front promised that when the regime fell, it would form a provisional government and a constituent assembly would be elected to write a constitution. Government by *shura* would be institutionalized in a strong elected parliament dominated neither by clergyman or politician (Sa'id Hawwa interview, *Die Welt,* Dec. 23, 1980). An independent judiciary of shari'a jurists would nullify all executive action and legislation contrary to Islamic law. Freedom of expression, the press, and party competition is guaranteed, except for parties against Islam or linked to foreign powers—e.g. communists. Since the majority is Muslim, Syria must be an Islamic state, but the rights of religious minorities would be guarded and all treated equally before the law, eliminating the partisan and sectarian favoritism supposedly prevalent under the Ba'th. Citizens would be protected against the current torture, repression and imprisonment without trial; freeing the judiciary from political pressures and appointments is crucial to this. The liberal features of this program, though accentuated to broaden support against the Ba'th, may be compatible with Muhammad al-Mubarak's Islamic regime. But other Islamic militants, such as Adnan Uqla's followers, envisioned no liberal state: they declared that men have no right to govern themselves and must be ruled by the command of God through a pious caliph (Perera 28).

The program's proposed economic order reflects a mixture of anti-statist free enterprise and a very diluted Islamic populism. Capitalism is said to have exploited the workers, but socialism, depriving them of the right to strike, is an even harsher tyranny. The Ba'th system mixes the worst of the West—rampant materialism—and of the East—an unproductive state sector which destroys incentives and is corrupted to enrich a small political clique. An Islamic economy would encourage private enterprise, investment, and the "natural incentives" of a fair profit, while avoiding excessive concentration of wealth and class conflict. Except for natural resources, public utilities and strategic industries, private enterprise, according to Sa'id Hawwa (Die Welt interview), would be the basis of the economy "as prescribed by the Quran." The program avoids calling for abolition of the huge public sector, advocating only the purging of corruption from it and giving its workers shares in their firms. But private investment in industry would be protected from further nationalizations. While workers in the private sector would be protected by a labor code, they had also to cease to malinger and to work for their wages—a sentiment which exposes the program's bourgeois worldview. The state should not encroach on the trade sector which is properly private and should be allowed to freely import and export. The bloated bureaucracy must be cut and people encouraged to work in the private sector. The implementation of land reform is said to have gone against the interests of the laboring masses and to have reduced agricultural output. While vast state-owned lands were neglected, the program charged, the "spiteful" Ba'th regime expropriated orchards (owned by the urban bourgeoisie), ruining their productivity. The issue of a land ownership ceiling is avoided but the program advocates giving uncultivated public lands to whoever cultivates them—which would most likely be entrepreneurs. State farms and cooperatives have failed and should be abandoned, peasants should be liberated from the state marketing system, which pays them low prices, and given title to land received in the reform. An extended criticism of Soviet collective agriculture argues, albeit obliquely, for a revival of the private agrarian sector in Syria. The pro-capitalist, anti-statist bias of most of this program is unmistakable. However, class gaps are to be narrowed through payment of zakat by the rich to support charitable endowments for the poor, aged, students, etc. and by a state guarantee of basic needs—food, clothing, shelter—for all citizens.

An Islamic foreign policy would be neutralist, "rejectionist," Pan-Arab, and Pan-Islamic. Unlike the Ba'th which, the Ikhwan asserts, has surrendered the country to the USSR, an Islamic government would regard the latter, for its occupation of Afghanistan (a crime blessed by Asad), as an enemy equally with the West for its support of Israel. To free Syria of Soviet dependence, a domestic armaments industry is needed. There can be no compromise over Palestine which must be liberated by jihad, but the road to Jerusalem lies through Damascus since the regime diverts the people from the struggle with Israel and tries to crush the Palestinian resistance. A major key to independence and liberation is Islamic unity, which could make the Muslims a world power and rally them behind the Palestinian and Afghan causes. But since the Islamic movement opposes all established regimes, a wave of Pan-Islamic revolution must first sweep these away. The Ikhwan initially saw the Iranian revolution as leading this wave, but its alliance with Asad disillusioned them. Increasingly, except for Adnan Uqla's partisans, the Syrian Ikhwan came to regard Iran as a sectarian Shiite regime. Indeed, in 1982, the mainstream Ikhwan struck an alliance with the Iraqi regime which, it claimed, was different in composition (Sunni) and orientation from the Syrian Ba'th.

As a strategy to rally a broad anti-regime front this program has some strengths but many weaknesses. Its economic provisions authentically reflect the interests of the movement's core constituency, a private sector embracing great families and small suq traders peripheralized by the state-run economy and frozen out of its patronage networks. The call for a state with both a central role for the shari'a and the ulama' and liberal political freedoms was designed to reconcile the desires of pious Muslims with the need for alliance with the secular opposition, but this compromise apparently satisfied neither hardline Islamics or liberals. The program's anti-Zionism is congruent with mass sentiment but its anti-Sovietism risks Syria's ability to confront Israel. Its anti-military and anti-bureaucratic biases threaten these powerful sectors of society. Its mass appeal seems problematic: rejecting everything Ba'thist, it has little of Saba'i's anti-aristocratic populism. Apart from scattered references to Islamic morality, there is, indeed, little distinctively Islamic about the program and much transparently expressive of the interests of the bourgeoisie.

By the mid-eighties, the Islamic movement was, in the wake of the unsuccessful 1982 showdown with the regime, in organizational and ideological disarray. In 1982 Adnan Uqla and the top Ikhwan leadership split over the latter's attempt to forge alliances with secular opponents of the regime. Uqla's more militant faction especially objected to the alliance Saad ad-Din had formed with Iraq, a secular regime fighting the world's only Islamic republic. He also rejected the compromise of the goal of an Islamic state forced by alliance with secular forces, and U.S. contacts which, he charged, demonstrated complacency toward imperialism. Thereafter he headed most of the fighters on the ground (Mayer 607–608; Perera). The mainstream Ikhwan, largely in exile, was itself soon split over whether to seek accommodation with the regime. "Moderates" led by Hasan Huweidi, who became General Supervisor in the mid-eighties, Ali Bayanuni, Munir Radban, and Shaikh Abu Ghuddah, argued that since the Ikhwan could not bring the regime down, it had to reach an agreement which would rescue its cadres from exile and prison; Adnan Saad ad-Din, deputy supervisor at this time, rejected all such accommodation. Negotiations were held with security chief Ali Duba, but came to little, although some Ikhwan may have come to terms with the regime. When no clear winner emerged in a 1986 election contest for General Supervisor between Saad ad-Din and Shaikh Abu Ghuddah, the organization split into two factions. Today Saad ad-Din is based in Iraq and Abu Ghuddah in Saudi Arabia, apparently allied with al-Attar. The movement's military wing is reportedly crippled by the "disappearance" of Adnan Uqla (*The Middle East,* April 1988, p. 21; *al-Watan al-Arabi,* May 1987).

The Social Base of Political Islam

An Islamic mobilization of Syrian society depends on the numbers and social composition of movement *activists.* The ulama' are one potential such cadre but their numbers are limited. In 1970 there were 2,843 ulama' in Syria, relatively concentrated in urban areas. Only 1,173 were available for over 6,000 villages, and few of these were educated, politically conscious, or with leadership status outside matters of ritual; by contrast, the Ba'th has cells in most villages (Batatu 1982:14). The Syrian ulama' lack the numbers, unity and organization of their counterparts in many other countries, such as the Iranian mullahs, and hence enjoy no comparable capacity to mobilize Islamic opposition. The numbers of lay militants have varied widely over time and area. In Aleppo they grew from about 500–700 in 1975 to ten times that in 1978 and before the heavy losses suffered at Hama there may have been 30,000 nationwide (Dekmejian 118–119). This rapid growth suggests there is a significant pool of passive sympathizers which can be mobilized in times of confrontation and who, given the risks, must be highly motivated.

Historically, Islamic activists in Syria have been drawn from middle and lower-middle class families of suq merchants, ulama', and petty employees, frequently recruited in mosque study circles. The school children of such families provided the main manpower for street demonstrations in the seventies. At an earlier time, these youth would have carried on their fathers' occupations, but as education became the key to success in Syria and they went to university, a growing proportion of Islamic activists came to drawn from educated middle class youth. Moreover, as the Ikhwan came to express opposition to Ba'th reforms, sons of higher status families who suffered under the Ba'th, often independent professionals who before 1963 would have filled the ranks of the notable parties, now began to join the Islamic movement. Reflective of these changes, a sample of 1,384 activists studied in the late seventies included 27.7% students, 7.9% teachers, and 13.3% professionals (79 engineers, 57 doctors, 25 lawyers and 10 pharmacists) (Batatu 1982:20). The apparently growing attraction of the Islamic movement for young professionals, such as the students of the medicine faculty where the Ikhwan appears strangely influential, has less to do with the subject of specialization than the fact that higher status or especially pious urban families tend to produce better prepared more diligent students who earn the grades needed for admittance to high status faculties. The general effect of these tendencies has been to shift the center of political Islam's recruitment pool upward in the stratification system as compared to the 1950s.

The broader receptivity of mass society to political Islam has varied widely over time. Historically, in Syria Islamic movements never took on dimensions comparable to those in Turkey, Egypt and Iran. Syria's modern political awakening, led by Westernized notables including many Christians and originally directed against Muslim Turkey, took the form of secular Arab nationalism. As political consciousness spread downward, Islamic activism appeared, but was contained by the clientage networks of the secular notable parties. Islamic expansion was also retarded by the rise of middle class parties such as the Ba'th, Syrian Nationalists, Arab Socialists, and Communists, which, counting many members of minority groups in their ranks, were also secular. Indicative of the limited appeal of the Ikhwan to the emerging salaried middle class, was its weakness in the army where politicized officers became Syrian Nationalists, Ba'thists, Nasirists, but—unlike Egypt—rarely Muslim Brothers.

Nonetheless, the Ikhwan carved out a durable place in the political arena centered on the traditional urban neighborhoods. In the elections of the 1940s and 1950s, it was able to elect a handful of deputies from the popular quarters of Damascus; 3 out of 13–16 Damascene seats went to the Ikhwan in the 1949 and 1954 elections—in contrast to Hama, which, despite its reputation for fundamentalism, was under the firm control of the great notable families. Ikhwan deputy Muhammad al-Mubarak served in several governments in the early 1950s. Later, when Nasirism was sweeping the area with powerful appeal to the urban masses, the Ikhwan was on the ideological defensive; yet Ikhwan leader Saba'i still got 47% of the vote in a losing 1957 contest with a pro-Nasir Ba'thist in Damascus. The fall of the UAR seemed to open new prospects for the movement. A military leader of the "separatist" coup, Lieutenant-Colonel Abd al-Karim al-Nahlawi, was close to it and offered Isam al-Attar a ministerial post. Despite being banned under the UAR, the Ikhwan won an unprecedented ten seats in the 1961 elections and, indicative of a broadening of its geographic base, seven were from outside Damascus. But Nasirism remained a powerful rival for the loyalty of the urban masses and in the 1962 uprisings against the "separatist" regime Nasirist and Ikhwan mobs of indistinguishable urban lower class composition fought in the streets (Hinnebusch 1982c:153–154; Batatu 1982:17–18).

With the decline of the notable parties under Ba'th rule and of Nasirism after Nasir, the Ikhwan had outlasted its major rivals for the support of the urban masses. The only remaining credible alternative to the Ba'th, it tended to inherit the parts of their mass bases not coopted by the regime. Under the Ba'th the social bases of political Islam have, thus, widened and altered. But they do remain unevenly distributed, both socially and regionally.

As before, the core support for political Islam is concentrated in the traditional urban quarters among merchants, artisans, ulama, and the laboring elements under their influence. Rich notable families whose clientage ties reach deep into these quarters have also gravitated to the Islamic coalition. This milieu is most sensitive to the minority and secular nature of the Ba'th for the ulama' and the mosque are concentrated here—as opposed to the modern city or the village. This part of Syrian society, from large notable to small trader, has also paid the heaviest costs of Ba'th policies. Land reform and the substitution of state agrarian credit and marketing networks for the old landlord-merchant ones deprived the latter of influence and wealth in the villages. Nationalization of industries, which in a few cases touched artisan workshops, was seen as an attack on business and property as a whole. The partial takeover of foreign and wholesale trade, restrictions on imports, and a growing state retail network, deprived big merchants of lucrative sources of wealth and because their distribution networks reached down to thousands of petty merchants, hurt or threatened many others. Indicative of the extent to which petty merchants, including itinerant peddlers who used to make their rounds of the villages, have felt threatened by government retailing networks, were the attacks on consumer cooperatives during the Islamic disturbances of the late seventies. Government price fixing and market regulation alienates merchants of all sizes. Asad's economic liberalization did reopen opportunities in foreign trade and small manufacturing, but business must still deal with inefficient government trading and banking bodies run by unsympathetic officials or pay off corrupt ones, must compete with the government for scarce foreign exchange, and remains insecure in the face of new state interventions in fields previously private (e.g. retailing of fruits and vegetables, insecticides and tractor spare parts).

In the late seventies, however, there was a clear geographic differentiation in the receptivity of urban Syria to Islamic opposition: while the northern cities, notably Hama and Aleppo, were hotbeds of unrest, Damascus remained quiescent. Hamawis and Aleppines may be more religious and volatile than the calculating, peaceable Damascenes, but Damascus was a center of anti-regime agitation in the sixties. Under Asad, however, Damascus was favored at the expense of the northern cities. Asad coopted into party and government ranks middle and even upper class Damascenes—such as former Prime Minister Abd al-Ra'uf al-Kasm. Close to the center of power, personal connection and corrupt influence, the Damascene bourgeoisie found ways to get around government regulations and enrich itself on cuts of the disproportionate share of public monies expended in the capital. The Damascene bourgeoisie may have been playing a double game, subsidizing the Ikhwan, but in return for concessions from the regime, ensuring that Damascus was quiet (Batatu 1982:16). This was perhaps the better part of valor because Damascus is no longer the preserve of the traditional bourgeoisie. The ubiquitous presence of the huge government apparatus and massive migration from the rural areas, much of it youth making claims on the spoils of the revolution, has shifted the balance of power there.

By contrast to Damascus, traditional Hama suffered under Ba'th rule. A historic center of Islamic piety and conservatism, Hama took particular offense at Ba'thi secularism. The city resented the favor shown the surrounding villages it used to dominate. The new factories around Hama largely recruited from rurals. Land reform and state credit eased the dependence of peasants on Hama landlords and money-lenders. Small inner city textile industries may have suffered from the competition of large state factories, from minimum wage laws, increases in prices paid cotton farmers, and from the priority given state firms by state cotton marketing agencies (Lawson 1982:24–27). The great families—the Keilanies, Barazis, Azms—which used to run Hama found the presence of Ba'th provincial officials in the heart of their once exclusive preserve galling. Similarly, the city of Aleppo suffered under the Ba'th relative to Damascus. The main seat of Syria's agrarian bourgeoisie, it especially suffered from agrarian reform. The centralization of power under the Ba'th disadvantaged Aleppo which was a powerful political bloc the equal of Damascus in the pre-Ba'th era (Devlin 1983:122). Moreover, Ba'thi political organization appears to be less dense in the whole Aleppo region than elsewhere (See Chapter 5, pp. 184–185).

Support, if chiefly in the form of passive sympathy, clearly broadened beyond this traditional core in the late seventies, however, when the educated urban Sunni middle class generally became more receptive to political Islam. With high aspirations, yet facing, with the rapid expansion of education, growing rural competition for scholarships and good jobs, it felt discriminated against by a minority/rural-dominated regime. Nevertheless, the Sunni middle class has not gone over to the Islamic opposition *en masse* and remains politically divided. This is so of a number of other social forces, too. Urban high school students played a role in Ikhwan street protests, but the Ba'th also has a massive organization in the schools which mobilized counter-demonstrations and it has had no trouble recruiting even pious Sunnis. The university campuses have not been swept by Islam as in Egypt: the Ba'th has a presence there and opposition to government is as likely to take a leftist form. The dislike of upper-middle class professionals for authoritarian, sectarian, and socialist rule led them into tactical alliances with the Ikhwan: thus the professional strikes against police repression of the Ikhwan in 1979 and 1980. But, generally liberal-minded, professionals have not been particularly receptive to Islamic ideology, although as the sons of the traditional quarters join their ranks, they may become more so. There is some sympathy for the Ikhwan among teachers and government employees, but their dependence on state employment, the strength of the secular center and left among them, and the anti-statist ideology of the Ikhwan deters active pro-Ikhwan opposition. The organized industrial working class and the peasantry remain little receptive to the Ikhwan. While the Ikhwan once had a modest following in the trade unions, the secular left, including the Ba'th, has contained it and in the sixties leftist trade unionists were able to mobilize workers against Islamic opposition to socialism. Nor has the Ikhwan much penetrated the countryside, except in a few larger villages near the cities. Rural recruitment was of low priority for the Ikhwan, and the landlord parties and later the Ba'th were obstacles to it (Abd-Allah 91–92). Rural imams were too thinly spread, uneducated, a-political, and dependent on their small government subsidies and too easily watched by village Ba'this to constitute a ready-made network of rural penetration. The Ikhwan was able to establish a few bridgeheads in the *rief* in areas where it found sympathetic support from a landlord or tribal leader, where part of the population was split from the local Ba'thist group by family, tribal, or localistic rivalries or where national level conflicts between Sunni and minority elements seeped down to the local level. It is also possible that the movement off the land will open the village to Ikhwan influence as migrants, recruited in the city, bring the Islamic message back to their families. Elsewhere in the Middle East recent rural migrants to the city, uprooted from the small community, alone in the larger more impersonal city environment, lacking the connections and opportunities of those earlier established and buffeted by inflation, have been especially receptive to fundamentalist Islam, finding in it a new identity and vehicle of discontent. Yet because many rural migrants in Syria already have relatives established in the city with connections in the Ba'th-run state, this environment may not be as inhospitable for them as in urban-dominated regimes; moreover, the Ikhwan, generally opposed to rural migration as a threat to its own urban constituency, has neglected recruitment of migrants. Up to now, there is no sign that the historic correlation between the Ikhwan-Ba'th cleavage and the urban-rural one has been effaced. In summary, there is a multitude of barriers to any rapid expansion of support for Islamic opposition to the Ba'th.

Although Syria's Islamic opposition is no exogenous creation, it has received revenue, sanctuary, and political support from Ikhwan branches elsewhere and external forces hostile to the Ba'th. It has close ties to the strong Ikhwan branch in Jordan where its top leaders established headquarters and training camps after fleeing Syria. Syrian efforts to make Jordan deny this sanctuary escalated into a major crisis between the states in 1980, with Syria massing troops on the border and sending agents into Jordan to seize Ikhwan leaders. Iraq has provided sanctuary, arms, money, and major encouragement, including broadcast facilities during the Hama uprising. The Lebanese Kataib, the Turkish National Salvation Party, and Arafat's PLO gave arms or training. The Egyptian government and the parent Ikhwan carried on a propaganda campaign trying to turn Sunnis against the "Alawite gangs" in the Ba'th regime. Saudi Arabia was a major source of Islamic funding in the sixties. On better terms with Syria under Asad, it may still have financed the Ikhwan to show the trouble it could make when he pursued policies it disliked; Saudi private sources certainly provided funds. The local Ikhwan branch almost got Kuwait's subsidy to the Syrian government cut off in protest at the repression in Hama. The Ikhwan may also have enjoyed covert American backing. This wide range of external support for anti-regime activity, making the regime feel besieged from all sides, was a measure of the Ba'th's regional isolation in the late 1970s. The state where the Ikhwan looked for inspiration and expected the strongest support, Islamic Iran, is the one place it did not get it. Iran, aligned with Asad, shocked the Ikhwan by denouncing it as "gangs carrying out the Camp David conspiracy against Syria."

Regime and Opposition: The Dynamics of Conflict

The Ba'th has survived six major urban revolts in which Islamic militants played a leading role. In early 1964 when the regime, having just come to power, lacked an organized base outside the army, the Ikhwan led violent resistance against the Ba'th's monopolization of power. The Ba'th coup had cut short the Ikhwan's own rising prospects under the "separatist regime," the Ba'th's secular and minority caste were repugnant to it, and the socialist policies it was unveiling threatened the Ikhwan's constituency. Banks and several large industries had been nationalized, worker profit sharing and participation in management of private firms declared, and a new land reform decreed. State controls imposed on trade sparked a crisis of business confidence, and a drying up of credit which plunged the suq into depression. Smoldering Nasirist resentment at the failure of union with Egypt and disaffection among liberals and leftists at the Ba'th's monopoly of power, brought enough of these various elements together with the Ikhwan to pose a major challenge to the Ba'th. Disturbances erupted in each of Syria's major cities. There were sectarian clashes in Baniyas between Sunnis from the town—both Nasirists and scions of the landlord-merchant families who had long dominated the surrounding villages—and Alawite Ba'thists from the villages emboldened by the rise of their comrades to power in the capital; this conflict expressed on a local level the same overlap of class and sectarian cleavages and the sudden disjuncture between political power and wealth that was apparent at the national level. In Hama, the Ikhwan, the ulama', and the great notable families, in tacit alliance with Nasirists and other dissidents, led an uprising that included attacks on government buildings, erection of street barricades, merchant strikes, and denunciations of the "godless" Ba'th from the mosques. Merchant strikes spread to Aleppo, Homs and Damascus, where the Chamber of Commerce demanded the repeal of restrictions on foreign trade and guarantees against further nationalizations. The regime, alarmed at the rapid spread of opposition across the political spectrum, attempted conciliation, denying it was atheistic and promising credit to small merchants. When this failed, tanks were used against barricades and artillery against a mosque in Hama, killing scores; in Damascus, Ba'thist militants forcibly opened shops and clashed with the Ikhwan in the *suq*. In the end, the disturbances were repressed, but the regime, isolated in the largely urban political arena, sought to mollify the opposition with a constitution enshrining Islam as a source of legislation and the right of private property. Never has the cleavage between a rural-based regime and the city seemed so total.

A year later, however, the regime, strengthened by the widened support base it was winning through agrarian reform and mass political organization in the village, struck at the economic power of the bourgeoisie with sweeping nationalizations. A new round of protests against socialism broke out, involving merchant strikes, protests from the Chamber of Commerce and the professional associations, denunciations of the regime from the mosques, and new clashes between Ba'th and Ikhwan militants. This time, the support of the leftist intelligentsia, peasants, and armed workers and the confiscation of struck shops enabled the regime to more readily isolate and suppress the opposition. Intense hostility, however, persisted between regime and *suq* especially after the Ba'th's 1966 leftward turn. In an effort to shift resources away from commerce and consumption toward investment and to force a redistribution of wealth in favor of its constituency, the regime tried to tighten its control over the market, limiting imports to essentials, raising taxes and fixing prices; as the *suq* responded with evasion and blackmarketeering, the regime countered with arrests of merchants and confiscations of stock, escalating animosity. The general hostility of the radical Ba'th toward capital, legal limits on the growth of private business, and the inefficiencies of state foreign trade bodies brought private economic activity to a virtual standstill. The regime's attempt to break the economic links between the bourgeoisie and the small merchants of the *suq* failed because state trading bodies could not effectively substitute for private merchants and because controls over trade and consumption hurt merchants of all sizes.

In May 1967, there was a third outbreak of Islamic-inspired opposition. When an article appeared in an army magazine urging the sweeping away of the traditions of the past—feudalism, capitalism, and religion—the ulama', led by Shaikh Habannakah took to the streets and strikes closed the markets. The assertion of Khalid al-Jundi, head of the workers militia, that religion was indeed the opium of the people, further inflamed conservative opinion. The regime, aware of the danger of being branded atheist in a still-religious society, silenced the radical secularists in its ranks, but also sent its workers' militia to force open shops and recover the streets from the opposition. This encounter expressed in most naked form the clash between an increasingly radical regime and the conservative bastions of traditional society. It was its populist base—peasant soldiers, partisans, and trade unionists—which enabled the regime to contain this opposition.

When Hafiz al-Asad led a faction of the Ba'th calling for an end to social polarization, the Damascene Ikhwan and merchant community both gave him their tacit backing and when he deposed his rivals in 1970 he set out to win durable support from urban society. Muting the secularism of the radicals, he portrayed himself as a pious Muslim, reintroduced abolished religious formula into public ceremonies, and cultivated the ulama' with honors and higher salaries. Economic liberalization measures revitalized the private sector. But a new round of protests against his 1973 constitution showed the limits of detente with the opposition. The protests were partly over the constitution's failure to make Islam the state religion, partly over the consecration of the Ba'th as "leading party," dashing hopes that Asad would end single party rule. The disturbances were led by Shaikh Habannakah in Damascus and the Ikhwan in Homs and Hama—where Sa'id Hawwa cut his teeth as a political activist, mobilizing the ulama' against the regime. Ba'th headquarters was attacked in Hama while merchant strikes and protest demonstrations swept other cities. While the violence in Hama was forcibly quelled—and Hawwa jailed—Asad tried to contain the opposition by changing the constitution to specify the religion of the President as Islam, while bolstering his own disputed credentials as a Muslim through distribution of copies of the Quran bearing his picture and publication of documents claiming Alawites were Muslims. This hardly satisfied the hard core opposition and disturbances continued until sufficient repression was brought to bear.

The 1973 war briefly united the country, but by the mid-seventies, the Ikhwan, pushed by Marwan Hadid, was growing more militant and indeed, his death in prison seems to have energized his followers and others to avenge him. It was, however, the growth of anti-regime grievances which created the climate in which an Islamic challenge to the Ba'th was favorably received by many Syrians. Sectarian favoritism in the distribution of scholarships and jobs became increasingly blatant under the influence of the president's brother, Rifat, whose unsavory life-style, open corruption and sectarianism, and reputation for heavy-handed repression made a mockery of the regime's professed secular socialism. Segments of the bourgeoisie thrived on the oil boom and widening economic liberalization, but had hardly been won over: indeed, resenting the payoffs required to do business with the state and the webs of economic regulation which still constrained it, the bourgeoisie felt vindicated that Ba'th socialism had never been more than a tool to soak the rich for the benefit of a "new class." It largely continued to reject the legitimacy of Ba'thist rule. The professional classes chafed under the heavy-handed security police. But the Ba'th's traditional middle and lower class support was also eroding. Growing inflation threatened the livelihood of broad strata, while the Damascene bourgeoisie and a corrupt officialdom enriched themselves. The Ba'th elite, visibly embourgeoised and corrupted, seemed to lose its populist commitments. Its murderous rivalry with other Arab nationalist forces—notably Iraq and the PLO—put its Arab nationalism in question. The 1976 Lebanon intervention against Palestinians and Muslims in defense of Christian rightists greatly damaged regime legitimacy among its own supporters and Sunni opinion generally.

Amidst this growing malaise, the Ikhwan launched a campaign of anti-government sabotage and assassinations, seeking to demoralize the regime, expose its vulnerability, and establish itself as a credible alternative. Scores of army and security officers, officials, and regime notables were killed. In August 1979, more than fifty Alawite military cadets at the Aleppo artillery school were massacred after having been separated from Sunnis by a Ba'thist officer of the school itself, an act particularly alarming because it seemed to signal a fraying of the regime's own base along sectarian lines. The same month large scale fighting between Alawis and Sunnis in Latakia, beginning as Alawite reprisals for growing anti-Alawite terrorism, necessitated the intervention of troops. Attacks on members of the Soviet mission expressed the antipathy of the Ikhwan for atheism, the invasion of Afghanistan, and Russia's support for the Ba'th regime. In all of this, the broader urban public, far from showing any inclination to assist in curbing anti-regime terrorism, tacitly sympathized with the Ikhwan. Islamic sentiment, measured, for example, by attendance at mosques, widened.

The initial regime response was to combine repression and conciliation. In reprisal for the cadet killings, some 300 Ikhwan were arrested and fifteen executed. The regime also moved to shore up eroding support among its Sunni urban middle class constituency. Salary increases were granted to bureaucrats and the military and price controls tightened to curb inflation. The regime promised to curb the arbitrary actions of the security forces, and permit "constructive criticism" by the small leftist and nationalist parties which made up the pro-regime National Progressive Front. It also opened negotiations with other Marxist and Nasirite opposition groups, generally seeking to win over the Left. Some of the regime's moderate leftist critics hoped the regime's vulnerability could be used to reform and democratize it, but more radical leftist groups calculated that the weakened regime could be brought down and entered into tactical alliances with the Islamic opposition. Twice, the regime launched anti-corruption campaigns, but public cynicism only increased and the discontent of the business community sharpened when the campaigns were limited to prosecution of some businessmen and minor officials while leaving corrupt figures in the power elite untouched; to many Syrians, this showed that corruption at the top, especially among key elements of the military and police, was so pervasive that the regime could not reform itself without virtually decimating its top cadres. The 1980 7th Regional Congress of the Ba'th Party met in an atmosphere of crisis in which delegates blamed the corruption of much of the incumbent party leaders—always excepting Asad's inner circle—for damaging the party and replaced many of them with new men; a new government of middle class technocrats was appointed under a wealthy but reputedly "clean" Damascene Sunni prime minister, Abd al-Ra'uf al-Kasm.

In early 1980, the Islamic opposition, buoyed by the Revolution in Iran and sensing the growing isolation of the regime, initiated a phase of resistance of an entirely new intensity and scale. In Aleppo a multitude of forces combined in demonstrations and strikes against the regime. The ulama' demanded the release of political prisoners, an end to martial law and the application of Islam. Professional associations went on strike against arbitrary security practices and for political freedoms and were joined by merchants protesting price and supply controls and leftist students at Aleppo University. A campaign of Ikhwan attacks on government installations and forces escalated into urban guerrilla warfare, while mass pro-Ikhwan demonstrations flooded the streets; for perhaps two weeks in early March whole quarters in the poorer less accessible parts of Aleppo were virtually out of government control. Similar, if less intense, unrest spread to Hama, Homs, Idlib, Latakia, Deir ez-Zor, Ma'arrat-an-Nu'man and Jisr esh-Shughur. The disturbances demonstrated that the Ikhwan could strike on a much wider and more intense scale than sporadic terrorism and that it could mobilize wide mass support against the regime. The adhesion of leftist and liberal middle class elements to an Islamic-led opposition made the prospects of a generalized anti-government movement under an Islamic umbrella, as in Iran, more real than ever before. While the regime made some gestures of appeasement— firing local governors, receiving petitions, making foreign exchange more readily available to merchants—its main response was coercive. A whole army division made a show of force on the outskirts of Aleppo while commando units fired on demonstrators attacking government buildings and assaulted anti-regime strongholds in the city. The regime attempted a counter-mobilization: the "popular organizations" mounted pro-government demonstrations to deny the Ikhwan the psychological domination of the streets and were recruited into armed units which buttressed the security forces in less contested areas of society. When the lawyers', engineers', and doctors' syndicates continued their protests, their leaders were purged and imprisoned; but the new regime-appointed head of the Lawyers' Syndicate was assassinated by the Ikhwan in retaliation. In mid-April, government security forces, 25,000 strong, backed by tanks and led by Rifat's *Saraya al-Difa'*, carried out a massive search of neighborhoods in the northern cities, in an effort to smash the Ikhwan network. Artillery was used against a mosque in Aleppo, and some 5,000 were arrested in house to house searches which met stiff resistance.

Although the large scale disturbances were repressed, opposition was not. Indeed, elements of the secular opposition, including veteran Ba'th political leaders (Salah al-Bitar, Akram al-Hawrani), who had been marginalized by Asad's consolidation of power, took encouragement from the regime's unprecedented isolation and began to organize in the hope of offering an alternative should the regime collapse. Nasirists led by Jamal al-Atasi, the "Riyad al-Turk" Communist faction, and followers of Salah Jedid, formed a National Democratic Grouping, demanding political freedoms, the withdrawal of the army from the cities, an end to repressive measures, civil rights, and free elections. None of these groups, however, accepted Ikhwan leadership: Atasi rejected terrorism and feared a possible sectarian civil war and Bitar claimed the Ikhwan had no credible program and lacked commitment to democracy. But they also admitted to representing only a handful of intellectuals and former politicians without the confidence of the people. Thus, the regime profited from the divisions in the opposition. Nevertheless, it evidently feared Bitar, in particular, as a possible alternative leader for disaffected Ba'this and even Alawis in the regime itself.

Inside the regime, a debate had long been waged as to whether reform and accommodation or repression could best cope with rising dissidence. Now the balance began to shift toward the hardliners led by Rifat and against Sunni moderates such as Mahmoud al-Ayubi. The hardliners argued that reactionaries had exploited the limited liberalization initiated by the regime after 1970 and that concessions, as the Aleppo events showed, only encouraged the opposition. They denounced the opposition as part of a "Camp David conspiracy" by the United States, Israel, and Egypt to break Syria's steadfastness against Arab capitulation to Israel; exhortations to patriotic Syrians to rally around the regime in the face of the Israeli threat became a major propaganda theme. The murder of a landowning family in Harim by armed pro-regime peasants and an atmosphere of intimidation which kept landowners from their estates in villages around Aleppo, was a warning to the old families that without the protection of the government they disliked, their property rights would prove unenforceable. A new land reform and a decree raising wages and favoring workers against their employers were part of a political strategy to exploit class cleavages against the opposition. At the same time, though, Asad called on conservatives to play a "patriotic role" and, in a bid to separate the militants from their broader support, conceded that not all Ikhwan were terrorists. But as disturbances widened, the regime shelved promised political reforms and tightened its political controls and, as such, its earlier bid to broaden its base among the progressive middle class bore little fruit.

An assassination attempt on the President in June 1980 decisively tipped the balance in favor of the hardliners who were apparently given a free hand to hunt down the regime's adversaries. Rifat al-Asad publicly threatened a bloodbath in defense of the regime, warning that people would have to choose and if they were not with the regime they were against it. Membership in the Ikhwan—after a amnesty period—was made a capital offense. There were reprisal killings of opponents in Jisr ash-Shughur and a massacre of prisoners at the Tadmur prison. Raids on Ikhwan hideouts in the cities in which weapons were seized, cadres killed and military field courts set up to deliver summary execution of prisoners, sometimes degenerated into indiscriminate killings. While such abuses may have expressed the personal brutality, fear, and animosity of Alawite troops for the Ikhwan, in the little care the security forces took to distinguish the activist Ikhwan from their passive supporters, they also demonstrated the lengths to which the regime would go and the costs it could exact to preserve itself: terrorism would be met by state terrorism. The regime also sent assassination squads abroad, apparently murdering Salah al-Bitar, the co-founder of the party it claimed to speak for, and the wife of Isam al-Attar. Raids into Jordan against Ikhwan exiles were meant to show that those directing the Ikhwan outside Syria enjoyed no safe refuge.

In the immediate term, this strategy only heightened and unified the opposition, apparently driving many less-political Islamic groups and ulama' into the Ikhwan-led Islamic Front which was founded in the fall of 1980. Militarily on the defensive, the Ikhwan nevertheless continued the attack: the murders of several friends of the president showed that it could make association with him as dangerous as he was making sympathy for the opposition. Bombings of government installations continued, some of them in their penetration of sensitive targets showing daring and apparent inside sympathizers. 1981 was, however, relatively quiet except for a provocative attempt by an emboldened Rifat to abolish the *hijab;* by sending his militant girls, "Daughters of the Revolution," into the streets of Damascus to tear veils from the faces of traditional women, he so outraged public opinion that the President had to publicly apologize. But an Ikhwan bombing in which more than a hundred by-standers were killed, allowing the regime to show grisly footage on TV, backfired against the movement. Interminable violence without prospect of resolution, in fact, enabled the regime to play on the fears of the middle class of a breakdown in public order. Regime propaganda, reminding Syrians how the Ikhwan had tried to kill Nasir, supported the *infisal*, opposed Arab nationalism, and wanted to return reform land to its owners, had some effect. But an abortive coup attempt in January 1982 by Sunni Ba'th officers, evidently followers of General Naji Jamil, a powerful Sunni politico who had apparently lost in a power struggle with Rifat al-Asad, showed that sectarian animosities were gnawing at the heart of the regime itself.

Both sides apparently wanted the showdown which came in Hama in February, 1982. The regime was conducting operations aimed at destroying the Ikhwan stronghold there. When several of its agents were murdered, the town was placed under military siege; as the regime went in to clean out its opponents, the Ikhwan concentrated its forces for a stand. The ulama' called on the city to rise. Members of the old families, such as the Barazis, were joined by followers of their old anti-feudalist enemy, Akram al-Hawrani, a sign of the extent to which the old class struggle was being superseded by a sectarian one. Militants under Adnan Uqla assaulted government centers, executing scores of officials and party members, and declared the city liberated. Since they could not penetrate the narrow streets and met mortar and anti-tank fire from the city, regime security forces used helicopter gunships, bulldozers, and artillery bombardment against the city, virtually razing whole quarters; Alawite units under Rifat and Ali Haydar reputedly went on the rampage. In part because military discipline unraveled in several units ordered into the city, it took at least three weeks for the government to win back control of Hama. At least five thousand Hamawis were killed and as many as a thousand government troops. Refugees from the city were scattered as far as Dera. In spite of a call by the Ikhwan for a nation-wide general strike in support of the Hama rebellion, the rest of the country remained quiet. The army had held firm while the armed strength of the Ikhwan was decimated in the fighting. At the beginning of March, the regime sponsored a mass mobilization of its supporters not just in Damascus, but Hama as well, symbolizing its victory. But such massive repression may well sow the seeds of future strife and revenge.

In the months after Hama it was clear that opposition to the regime had been dealt a major blow. While abhorrence at the slaughter did bring the Islamic Front together was some nineteen small secular opposition groups, in a "National Alliance for the Liberation of Syria," it has shown little effectiveness and, indeed, was the occasion for the split off of Adnan Uqla from the Ikhwan itself. Hama was more than people bargained for: those who had joined the opposition less out of Islamic zeal than dislike of the regime, melted away and people who had given succor to Ikhwan cadres now sought to distance themselves. The *mukhabarat* had learned to penetrate Ikhwan camouflage more effectively. Adnan Saad ad-Din acknowledged that new tactics had to be adopted to avoid reprisals against civilians. The replacement in the movement's newspaper of local reporting on activities in the provinces by foreign sources on Syrian conditions suggested the Ikhwan's countrywide network was crumbling (Mayer 608). By the mid-eighties, the organized Ikhwan threat seemed to have melted away. But the return of peace to Syria's cities no more signified than ever before urban acceptance of Ba'th rule.

A multitude of factors account for the failure of the Islamic challenge to the Ba'th. The Ba'th regime itself has consistently proved stronger and more durable than superficial observers have expected. Alawi control over the security forces represents a powerful bulwark against opposition, but the regime also dominates the largest and best organized institutions in society— army, party, and state—and is deeply rooted in the village. Against these formidable resources, the opposition can only prevail by the mobilization of a far wider coalition than it has so far done, indeed, one which would pit most of the Sunni majority, including those in the Ba'th, against the numerically inferior Alawites who dominate the regime. But this means breaking the cross-sectarian elite coalition around Asad, destroying party solidarity and military discipline, and unraveling the regime's organized mass base. This seems beyond the present ability of the Islamic movement.

Indeed, the Islamic movement suffers from many vulnerabilities. Its leadership has been plagued by factionalism. It lacks a durable outstanding leader of the caliber of an al-Banna or Khomeini capable of uniting the movement, attracting wider support, and posing as a credible alternative to Hafiz al-Asad. These weaknesses may be a function of Syria's fragmented, individualistic, political culture and its lack of a hierarchic cohesive religious elite. The leadership's incapacity to sustain a physical presence in Syria, a function of insufficient popular support and (unlike Afghanistan) a terrain offering little obstacle to government penetration, has continually forced operation from exile. The movement is too urban, private sector, and regionally based and the Islamic program lacks sufficiently broad appeal and credibility to gain wider backing. The secular left, organized workers, government employees, and the peasantry are likely to be wary of any return of power to merchants and landlords. The secular middle class and the minorities— the latter a fourth of the population—cannot favor the widened role for the clergy and religious law in public life which an Islamic victory would bring; liberal modernist Islam compatible with the secular state remains dominant among educated Syrians. Many Sunnis feared the insecurity and violence incipient civil war unleashed. Where political Islam has been most successful, it has fused religious zeal with nationalist revolt against a foreign or foreign-dependent regime (as in pre-1952 Egypt, Algeria, and Iran), but the Ba'th has enough of a nationalist character to largely deprive Syrian Islam of this weapon; indeed the Ikhwan's attacks, with covert Western backing, on the last Arab regime standing against Israel called in question its own nationalism. Arab nationalism, rather than Islamism, probably remains the dominant political identity in Syria. Unlike political Islam in Iran, Syria's variant can take little nurture from a rejection of modernity, for in Syria modernization, nationalized and nativized, has advanced devoid of blatant Westernization.

Although political Islam has entered another phase of passivity in its cyclical history of rebellion and quiescence, it is certainly not dead: it is deeply rooted in the *suq* and the families which carry on its age old mercantile traditions, and in the pervasive religious sensibility nurtured by the ulama'—interests too durable, sentiments too diffuse to be eradicated by coercion alone. The Ba'th, has failed to create a viable "socialist" alternative to the capitalist milieu which nourishes these interests. Moreover, having failed to establish political institutions capable of absorbing broad participatory demands, the Ba'th cannot win the unchallenged legitimacy needed to deprive Islamic counterelites of their mass support. Indeed, the Islamic uprising was, in one sense, a symptom of a "participatory crisis" which has not been solved. As the Ba'th party evolved from an ideological movement into a patronage network and as corruption and indiscipline grew in party ranks, it had become a less effective instrument of mobilization and control. Asad's cautious experiments with a multi-party front and with parliamentary and local council elections in the early seventies had failed to open the access to real power needed to satisfy those outside the Ba'th's constituency. The regime has since failed to widen its frayed base or reform its political institutions. Asad made none of the concessions needed to win over middle class opinion, such as a serious anti-corruption purge and greater political freedoms, although the curbing of Rifat al-Asad may have appeased some. The relentless authoritarianism of the regime seems likely, therefore, to continue generating dissidence which can find no outlet save violence.

Thus, the Islamic opposition is likely to survive, if only because it presently offers the only credible alternative to the regime. Whether it remains quiescent depends to a great extent on the regime's performance. Issues of nationalist legitimacy remain crucial to the balance of power between regime and opposition. Thus, the 1982 war in Lebanon and Asad's subsequent thwarting of Israeli-American plans there rallied nationalist opinion to the regime. But Asad also persisted in policies offensive to Arab nationalism, such as the Iranian alignment and the feuding with the PLO. Economic conditions are also crucial and the economic stagnation of the eighties has made life increasingly difficult for ordinary people. Revived prosperity and reform could undercut opposition, but the regime seems likely to face growing economic problems along the uncertain road of modernization and it appears incapable of eradicating the endemic corruption which makes austerity far less bearable. Thus the breeding grounds for receptivity to the Islamic *da'wa* or some other opposition movement are likely to persist. If combined with defeat in war or a succession crisis which splits the top elite, this could still create conditions for toppling the regime. But, in the immediate term, the most likely prognosis is the indefinite stalemate of a politically split society.[4]

Notes

1. This chapter is an expanded version of my article "Syria," which appeared in Shireen T. Hunter, ed., *The Politics of Islamic Revivalism.* Bloomington: Indiana University Press, 1988, pp. 39–56.

2. The Khumasiya refers to Syria's largest capitalist firm until its nationalization.

3. A similarly named group was separately founded by an Ikhwan leader in Aleppo, but attempts to form them in Damascus were smashed by the regime.

4. On the struggle of regime and opposition see: Rabinovich, 109–145; Petran, 175–179, 197–198; Tibawi, 415–420; Donahue; Kelidar; Kramer, 1980; Drysdale, 1982; Abd-Allah, 108–120; Mayer; Hudson, 1983; Hinnebusch 1982c, 1988.

10

Authoritarian-Populism and State Formation Under the Ba'th

Since 1963 Syria has undergone a political and social transformation of major magnitude. Both the rise of populist forces from below and state building and revolution from above contributed to this outcome.

Populist Revolt: The Roots and Forces of System Transformation

The rise of the Ba'th must be viewed not as a mere manifestation of military praetorianism, communal conflict, or even middle class breakthrough, although all of these elements are ingredients in the complex mixture of forces which produced it. It can only be fully understood as an outcome of societal crisis with roots in both Syria's pre-modern social formation and its incorporation into the modern world system.

The failure of the "traditional" elite, owing to profound liabilities rooted in Syria's long history, opened the door to the Ba'th. Syria, ruled for centuries by imperial elites, never developed an indigenous landed aristocracy able to integrate state and society: the elites of the patrimonial conquest states, in the absence of private property in land, largely failed to establish strong local roots in the countryside, and would not tolerate the rise of independent landed elites from local society. Nor did the traditional elite, oriented to war and extraction in a land with a precarious agrarian base, foster the agricultural revolution or produce the dynamic bourgeoisie needed for capitalist development. Hence, well into modern times, Syria remained a fragmented mosaic society, agriculturally backward, with a great cleavage between the dominant elite of wealth and power in the cities and the mass of peasantry and tribesmen in their patriarchal communities. This unmobilized society was extremely vulnerable to Western imperialism; even when the imperialist tide receded, the local elite would lack the traditions and resources needed to overcome these liabilities.

Almost a century of imperialist penetration and occupation reshaped Syria, simultaneously sweeping it into the world capitalist market and creating new obstacles to its development. Imperialism fostered a parasitic large landowning class at the expense of the peasants which became the indigenous ruling elite. It dismembered historic Syria, leaving a truncated "little Syrian" state, imposing artificial boundaries and imported liberal institutions. The elite which inherited power at independence was thus of precarious legitimacy, its mass roots shallow, the state fragile. The Palestine disaster and the elite's inability to cut its economic and ideological dependency on the West deprived it of the nationalist legitimacy needed to respond to the challenges it faced. So damaging was the impact of imperialism on Syria that a unusually intense nationalism gave powerful impetus to counter-regime movements.

Social change, driven by capitalist penetration and state formation, accelerated after independence. Some capitalist development did get started, sparking agrarian revival and early industrialization. But it failed to lay the basis for sustained modernization while eroding the self-contained communities and patriarchal authority on which the old regime was erected. State formation was supposed to provide a new order to contain the tensions of capitalist development, but, in promoting the spread of education and state employment, it accelerated social mobilization disruptive of the old regime. Out of these developments grew new classes—a tiny entrepreneurial bourgeoisie, a salaried new middle class, a proletariat—sandwiched between the traditional landed elite and the peasant masses. The new middle class, barely incorporated into the old order and radicalized by its failures, challenged the dominance of the landed elite and sought to mobilize the mass public on its side.

Capitalist penetration disrupted the village and created the conditions of landlord-peasant conflict. At first, land concentration gave rise to great latifundia and a tightened grip of the city over the village surplus, but little agrarian modernization. Landlords were content to live off the harvest extracted from tenants who, impoverished, fatalistic, and resenting their overlords, produced a meager surplus. Even the small-holding peasants were typically indebted and threatened by dispossession. Later, the erosion of traditional tenure, under impact of capitalist farming and population growth, led to proletarianization and urban migration. These changes generated a profound agrarian crisis which the ruling elite, lacking leadership and functions in the village, was ill-equipped to contain.

Agrarian crisis and landlord weakness created conditions for a certain political mobilization of the peasantry as a class. It was, however, a limited, uneven mobilization, with two distinct bases which had to come together before it represented a real threat to the established order. Among the small-holding peasantry, especially in mountainous areas, encroachment by landlords and merchants, sometimes combined with sectarian cleavages, translated into alienation from the established order. The isolation of small-holders, primordial divisions, and small landownership may have retarded overt small-holder revolt; but relative freedom from direct landlord control and minimal village stratification allowed a drive by peasant youth for education and employment outside agriculture which ended in politicization and party recruitment. The plains sharecroppers, despite their intense resentment of the established order, were initially too powerless for more than sporadic rebellion. Only when the whole fabric of village society began to fray under the forces of proletarianization and after radical middle class leadership—some of it provided by ex-peasant youth—penetrated the village, did the conditions for village mobilization come about. Once organized into a radical party and entrenched in the lower echelons of the state apparatus, ex-peasants provided the leadership, ideology, and organization needed to contest landlord control of the village, broaden peasant mobilization, and concentrate rural grievances against the established order. To be sure, this movement never achieved the breadth or intensity of major peasant revolution or even of large scale revolt; peasant ferment was channeled into party and electoral mobilization which petered out without leading directly into the overthrow of the agrarian order. But the rise of agrarian radicalism shattered the conservative ideology and peasant passivity on which the landlord-led regime rested and decisively discredited the mixed feudal-capitalist model of development over which it presided. It shaped a new rural counterelite dedicated to the overthrow of the old order and was the crucible of the coalition between this elite and the peasantry, without which the post-1963 Ba‘th state could not have consolidated itself and would have remained a mere military or middle class regime susceptible to praetorian collapse. Thus, the two separate bases of peasant revolt came together, with explosive consequences. These developments are consistent with empirical generalizations on peasant mobilization elsewhere; indeed, the two groups often considered most susceptible to rural revolt, sharecroppers and small holders under pressure, each contributed to the outcome. But their ultimate political impact issued not so much from peasant revolt as from a rural capture of strategic instruments of political power.

In this mosaic society, peasant mobilization meant mobilization of the peripheral compact minorities. Colonial divide and rule and the territorial concentration of the minorities had at first sharpened their separate identities. But, with social mobilization, traditional sectarian leaders were displaced, minority youth embraced the secular universalistic Arab nationalism of the dominant community, and revolt of the periphery against penetration by the center gave way to a drive for integration of the periphery into the center. Minority mobilization took an assimilationist form in part because little cultural distance separated the minorities and the majority and they shared a common Arab language, culture, and, except for the Christians, a parent religion. The Alawis, in particular, being initially less advanced, sought assimilation into high Arab culture as they acquired education. As Hudson (1977:38–39) argues, the Arabic language and the common culture it shapes are powerful forces for social cohesion in the Arab world. Socialization of the new minority generation took place through national institutions— government schools, the army, and the Ba‘th Party, a secular political movement. For minority youth, the career rewards of integration far exceeded those of an economically unviable separatism. That cultural assimilation partly preceded and partly accompanied social mobilization played a crucial role in overcoming the effect of the minorities' territorial concentration.

Though the Syrian state, corresponding to no felt national community, offered no powerful focus for broader loyalties, Arab nationalism, sharpened by a common perception of external threat from imperialism and Israel, came to be shared by most Syrians regardless of sectarian origins. Finally, because their disadvantaged status had more of a class—as peasants and ex-peasants—than a communal origin, Ba'thism's fusion of anti-establishment populism and Arab nationalism was able to channel minority social grievances in a universalistic direction, merging their protest with that of the peasantry and middle class as a whole. Indeed, overlapping cleavages—the minorities' separation from the establishment on sectarian, class, and urban-rural grounds—translated into a particularly intense alienation, making them shocktroops of radical social change, but under the banner of populist anti-feudalism, not anti-Sunni particularism. Communal identities persisted but the national and class mobilization of the fifties submerged them. The prior or more intense mobilization of the small-holding minority peasantry, leading to their disproportionate representation in the two future power institutions—the Ba'th Party and army—would regenerate sectarian conflict and solidarity after 1963. But the fact that these minorities were socialized in the ideological ferment of the fifties imparted a durable Arab nationalist and populist orientation to the post-1963 political elite. Had their mobilization taken a different form—that of separatism or attachment to overtly minority parties—the whole course of modern Syrian history would have been different and probably closer to that of Lebanon.

The contradictions in which Syria's capitalist development snared her propelled the class polarization of society, generating, by the mid-fifties, a system crisis. The agrarian-commercial ruling class seemed incapable of sustaining industrialization, of undertaking agrarian reform, and of leading independent national development able to satisfy the aspirations of the new middle class and the peasantry. The benefits and burdens of capitalist development were so unevenly distributed that growth only accentuated the already substantial inequality of pre-capitalist times, itself de-legitimized by the decline of traditional bonds. A privileged few at the top were further enriched; the expectations of the middle strata, increasing faster than upward mobility, were frustrated when economic growth reached a limit; and the lives of those at the rural base of society were further impoverished and disrupted. Social crisis was intimately linked to the nationalist struggle since, as counterelites like the Ba'thists preached to a whole generation, social revolution and true national independence were mutual requisites. The special circumstance of Israel and the strong Western pressures on Syria in the late fifties gave nationalism a special intensity which, in turn, aggravated social conflict. By the mid-fifties the segmental cleavages of a pre-mobilized era were superseded by a broad struggle aligning Syria into great antagonistic camps, self-described as *yamin* (right) and *yasar* (left), defined by national issues and class interests rather than parochial rivalries. But instead of taking the form of mass uprising, this class-shaped struggle was channeled by the peculiar processes of state formation in Syria. The recruitment of cohorts of middle class and peasant youth into the new state's bureaucracy, military and educational system, never fully under control of the ruling landed class, led to the partial capture of these institutions by the middle class and then their gradual infiltration from below by rural youth; while the ruling elite retained control of land, wealth, and parliament, their power base in the state apparatus itself was decisively undermined. Once they lost control of the apparatus of coercion, their hold over the streets, campuses, and villages, always precarious, rapidly eroded. Thus, state formation created institutional vehicles through which a middle-class-peasant alliance against the ruling agrarian bourgeoisie took form. In short, the post-independence combination of agrarian crisis, capitalist deadend, national trauma, and system de-legitimation created the conditions for a class conflict which superseded, for a crucial period, the segmental and clientelist politics which perpetuated the status quo and generated an anti-regime movement which would end in its radical transformation. But the gradual capture of the state by this movement obviated the need for mass revolution to overturn it: in the end, a coup would be enough to set off a pent-up transformation directed from above.

Class conflict came to be most concentrated and "institutionalized" in two phenomenon, the radicalization of the army and the rise of anti-system parties. The intensity of politicization and radicalization of the Syrian army has few parallels. The lack of an indigenous military aristocracy and the army's consequent autonomy of the dominant economic classes was a necessary condition of radicalization. But the special pressures of Syria's inter-state environment—above all, the Palestine defeat—were also crucial. The defeat discredited traditional rule in military eyes and led to a continuous expansion of the army under middle class leadership, resulting in the exceptional depth in the stratification system from which the officer corps came to be drawn. Recruitment was indeed from elements most susceptible to radicalization: minorities, the hinterland petite bourgeoisie, many with links to radical civilians, and from the mainstream peasantry. The consequence was the infection of the army with middle class radicalism and agrarian populism. Initially, military politicization translated into instability: military coups, dictatorships, and struggles among civil-military coalitions which split the army into rival blocs. But, ultimately, it ended in the capture of the army from below, turning it from a ruling class shield into a vehicle of system-transformation. Once captured by a radical party—the Ba'th—the army would show an unexpected capacity for imposing revolution from above.

Of the many possible candidates, it was to be the Ba'th Party, in tandem with the ultimately Ba'thized army, which was to be the vehicle of system change. The Ba'th exhibited many of the features of system challenging movements. It began with philosopher-intellectuals who developed an ideology embodying a critique of traditional society and a vision of radical change which raised political consciousness. Its combination of nationalism and populism offered plausible solutions to Syria's crises which proved appealing to a multitude of social forces and shaped the attitudes of a whole generation. Around the founding leaders, gathered a core of "militants," typically drawn from "marginals" alienated from traditional authority and insecure: educated ex-peasants, students, minorities, etc. In the next stage, politicians began to displace the philosopher-ideologues—thus, the growing dominance of Hawrani and later of the second generation radicals; under them, the Ba'th developed modern party organization, a new "political technology" going well beyond traditional kinds of political cement. Ideology and organization enabled the Ba'th to undertake a broader mobilization than any of its rivals and to partially incorporate a coalition linking important elements of the intelligentsia and the officer corps and substantial sections of the small but mobilized urban working class and of the peasantry. The strength of these ideological and organizational traditions enabled the party to survive the splits among its leaders and the dissolution of the 1958–1963 period and permitted its relatively rapid reconstruction after 1963.

Nevertheless, Ba'thist mobilization was uneven and sporadic. In part, this was due to social structural factors. Uneven mobilization is a universal product of uneven development and Syria's geographical and social heterogeneity only accentuated this. Thus, the independent peasant minorities early produced a radical intelligentsia and the share-croppers of the north-central plains provided the mass base of rural revolt, while many other areas remained quiescent. But the most striking manifestation of unevenness was the relative immunity of Syrian cities to Ba'thism. To be sure, the city—the campus, barracks, streets—was the origin of radical and Ba'thist thought and the ultimate focus of radical action. But it was in the countryside that Ba'thism put down real roots while the city remained a bastion of conservatism. Having failed to produce a dynamic anti-feudal bourgeoisie and with only a small proletariat, Syria's cities long remained under the sway of the landed notability and the clergy, historically concentrated there, not in the countryside; moreover, as its trading wealth declined and the city became parasitic on the agrarian hinterland, the urban petite bourgeoisie and masses developed a certain stake in preserving the status quo, too, and under assault by Westernization, retreated into religious traditionalism. Thus, the Ba'th ended up with a predominately rural and regionally concentrated base. The unevenness of Ba'th mobilization was, however, accentuated by the party's own organizational weaknesses: its structure, a mixture of modern and traditional ties, was incapable of sustaining the organizational incorporation of its mass base. Its failure to recruit cadres uniformly from a broad base meant that the dominant elements of its leadership would come from those rural sectors most advanced in producing an educated leadership and most alienated from the old order—the small holding peasantry of specific areas, much of it minoritarian. The defection of much of the party's luke-warm urban Sunni middle class base to Nasirism and the party's post-1958 dissolution greatly exacerbated the party's uneven composition. Without a broad organized urban-rural base, the party could not come to power through mass revolution or votes and ended up doing so on the back of the army. That the same minorities were being disproportionately recruited into the military meant it was *they* who would combine party and army as the tandem vehicles of system challenge.

The combination of social crisis and political mobilization produced a classic case of a "praetorian state" in post-independence Syria. Even as traditional authority was breaking down, the entrenchment of constitutional institutions capable of absorbing political mobilization was obstructed by the absence of supportive traditions and the failure to open them to new social forces at a satisfactory pace. The resulting military interventions were symptoms of the elite's loss of control over the repressive apparatus and of breakthrough into the political arena by the new middle class. The middle class was at first too fragmented and incapable of mass mobilization to challenge the old elite through electoral channels or popular revolt; but because politics was still limited to a small urban political arena, it could exact a share of power through street protests or occasional coups curbing the upper class elite. By the late fifties, the praetorian crisis deepened as rural forces were mobilized under middle class leadership, shifting the power balance against the establishment. Thus, political conflict moved from being a mere urban tempest in a tea cup to reflect the deeper agrarian crisis agitating the countryside. But the demands of rural forces for agrarian reform, appearing to challenge the very foundations of the old regime, could not be accommodated by the system: thus, the failure of the elite to permit evolutionary reform through established institutions prepared the way for populist revolt against them. Exacerbating class and ideological rivalries, was the intervention of external forces, readily penetrating a weak state. Syria during this period was reckoned one of the most unstable countries in the world, threatening to pass, in Huntington's terms, from radical middle class to mass praetorianism. The ease with which the old regime was swept aside by the UAR and the utter failure of the "separatist" attempt to turn back the political clock exposed the bankruptcy of the old order. But the national-left coalition which in 1958 appeared on the verge of displacing it, collapsed thereafter, and its core, the Ba'th, became a victim of organizational dissolution and de-mobilization under the UAR. Any possibility of system transformation through mass mobilization from below vanished. In the end, however, the very fragmentation of the political arena would aid a determined Ba'thi counter-elite, armed with ideology and guns, to seize power in March 1963.

The Road to Power: The Rise of a New Elite

Thus, the final collapse of the old regime came through military coup, ostensibly yet another episode of radical praetorianism or, at most, the beginning of "revolution from above" on the Turkish or Egyptian models. The seizure of power by coup, unaccompanied by mass revolt or mobilization and without benefit of a cohesive movement which could take over governance, meant state-building would take place "from above." Relying on army officers to take and keep power, the regime would never mobilize the ideological activism of a revolution from below. Moreover, the elite had a minority character, the product of the prior unevenness of mobilization and the splits and dissolution under the UAR which put party reconstruction after 1963 in the hands of the most determined and least de-mobilized elements, minority Ba'thi officers and those civilian branches, notably in Alawite Latakia, which had been informally preserved.

Yet, March 1963 was far more than a mere military coup or sectarian power seizure: it was a delayed outcome, cut short by the 1958–1963 interregnum, of forces generated in a decade and a half of prior political struggle rooted in the profound crises of Syrian society. The coup makers were a product of the forces mobilized by this struggle. They were plebeian elements, junior officers from modest rural backgrounds who had infiltrated and captured parts of the military apparatus, had been purged for their radicalism and—far more than an Ataturk or even a Nasir—were "outsiders" alienated from the establishment. More the products of rural disruption and mobilization than bureaucratic elites identified primarily with the state, their outlook was shaped by intense anti-feudal, anti-capitalist, and anti-imperialist sentiments. Moreover, they had a potential popular base, for though the middle-class peasant coalition the Ba'th mobilized in the fifties was fragmented and demobilized after 1958, its constituent elements remained in being, some of them available for reconstruction in the post-coup period.

In consequence, the goals of the new regime were far broader than sectarian or military aggrandizement. Its radical nationalist-populist ideology was, indeed, an authentic reflection of its roots in major segments of society. Secular nationalism united the officer corps, intellectuals, peasantry and minorities; populist etatism, reformist but tolerant of small property, expressed the interests of petit bourgeois officials and peasants as well as their hostility toward "feudalists" and "middlemen." The regime would attempt a populist revolution expressing the interests of these social forces. The subsequent incorporation into the new state of an alliance of officers, intellectuals, and peasants would give it formidable assets—the guns, brains, and numbers— to concentrate, direct, and expand the revolutionary power needed for this enterprise. All of this would give the Ba'th a more intense and enduring policy direction than any mere coup could have generated. The consequent transformation of Syria had, indeed, many of the symptoms of revolution: the displacement of an old elite by one of quite different plebeian origin, the transformation of state structure and social composition, a radical change in public policy, social structural reform, decisively altering the balance of class power to the disadvantage of the upper classes, a challenge to the surrounding world order, and the emergence of a stronger state.

The Ba'th case does not fit the model of peasant revolution from below; but it far exceeds the dimensions of a "reform coup." Trimberger's military-bureaucratic revolution from above captures part of the outcome, a forced social transformation led by state elites, but it does not adequately account for the rural mobilization which preceded and precipitated the Ba'th's power seizure. If the anti-regime mobilization of the fifties is considered an organic precondition of the 1963 coup, the case has features of Walton's "national revolt," but because counter-elites gradually captured the state, violent encounter between state and opposition was far milder. The Syrian case thus appears mixed, combining features of both the Trimberger and Walton types: one in which a radicalized military was captured by—or captured—a populist party with mass roots. The power seizing coup was an outgrowth of revolt from below; the forces generated by this revolt were then incorporated into the regime by the "revolution from above" which followed.

The Ba'th in Power: State Formation

Struggle for Power, Revolution from Above

The Ba'th regime's first challenge, confronted from 1963–1965, was the concentration of power over the command posts of the state and the exclusion of rival elites. Its lack of an organized base and intense opposition in the cities initially forced the regime to rule chiefly by force; establishing control over the army and government apparatus was hence its first priority. The heavy reliance on recruitment of the friends and kin of leading Ba'th officers in the Ba'thization of the military "institutionalized" from the outset the dominance of rural minorities, especially Alawis, over it. They gave a militancy and tenaciousness to the regime in the intense conflicts with the Sunni establishment in the sixties, but they also limited the regime's ability to appeal to the urban masses and broaden its base beyond the village.

The struggle for power was in essence over the "revolution from above" envisioned by the new elites. The opposition was led by a patrician coalition of the notability, merchants and the Ikhwan, defending the interests of traditional urban society in the language of free enterprise and conservative Islam; the inclusion of urban middle class Nasirites in the opposition initially gave the cleavage between it and the regime an urban-rural character. A second struggle inside the regime itself pitted rural radicals who wanted a socialist revolution against urban middle class moderates advocating a reformist model which could secure the cooperation of urban capital. This struggle often had a civil-military and sectarian dimension, but sectarianism and militarism were not ends in themselves but means used in the struggle over the leadership and course of the "revolution." The victories of the radicals in the see-sawing internal power struggle were associated with policy initiatives—radicalized land reform, nationalizations, government controls over the market—which challenged the urban bourgeoisie's control of the means of production and the market. The regime's 1965 assault on the economic bases of opposition power and the 1966 ousting of the old Ba'this were watersheds in the struggle over the concentration and purposes of power.

In a second phase (1965–1970), even as power was more tightly concentrated at the top, the regime began to expand it by widening the scope of conflict, bringing in new actors, and thereby shifting the balance of power in the political arena in its own favor. It set about remobilizing its peasant base, the roots of which persisted in the villages. It decreed radical social reforms and forged Leninist-like political structures from the top down, but the reforms were responses to long standing demands from below and the formation of new state structures also entailed a building upward from village bases; mobilization and social transformation took place, from both "above" and "below." Thus, in Leninist fashion, the regime narrowed the distribution of power at the center, in the inter-elite arena, while widening it at the base. Ba'th party dominance of the regime, the Ba'thization of the army and bureaucracy, and the incorporation of a rural constituency transformed the social composition of the state, resting it on a "populist coalition"—of radical officers and intellectuals, workers, petty bureaucrats, and peasants—which had its deepest roots in the countryside. The policies of the regime had a corresponding social bias, favoring its plebeian rural constituency at the expense of the notability and the *suq*. A ruralized state took form, ruling over a hostile city. Thus, the historic urban-rural gap, long the most important cleavage in Syrian society, had been turned on its head, putting the previously subordinate "village" on top.

This regime had three clear weaknesses. The center remained barely institutionalized and military praetorianism barely contained. The use of sectarian, regional, and kinship ties in the intra-elite struggle for power had sharpened sectarian identities, making the elite more susceptible to a fragmentation which increasingly narrowed it. Secondly, the regime lacked the power to back its revisionist foreign policy. Thirdly, opposition remained intense among broad cross-class sectors of urban society. The rule of a rural plebeian regime over a higher-status led urban opposition could not be indefinitely sustained without some accommodation of urban forces and in the aftermath of the 1967 war, Syria could no longer afford such internal polarization. General Hafiz al-Asad's demand for a restoration of national unity set off another power struggle inside the Ba'th in which the opposing sides were similar cross-sectarian and civil-military coalitions, but otherwise appealed to differing constituencies: Syria's bourgeoisie and the army high command backed Asad, while leftist intellectuals and trade unionists supported the radicals. With the main levers of military power in his hands by 1970, al-Asad deposed the radicals in an intra-party coup. It is, however, a measure of the success of the radical leadership in consolidating power that no group outside the Ba'th could challenge the party's grip on the state. This compared favorably with the weak unstable regimes of the pre-1963 period.

The Outcome of Regime Consolidation:
A Semi-"Bonapartist" State

Regime Center: Presidential Monarchy: Asad set out to remedy the structural weaknesses of the Ba'th state, largely through the creation of a patrimonial core inside the universalistic but fragile Leninist institutions inherited from his predecessors. Collegial leadership gave way to a "Presidential Monarchy" in which power was personalized and concentrated. Asad's intra-elite power rested on a cross-sectarian team of close "comrades-in-arms," and on the formation of a personally loyal Alawi clientelist network at the levers of state coercion, each cemented by the dispensation of patronage and tolerance of corruption among the elite.

The resulting "patrimonialization" of the regime center was manifest in a number of phenomenon. The personalization of power was, perhaps, a return to the dominant indigenous tradition of leadership. The Alawi military chiefs around the president, a formidable shield against his enemies, abusing their power and favoring their own sect, had analogues in earlier patrimonial states in the area. Alawis in general became a privileged recruitment pool based more on ascriptive criteria than ideological commitment or skills. The Asad elite as a whole used state power to enrich itself in true patrimonial fashion and turned the regime from a command post of revolution into an instrument of more traditional pursuits—war abroad and social stability at home. This patrimonialization appeared, however, to give the center a greater cohesion than heretofore.

But patrimonialization was never complete. The solidarity of the Asad elite rested on more than mere sectarian and personal loyalties: raison d'état was always an important element governing elite behavior, often in conflict, to be sure, with the use of sectarian and class ties for personal or group aggrandizement. Nor was elite politics exclusively a matter of clientelist and sectarian factionalism: ideological issues and debates over the requisites of national security and the proper strategy of development still played a role in the policy process. Intra-elite relations were not exclusively zero-sum ones—Alawis against Sunnis, military against civilian; indeed state structures fostered a certain cooperation serving common elite interests. In short, the level of cohesion attained by the elite, inspite of its sectarian heterogeneity, resulted not exclusively from primordial ties, but also from a certain shared ideology, even some accepted rules of the game embodied in the legal-rational structures of the state. Finally, the power of Asad's team over society rested not simply on minority solidarity and clientelist networks but on its command of the levers of three major state institutions, the army, the state bureaucracy and, not least, the party machine through which the regime incorporated and controlled a mass constituency.

The Structures of Power: The military has played a central role in the Ba'th state, but the military is not simply some new Mamluk class dominating civil society: its role is much more ambiguous. On the one hand, the military advanced state formation in certain important ways: under the radicals populist officers sustained the state's autonomy of the dominant classes without which radical reform would have foundered and backed the use of Leninist techniques in the mobilization of a popular base. Under Asad, the military forged a national security apparatus which turned Syria from a victim of its international environment into a formidable actor. Yet, perhaps a function of the continuing state of war, Syria has little advanced in the "de-militarizing" of the state necessary to bury praetorianism. As a result, the military remains the final arbiter of intra-elite political conflicts and, up to now, the coup is the only leadership succession mechanism of record; the politicized military, reflecting the fragmentations of the society in which it is rooted, has kept praetorianism alive in the heart of the state. The military constrains even modest political liberalization, while burdening the economy and sometimes encroaching on civilian domains.

But Syria is no mere praetorian regime for military-politicians and military institutions operate within a wider political system which both sustains and constrains their dominant role. The Presidency subordinates and contains military power. The military shares power with civilian "politicos" and "technos," and most elite factions are military-civil coalitions. A certain military professionalism and the functional autonomy of party and bureaucracy are significant obstacles to military aggrandizement. The two leadership succession coups came from within the Ba'th itself, in the name of civil-military ideological factions, not military corporate interest, altering but never effacing the main thrust of Ba'thism; moreover, in the last eighteen years no such military intervention has succeeded. A mixed military-party state has emerged in which praetorianism remains below the surface but is normally contained by the partial institutionalization of the Ba'th political system.

That the Ba'thist political system has achieved a *partial institutionalization* is manifest in a number of "indicators" (Huntington 1968:12–32).

1. It is a *structurally complex* regime with multiple centers of power—presidency, army command, party politburo, council of ministers—rather than a simple or purely personal one. These power structures, far from being mere facades for clientelism, have many of the rules, roles, and functions of authentic institutions. The party is a real party with a long history, not a mere creation or appendage of leader, army or bureaucracy. It performs crucial political functions, initially those of a vanguard party—elite recruitment, mass mobilization—now increasingly those of a patronage party; presidency and military constrain its role, patrimonialization and bureaucratization enervate it, but they do not negate it. The role of ideology in party recruitment and mobilization is increasingly eroded by careerism and primordial ties, weakening the muscle of political structures and diluting political activism. But specifically political phenomena—ideology, organization, cadres, votes, debates, etc. reached and retain a significant level of development in the party's internal life. It is the party's viability and role which permits the regime to transcend pure patrimonialism and praetorianism. Unlike the Egyptian ASU, which Sadat abolished with ease, the Ba'th party could no more be abolished tomorrow than Stalin could have abolished the Communist Party. The state bureaucracy is a less powerful institution, more an instrument than an autonomous center of power. But it has also achieved a significant measure of legal-rationality: power is based to a great extent on office and control of organizational levers and is channeled by plans, rules, and operating procedures which organize the work of thousands of officials toward publicly defined goals, even if clientelism and the drive for patronage make for a hidden second agenda in conflict with the official one. This gives the state a structural base and a policy-implementing capability which go well beyond those of a merely patrimonial regime.

2. Regime structures enjoy a certain *autonomy*. Most obviously, the state enjoys a considerable measure of autonomy from the dominant classes: the leveling of the economic sources of their power, the fluidization of the social structure and the incorporation of a mass base into the state, raised the regime above these forces. The societal resources by which the dominant classes had hitherto virtually colonized the state—wealth, traditional family status—were initially excluded from the political sphere; the doors to wealth have, of course, re-opened but even today these resources cannot be as directly translated into political influence as before.

Nor are regime political institutions simply the tools of particular elites—such as Alawi generals or a "state bourgeoisie." Political elites, to be sure, command, deploy and sometimes privately appropriate the resources of these institutions. But certain interests attach to the roles and offices constituting the state which are distinguishable from those of the elite. Regime structures incorporate the interests of a variety of social forces: rural party apparatchiki, Sunni urban middle class bureaucrats, and through their syndical organizations, masses of peasants, workers, and school-age youth; it strains credibility to think that these elaborate structures can be readily manipulated by elites without accommodating the interests of the thousands of activists and officials who make them up. Moreover, it is possible to identify a "state interest," distinct from the private interests of elites and shared by all these forces, which shapes political behavior within the regime, although this may mean somewhat different things to different actors: to top elites maintenance of regime legitimacy, and of the coercive, resource mobilization, and national security capacities of the state; to a wider officialdom, protection of the state's revenue base and capacity to enforce policies; for party *apparatchiki*, maintenance of the organizational and ideological integrity of the party; for the officer corps, advancement of the defense capabilities and professional integrity of the military; and, at the yet wider level of the regime and its constituency, the maintenance of populist policies and defense of Syrian territory and national prestige. One manifestation of a common state interest at work is the tendency of these forces to close ranks when these interests are threatened by outsiders.

3. There are several indicators of a significant measure of regime *coherence*. The Ba'thist ideological paradigm, though altered, has continued to give a recognizable and distinct thrust to public policy for over a quarter century. The regime has also shown an ability to adapt and survive in different and difficult environmental conditions and has attained a measure of stability and durability in spite of intense internal opposition and formidable external enemies: this is no longer, as in 1949, a regime which can be overthrown by "the exchange of a few words and a few thousand dollars between a foreign ambassador and some disaffected colonel" (Huntington 1968:21). The state's much increased societal penetration, resource mobilization, and functional responsibilities and its greater ability to better hold its own in the international arena suggest a credible level of policy implementation capability.

The institutionalization of power is, of course, only partial and there are also plenty of indicators of praetorianism and patrimonialism. The dominant role of the military, the manipulation or breaking of the rules of the political game by elites, the lack of effective accountability mechanisms, and the clientelism and primordialism which indisputably infect political structures are all signs of these ills. But the Achilles' heel of the regime lies in the failure to institutionalize leadership succession, each case of which has so far been brokered by military violence and shows every sign of doing so again after Asad.

The mobilizational and mass incorporating capacity of the regime is a similar "mixed" story: it has accommodated *limited participation,* but has failed to "solve" the "crisis of participation." Initially, the regime sharply constrained participation, repressing the urban centered pluralism of the fifties while, at the same time, generating a measure of ideological-oriented pro-regime activism. The regime also penetrated the rural areas in a relatively uniform way, by-passing gatekeepers who kept the peasantry encapsulated, drawing previously inactive peasants into the political arena, opening up new recruitment channels for rurals, and establishing new centers of village leadership, thereby pluralizing power in the *rief.* This mobilization, widening the political arena (and reducing the relative weight of the urban opposition), shifted the balance of power in favor of the Ba'th state. In several respects the Ba'th also enhanced political equality. A more equitable distribution of participatory resources (e.g. literacy, political consciousness) was effected and social structural barriers to mass politicization—rigid stratification, segmental encapsulation—eased. Through the party and mass syndicates, political association on a scale hitherto unknown was fostered. A populist form of corporatism institutionalized access to the political center for the regime's mass constituency. The exclusion of formerly privileged groups from access and this rural incorporation produced much greater elite responsiveness to the rural majority than that under the landlord regime. This contrasts with the more common Third World situation in which the city enjoys some political power while the village does not.

But, subsequently, Asad's power strategy had a contradictory effect on the regime's incorporative capacity. He tried with some success to widen the regime's base through political relaxation, cooptation of opposition and economic rewards—government jobs for the middle class, liberalization and enrichment opportunities for the bourgeoisie. But the economic payoffs to urban interests narrowed responsiveness to the regime's rural constituency and alienated part of the regime's activist support. Moreover, as, after 1970, class conflict and class ideology faded, while Asad used communal ties to consolidate the elite core, the persistence of a strong religious and kinship culture made communal solidarities into "natural" vehicles of political action. In this climate, the Alawis turned from a deprived into a privileged group, narrowing access for all others. Then, as fundamentalist Islam became a vehicle of anti-regime mobilization for those feeling most excluded, the regime, faced with a formidable challenge to its survival, narrowed the modest scope of participation previously permitted and jettisoned all tolerance of dissent in a burst of repression. Accommodation between state and private sector, city and regime, was set back and the regime's cooptative capability seriously enervated.

On the whole the regime has shown little capacity to politically incorporate urban society. Much of the old upper classes, large segments of the urban middle class, and the masses of the traditional quarters are alienated and feel deprived of political rights. But, unlike totalitarian regimes, the Ba'th has neither the will or capacity to destroy the economic bases of the opposition elites or snap mass links to them. Thus, it faces a permanent opposition coalition joining old money, the *suq,* and youthful militants around a powerful "counter-ideology"—fundamentalist Islam. Virtually excluded from participatory channels, apparently invulnerable to economic appeasement, the opposition periodically resorts to anti-system activities—the riot, demonstration, merchant strike, the black market, the brain drain, assassination, finally, the mass armed uprising; while "anomic" and often costly to those who engage in them, these forms of protest have deterred the regime from certain initiatives, wrested concessions from it, even forced it to change course: they helped de-rail the socialist experiment and forced a muting of secularization.

The participatory efficacy of even the regime's own constituency is currently limited though it is still of some significance. Intra-party politicking through which activists move upward in the political structure, controlled interest group activity, and clientelist access ("individual contacting") remain viable avenues of access for it. In countries like Syria where many societal interests are literally incorporated into the state itself, the informal lobbying of officials themselves is a crucial part of politics. All these forms of politics have, in the aggregate, an effect on outcomes. Moreover, the pro-regime activism of significant numbers of lower-middle and lower class elements in the party bases, often dismissed as a "mobilized," hence meaningless form of participation, has had strategic consequences: it is crucial to the durability of Ba'thism. But even "legitimate" pro-regime participation is tightly constrained. Many of the crucial issues are excluded from intra-party political debate, which takes place largely on terms set by the elite, and participants lack institutionalized mechanisms to keep elites responsive. In their absence, informal mechanisms may operate, notably the need of a regime lacking much customary or procedural legitimacy to satisfy its constituency, especially in periods of sharp opposition challenge. Yet, since the most dangerous threat to regime survival is the prospect of military coup the regime's first priority is satisfying the military, turning the latter into a privileged force sometimes immune from the law and with priority claims on the country's resources.

Politicization has clearly outrun the limited institutionalization of participation in Syria. The middle class praetorianism of the fifties and early sixties was initially superseded as Ba'thist political mobilization expanded the small highly fragmented urban political arena and incorporated a rural mass base into the state. By the late seventies, the arena was much enlarged and more mobilized, but the declining incorporative capacity of the regime bifurcated it between the Ba'th and a largely Islamic opposition, resulting in sporadic mass praetorianism. But the regime retained enough of a political base to contain this concentrated, intense opposition. The repression of Islamic opposition ended in the uneasy passivity of the eighties. The regime seems to lack the broad legitimacy necessary to defuse the praetorian potential of the now submerged opposition by widening institutionalized participation; hence the "crisis of participation" remains on the political agenda.

Populist Statism and Ba'thist Power

The Ba'th's populist-statist "modernizing strategy"—social leveling, the concentration of economic power in the state—was shaped by its origins in a populist revolt against the old oligarchy. It was in part an instrument for relaunching the socio-economic development which had faltered with the breakdown of Syria's capitalist experiment. But, in responding to the expectations of the constituency the Ba'th was incorporating and in breaking the economic dominance of its rivals, the Ba'th was also deploying development policy as an instrument of regime power consolidation.

The public sector became a lever of state control over the economy, a vehicle for channeling significant investment into infrastructure and industry which sparked a burst of economic expansion, and an instrument of political cooptation, incorporating thousands of middle and working class constituents who thereby acquired a certain stake in a statist regime. In agriculture the regime pursued both populist leveling and bureaucratic expansion. Land reform, in breaking the hold of the great notables over land and peasant, broadened and consolidated a small holding sector beholden to the regime. In deploying the agrarian bureaucracy in a series of rationalizing innovations and forging a state-cooperative agricultural infrastructure, state control replaced commercial dominance over agriculture while fostering a certain peasant security and prosperity. In this way the Ba'th broke through traditional barriers to state penetration, institutionalized linkages to peasants and incorporated a large portion of them into the state. None of this would have been possible without concentrated and populist authoritarian power.

But the "socialist" experiment ultimately reached its limits and the regime exhausted its ideological energies without having created viable economic institutions which could substitute for capitalism. In industry, inefficient management, an undisciplined work force, and the subordination of profit to political goals such as patronage deprived the public sector of the capacity to mobilize the capital for its own reproduction without costly dependence on outside sources. In agriculture, the bureaucracy also failed to extract much surplus and the cooperatives to foster collective investment and cultivation. The regime over-committed its resources—to national defense, welfare, development investment—without attaining a commensurate resource mobilization capability. The internal accommodation with capital under Asad—economic liberalization, social stabilization—was an effort to create safety valves and stimulate an alternative private economic motor to supplement the public sector; but liberalization chiefly fostered consumption, corruption, and inflation which led to widening trade deficits and inequality. Since this was accompanied by a buttressing of the state sector through which petro rent continued to be funneled, the new strategy did not so much reverse etatism as erode its populist character. Populism persists, however, in the servicing of the regime's plebeian constituency through such instruments as subsidization of popular commodities and cheap credit to peasants and development policy has not been "captured" by the bourgeoisie or put in the service of capitalist resurgence at the expense of the masses. Rather, the state seeks to reconcile and appease the interests of capital and labor, state and merchant, city and peasant. The combination of initial leveling and the renewed inequalities which the Ba'th has fostered amounts to a major re-stratification of society. As the weight of old wealth and family name was curbed, while that of political loyalty and activism, state service, and military power were enhanced, "making it" in Syria came to depend for many on making it in or with the state, a major explanation for the regime's durability. Thus, although its economic rationality is in some respects questionable, the state's development strategy proved an effective instrument of political consolidation for the Ba'th.

The limits of this strategy have, however, been reached and perhaps overreached. The burden of the national security state combined with patronage and corruption dissipate resources needed for investment and under the economic stagnation and inflation which has resulted in the eighties, the mobilization of aspirations and demands is outrunning the capacity to satisfy them; indeed the situation of the plebeian strata seems to be eroding. The regime has no easy way out: it is loath to squeeze its own constituency very far—whether the new bourgeoisie or the masses—for fear of losing its precarious political base and it cannot extract from a private bourgeoisie able to evade its bureaucratic reach and threaten disinvestment. Oil wealth and the exit of the most ambitious have provided safety values but as these narrow, the regime has been forced into an austerity policy which shrinks patronage and populism. In creating or mobilizing whole sets of new interests, then accommodating old ones, the regime had, by the eighties, been caught in a web of its own making, depriving it of capacity for major innovation.

Classifying the Ba'th State and Its Evolution

The evolution of the Ba'th state can be summarized and classified in terms of the categories in the introduction.

1. Immediately after 1963, the regime had all the symptoms of a "radical praetorian" state: seizure of power by coup against a landlord regime, ideological intensity, military rule, little institutional development or organized popular base, reform by decree from above, instability—military factionalism inside the regime and class hostility outside.

2. Subsequently (1965–1970), the regime moved toward the mature "authoritarian-populist" type. Limited Leninization gave rise to a strong

ruling party and mass organizations incorporating a support base and generating the power to implement major reforms. But the regime, only partially institutionalized, never decisively subordinated the military to political leadership and soon abandoned rule through collegial party institutions. In its place an authoritarian presidency emerged (1970–1975), resting on both an elite core forged through *asabiya* and party and bureaucratic structures. The state incorporated a major array of bureaucratic and populist interests and their defense eclipsed radical change as the major goal of policy.

3. Thereafter (1976–1989), patrimonial tendencies began to infect the regime, manifest in the aggrandizement of presidential monarchy and of the Alawi core around it at the expense of party and state institutions, the decline of ideology, the transformation of the party into a patronage machine, the enervation of state rationality and development capacity by corruption and inertia, the compromising of populist-etatist development, and a certain reconciliation with traditional forces in the villages. But patrimonialization has not decisively traditionalized the elite, wholly effaced ideology or gutted prior institutional development.

4. Simultaneously, the regime moved in a conservative direction. Conservatization grew out of the post-1970 halt in "socialist transformation," construction of a national security state, and revival of the private economy. By the mid-seventies, these policies had resulted in embourgeoisement of the plebeian elite, a certain incorporation of bourgeois elements into the regime, a tolerance of new inequalities, and increased repression of leftist as well as rightist dissidents. Patrimonial corruption accelerated these tendencies. The regime, thus, showed the symptoms of post-populist transformation. But state power has yet to be put in the service of a reconstructed bourgeoisie, a return to capitalist development, or the de-mobilization of the masses, and, in the absence of limited liberalization, the access of the bourgeoisie to power remains uninstitutionalized and unreliable.

5. By the mid-eighties, the regime had passed the apex of its institutional development, but neither structural deterioration or policy transformation were advanced enough to move it fully into the neo-patrimonial or post-populist categories. It resembles a "Bonapartist" regime hovering near the center of the matrix of four types depicted in chapter one: structurally, it is headed by a nationalist general turned Presidential Monarch, backed by the army and bureaucracy, and with a mass incorporating populist party; in orientation it is the product of both a leveling revolution and the generation of a new stratification system, including a new "state bourgeoisie," and thus stands "above" rather than taking sides between social classes.

6. Eventually the regime must depart in one direction or the other. It seems incapable of reforming and re-vitalizing itself along populist lines. Yet the conditions of intensified praetorianism and system collapse do not yet exist: disparate counter-elites would have to develop greater unity and mobilizational capacity, notably one able to overcome the urban-rural gap, state institutions would have to crumble, and the Ba'thist elite split along sectarian lines. A succession crisis might result in such a division, but it

would take a broader crisis for the state's structures to unravel. The obstacles to a limited political liberalization opening the regime to bourgeois penetration remain formidable, especially the Alawi core of the regime, the party apparatus, the continuing conflict with Israel, and the risks of enhancing the power of the anti-regime city at the expense of the regime's village base. The most likely immediate prospect is therefore continuing neo-patrimonial drift, enervating the regime's institutions and narrowing its base. But the simultaneous crisis of the statist economy and development of capitalist forces in society and within the regime itself, will, in the long run, probably force a certain "liberal" transformation of an exhausted Bonapartist regime: perhaps an opening of the state, as in France's "Liberal Empire" or Sadat's Egypt, to power-sharing with the capitalist bourgeoisie-in-parliament.

Observations on Political Theory from the Syrian Case

1. The origins of authoritarian-populism in Syria, a dominant route of state formation in the Middle East, throws some light on the nature of *political change* there. It is evident that the root explanation for the widespread displacement of traditional by authoritarian-populist regimes must be sought in basic structural variables. Some are fairly specific to the region, in particular, the inherited structure of urban-rural relations which defined the pre-capitalist order. The slim agrarian roots of traditional elites made the old regime very vulnerable to rural revolt, as analysts like Moore and Anderson argued in other "Asian" cases. Others are familiar from analyses of radical change throughout the Third World, namely the disruptions accompanying the incorporation of an agrarian society into the world capitalist system. The impact of imperialism on Syria's fragile traditional order ended in a severe case of regime de-legitimation. Capitalist penetration undermined traditional authority, generated new classes and an agrarian crisis and set off the class conflict which fed anti-regime political mobilization.

The class variable is central to understanding these developments and the nature of politics and the state throughout them. Class structure shaped the nature of the early post-independence state: in an unmobilized society topped by a class of large landed magnates it could be little more than the instrument of dominant class power. But once new classes mobilized, the state was transformed into an arena of ideological struggle over system transformation. Thereafter, the political conflicts of greatest consequence for systemic change pitted actors shaped by class identities in battles over class-related issues: the distribution of wealth and the proper model of development, matters having direct bearing on the mode of production. The Middle East appears, far from being exceptional, to replicate in important ways the role of class in historic regime transformations elsewhere.

But because of the special features of Syrian social structure, the anti-regime coalition grew more out of urban-rural conflict than a straightforward class lineup. The dominant classes were exceptionally concentrated in the city: the landed elite was urban, and it, the merchants and much of their clients at the bottom of urban society shared, though very unequally, an interest in dominating the village through exploitative relations of production. On the other hand, the radical forces were rooted in the village: rural elements of the middle class made up their vanguard, peasants their most durable base, and agrarian populism the ideological cement of the middle-class–peasant coalition which brought the Ba'th to power. In some respects the Ba'th case appears an instance of Ibn Khaldun's specifically Middle Eastern scenario in which a new state rises out of hinterland revolt against the exaggerated concentration of power and wealth in the city. But the intimate linkage of rural alienation to class relationships arising from the penetration of capitalism is quite different from the traditional syndrome he charts. Thus, in the modern Middle East the inherited urban-rural cleavage is filled with a new class content hitherto lacking.

Under the radical Ba'th, the state again became an instrument of class power—but this time wielded by lower, rural classes. Class origins shaped the populist ideology of political elites who made the state an instrument of war on the dominant classes. In turn, the transformations in class structure issuing from this revolution shaped changes in the state: leveling and restratification cleared the way for a Bonapartist-like state "above" classes.

The Syrian case also gives some clues as to why the factors which produced populist regimes did not generally come together in full scale peasant revolution in the Middle East. The reasons do not appear to be particularly cultural-specific. Neither Islam, sectarianism, or segmentalism were unsurmountable obstacles to anti-regime mobilization; segmentalism may have slowed it but communalism seems to have fed into broader class-based mobilization. The urban-rural cleavage appears to have been decisive: on the one hand, it obstructed the formation of the broad urban-rural mass coalition needed for revolution; on the other hand, the narrow urban base of the *ancien regime* gave it little staying power and allowed a capture of the armed forces by alienated rural plebeians, factors making it possible to topple the regime with much less than a "great" revolution. The subsequent "revolution from above" launched by radical officers preempted and substituted for revolution from below. The later failure of an Islamic form of revolution in Syria can also partly be understood as a outcome of a special social structure. Islam's exaggerated concentration in the city and the solid grounding of the populist regime in the village blocked the construction of the urban-rural coalition needed for such massive upheaval; indeed, despite certain similarities with Islamic movements elsewhere, in Syria the mass base of Islamic revivalism was limited by its roots in formerly privileged rather than deprived social forces.

2. The transformation in the forms of *political association* from the anti-regime mobilization of the fifties to the post regime-consolidation of the seventies gives insights into the complexity of political behavior in the Middle East. Much of the literature on the bases of political solidarity and cleavage there is schizophrenic: it tends to stress either secular (class, universalistic ideologies) or primordial (kinship, sectarian, ethnic) factors to the exclusion

of the other. Whereas it was once expected that communal and religious identities would be superseded by secular ones, it is now common to argue that the former are the natural and culturally specific bases of politics in the Middle East. But if the Syrian case is any indicator, secular and primordial bases of association are not mutually exclusive and complex mixes of associational forms are more typical than pure cases. There are many manifestations of this complexity in the Syrian case.

Just as modernization theorists expected, social mobilization widened the hitherto very limited associative capacity of political life in Syria. Thus, once peasant youth were exposed to education, the segmental barriers to their political mobilization began to give way. Similarly, initially separatist sectarian minorities, once socially mobilized, chose to pursue their interests through integration, embracing the dominant universalistic Arab nationalism and a reformism expressed in class terms. Moreover, as Marxist analysis predicts, capitalist penetration generated class conflict and solidarity, for a time displacing segmental politics, and giving rise to a broad anti-regime coalition. To be sure, social structural complexity gave this anti-regime mobilization its own complexity: a mobilization of the Sunni peasantry on relatively pure class grounds was paralleled by one among the minorities where class and communal cleavages overlapped; the political arena was never blocked off into exclusively class determined political formations and Syria's mosaic society and kinship culture made class alliances vulnerable to fragmentation. But it was essentially class conflict which propelled the rise of the Ba'th and the transformation of the state under the Ba'th was, at base, a transformation in its class composition. The fact that the Ba'th state, despite its heavily minoritarian leadership, incorporated Sunni villages but not Sunni urban quarters shows the essential importance of class-shaped urban-rural conflict in the formation of the new regime. Modernization and class formation did not, however, efface narrower identities and once class conflict receded, they revived.

The consolidation of the new regime can only be explained by a complex interaction between more particularistic and universalistic forms of political association. Sectarianism and clientelism played a pivotal role in forging the elite core. But coexisting or overlapping with such ties were the class and national shaped ideological preferences and career interests through which thousands of Ba'th party activists were mobilized and political organizations of unprecedented scale constructed: this organization-building, indeed, went far to overcome the fragmentation of a historically mosaic, tribal society lacking natural unifying forces. While the use of traditional forms of political cement needs no explanation, the regime's successful institution-building can only be explained by the broadening of loyalties and dilution of primordialism associated with social mobilization combined with the elite's adoption of the modern "political technology" of ideology and party organization.

Then as, after 1970, reform eased class rigidities and state patronage became the focus of social competition, class conflict gave way to group politics in which reactivated sectarian ties became natural lines of clientelistic access. Alawite sectarianism stimulated a reactive solidarity among Sunnis lacking equal access to the font of state patronage. Yet, even in these conditions of communal conflict, the two sides expressed themselves in universalistic ideologies, Arab nationalism and fundamentalist Islam, and these ideologies expressed less cleavages over community and identity, per se, than over power and distribution: they were vehicles of regime legitimation and anti-regime protest.

Syria is clearly a case where multiple loyalties—personal, communal, class, state, Arab national and Islamic umma—compete, their relative ascendence changing over time according to socio-political conditions. Political ties are a mix of "modern" (class and national ideology) and "traditional" (communal, clientelist). Why this complexity is so seldom recognized is difficult to fathom: it is exactly what should be expected in newly created states where modern political and bureaucratic technology is adapted to "transitional" societies historically built on kinship and segmentalism.

3. The Syrian case throws some light on the nature of the *authoritarian state in the Middle East.* Much of the literature, applying Weberian (neo-patrimonial/legal-rational), or functionalist (praetorian/institutionalized) concepts in a simplistic way, tends to view these states as pure cases— typically praetorian or patrimonial—of these types. A close look at Syrian realities, however, makes clear what Weber himself insisted: that most real regimes are mixes of the ideal types. The Ba'th, relying on a mixed patri-monial/organization-building strategy, produced a mixed state, part-Bona-partist, part-Leninist. Whatever the contradictions introduced into the political system by this fusion, the mixed strategy proved, just as Weber suggested, more effective, durable and flexible than a "pure" one. Leninist organization alone proved incapable of forging a solid elite core while sectarianism and clientelism were irrelevant to the mobilization and incorporation of a mass base. Nor does Syria fit comfortably into Huntington's praetorian/institu-tionalized dichotomy as regards the role of military violence. The military has played an ambiguous role, a source of praetorianism but also of leadership which forged the institutions to contain praetorianism and give Syria a far more stable state than hitherto. The Syrian experience seems, thus, to show the utility of the intermediate category of *partial institutionalization.*

The Syrian case also calls into question the sharp dichotomy often assumed between democratic regimes, supposedly responsive, participatory and based on consent, and authoritarian ones, supposedly based on coercion and neither responsive or participatory. It is indisputable that the democratic ideal of a conscious citizenry able to make choices among policies and hold leaders accountable is absent in authoritarian regimes (and indeed only more or less approximated in democratic ones); but between this and total mass passivity, there may be a whole range of participatory possibilities. This case suggests that even authoritarian regimes little tolerant of dissent, may, *if they have populist roots and a strong party system,* nevertheless institutionalize a certain *limited* participation which enhances responsiveness, permits them to incorporate a support base under much less than ideal democratic conditions, and reduces their dependence on coercion. Moreover, in contracting the participation of the more urban, educated, and privileged elements which in developing countries take disproportionate benefit from liberal politics (Nelson 1987:139), they may actually expand responsiveness to less privileged strata. And, while protest against authoritarian regimes may be un-institutionalized, it is no less a form of participation, often effective in winning concessions. It is time, as Nelson (1987:104–105) puts it, to "decouple" the concept of participation (and responsiveness, for that matter) from democracy. The growing scope of dissent and repression in Syria does, of course, support the belief that participatory propensities inevitably grow with societal development and that even an authoritarian regime possessing an effective single party will, given the lack of choice, only be able to incorporate a *portion* of society and hence do no more than contain, not "solve" the "crisis of participation." Because of this, military coercion remains central to the survival of such regimes.

Another important question concerning authoritarian states is their relation to society, usually evaluated according to their "strength" in imposing policy on society and their "autonomy" from societal pressures. In regard to "strength," the literature tends to waver between considering such regimes strong, because of their concentration of power and weak because of their supposed lack of legitimacy and institutionalization. The Syrian case shows the complexity of the question of state strength. The Ba'th came to power in a country where the state was, by any measure, very weak and society dominated by plural centers of private power outside its control. The new regime smashed these centers, concentrated and expanded power, acquired some legitimacy, and developed many of the attributes of a "strong" state: autonomy of the dominant landed-commercial classes, a complex organizational structure, widened government function, innovation, regulation, and penetration, and significant state-sponsored re-stratification. The attachment of a much wider array of interests to the state gave it a new weight in society and an increased ability to mobilize and coordinate manpower and resources made it a formidable actor in the international arena. Yet, paradoxically, developing these very capabilities had costs which, as they mounted, began to enervate the state. The autonomy of dominant classes was purchased in part through the liberal use of *asabiya* in the creation of coercive "centers of power" which now threaten to colonize the state and subvert its policies. Government control over society was accompanied by the growth of bureaucracies whose control is itself now a major problem, whose functions exceed their capabilities, and whose regulation is often counterproductive. The populist-etatist policies, patronage, and military buildup which satisfied and incorporated various constituencies resulted in excessive consumption, resource overcommitment, and vested interests which, eroding the extraction capacity of the state and burdening the productive bases of society, have resulted in external dependence and economic stagnation. Thus, it may be typical of populist authoritarianism that the bureaucratization, restratification, and distribution through which the state develops its power undermines its own resource base and may in time force a certain retreat of the state or even its recapture by powerful societal forces. The Syrian case suggests that little is gained by insisting on either the strength or weakness of authoritarian regimes: not only do these regimes vary widely, but the same state may be "strong" on certain dimensions during certain periods, but at the possible cost of weakness in other respects or in future periods.

The question of "autonomy," largely having to do with the extent of dominant class control over the state, is also complex. Marxist tradition, while viewing the state as normally an instrument of such classes, acknowledges that in certain circumstances the state may attain some autonomy; the Syrian case suggests that authoritarian-populism produces one of those episodes. Certainly, if autonomy means the state is no mere servant of a dominant class (whether old or regime-created), or that it is not dependent on the mediation of traditional notables to link it to the masses, or that raison d'état is a more crucial ingredient in policy-making than the class interest of elites or the pressures of social classes, then the Syrian regime ranks fairly high on autonomy. The Ba'thist state was consolidated in a period conducive to state autonomy: when societal crisis and international threat legitimized the concentration of state power, when an old dominant class was in decline and readily attacked and new forces on the rise could be harnessed. Nevertheless, in the real world state autonomy is only relative: no state, however authoritarian, exists in a vacuum and if autonomy is construed to mean elites are under no constraints from the groups and classes of their own constituency or the pressures of the opposition, or even the demands of their own putative "instruments," then the Syrian state lacks autonomy; indeed the case suggests that autonomy of part of society can only be purchased at the price of dependence on other parts. Moreover, the case supports the Marxist expectation that a high level of autonomy is a temporary, transitional phenomenon, for constraints on the Ba'th state are increasing and economic pressures may soon force it to come to terms with the bourgeoisie. But the decline of autonomy need not mean the state is captured by one social force, even the dominant class. In the Syrian case, declining autonomy so far means that the state is constrained by the demands of a multitude of social forces; it is certainly premature to speak of the restoration of the political power of a capitalist bourgeoisie over it and, in fact, the state is probably entirely too complex and too conscious of distinct interests of its own to be wholly captured by any one social force—sectarian, corporate or class.

The record of strength and autonomy in the Syrian case suggests there may be a certain cycle in state-building: in its effort to create authority and autonomy where it is lacking the state may go too far and after a period the costs of patrimonialization and bureaucratization come to outweigh the benefits. The outcome may be stagnation or, alternatively, rationalizing and democratic reforms which redress the imbalance of state and society. The conflict between these alternatives may be the essence of Syrian politics today.

Bibliography

Abd-Allah, Umar F. (1983) *The Islamic Struggle in Syria.* Berkeley: Mizan Press.

Abd al-Salam, Adil. (1973) *Jughrafiyat Suriya* [Geography of Syria]. Damascus: University of Damascus Press.

Abu Jaber, Kamel S. (1966) *The Arab Ba'th Socialist Party: History, Ideology, and Organization.* Syracuse: Syracuse University Press.

Abyad, Malikah. (1968) "Values of Syrian Youth: A Study Based on Students in Damascus University," M.A. Thesis: American University in Beirut.

Aflaq, Michel. (1959) *Fi sabil al-Ba'th* [On the Road to the Resurgence]. Beirut: Dar al-Tali'a.

———. (1971) *Nuqtat al-bidaya: ahadith ba'da al-khamis min haziran* [The Beginning Point: Discourses after the 5th of June].Beirut.

al-Akhrass, Safouh. (1969) "Revolutionary Change and Modernization in the Arab World: A Case from Syria." Ph.D. Dissertation, University of California, Berkeley.

Allouni, A. Aziz. (1959) "The Labor Movement in Syria," *Middle East Journal,* v. 13, Winter, pp. 64–76.

Allush, Naji. (1962) *al-Thawra wal-jamahir* [The Revolution and the Masses]. Beirut: Dar al-Tali'a.

Almond, Gabriel and Powell, G. Bingham. (1966) *Comparative Politics: A Developmental Approach.* Boston: Little, Brown & Co.

———. (1978) *Comparative Politics: Structure, Process and Policy.* Boston: Little, Brown & Co.

Anderson, Charles W., von der Mehden, Fred R., and Young, Crawford. (1967) *Issues of Political Development.* Englewood Cliffs, N.J.: Prentice-Hall.

Anderson, Perry. (1974) *Lineages of the Absolutist State.* London: Verso Editions.

Antaki, Ikram. (1973) *Deir Atieh.* Paris.

Antoun, Richard and Harik, Iliya, eds. (1972) *Rural Politics and Social Change in the Middle East.* Bloomington, Ind.: Indiana University Press.

Apter, David. (1965) *The Politics of Modernization.* Chicago: University of Chicago Press.

Arab Ba'th Socialist Party (ABSP). (1962) "Constitution" in Sylvia Haim *Arab Nationalism: An Anthology.* Berkeley: University of California Press, pp. 233–241.

———. (1963) *Nidal al-Ba'th fi sabil al-wahda wal-hurriya wal-ishtirakiya* [The Struggle of the Ba'th for Unity, Freedom and Socialism]. ed., Bashir Da'uq. Beirut: Dar al-Tali'a, 3 vols.

———. (1963b) *Abhath fi tanzim al-hizbiya* [Studies in Party Organization]. Damascus.

———. (1964) "Resolutions of the 6th National Congress of the Arab Ba'th Socialist Party" in *Arab Political Documents, 1963,* pp. 439–442, Beirut.

———. (1965) *al-manhaj al-marhali* [The Phased Programme]. Damascus.

———. (1965b) *Programme du Parti.* Damascus.

———. (1968) "Statement of the National Leadership on the Results of the 10th National Congress." Damascus.

————. (1969) *al-Suqut fi al-hizb al-thawri* [Decline in the Revolutionary Party]. Damascus.

————. (1970) *al-taqrir al-siyasi lil-mu'tamar al-qaumi al-istithna'i al-'ashir* [Political Report of the 10th Extraordinary National Congress]. Damascus.

————. (1971) "Statement of the National Leadership on the Work and Results of the 11th National Congress." Damascus.

————. (1972a) *Dirasat tarikhiya tahliliya li-nidal Hizb al-Ba'th al-Arabi al-Ishtiraki* [Analytical Historical Study of the Struggle of the Arab Ba'th Socialist Party]. Damascus.

————. (1972b) *al-hizb wal-mas'ala al-zira'iya* [The party and the agrarian question]. Damascus.

————. (1972c) *Nidal Hizb al-Ba'th al-Arabi al-Ishtiraki abr mu'tamaratihi al-qaumiya* [Struggle of the Arab Ba'th Socialist Party Through its National Congresses]. Beirut: Dar al-Tali'a

————. (1973) *Some Theoretical Points of Departure.* Damascus.

————. (1975) *al-Mu'tamar al-qutri as-sadis* [The Sixth Regional Congress]. Damascus.

————. (1980) "Statement by the National Leadership of the Baath Arab Socialist Party on the Proceedings of the Party's 13th National Congress." Damascus.

————. (1985a) *al-Ikhwan al-Muslimun.* Damascus: Maktab al-i'dad.

————. (1985b) *Taqarir al-mu'tamar al-qutri al-thamin wa muqarraratihi* [Reports and Resolutions of the 8th Regional Congress]. Damascus.

Arudki, Yehya. (1972) *al-Iqtisad al-Suri al-hadith* [The Modern Syrian Economy]. v. 1., Damascus.

Atasi, Nadr. (1968) "Wage Fixing and Wage Structure in Syria," *International Labor Review,* [Geneva], v. 98, n. 4., pp. 337–353.

Babikian, N. Salem. (1977) "A Partial Reconstruction of Michel 'Aflaq's Thought," *The Muslim World,* v. 67 (4), pp. 280–294.

Baer, Gabriel. (1966) "The Evolution of Private Landownership in Egypt and the Fertile Crescent," in Charles Issawi, *The Economic History of the Middle East, 1800–1914.* London: Oxford University Press, pp. 80–113.

Bakour, Yehia, et. al. (1977) "Qanun al-tanzim al-fallahi" [The Law on Peasant Organization]. Damascus: Working Paper of the Agricultural Symposium.

Batatu, Hanna. (1981) "Some Observations on the Social Roots of Syria's Ruling Military Group and the Causes of its Dominance," *Middle East Journal* v. 35, no. 3, Summer.

————. (1982) "Syria's Muslim Brethren," *MERIP Reports,* n. 110, November–December, pp. 12–20.

Be'eri, Eliezer. (1970) *Army Officers in Arab Politics and Society.* New York & London: Praeger and Pall Mall.

Bendix, Reinhard. (1977) *Max Weber: An Intellectual Portrait.* Berkeley and Los Angeles: University of California Press.

Ben Tzur, Avraham. (1965) "What Is Arab Socialism," *New Outlook* vol. 8, no. 5, pp. 37–45.

————. (1968) "The Neo-Ba'th Party of Syria." *Journal of Contemporary History,* v. 3, n. 3, pp. 161–181.

————. (1968a) "The Composition and Membership of the Ba'th Party in the Kuneitra Region," *The New East,* XVIII, pp. 269–273.

Berger, Morroe. (1962) *The Arab World Today.* Garden City, N.Y.: Doubleday & Co.

Bianquis, Anne-Marie. (1979) "Les Cooperatives Agricoles en Syrie: l'exemple de l'oasis de Damas," *Revue de Geographie de Lyon,* n. 3.

_____ . (1980) "Reforme Fonciere et Politique Agricole dans la Ghuta de Damas," These, Universite Lyon II.

Bill, James and Leiden, Carl. (1984) *Politics in the Middle East.* Boston: Little, Brown & Co.

Binder, Leonard. (1959) "Radical Reform Nationalism in Syria and Egypt," *Muslim World,* April and June, pp. 96–109, 213–231.

_____ . (1964) *The Ideological Revolution in the Middle East.* New York: Wiley.

Blau, Peter. (1964) *Exchange and Power in Social Life.* New York: John Wiley & Sons, Inc.

Bonne, Alfred. (1955) *State and Economics in the Middle East.* London: Routledge & Kegan Paul.

Brinton, Crane. (1952) *The Anatomy of Revolution.* Englewood Cliffs, N.J.: Prentice-Hall.

Carleton, Alford. (1950) "The Syrian Coups d'Etat of 1949," *Middle East Journal,* v. 4, no. 1, January, pp. 1–11.

Chalmers, Douglas. (1977). "The Politicized State in Latin America," in Malloy, James, *Authoritarianism and Corporatism in Latin America.* Pittsburgh: University of Pittsburgh Press, pp. 23–45.

Chamy, Georgio. (1957) "Men and Parties in Syria," *Etudes Mediterraneenes,* Autumn.

Coleman, James S. (1975) "Tradition and Nationalism in Tropical Africa," in Martin Kilson, ed., *New States in the Modern World.* Cambridge, Mass.: Harvard University Press, pp. 3–36.

Coon, Carleton. (1958) *Caravan: The Story of the Middle East.* New York: Holt.

Crow, Ralph. (1964) "The Civil Service of Independent Syria." Ph.D. Dissertation, University of Michigan.

ad-Dahr, Nafi Sayyem. (1952) "Agrarian Structure and Economic Development in Syria," Ph.D. Dissertation, Columbia University.

Daoud Agha, Adnan. (1970) "Military Elites, Military-Led Social Movements and the Social Structure of Developing Countries: A Comparative Study of Egypt and Syria," Ph.D. Dissertation, University of California.

Davis, James. (1962) "Toward a Theory of Revolution," *American Sociological Review,* XXVII, February, 1–19.

Dawisha, Adeed. (1978a) "Syria Under Asad, 1970–1978: The Centres of Power," *Government and Opposition,* v. 13, n. 3, Summer, pp. 341–354.

_____ . (1978b) "Syria's Intervention in Lebanon, 1975–1976," *Jerusalem Journal of International Relations,* v. 3, nos. 2–3, pp. 245–264.

Dawn, Ernest. (1962) "The Rise of Arabism in Syria," *Middle East Journal,* v. 16, no. 2, pp. 145–68.

Dekmejian, R. Hrair. (1985) *Islam in Revolution.* Syracuse: Syracuse University Press.

Deutsch, Karl. (1953) *Nationalism and Social Communication.* Cambridge, Mass.: MIT Press.

_____ . (1961) "Social Mobilization and Political Development," *American Political Science Review,* v. LV, n. 3, September, pp. 493–514.

Devlin, John. (1976) *The Ba'th Party: A History from its Origins to 1966.* Stanford: Hoover Institution Press.

_____ . (1983) *Syria: Modern State in an Ancient Land.* Boulder, Colorado: Westview Press.

Donahue, John. (1973) "La nouvelle constitution syrienne et ses detracteurs," *Traveux et Jours,* April–June.

Drysdale, Alasdair. (1979) "Ethnicity in the Syrian Officer Corps: A Conceptualization," *Civilisations,* XXIX, 3–4, pp. 359–373.

———— . (1981a) "The Regional Equalization of Health Care and Education in Syria since the Ba'thi Revolution," *International Journal of Middle East Studies*, v. 13, pp. 93–111.

———— . (1981b) "The Syrian Political Elite, 1966–1976: A Spatial and Social Analysis," *Middle Eastern Studies*, v. 17, n. 1, pp. 3–30.

———— . (1982) "The Asad Regime and its Troubles," *MERIP Reports*, v. 12, n. 9, November–December.

———— . (1984) "Syria's Sectarian Schism and the Struggle for Power," *Middle East Insight*, v. 3, n. 4., pp. 24–29.

Eisenstadt, S.N. (1964) "Breakdowns of Modernization," *Economic Development and Cultural Change*, v. 12, n. 4, July, pp. 345–367.

Eisenstadt, S.N. and Lemarchand, Rene. (1981) *Political Clientalism, Patronage and Development.* Beverly Hills, Calif.: Sage Publications.

Epstein, Eliahu. (1936) "Notes from a Paper on the Present Condition of the Hauran," *Journal of the Royal Central Asia Society*, v. 23.

Faksh, Mahmud A. (1984) "The Alawi Community of Syria: A New Dominant Political Force," *Middle Eastern Studies*, v. 20, n. 2, April, pp. 133–153.

Farsoun, S. and Carroll. W. (1978). "State Capitalism and Counter-Revolution in the Middle East: A Thesis," in *Social Change in the Capitalist World Economy*, ed. Barbara H. Kaplan, Beverly Hills: Sage Publications.

Fedden, Robin. (1946) *Syria: A Historical Appreciation.* London: Robert Hale.

Gaspard, J. (1969a) "Penetrating the Ba'th: An Ideology in Search of Leadership," *New Middle East*, May.

———— . (1969b) "Troubled Waters in the Ba'th," *New Middle East*, May.

———— . (1971) "Damascus After the Coup: Syria's New Master Breaks with the Past," *New Middle East*, v. 28, January.

Geertz, Clifford. (1963) "The Integrative Revolution: Primordial Sentiments and Civic Politics in the New States," in C. Geertz, ed. *Old Societies and New States: The Quest for Modernity in Asia and Africa.* New York: The Free Press.

General Federation of Peasants (GFP). (1967) *Mu'tamar ittihadat al-fallahin al-thani* [The Second Conference of the Peasant Federations]. Damascus.

———— . (1969) *al-Nizam al-dakhili lil-ittihad al-'amm lil-fallahin* [Internal Rules of the General Federation of Peasants]. Damascus.

———— . (1970) *Muqarrarat al-mu'tamar al-thalith lil-ittihad al-'amm lil-fallahin* [Decisions of the Third Congress of the General Federation of Peasants]. Damascus.

———— . (1974) "Decree 21 on the Peasants' Organization." Damascus.

———— . (1977) *al-Mu'tamar al-'amm al-rabi' lil-ittihad al-'amm lil-fallahin* [The Fourth General Congress of the General Federation of Peasants]. Damascus.

———— . (1977b) *al-Nashra al-ihsa'iya lil-qita' al-fallahi al-ta'awuni* [Statistical Bulletin of the Peasant Cooperative Sector]. Damascus.

———— . (1981) *al-Mu'tamar al-'amm al-khamis lil-ittihad al-'amm lil-fallahin* [The Fifth General Congress]. Damascus.

Gubser, Peter. (1979a) "Minorities in Isolation: The Druze of Lebanon and Syria," in R.D. McLaurin ed., *The Political Role of Minority Groups in the Middle East.* New York, pp. 109–134.

———— . (1979b) "Minorities in Power: The Alawites of Syria" in R.D. McLaurin, ed., *The Political Role of Minority Groups in the Middle East.* New York, pp. 17–48.

Gurr, Ted Robert. (1970) *Why Men Rebel.* Princeton: Princeton University Press.

Haddad, George. (1971) *Revolutions and Military Rule in the Middle East: The Arab States.* New York: Robert Speller & Sons.

Halpern, Manfred. (1962) "Middle Eastern Armies and the New Middle Class," in *The Role of the Military in Underdeveloped Countries,* ed. John J. Johnston. Princeton: Princeton University Press, pp. 277–315.

———. (1963) *The Politics of Social Change in the Middle East and North Africa.* Princeton: Princeton University Press.

Hamide, Abdul Rahman. (1959) *La region d'Alep, Etude de geographie rurale.* Paris.

Hammadi, Sadoon. (1966) *Comments on the Results of the Agrarian Reform in Syria.* Damascus: Planning Institute for Social and Economic Development.

Hanna, Abdullah. (1978) *al-Qadiya al-zira'iya wa al-harakat al-fallahiya fi Suriya wa Lubnan, 1920–1945* [The Agricultural Problem and the Peasant Movements in Syria and Lebanon]. Beirut: Dar al-Farabi.

Hannoyer, Jean. (1980) "Le monde rural avant les reformes," in Andre Raymond, *La Syrie d'aujourd'hui.* Paris: CNRS, pp. 273–295.

Hansen, Bent. (1972) "Economic Development of Syria" in Charles A. Cooper and Sidney Alexander, *Economic Development and Population Growth in the Middle East.* New York: American Elsevier, pp. 333–366.

Harik, Iliya. (1972a) "The Impact of the Domestic Market on Rural- Urban Relations in the Middle East," in Richard Antoun and Iliya Harik, *Rural Politics and Social Change in the Middle East.* Bloomington Indiana: Indiana University Press, pp. 337–363.

———. (1972b) "The Ethnic Revolution and Political Integration in the Middle East," *International Journal of Middle East Studies,* v. 3, pp. 303–323.

———. (1973) "The Single Party as a Subordinate Movement," *World Politics,* 26, pp. 80–105.

Havens, Eugene. (1980) "Technology, Relations of Production, and Change in Syrian Villages," in US Department of Agriculture and USAID, *Syria: Agricultural Sector Assessment,* v. 5., Washington.

Hilan, Rizkallah. (1969) *Culture et developpement en Syrie et dans les pays retardes.* Paris: Editions Anthropos.

———. (1973) *Suriya bayna al-takhalluf wa al-tanmiya* [Syria between Backwardness and Development]. Damascus.

Hinnebusch, Raymond A. (1976) "Local Politics in Syria: Organization and Mobilization in Four Village Cases," *Middle East Journal,* v. 30, n. 1, Winter, 1–24.

———. (1979) "Party and Peasant in Syria," *Cairo Papers in Social Science,* v. 3, n. 1., November.

———. (1980) "Political Recruitment and Socialization in Syria: The Case of the Revolutionary Youth Federation," *International Journal of Middle East Studies,* v. 11, pp. 143–174.

———. (1982a) "Rural Politics in Ba'thist Syria," *The Review of Politics,* v. 44, n. 1, January, 110–130.

———. (1982b) "Syria under the Ba'th: State Formation in a Fragmented Society," *Arab Studies Quarterly,* v. 4, n. 3, Summer, 177–199.

———. (1982c) "The Islamic Movement in Syria: Sectarian Conflict and Urban Rebellion in an Authoritarian-Populist Regime," in Ali E. H. Dessouki, *Islamic Resurgence in the Arab World.* New York: Praeger, pp. 138–169.

———. (1984a) "Revisionist Dreams, Realist Strategies: The Foreign Policy of Syria," in Bahgat Korany and Ali Dessouki, eds., *The Foreign Policies of Arab States.* Boulder, Colorado: Westview Press, pp. 283–322.

———. (1984b) "Political Participation and the Authoritarian-Modernizing State in the Mideast: Activists in Syria and Egypt," *Journal of Arab Affairs,* v. 3, n. 2, Fall, pp. 131–156.

———— . (1986) "Syria under the Ba'th: Social Ideology, Policy, and Practice," in Laurence Michalak and Jeswald Salacuse, eds., *Social Legislation in the Contemporary Middle East.* Berkeley: University of California Press, pp. 61–109.

———— . (1986b) "Syrian Policy in Lebanon and the Palestinians," *Arab Studies Quarterly,* v. 8, n. 1, Winter, pp. 1–20.

———— . (1988) "Syria," in *The Politics of Islamic Revivalism,* ed. Shireen Hunter, Bloomington: Indiana University Press, 1988, 39–55.

———— . (1989) *Peasant and Bureaucracy in Ba'thist Syria: The Political Economy of Rural Development.* Boulder, Colo.: Westview Press.

Hitti, Philip. (1959) *Syria: A Short History.* London: Macmillan & Co.

Hobsbawm, E.J. (1959) *Primitive Rebels.* New York: W.W. Norton.

Holt, P.M. (1966) *Egypt and the Fertile Crescent, 1516–1922: A Political History.* Ithaca, New York: Cornell University Press.

Horowitz, Irving Louis. (1982) *Beyond Empire and Revolution: Militarization and Consolidation in the Third World.* Oxford: Oxford University Press.

Horton, Alan. (1961) "A Syrian Village in Its Changing Environment," Ph.D. Dissertation, Harvard University.

Hourani, Albert. (1946) *Syria and Lebanon.* London: Oxford University Press.

———— . (1966) "The Fertile Crescent in the 18th Century," in Charles Issawi, *The Economic History of the Middle East, 1800–1914.* Chicago: University of Chicago Press.

———— . (1968). "Ottoman Reform and the Politics of Notables," in William Polk and Richard Chambers, *The Beginnings of Modernization in the Middle East,* Chicago: University of Chicago Press, pp. 41–68.

Howard, Diana. (1972) "Syria's New Nationalists Move toward Democracy," *New Middle East,* March-April.

Hreib, Alaeddin Saleh, "The Influence of Sub-Regionalism (Rural Areas) on the Structure of Syrian Politics, 1920–1973," Ph.D. Dissertation, Georgetown University.

Hudson, Michael. (1977) *Arab Politics: The Search for Legitimacy.* New Haven: Yale University Press.

———— . (1983) "The Islamic Factor in Syrian and Iraqi Politics," in James Piscatori, *Islam in the Political Process.* Cambridge: Cambridge University Press, pp. 73–95.

Humphreys, R. Stephan. (1979) "Islam and Political Values in Saudi Arabia, Egypt, and Syria," *Middle East Journal,* v. 33, Winter.

Huntington, Samuel P. (1962) *Changing Patterns of Military Politics.* New York: Free Press.

———— . (1968) *Political Order in Changing Societies.* New Haven: Yale University Press.

———— . (1974) "Social and Institutional Dynamics of One-Party Systems," in Louis J. Cantori, *Comparative Political Systems.* Boston: Holbrook Press, pp. 323–370.

Huntington, Samuel and Nelson, Joan. (1976) *No Easy Choice: Political Participation in Developing Countries.* Cambridge Mass.: Harvard University Press.

Ibn Khaldun. (1967) *The Muqaddimah: An Introduction to History,* ed. N.A. Dawood. Princeton, N.J.: Princeton University Press.

International Bank for Reconstruction and Development (IBRD). (1955) *The Economic Development of Syria.* Baltimore: Johns Hopkins University Press.

Ismail, Kamil. (1975) *Die Sozialokonomischen Verhaltnisse der Bauerlichen Bevolkerung in Kustengebirge der Syrischen Arabischen Republik.* Berlin.

Issawi, Charles. (1966) *The Economic History of the Middle East, 1800–1914.* Chicago: University of Chicago Press.

Jabber, Fuad. (1973) "The Palestinian Resistance and Inter-Arab Politics" in Quandt, et al., *The Politics of Palestinian Nationalism*. Berkeley and Los Angeles: University of California Press, pp. 155–216.

Jabbur, George. (1987) *al-Fikra al-siyasi al-mu'asir fi Suriya* [Contemporary Political Thought in Syria]. London: Riad al-Rayyes.

Jadaane, Fahmi. (1987) "Notions of the State in Contemporary Arab-Islamic Writings," in Ghassan Salame, ed., *The Foundations of the Arab State*. London: Croom Helm.

Janowitz, Morris. (1964) *The Military in the Political Development of New Nations*. Chicago: University of Chicago Press.

al-Jundi, Sami. (1969) *al-Ba'th*. Beirut: Dar al-Nahar.

Kabbarah, Muhammad Bashshar. (1972) "Scope and Sequence of Industrial Development in Syria," Ph.D. Dissertation, University of Pennsylvania.

Kannan, Taher. (1960) "Introduction to the Ba'th," *New Outlook* III, (July-August), pp. 24–29.

Kapeliuk, Amnon. (1964) "Setback for the Ba'th," *New Outlook*, January.

———. (1966) "Dissension in the Syrian Ba'th," *New Outlook*, February.

Karpat, Kemal H. (1968) "The Land Regime, Social Structure, and Modernization in the Ottoman Empire," in William Polk and Richard Chambers, eds., *The Beginnings of Modernization in the Middle East*. Chicago: University of Chicago Press, pp. 69–90.

Kaylani, Nabil M. (1972) "The Rise of the Syrian Ba'th, 1940–1958: Political Success, Party Failure," *International Journal of Middle East Studies*, v. 3, n. 1, January, pp. 3–23.

Keilany, Ziad. (1968) "The Role of National Planning in Economic Development, Syria: A Case Study, 1960–1964." Ph.D. Dissertation, Indiana University.

———. (1970) "Economic Planning in Syria, 1960–1965: An Evaluation," *Journal of Developing Areas*, April.

———. (1973) "Socialism and Economic Change in Syria," *Middle Eastern Studies*, v. 9, n. 1, January, pp. 61–72.

———. (1980) "Land Reforms in Syria," *Middle Eastern Studies*, v. 16, pp. 208–224.

Kelidar, A.R. (1974) "Religion and State in Syria," *Asian Affairs*, v. 61, part 1, February, pp. 16–22.

Kerr, Malcolm. (1963) "Arab Radical Notions of Democracy," in *St. Anthony's Papers, No. 16, Middle Eastern Affairs, n. 3*. London: Chatto and Windus, pp. 9–40.

———. (1971) *The Arab Cold War*. London: Oxford University Press.

———. (1975) "Hafiz al-Asad and the Changing Patterns of Syrian Politics," *International Journal*, v. 28, n. 4, pp. 689–707.

Khadduri, Majid. (1953) "The Role of the Military in Middle East Politics," *American Political Science Review*, v. 47, June, pp. 516–517.

———. (1970) *Political Trends in the Arab World*. Baltimore: The Johns Hopkins Press.

Khader, Bichara. (1975) "Propriete agricole et reforme agraire en Syrie," *Civilisations*, n. 25, pp. 62–83.

Khalaf, Sulayman Najm. (1981) "Family, Village and the Political Party: Articulation of Social Change in Contemporary Rural Syria," Ph.D. Dissertation, University of California, Los Angeles.

Khalidi, Rashid. (1988) "Social Transformation and Political Power in the Radical Arab States" in Adeed Dawisha and I. William Zartman, *Beyond Coercion: The Durability of the Arab State*. London: Croom Helm, pp. 203–219.

Khalidi, Tarif. (1966) "A Critical Study of the Ideas of Michel Aflaq," *Middle East Forum,* v. 42, no. 4., pp. 55–67.

Khalidi, Walid. (1958) "Political Trends in the Fertile Crescent," in Walter Laqueur, *The Middle East in Transition.* New York: Praeger.

Khalil, Ali Yusef. (1962) "The Socialist Parties in Syria and Lebanon," Ph.D. Dissertation, American University.

Khoury, Philip. (1984) "Syrian Urban Politics in Transition: The Quarters of Damascus During the French Mandate,"*International Journal of Middle East Studies,* v. 16, no. 4, pp. 507–540.

Klat, Paul. (1958) "The Origins of Landownership in Syria," in *Middle East Economic Papers, 1958.* Beirut: American University of Beirut, pp. 51–66.

Koury, Enver. (1970) *The Patterns of Mass Movements in Arab Revolutionary-Progressive States.* The Hague: Mouton.

Kramer, Martin. (1980) "Political Islam," *The Washington Papers,* n. 73, Sage Publications.

———. (1987) "Syria's Alawis and Shi'ism," in Martin Kramer, ed., *Shi'ism, Resistance, and Revolution.* Boulder, CO: Westview Press, pp. 237–254.

Latron, Andre. (1936) *La vie rurale en Syrie et au Liban.* Beyrouth: Imprimerie catholique.

Lawson, Fred. (1982) "Social Basis of the Hamah Revolt," *MERIP Reports,* v. 12, n. 9, November–December.

Leca, Jean. (1988) "Social Structure and Political Stability: Comparative Evidence from the Algerian, Syrian and Iraqi Cases," in Adeed Dawisha and I. William Zartman, *Beyond Coercion: The Durability of the Arab State.* London: Croom-Helm, 164–202.

Lenczowski, George. (1966) "Radical Regimes in Egypt, Syria and Iraq" *Journal of Politics,* v. 28, n. 1, February, pp. 29–56.

Lerner, Daniel. (1958) *The Passing of Traditional Society: Modernizing the Middle East.* New York: The Free Press.

Lewis, Norman. (1952) "The Isma'ilis of Syria Today," *Journal of the Royal Central Asia Society,* London, v. 39, January, pp. 69–77.

———. (1955) "The Frontier of Settlement in Syria, 1800–1950," *International Affairs,* v. 31, n. 1, January, pp. 48–61.

———. (1987) "Syria: Land and People." in *Politics and the Economy in Syria,* ed. J.A. Allen, London: School of Oriental and African Studies, pp. 1–19.

Longuenesse, Elizabeth. (1978) "La classe ouvriere au Proche Orient: La Syrie," *Pensee,* n. 197, February, pp. 120–132.

———. (1979) "The Class Nature of the State in Syria," *MERIP Reports,* v. 9, n. 4. pp. 3–11.

MacIntyre, Ronald Robert. (1969) "The Arab Ba'th Socialist Party: Ideology, Politics, Sociology, and Organization." Ph.D. Dissertation, Australian National University.

Makdisi, Samir. (1971) "Syria: Rate of Economic Growth and Fixed Capital Formation, 1936–1968," *Middle East Journal,* v. 25, n. 2.

Makhoul, Ivanho Toufic. (1970) "The Ba'th Arab Socialist Party: Reasons for Unity with Egypt in 1958." M.A. Thesis, Duquesne University.

Malloy, James. (1977) "Authoritarianism and Corporatism in Latin America: The Modal Pattern," in Malloy, ed. *Authoritarianism and Corporatism in Latin America.* Pittsburgh: University of Pittsburgh Press, pp. 3–19.

Manzardo, Andrew E. (1980) "Agricultural Extension." in US Department of Agriculture and USAID, *Syria: Agricultural Sector Assessment,* v. 5., Washington.

Ma'oz, Moshe. (1968) *Ottoman Reform in Syria and Palestine, 1840–1861.* London: Oxford University Press.

———. (1972) "Attempts at Creating a Political Community in Modern Syria," *Middle East Journal,* v. 26, n. 4., pp. 389–404.

———. (1975) "Syria under Hafiz al-Asad: New Domestic and Foreign Policies," in *Jerusalem Papers on Peace Problems,* Hebrew University of Jerusalem, pp. 5–29.

———. (1976) "Alawi Military Officers in Syrian Politics: 1966–1974," in Harold Schiffrin, *Military and State in Modern Asia.* Jerusalem: Jerusalem Academic Press, pp. 277–298.

———. (1978) "Hafiz al-Asad: A Political Profile," *Jerusalem Quarterly,* 8, Summer, pp. 16–31.

Marsh, R. M. (1953) "Marginal Projectivity and Communication Behavior in Modern Syria," M.A. Thesis, Columbia University.

Mayer, Thomas. (1983) "The Islamic Opposition in Syria, 1961–1982," *Orient,* v. 24, n. 4, December.

Metral, Francoise. (1980) "Le monde rural syrien a l'ere des reformes (1958-1978)" in Andre Raymond, et al., *La Syrie d'aujourd'hui.* Paris: CNRS, pp. 297–325.

———. (1984) "State and Peasants in Syria: A Local View of a Government Irrigation Project," *Peasant Studies,* v. 11, no. 2, pp. 69–89.

Metral, Jean and Sanlaville, Paul. (1979) "L'Eau, la Terre, et les Hommes Dans les Campagnes Syriennes," *Revue de Geographie de Lyon,* v. 3, pp. 229–237.

Michels, Robert. (1962) *Political Parties: A Sociological Study of the Oligarchical Tendencies of Modern Democracy.* New York: The Free Press.

Migdal, Joel. (1987) "Strong States, Weak States: Power and Accommodation," in M. Weiner and S. P. Huntington, *Understanding Political Development.* Boston: Little, Brown.

Moore, Barrington. (1966) *Dictatorship and Democracy: Lord and Peasant in the Making of the Modern World.* Boston: Beacon Press.

Moore, Clement Henry. (1974) "On Theory and Practice Among the Arabs" *World Politics,* 24, October, pp. 106–126.

Mourad, Ahmad. (1970) "La Propriete Agricole en Syrie." in *L'Agriculture Syrienne.* Damascus: L'Office Arabe de Presse et de Documentation.

Musallem, Adnan. (1983) *al-mas'ala al-zira'iya fi al-qutr al-arabi al-suri* [The Agricultural Question in the Syrian Arab Republic]. Damascus: Matba' al-'Ulama.

Naaman, Anwar. (1950) "Precisions sur la structure agraire dans la region de Homs-Hama (Syrie)," *Bulletin de l'Association de Geographes Francais.*

Nassar, Nadim. (1971) "Analysis of Syrian Agricultural Development: A Case Study 1958–1965." M.A. Thesis, University of Pittsburgh.

Nelson, Joan. (1987) "Political Participation," in Myron Weiner and Samuel P. Huntington, *Understanding Political Development.* Boston: Little, Brown, pp. 103–159.

Nyrop, Richard, et al. (1971) *Area Handbook for Syria.* Washington, D.C.: U.S. Government Printing Office.

O'Donnell, Guillermo. (1977) "Corporatism and the Question of the State," in James Malloy, ed., *Authoritarianism and Corporatism in Latin America.* Pittsburgh: University of Pittsburgh Press, pp. 47–87.

Olson, Robert W. (1978–1979) "The Ba'th in Syria, 1947–1979: An Interpretative Historical Essay,"*Oriente Moderno,* LVIII, n. 12, December 1978, pp. 645–681 and LIX, n. 6, June 1979, pp. 439–475.

———. (1982) *The Ba'th and Syria, 1947–1982.* Princeton, N.J.: The Kingston Press.

Orgels, Bernard. (1962) "Contribution a l'etude des problemes agricoles de la Syrie," *Correspondance d'Orient*, n. 4, Bruxelles.

Owen, Wyn F. (1980) "Land Tenure in the Euphrates Basin." in US Department of Agriculture and USAID, *Syria: Agricultural Sector Assessment*, v. 5, Washington.

Paige, Jeffery M. (1975) *Agrarian Revolution*. New York and London: Free Press.

Palmer, Monte. (1966) "The United Arab Republic: An Assessment of its Failure," *Middle East Journal, v. 20, n. 1*, Winter, pp. 50–67.

Perera, Judith. (1983) "The Shifting Fortunes of Syria's Muslim Brothers," *The Middle East*, May, pp. 25–28.

Perlmutter, Amos. (1969) "From Obscurity to Rule: The Syrian Army and the Ba'th Party," *Western Political Quarterly*, v. 22, n. 4.

————. (1981) *Modern Authoritarianism: A Comparative Institutional Analysis*. New Haven: Yale University Press.

Petran, Tabitha. (1972) *Syria*. London: Ernest Benn.

Picard, Elizabeth. (1979a) "Clans militaires et pouvoir ba'thiste en Syrie," *Orient*, Hamburg, 49–62.

————. (1979b) "Ouverture economique et renforcement militaire en Syrie," *Orient Moderne*, v. 59, nos. 7–12, pp. 663–676.

————. (1988) "Arab Military in Politics: From Revolutionary Plot to Authoritarian State," in Adeed Dawisha and I. William Zartman, *Beyond Coercion: The Durability of the Arab State*. London: Croom-Helm, pp. 116–146.

Planhol, Xavier de. (1972) "Regional Diversification and Social Structure in North Africa and the Islamic Middle East: A Geographical Approach" in Richard Antoun and Iliya Harik, *Rural Politics and Social Change in the Middle East*. Bloomington, Indiana: Indiana University Press, pp. 103–117.

Porter, R. S. (1963) "The Growth of the Syrian Economy," *Middle East Forum*, November.

al-Qazzaz, Ayad. (1969) "Political Order, Stability and Officers: A Comparative Study of Iraq, Syria and Egypt from Independence to June, 1967." *Middle East Forum*, n. 2.

Rabinovich, Itamar. (1972) *Syria Under the Ba'th, 1963–1966: The Army-Party Symbiosis*. New York: Halstead Press.

Ratnatunga, R.T. (1968) "Report on Land Tenure, Land Settlement and Institutional Considerations." Damascus: FAO (Ghab Development Project).

Razzaz, Munif (1967) *al-Tajriba al-murra* [The Bitter Experience]. Beirut: Dar al-Ghandur.

Riggs, Fred. (1964) *Administration in Developing Countries: The Theory of Prismatic Society*. Boston: Houghton-Mifflin.

Rodinson, Maxime. (1968) *Israel and the Arabs*. Middlesex, England: Penguin Books.

Rouleau, Eric. (1967) "The Syrian Enigma: What is the Ba'th," *New Left Review*, n. 45, pp. 53–65.

Russett, Bruce. (1964) "Inequality and Instability: The Relation of Land Tenure to Politics," *World Politics*, 16, April, pp. 442–454.

Saab, Edouard. (1968) *La Syrie ou la Revolution dans la rancoeur*. Paris: Julliard

Sadowski, Yehya. (1985) "Cadres, Guns and Money: The Eighth Regional Congress of the Syrian Ba'th," *MERIP Reports*, July/August.

Safadi, Muta'. (1964) *Hizb al-Ba'th: ma'sat al-mawlid, ma'sat al-nihaya* [The Ba'th Party: The Tragedies of its Birth and End]. Beirut: Dar al-Adab.

Salamah, Ibrahim. (1969) *al-Ba'th min al-madaris ila al-thakanat* [The Ba'th from the School to the Barracks]. Beirut.

Sayyid, Jallal. (1973) *Hizb al-Ba'th al-Arabi*. Beirut: Dar al-Nahar.

Schatkowski-Schilcher, Linda. (1978) "Government Policy, Local Politics, and Economic Integration in Syria: The Hauran in the 19th and 20th Centuries," paper given to conference on Local Politics in the Middle East, University of Maryland, Baltimore.

Seale, Patrick. (1965) *The Struggle for Syria.* London: Oxford University Press.

Seymour, Martin. (1970) "The Dynamics of Power in Syria since the Break with Egypt," *Middle Eastern Studies,* v. 6, n. 1, January, pp. 35–47.

Shakra, Akram. (1966) "Land Reform in Syria." Ph.D. Dissertation, University of Oklahoma.

Shamir, Shimon. (1968) "The Modernization of Syria: Problems and Solutions in the Early Period of Abdulhamid," in William Polk and Richard Chambers, *Beginnings of Modernization in the Middle East.* Chicago: University of Chicago Press, pp. 351–381.

Shanin, Teodor. (1966) "The Peasantry as a Political Factor," *Sociological Review,* n. 14, March, pp. 5–27.

Sheehan, Edward. (1976) *The Arabs, Israelis, and Kissinger: A Secret History of American Diplomacy in the Middle East.* New York: Reader's Digest Press.

Skocpol, Theda. (1979) *States and Social Revolution.* Cambridge: Cambridge University Press.

Springborg, Robert. (1981) "Ba'athism in Practice: Agriculture, Politics, and Political Culture in Syria and Iraq," *Middle Eastern Studies,* v. 17, n. 2, April, pp. 191–209.

Suleiman, Michael. (1967) *Political Parties in Lebanon.* Ithica, New York: Cornell University Press.

Sweet, Louise. (1957) "Tell Toqaan: A Syrian Village." Ph.D. Dissertation, University of Michigan.

Syrian Arab Republic (SAR), Central Bureau of Statistics. (1970) *Population Census in Syrian Arab Republic.* v. 1, Damascus.

_____. (1970–1971) *1970–1971 Agricultural Census Data: First Stage Basic Data in Syrian Arab Republic.* Damascus.

_____. (1971) *Agricultural Census Data: Second Stage, Detailed Data.* Damascus.

_____. (1976) *Statistical Abstract, 1976.* Damascus.

_____. (1984) *Statistical Abstract, 1984.* Damascus.

_____. (1986) *Statistical Abstract, 1986.* Damascus.

Syrian Arab Republic, Ministry of Agriculture. (1972) *al-Nashra al-ihsa'iya al-sanawi lil-qita' al-ta'awuni [Annual Statistical Bulletin of the Cooperative Sector].* Damascus.

Syrian Arab Republic, Ministry of Information. (1965) Documents sur la Transformation Socialiste en Republique Arabe Syrienne. Damascus.

_____. (1973) *Suriya al-thawra fi ammha al-ashir* [Revolutionary Syria in its Tenth Year]. Damascus.

Syrian Arab Republic, Ministry of Labor and Social Affairs. (1969) "La Loi de L'Organisation Syndicale Paysanne, No. 253." Damascus.

al-Tal, Muhammed Fayez. (1967) *al-Mujtama' al-Arabi al-Suri fi al-dawlah al-haditha* [Syrian Arab Society in the Modern State]. Damascus: al-Matba' al-Ta'awuniya.

Thoumin, Richard. (1936) *Geographie humaine de la Syrie centrale.* Paris: Librairie Ernest Leroux.

Tibawi, A.L. (1969) *A Modern History of Syria.* London: Macmillan.

Torrey, Gordon. (1964) *Syrian Politics and the Military, 1945–1958.* Columbus: Ohio State University.

_____. (1969) "The Ba'th: Ideology and Practice," *Middle East Journal,* v. 23, n. 4, Autumn, pp. 445–470.

————. (1970) "Instability in Syria," *Current History*, LVIII, n. 341, January, pp. 13–15, 47–48.

Tower, Allen J. (1935) *The Oasis of Damascus*, Beirut.

Trimberger, Ellen Kay. (1978) *Revolution from Above: Military Bureaucrats and Development in Japan, Turkey, Egypt and Peru*. New Brunswick, N.J.: Transaction Books.

United Nations. (1971) "Development Planning and Social Objectives in Syria," in *Studies on Selected Development Problems in Various Countries in the Middle East, 1971*. New York, pp. 1–26.

Van Dam, Nikolaos. (1981) *The Struggle for Power in Syria: Sectarianism, Regionalism and Tribalism in Politics, 1961–1980*. London: Croom-Helm.

Van Dusen, Michael. (1971) "Intra- and Inter-Generational Conflict in the Syrian Army." Ph.D. Dissertation, Johns Hopkins University.

————. (1972) "Political Integration and Regionalism in Syria," *Middle East Journal*, XXVI, n. 1., pp. 123–136.

————. (1975) "Downfall of a Traditional Elite," in Frank Tachau, ed., *Political Elites and Political Development in the Middle East*. Cambridge, Mass: Schenkman/Wiley, pp. 115–155.

Victorov, F.B. (1970) *Iqtisad Suriya al-Haditha* [The Economy of Modern Syria] (Translated into Arabic from Russian). Damascus: Dar al-Ba'th.

Volney, C.F. (1966) "Travels through Syria and Egypt" in Charles Issawi, *Economic History of the Middle East, 1800–1914*. London: Oxford University Press, pp. 213–220.

Walton, John. (1984) *Reluctant Rebels: Comparative Studies of Revolution and Underdevelopment*. New York: Columbia University Press.

Warriner, Doreen. (1948) *Land and Poverty in the Middle East*. London: Royal Institute of International Affairs.

Warriner, Doreen. (1962) *Land Reform and Development in the Middle East*. London & New York: Oxford University Press.

Waterbury, John. (1976) "Corruption, Political Stability and Development: Comparative Evidence from Egypt and Morocco," *Government and Opposition*, 11, pp. 426–445.

Weber, Max. (1964) *The Theory of Social and Economic Organization*. New York: Free Press.

Weiner, Myron. (1965) "Political Integration and PoliticalDevelopment," *The Annals*, v. 358, March, pp. 52–64.

Weulersse, Jacques. (1940) *Le Pays des Alaouites*. Tours: Institut Francais de Damas.

————. (1946) *Paysans de Syrie et du Proche-Orient*. Paris: Gallimard.

Winder, R. Bayly. (1962–1963) "Syrian Deputies and Cabinet Ministers: 1919–1959," *Middle East Journal*, XVI, August, 1962, pp. 407–429 and XVII, Winter-Spring, 1963, pp. 35–54.

Wirth, Eugen. (1966) "Damaskus–Aleppo–Beirut; ein geographischer Vergleich dreier nahostlicher Stadte im Spiegel ihrer sozial undwirtschaftlich tonangebenden Schichten." *Die Erde*, 96, pp. 96–202.

Wolf, Eric. (1969) *Peasant Wars of the Twentieth Century*. New York: Harper & Row.

Wolpin, Miles. (1981) *Militarism and Social Revolution in the Third World*. Totowa, N.J.: Allenheld and Osmun.

World Bank. (1980) *Syrian Arab Republic Development Prospects and Policies*, 4 vols., Washington, D.C.

Yodfat, Aryeh. (1971) "The End of Syria's Isolation?," *The World Today*, August.

Zagoria, Donald, "Rice and Feudal Communism in India," unpublished paper.

el-Za'im, Issam. (1967) "Le probleme agraire Syrien: Etapes et bilan de la reforme," *Developpement et Civilisations*, n. 31., pp. 68–78.

Zakariya, Khodr. (1984) *Some Peculiarities of the Class Construction in the Syrian Society*. Tokyo: Institute of Developing Economics.

Ziadeh, Nicola A. (1957) *Syria and Lebanon*. New York: Praeger.

Zoubi, Ahmad. (1971) "Agricultural Extension and Rural Development in Syria, 1955-1968," Ph.D. Dissertation, Ohio State University.

Zoubi, Ahmad; al-Attar, Hassan; and al-Jam, Mehdi. (1969) *The Question of Agrarian Reform through Legislation and Action in the S.A.R.* Damascus.

Index